HAPTICS RENDERING AND APPLICATIONS

Edited by **Abdulmotaleb El Saddik**

Haptics Rendering and Applications
Edited by Abdulmotaleb El Saddik

Published by InTech
Janeza Trdine 9, 51000 Rijeka, Croatia

Publishing Process Manager Adriana Pecar

Technical Editor Teodora Smiljanic

Cover Designer InTech Design Team

Additional hard copies can be obtained from orders@intechopen.com

Haptics Rendering and Applications, Edited by Abdulmotaleb El Saddik
p. cm.
ISBN 978-953-307-897-7

For EU product safety concerns:
IN TECH d.o.o., Prolaz Marije Krucifikse Kozulić 3, 51000 Rijeka, Croatia,
info@intechopen.com or visit our website at intechopen.com.

Meet the editor

Professor Abdulmotaleb El Saddik is a University Research Chair and Professor in the School of Electrical Engineering and Computer Science at the University of Ottawa. He is an internationally-recognized scholar who has made notable contributions to the knowledge and understanding of multimedia computing, communications and applications - particularly in the digitization, communication and security of the sense of touch ("haptics") which is a new medium that is significantly changing the way in which human-to-human and human-computer interactions are performed. He has authored and co-authored four books, more than 350 publications and received research grants and contracts totaling more than $16 Mio. More than 90 researchers were under his mentorships and he received several international awards. He is currently a fellow of the Engineering Institute of Canada, The Canadian Academy of Engineers and IEEE.

Contents

Preface

Society is becoming based on information gathering, manipulation, and dissemination. We are witnessing an ever-growing and evolving content delivery market accompanied by significant restructuring worldwide. Such continuous changes reflect the need for specialization of new content, dynamic access to content to enable timely reaction, flexible delivery, customized presentation structures, interactivity and collaboration. These changes are caused and enabled by the transformation in the delivery mode from paper to electronic media formats and the growing trends towards interactive services delivering information in full accordance with the declared interests of the end-user. Haptics, a term that was derived from the Greek verb "haptesthai", meaning "to touch", refers to the science of sensing and manipulation through touch. This word was introduced at the beginning of the twentieth century by researchers in the field of experimental psychology to refer to the active touch of real objects by humans. In the late nineteen eighties, the term was redefined to enlarge its scope and to include all aspects of machine touch and human-machine touch interaction. The 'touching' of objects can be by humans, machines, or a combination of both; the environment can be real, virtual, or a combination of both. Currently, the term has brought together many disciplines including biomechanics, psychology, neurophysiology, engineering and computer science to refer to the study of human touch and force feedback with the external environment.

It is worth mentioning that even with the significant progress in haptic technologies, the incorporation of haptics into virtual environments is still in its infancy. A wide range of the new society's human activities including communication, education, art, entertainment, commerce and science would forever change if we learned how to capture, manipulate and reproduce haptic sensory stimuli that are nearly indistinguishable from reality. For the field to move forward, many commercial and technological barriers need to be be overcome. First, business models/frameworks are needed to make haptic devices practical, inexpensive and widely accessible; ultimately, a haptic device should be as easily pluggable as the mouse in a computer. Moreover, multipoint, multihand and multiperson interaction scenarios need further investigations to reach enticingly rich interactivity. Finally, we should not forget that touch and physical interaction are fundamental in haptic systems development. By rendering how objects feel through haptic technology, we communicate information that might reflect a desire to speak a physically-based language that has never been explored before.

Traditionally, the most typical style of human-computer interaction has been the visual style, which means people mainly interact with computers via texts, data, and images on the screen. There has only been indirect manipulation between human and computers. Keyboards and mouses have been used to translate human body languages and project these movements into actions on the screen. Using such indirect manipulation input devices, human don't receive any force feedback about these actions. Haptics technology, on the other hand, provides a new style of interaction and facilitates the perception of objects through the sense of touch.

The complexity of haptics applications is usually the very first obstacle for both developers and users. Haptics technology requires highly specialized hardware and software. This equipment is expensive for single daily users to obtain, not to mention the prototypes of these devices which are usually too large and not easily portable. Moreover, to complete a haptics project, experts from many different disciplines need to co-operate. To sum up, haptics technology nowadays is still in its early stage, there are still many problems waiting to be solved and obstacles to be surmounted.

Without question, haptics technology is a revolution in the way in which we interact in the virtual world. Haptics prototypes will continue to be refined and there will be further research into the human-computer interface. User patterns and preferences will also be further investigated. Meanwhile, researchers and developers will continue to improve the accuracy of capturing human movements and providing the proper force feedback.

Experts are also working on producing portable and consumer-grade haptic devices. Hopefully, with the arrival of these consumer-grade haptic devices on the markets, researchers will be able to obtain more real-time information, as well as feedback from customers and they can then further improve the haptic technology. With related technology improving every day, more and more pieces of research on haptics topics are being published. I believe there is a promising future for haptics technology.

Dedication
For my wife Ligia and my beloved kids Ikram, Yasmin, Hamdi and Aisha
With Love

Prof. Dr.-Ing. Abdulmotaleb El Saddik,
FIEEE, FCAE, FEIC, P.Eng. University Research Chair
in Ambient Interactive Media & Communications,
Director: Multimedia Communications Research Laboratory (MCRLab),
School of Information Technology and Engineering (SITE),
University of Ottawa,
Canada

Part 1

Haptic Perception

1

Haptic Concepts

Phuong Do, Donald Homa, Ryan Ferguson and Thomas Crawford
Arizona State University, United States of America

1. Introduction

A concept may be defined as a collection of objects grouped together by a common name whose members are usually, but not always, generated by a plan or algorithm. All words are concepts, as are the natural categories, esthetic style, the various diseases, and social stereotypes. In virtually all cases, an endless number of discriminably different examples of a concept has been rendered equivalent. A striking example was provided by Bruner, Goodnow, and Austin (1956), who noted that humans can make 7 million color discriminations and yet rely on a relative handful of color names. We categorize, according to Bruner et al., for a number of reasons – it is cognitively adaptive to segment the world into manageable categories, categories once acquired permit inference to novel instances, and concepts, once identified, provide direction for instrumental activity. For example, we avoid poisonous plants, fight or flee when encountering threat, and make decisions following a diagnosis. With rare exceptions, all concepts are acquired by experiences that are enormously complex and always unique.

However, the substantial and growing literature on formal models of concepts (e.g., Busemeyer & Pleskac, 2009) and the discovery of variables that shape concepts (e.g., Homa, 1984) has been acquired, almost exclusively, from studies that investigate the appearance of objects, i.e., the presentation of stimuli that are apprehended visually. Yet a moment's reflection reveals that our common concepts are associated with inputs from the various modalities. The taste, texture, odor, and appearance of food might critically inform us that this food is spoiled and not fresh; that the distinctive shape, gait, and sound marks this stray dog as probably lost and not dangerous; and the sounds, odors, and handling might be telling us that the family car needs a tune-up. Little is known about haptic or auditory concepts and virtually nothing is known about cross-modal transfer of categorical information between the different modalities, at least not from formal, experimental studies.

In contrast to the dearth of studies involving multimodal input and cross-modal transfer in category formation, there exists ample, albeit indirect, support for the role of multimodal properties revealed from other cognitive paradigms, ranging from feature and associative listing of words and category instances to the solution of analogies and logical decision-making. When asked to list attributes of category members (e.g., Garrard, Lambon, Ralph, Hodges, & Patterson, 2001; Rosch & Mervis, 1975), subjects typically include properties drawn from vision, audition, touch, olfaction, and taste. Similarly, the solution of analogies (e.g., Rumelhart & Abrahamson, 1973) and category-based induction (e.g., Osherson, Smith,

Wilkie, & Lopez, 1990) involve properties reflecting the various modalities. More direct support has been obtained from motor control studies involving olfaction and vision (Castiello, Zucco, Parma, Ansuini, & Tirindelli, 2006), in which the odor of an object has been shown to influence maximum hand aperature for object grasping, and mental rotation of objects presented haptically and visually (Volcic, Wijnjes, Kool, & Kappers, 2010). Each of these studies suggests that our modalities must share a common representation.

1.1 Summary of proposed studies

In the present chapter, we report the results of experiments, including recent results from our laboratory, that explore whether concepts learned haptically or visually can transfer their information to the alternate modality. We also report whether categorical information, simultaneously perceived by the two modalities, can be learned when put into conflict. Specifically, the objects explored visually and haptically belonged to the same category but were, unbeknownst to the subject, different objects. In the latter situation, we are especially interested in whether intermodal conflict retards or even precludes learning or whether the disparities provided by touch and vision are readily overcome. We also report the results of a preliminary study that addresses whether concepts can be learned when partial information is provided. Finally, we explore whether the representation of categories acquired haptically or visually differ minimally or dramatically and whether the structures are modified in similar ways following category learning.

The lack of research into multi-modal concepts should not imply that little is known about haptic processing. The classic Woodward and Schlosberg (1954) text devoted a chapter to touch and the cutaneous senses, and a recent textbook on haptics (Hatwell, Streri, & Gentaz, 2003) lists 17 subareas of research with over 1000 references. There is now an electronic journal devoted to haptics (Haptics-e), the IEEE Transactions on Haptics was established in 2009, and numerous labs have been formed both nationally and internationally that are dedicated to haptics and haptic interfaces. A brief summary of pertinent research on haptic processing is presented first.

1.2 Brief summary of haptic processing

Haptic perception requires active exploratory movements derived from proprioceptive information. Unlike vision, which provides useful information from a single glance and at a distance (e.g., Biederman, 1972; Luck & Vogel, 1997), haptic perception relies on sequential examination in which tactile-kinesthetic reafferences can be generated only by direct contact with the stimulus. The absence of vision, however, does not preclude the coding of reference and spatial information (Golledge, 1992; Golledge, Ruggles, Pellegrino, & Gale, 1993; Kitchin, Blades, & Golledge, 1997). Haptic perception enables the blind to identify novel stimuli (Klatzky & Lederman, 2003), detect material properties of objects (Kitchin *et al.*, 1997; Gentaz & Hatwell, 2003; 1995), and to acquire abstract categories (Homa, Kanav, Priyamvada, Bratton, & Panchanathan, 2009). For example, we (Homa et al., 2009) demonstrated that students who are blind can learn concepts whose members vary in size, shape, and texture as rapidly as sighted subjects who were permitted to both touch and view the same stimuli. Interestingly, the blind subjects exhibited lower false alarm rates than normally-sighted subjects who were permitted to view and handle the stimuli or who were blindfolded and relied on touch alone, rarely calling 'new' stimuli 'old', but with one curious exception - they invariably false alarmed to the category prototypes and at a much higher rate than any other subjects.

Numerous studies have explored how shape (Gliner, Pick, Pick, & Hales, 1969; Moll & Erdmann, 2003; Streri, 1987), texture (Catherwood, 1993; Lederman, Klatzky, Tong, & Hamilton, 2006; Salada, Colgate, Vishton, & Frankel, 2004), and material (Bergmann-Tiest & Kappers, 2006; Stevens & Harris, 1962) are coded following haptic exploration. Researchers have embraced the possibility that learning and transfer are mediated by an integration of information from multiple sensory modalities (Millar & Al-Attar, 2005; Ernst & Bulthoff, 2004), and that visual and tactile shape processing share common neurological sites (Amedi, Jacobson, Hendler, Malach, and Zohary, 2001). Ernst and Banks (2002) concluded that the lateral occipital complex is activated in similar ways to objects viewed or handled. More recently, Ernst (2007) has shown that luminance and pressure resistance can be integrated into a single perception "if the value of one variable was informative about the value of the other". Specifically, participants had a lower threshold to discriminate stimuli when the two dimensions were correlated but not when they were uncorrelated.

1.3 Stimuli for Experiments 1-3

The initial studies used complex 3D shapes, shown in Figure 1, that were composed of three abstract prototypical shapes and systematic distortions. Objects were originally modeled in the Maya 3D modeling software produced by Autodesk. Initially, 30-40 3-dimensional virtual forms were generated using a shape growth tool within the Maya suite, and 20 were chosen for multidimensional scaling. Three forms were then selected from the multidimensional space (MDS) that were moderately separated from each other and which appeared to be equi-distant from each other in three dimensions. These 3 forms become the prototypical forms for three categories. The surface of each prototype was then subdivided into a very small polygon mesh which gives objects a more organic appearance.

The Maya's shape blend tool was used to generate forms that were incremental blends between all pairs of the 3 prototype forms. This resulted in a final category population of 24 3-dimensional objects, where each prototype was transformed, along two paths into the other two prototypes. The distortion setting used in the shape blend tool was set to .14, which allowed for 7 forms to be generated between each prototype pair. The forms were then converted from Maya's file format which could then be steriolithographically printed using a ZCorperation Zprinter. Each of the objects was smooth to the touch and of the same approximate weight and overall size.

1.4 Theoretical issues

This structure was selected to address a number of additional issues. First, each prototype occupied the endpoints of two transformational paths and was the only form capable of readily generating its distortions. However, unlike the vast majority of studies in categorization, each prototype was not otherwise central to its learning (or transfer) patterns but was positioned at the endpoints of two transformational paths. We were interested in whether these prototypical objects would, nonetheless, exhibit characteristics typically found in recognition and classification. For example, the prototype is often falsely recognized as an old pattern and classified better than other new exemplars (Metcalfe & Fisher, 1986; Nosofsky, 1991; Shin & Nosofsky, 1992). However, exceptions in recognition to this outcome have been obtained (Homa, Goldhardt, Burruel-Homa, & Smith, 1993; Homa, Smith, Macak, Johovich, & Osorio, 2001), apparently when the prototype is a unique pattern rather than composed of features identically contained in its exemplars.

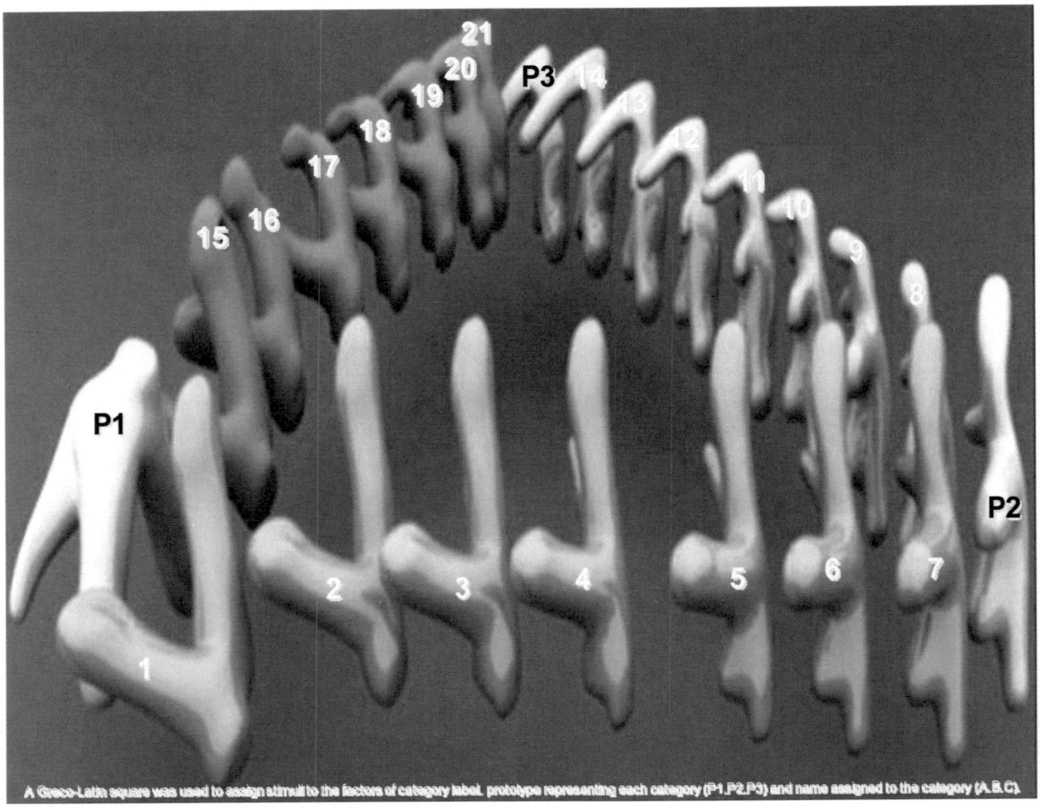

Fig. 1. The categorical space composed of 24 shapes; each category prototype is located at the vertex

In the present experiments, all objects including the prototypes were unique patterns, composed of novel and not identically repeated features or components. Second, two types of new patterns were used in transfer, those that were positioned between old training forms and those that were located at the midpoint of the transformational paths generated from different prototypes. In effect, each midpoint stimulus was a form that was positioned within a 'gap' that was positioned in the middle between two prototypes. We were interested in whether an object that fills a gap and flanked by two training patterns from different prototypes would be less likely to be falsely recognized as old than other new patterns that were similarly flanked by two training patterns but which was closer to the category prototype. If similarity to close training neighbors in learning dictates (false) recognition, regardless of the category membership of the neighbors, then recognition of the midpoint objects should be similar to recognition of the new objects. Alternatively, if ambiguity of category membership also plays a role, as well as similarity to old training objects, then (false) recognition should be reduced, compared to the new objects. This was because the midpoint objects could not be unambiguously classified into a single prototype, since either of two prototype classes would be correct.

2. Cross-modal category transfer

Experiment 1 examined visual (V) or haptic (H) category learning followed by a transfer test in the same or alternate modality (VV, VH, HV, HH). Half of the subjects received random or systematic training. Particular contrasts were of special interest: (a) Transfer differences between the VV and HH conditions should reveal whether visual concepts are learned better than concepts learned haptically; (b) VV vs. VH and HH vs. HV should indicate how much information is lost when tested in an alternate modality; and (c) VH vs. HV would indicate whether information is transferred more readily from one modality to the other.

2.1 Method

Objects were placed on a small table next to the participant. An opaque dark blue curtain was hung between the stimuli and participant and could be slid back and forth along a rod situated 10 feet above, allowing the participant to view or handle the object. This allowed the experimenter to select a designated stimulus to present to the subject, while hiding the remaining 23 stimuli. The stimuli were shown one at a time. Four types of objects can be identified: (a) 12 old objects, 4 from each category prototype, that were presented during learning; (b) 6 new patterns, 2 from each category; (c) 3 prototypes; and (d) 3 midpoint objects. The latter objects were midway between either of two prototypes and, therefore, could not be unambiguously assigned to a single prototype category. A schematic representation of the 24 objects, separated by the three categories and transformational paths is shown in Figure 2.

2.2 Procedure

The learning phase was composed of four study-test trial blocks. On each study block, the 12 learning objects were shown randomly or systematically blocked by category, labeled as A, B, or C for the subject. Following this, the objects were presented in a random order and required verbal classification of the object (A, B, or C). Following their judgment, corrective verbal feedback was provided. For subjects in the systematic condition, the three categories were presented in a counterbalanced order, although patterns belonging to a given category were shown in a random order.

On the transfer test, all 24 objects were presented in a random order, which included the four training patterns in each category (old), the three category prototypes, and nine new objects. As indicated in Figure 2, three of the new patterns were located midway between the two prototypes and were, as a consequence, analyzed separately from the remaining new objects. On the transfer test, the subject was required to make a double judgment to each object. The first judgment was a recognition judgment – is this object old or new? The second judgment was a classification judgment (is it an A, B, or C pattern?).

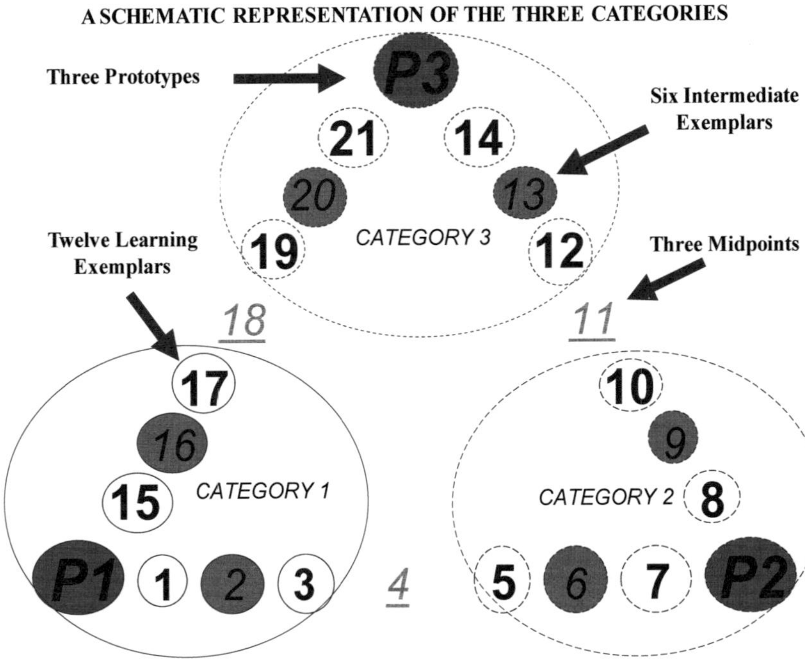

Fig. 2. A schematic representation of the three categories and 24 objects

2.3 Results - Learning

Figure 3 shows the mean correct classification rate across learning blocks as a function of input modality and training order (systematic, random). The main effects of learning blocks, modality of training, and order of stimulus presentation during learning were each significant.

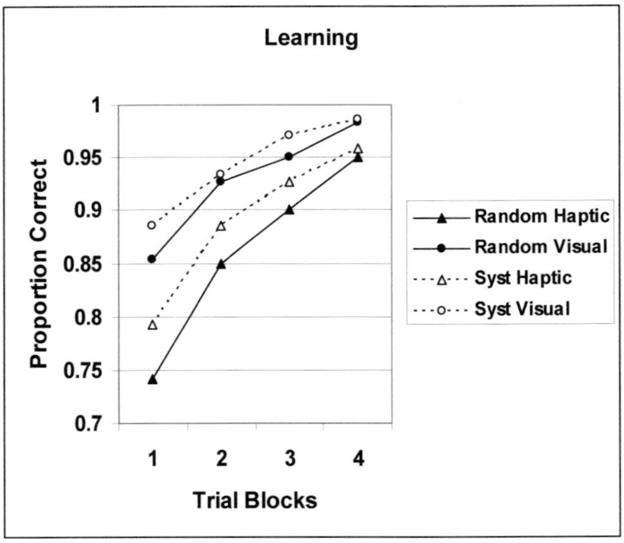

Fig. 3. Learning across training blocks as a function of modality and order of presentation.

In general, performance improved across learning blocks, learning was more efficient with visual than haptic inspection, and performance was enhanced when study presentation was systematic.

2.4 Results – Transfer classification and recognition

Classification errors were unexpectedly rare, with overall error rates ranging between 3-10% among the four modality conditions, with accuracy highest in the VV condition and worst in the HH condition (participants were also tested one week later, and performance deteriorated a slight 4%).

Figure 4 shows the mean hit and false alarm rates as a function of study and test modality (VV, VH, HV, HH), training order (random, systematic), and time of test (immediate, week delay). In general, subjects were able to discriminate old from new objects with fair accuracy, with an overall hit rate of .715 and a false alarm rate of .543. The conditions ordered themselves, from best to poorest old-new discrimination, as VV > VH = HH > HV, with a mean difference between hits and false alarms of .304, .176, .167, and .100, respectively.

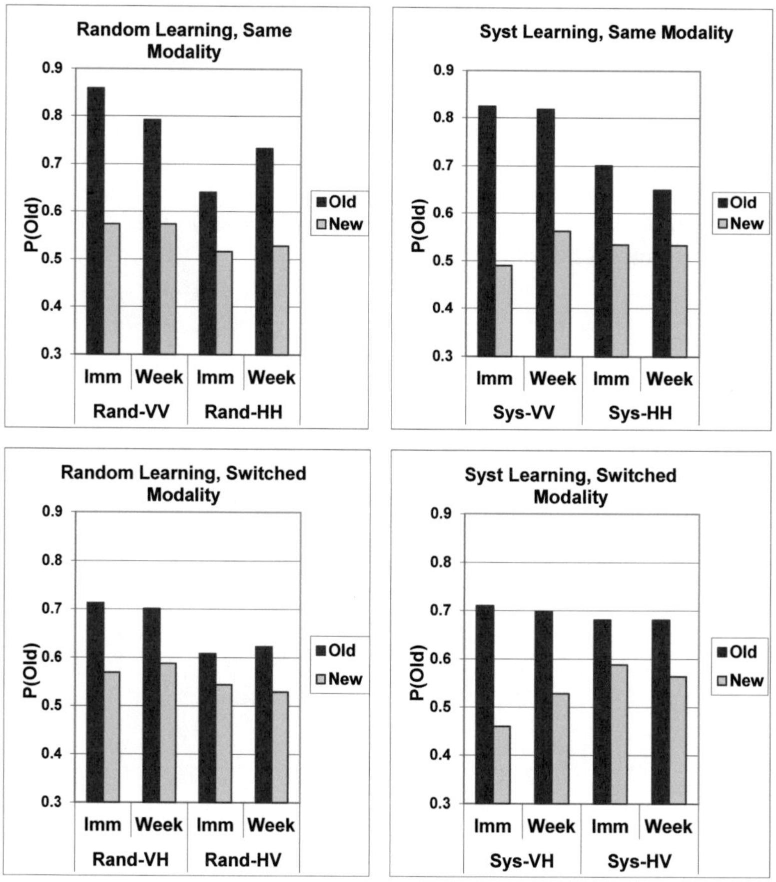

Fig. 4. Mean hit and false alarm rates as a function of study and test modality (VV, VH, HV, HH), training order (random, systematic), and time of test (immediate, week delay).

Testing in an alternate modality provides an index of level of transfer between these modalities. The overall level of discrimination between old and new objects was .304 for the VV condition versus .176 for the VH, which suggests that transfer was substantial but with some loss of information from the visual to the haptic modality. The HH/HV contrast provides an index of conceptual transfer from the haptic to the visual modality. The overall level of discrimination between old and new was .167 for HH; for HV, discrimination dropped to .100. Differences in performance between the HH and VH must reflect encoding (and transfer) from one modality to the other, given a common test modality. No overall differences in recognition discrimination emerged between these conditions (HH = .167; VH = .176), either as main effects or interactions. For the VV vs. HV condition, the difference in discrimination accuracy (VV = .304; HV = .100) was substantial.

In spite of the wide variations in transfer, each of the conditions - transfer to the same or alternate modality - revealed that the ability to discriminate old from new objects was significant even after a week delay. In particular, our expectation that discrimination in the alternate modality would vanish after one week was not supported.

Figure 5 shows the probability each object type (old, new, prototype, midpoint) was called old as a function of learning and transfer modality. In general, subjects were most accurate in identification of old patterns as 'old'; the midpoint, prototype, and new objects were (incorrectly) called 'old' at rates of .459, .539, and .586, respectively. A notable result was that the category prototype, often false alarmed at a higher rate than other new patterns (e.g., Metcalfe & Fisher, 1986), was incorrectly called 'old' no more often than other new objects. This replicates previous studies which have found that the prototype, when composed of continuously variable features, is likely represented as a novel, ideal pattern, not a familiar one (Homa et al., 1993; 2001).

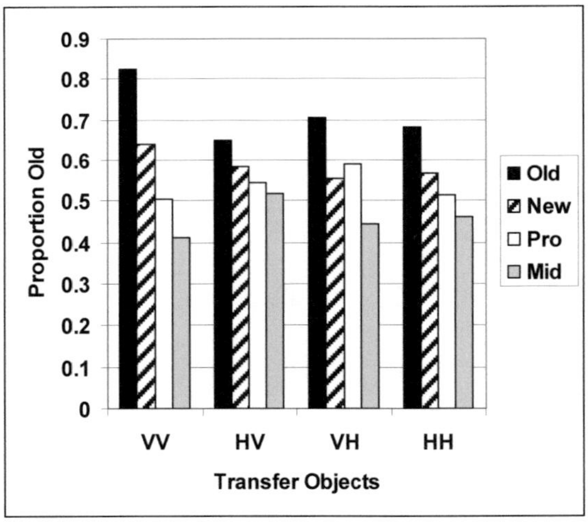

Fig. 5. Probability of calling a stimulus 'old' as a function of condition.

2.5 Conclusion

As expected, the categories were learned more rapidly when presented visually than haptically and when presented in a systematic rather than a random order. However, the terminal level of learning was virtually the same in each case. Surprisingly, classification on the transfer test, even when switched to a different modality, was remarkably accurate, with error rates ranging from 2-10%; the impact of a test delayed by one week was statistically significant but minimal in terms of absolute loss.

The greatest differences occurred in recognition, where again the visual modality generally resulted in superior performance. The visual-visual (VV) condition, compared to the haptic-haptic (HH) condition, revealed the general advantage of the visual modality for the same objects, and would be consistent with the general hypothesis that the visual modality encodes more (or more accurate) information than the haptic modality.

Recognition accuracy was slightly worse in the cross-modality conditions, with better discrimination found for visual study and haptic test than the reverse. This suggests that visual encoding provides considerably more information than haptic encoding, and that this difference remains even following haptic testing. A simple model is to assume that the visual modality encodes more features than does the haptic modality, and that each modality can transfer a proportion of these features to the alternate modality. For example, suppose that 80 features have been encoded and stored for each category following visual learning; for the haptic modality, 40 features are encoded. If 50% of all features can be transferred to the alternate modality, then the number of features available at the time of transfer would be 80(1.0) = 80 for VV, 80(.50) = 40 for VH, 40(1.0) = 40 for HH, and 40(.50) = 20 for HV, an ordering that matched that obtained in recognition.

3. Intermodal conflict in category learning and transfer

This experiment addressed whether categories can be learned when the objects, simultaneously explored visually and haptically, were actually different although from the same category. Following each study block, the subject was tested by presenting the study objects either visually, haptically, or both visually and haptically. This was repeated four times, followed by a transfer test similar to that used in Experiment 1.

One hypothesis is that cross-modal conflict should retard learning, because of the inconsistency of information available during study. Alternatively, presenting information that is available to both modalities, even when in conflict, could provide additional cues for learning. Since subjects were not told that the objects would be different, and since the differences among the patterns belonging to the same category were not strikingly obvious and encoded by different modalities, it is possible that the visually sensed and felt information for a given 'stimulus' might be integrated into a coherent percept. Since the features encoded visually and haptically could differ, at least for some percentage of the encoded features (Miller, 1972), any integration from the two modalities could, in principle, result in a more robust concept.

Alternatively, the subject could learn two versions for each category, one visual and one haptic, with integration between the modalities playing no role. It is worth stressing that the objects studied visually and haptically for each category were identical; only the pairing on each study trial was inconsistent. Since learning more categories has been found to retard learning but enhance later transfer (Homa & Chambliss, 1975), the formation of multiple-modality categories would predict that learning rate would be slowed by this manipulation but produce more accurate later transfer.

On the transfer test, subjects were either provided with the objects to be recognized and classified, based only on its visual appearance, from touch alone, or with both vision and touch provided. As was the case in learning, when an old object was presented to both modalities, the object matched its training pairing. Finally, as was the case in Experiment 1, objects were learned in a systematic or random manner, with testing occurring either immediately or after a delay of one week.

3.1 Method

The learning phase again consisted of a series of four 4 study-test trials with corrective feedback. On each learning trial, the participant visually perceived an object of a category (e.g., A1) and at the same time haptically explored, under an opaque black foam board, another object of the same category (e.g., A15). Presentation order for the systematic training condition again presented the objects blocked by category; in the random condition, category pairing was maintained but randomly selected in terms of the category presented. Following a given study block, the objects were randomly presented and the subject was asked to identify the category. In the visual condition, the objects were presented visually but could not be touched; in the haptic condition, each object could be manipulated but not seen. In the visual + haptic condition, the objects could be inspected both visually and haptically. Following each response, corrective feedback was provided. This procedure was repeated 3 additional study/test times. Participants were only informed of a category label and told to form each category by using both the appearance and felt conformations of each presented object. Participants were instructed to haptically explore and visually perceive the two conflicting stimuli simultaneously.

The transfer phase began either immediately or one week after completion of the learning phase. Participants were instructed to classify each object to its appropriate category learned during training (A, B, or C), and recognize whether this object was old or new using vision only, touch only, or both vision and touch. To each randomly presented object, participants gave a double-response after each presentation, recognition (Old or New) followed by classification (A, B, or C). Response time was self-spaced but restricted to 15 sec and feedback was not given during transfer test.

3.2 Results – Learning

Figure 6 shows the mean accuracy across learning blocks as a function of order of presentation and modality of test following each study trial. The main effect of learning blocks, order, and modality at test, were significant. In general, performance improved across learning blocks, with systematic presentation again facilitating rate of learning. Learning following visual + haptic test produced faster learning than visual alone or haptic alone ($p < .05$ in each case, Bonferroni test); visual alone also resulted in significantly fewer errors than haptic alone.

3.3 Results – Classification and recognition

Classification errors were again rare, averaging between 2% on the immediate test following systematic training and visual testing to 11.0% on the delayed test following random training and a haptic test.

On the recognition, test, the overall hit and false alarm rates were .794 and 533, respectively, which demonstrated that subjects discriminated old from new objects on the transfer test. The best discrimination occurred when recognition was tested visually (P(Hit) = .860, P(FA) = .532), or when both haptic and visual information were available (P(Hit) = .819, P(FA) = .468); when tested by the haptic modality alone, the difference between hits and false alarms remained significant but the level of discrimination was reduced (P(Hit) = .702, P(FA) = .600). A post-hoc Bonferronni test revealed that recognition discrimination was ordered V+H = V > H. Discrimination between old and new objects was also enhanced by systematic presentation during study, P(Hit) = .791 and P(FA) = .502; following random presentation, these values were P(Hit) = .796 and P(FA) = .565.

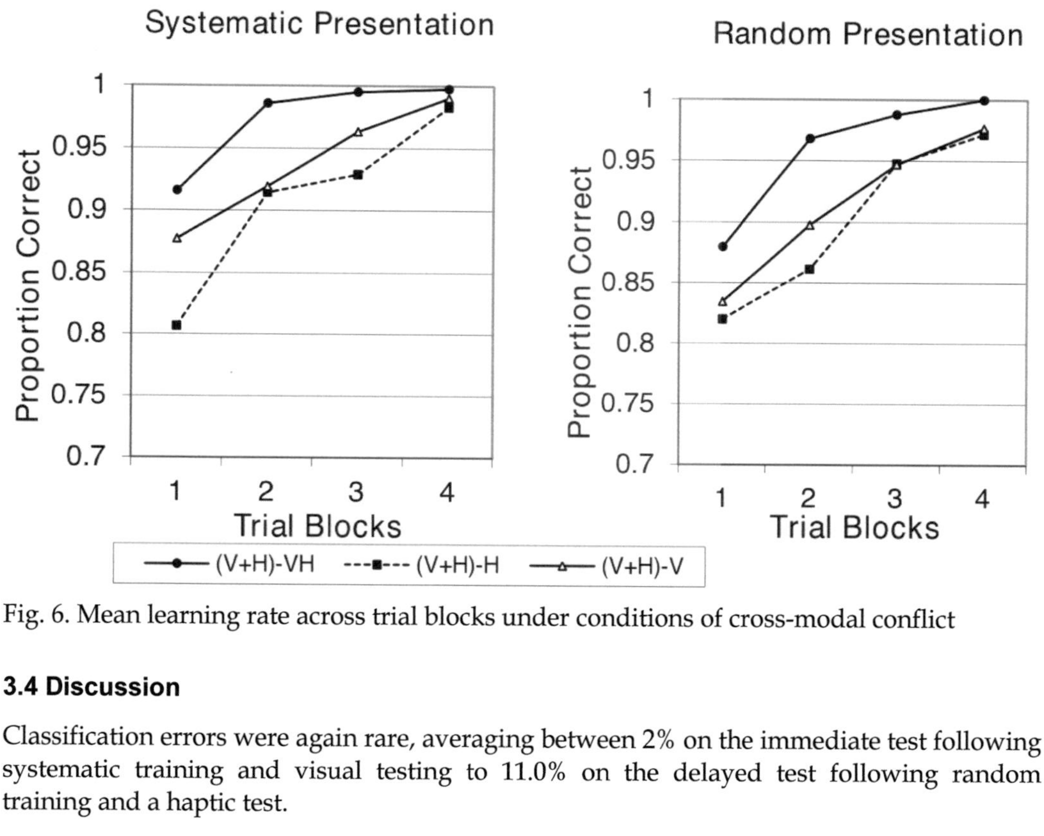

Fig. 6. Mean learning rate across trial blocks under conditions of cross-modal conflict

3.4 Discussion

Classification errors were again rare, averaging between 2% on the immediate test following systematic training and visual testing to 11.0% on the delayed test following random training and a haptic test.

Inter-modal conflict neither retarded learning nor degraded recognition. In fact, learning was speeded slightly by intermodal conflict, with learning rates comparing favorably to those obtained in any of the conditions in Experiment 1. Similarly, classification and later recognition was largely unperturbed by this manipulation. The results do show clear dominance by the visual modality, since recognition accuracy for touch alone, following learning with both modalities present, was significant but substantially reduced relative to recognition based on vision alone or when both vision and haptic information was available. This would suggest that, when both visual and haptic information are simultaneously available in the learning of concepts that the resulting concepts are biased by visual information, with haptic information available but playing a reduced role. Finally, as was the case in Experiment 1, false recognition of the midpoint and prototype objects was lower than for the new objects closest to the category prototype.

4. The effect of partial exemplar experience on multi-modal categorization

An unexplored issue in human categorization is whether concepts can be learned when less than complete information is available. Partial information, of course, arises in most common situations - occlusion, as in ordinary perception when one object partially covers another, thereby obscuring the object, or circumstance, as when an object can be seen but not touched or touched but not seen. In the present study, we investigated the learning of concepts when an object could be viewed but not touched or the reverse. An added manipulation was the criticality of the missing information. In one condition, texture was critical to the separation of the two categories to be learned; in another, the length of the stimulus was critical. The dimensions were the length, width, and texture of the objects to be classified (the stimuli were simple elliptical shapes, with texture variations on the backside of the stimulus). When length was critical, it needed to be combined with width or texture of the same object to unambiguously classify it into category A or B. That is, length (when critical to classification) could not be used by itself; it had to be combined with either width or texture to classify the stimulus with 100% accuracy. Figure 7 shows the overall structure of the two categories in the length critical condition (not shown is the length x texture figure, which was similarly structured as length x width). Note that texture and width was not informative for classification in this condition, since the integration of these two dimensions resulted in ambiguous classification. When texture was critical, it needed to be combined with length or width for unambiguous classification (essentially the same figure but substitute texture for length). In the control condition, all three dimensions were always available for inspection, i.e., the subject was free to view and touch (the backside) of each stimulus (which varied in texture) during learning, and either length or texture was critical to classification. In all, there were 20 stimuli, 10 in each category. In the partial condition, the subject was provided partial information only on each stimulus, being able to view but not touch half the stimuli; the remaining half could be touched but not viewed. In the 'length critical' condition, the categories could be separated if length was integrated with width or texture; in the 'texture critical' condition, the categories could be separated only if texture was integrated with either length or width.

We hypothesized that the modality of the crucial dimension should have no effect in learning if all dimensions are presented simultaneously. Ernst (2007) showed that normally non-related experiences of vision and touch, namely luminance and resistance to pressure, can be integrated by showing that participants who experienced the two dimensions as being correlated had a lower threshold to discriminate stimuli than stimuli with non-correlated dimensions. Therefore, we predicted that there should be no difference in learning categorization performance between participants in the length and texture crucial dimension conditions if they have full experience with the learning stimuli. If there is a difference we would assume participants in the texture crucial dimension condition would perform worse in categorization tests across learning and transfer than subjects who studied stimuli with length as the crucial dimension due to a potential difficulty resulting from forcing participants in the texture as the crucial dimension condition to integrate across modalities.

Second, when texture is the crucial dimension there should be reliable differences in categorization performance across learning trials and transfer between subjects in the partial and complete experience conditions. The integration of the crucial dimension with its related dimensions should become more difficult, if not impossible, if the related dimensions are not simultaneously provided with the crucial dimension, as when texture is the crucial dimension, as opposed to if one of the related dimensions is provided simultaneously with the crucial dimension, as when length is the crucial dimension. As such, for participants with partial experience, those that studied categories with texture as the crucial dimension should have worse categorization performance in learning compared to participants whose crucial dimension was length.

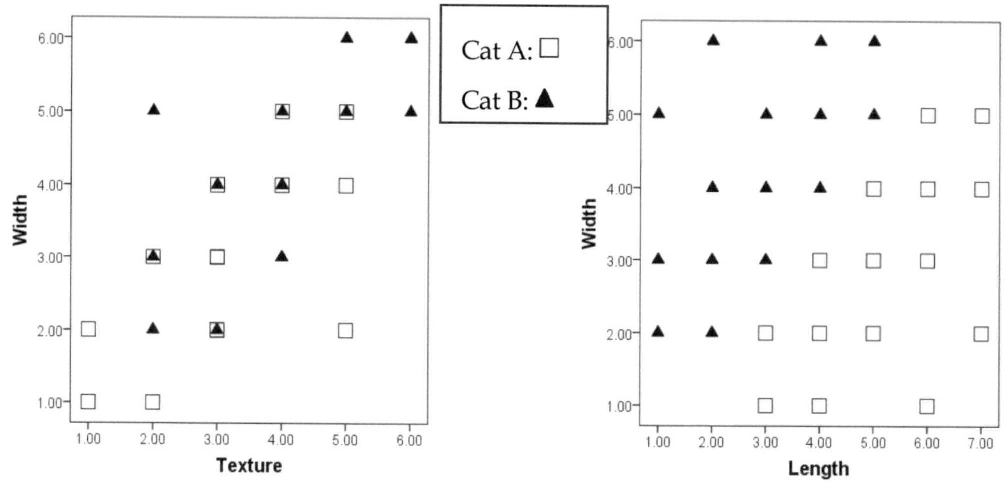

Fig. 7. Categorical structure in the length-critical condition

These two predictions would result in little difference in categorization accuracy across learning trials between participants with full experience and length as their crucial dimension, participants with partial experience and length as their crucial dimension, and participants with full experience and texture as their crucial dimension, yet all three of those groups of participants would perform very differently across learning trials from participants with partial experience and texture as their crucial dimension.

4.1 Method, procedure, and results

Subjects received 6 learning trials, the results of which are shown in Figure 8. Overall, learning was as predicted - when length was the critical dimension and learning was partial, learning was unaffected, i.e., being deprived of texture (even though texture and length could also be used to discriminate the categories) did not degrade learning, since length could always be combined with width for categorical separation. Similarly, when texture was critical, it was readily learned in the complete condition but learning was severely retarded in the partial condition. That is partial experience inhibited access to diagnostic categorical information only when texture was the crucial dimension.

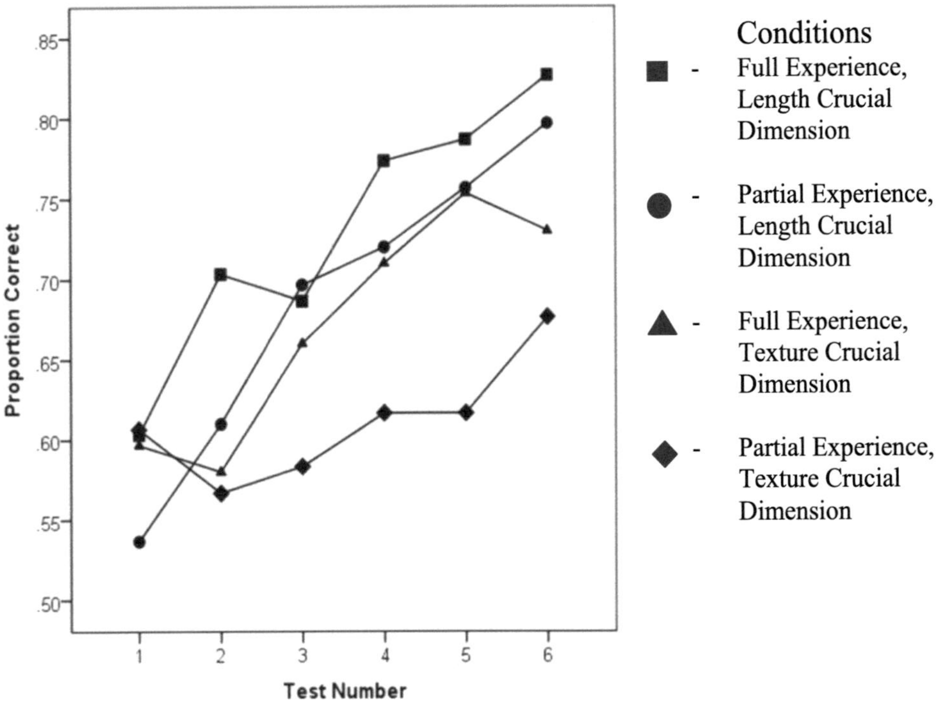

Fig. 8. Learning rate as a function of full and partial experience with length or texture as the crucial dimension.

5. Multidimensional scaling of a haptic vs. visual space

Insight into the patterning of results was further explored by multidimensional scaling of the objects. A total of six different scalings was performed, determined by haptic or visual inspection and following either no learning, random learning, or systematic learning. In each condition, the subject made similarity judgments to object pairs. We were especially interested in whether the space generated from visual judgments mirrored that when judgments were made haptically, and whether this space was further altered by prior learning. Since vision appeared to dominate haptic categories, and since more information appears to be available following visual examination, we expected that the haptic space would be structured more tightly than the visual space. This would be consistent with the hypothesis that the visual modality provides more, perhaps idiosyncratic, information than haptic exploration, and this additional information might be expected to increase stimulus discrimination and reduce overall categorical structure.

5.1 Method

Ninety Arizona State University undergraduates were drawn from the same subject pool as in previous experiments and randomly assigned to one of the six conditions. For two conditions, the similarity judgments were made either haptically or visually and followed no learning. For the remaining four conditions, learning was either systematic or random, as in Experiment 1, in the visual or haptic modality, followed by similarity judgments in the same modality as training.

Participants were either exposed to no learning or the same learning procedure used previously. They were individually tested and randomly assigned to one of the 6 conditions. Followed learning or no learning, participants were asked to make similarity judgments to the 105 possible paired-objects on a Likert-scale ranging from 1 to 9, with 1 = minimal similarity and 9 = maximal similarity. These 105 paired objects were presented randomly. For the haptic judgments, the objects were presented sequentially, with each object presented first or second about the same number of times. Ratings were self-paced but restricted to a maximum duration of 15 sec. When objects were presented visually, a similar procedure was used in which first one object was presented for inspection followed by the second object of the rating pair.

5.2 Results

The learning data mirrored that found previously, with more rapid learning for visual than haptic presentation but with terminal levels reaching nearly 100% in all learning conditions. As a consequence, the multidimensional spaces derived from similarity ratings following learning were based on comparable and near-errorless performance.

For each of the six conditions, the objects were multidimensionally scaled in dimensions 1-6. The three dimensional solutions were selected for further analysis because stress levels were low (none exceeded .05), of comparable value, and were the highest dimensionality that could be visually inspected. Three analyses were performed: (a) computation of the structural ratio (Homa, Rhodes, & Chambliss, 1979) for 15 objects as well as overall for each condition; (b) a comparison of the structural similarity among the six conditions; and (c) computation of each object to the centroid of its learning exemplars. The first measure tells us how structured each space was and whether the psychological structure mirrored objective structure. The second measure tells us whether the various scalings produced similar or different representations. The third measure assesses whether the prototype for each category was positioned away from or near the centroid of each category

The structural ratio was calculated for each of the 15 objects in a given condition by calculating the mean distance of that item to members of the same category, relative to the mean distance to objects from the other two categories. The mean of these 15 ratios for a given condition defined the mean structural ratio and represented level of conceptual structure, with smaller values indicating greater structure and values approaching 1.00 indicating a random structure. Figure 9 shows the mean structural ratio for each of the six conditions.

The structural ratios (SRs) ranged from (poorest) the space determined from visual inspection of the objects following no learning (SR = .414) to haptic inspection following systematic learning (SR = .223). In general, the structural ratios decreased with degree of learning, with the weakest structure associated with no learning (SR = .381), greatest structure with systematic learning (SR = .297), and intermediate structure with random learning (SR = .332). Overall, the haptic conceptual spaces were more structured than were the visual spaces (.301 vs. .381). To assess the similarity among the six conditions, correlations were computed among the six conditions, using as input the individual structural ratios for each object. These 15 correlations were positive and high, ranging from r = + .817 to r = + .981; the average correlation was r = +.924. A sample space – in this case, the MDS space following systematic learning in the haptic modality - is shown in Figure 10. What is clear is that the three haptic categories are clearly defined. Comparison with the original space (Figure 1) clearly reveals that the category prototype (P1, P2, P3) has become centered within each category rather than occupying the location at the extreme points of the two transformational paths.

5.3 Discussion

The results show that the haptic and visual representations of the same 3D objects were remarkably similar, suggesting that information critical to visual concepts were generally maintained following haptic inspection. As was the case in our previous studies that explored multidimensional scaling following the learning of categorical structure, the degree of structure was generally enhanced following learning (Homa et al., 1979; Zaki & Homa, 1999). As predicted, the conceptual spaces were more tightly structured following haptic examination. What seems likely is that there exists a dominant set of features critical to similarity that are comparable to the visual and haptic modality but that additional information, perhaps idiosyncratic, is more available in the visual modality. This would explain why the spaces were highly correlated and yet why the haptic space was more tightly structured.

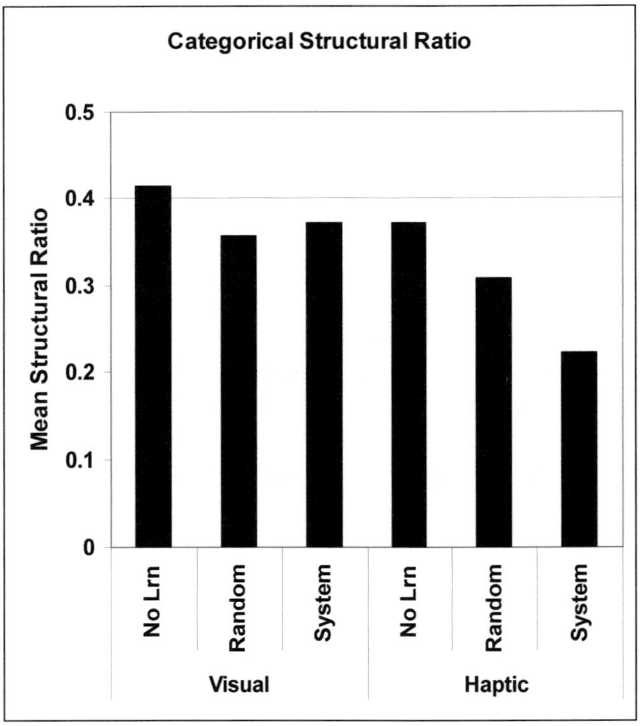

Fig. 9. Mean Structural Ratio for the six MDS solutions

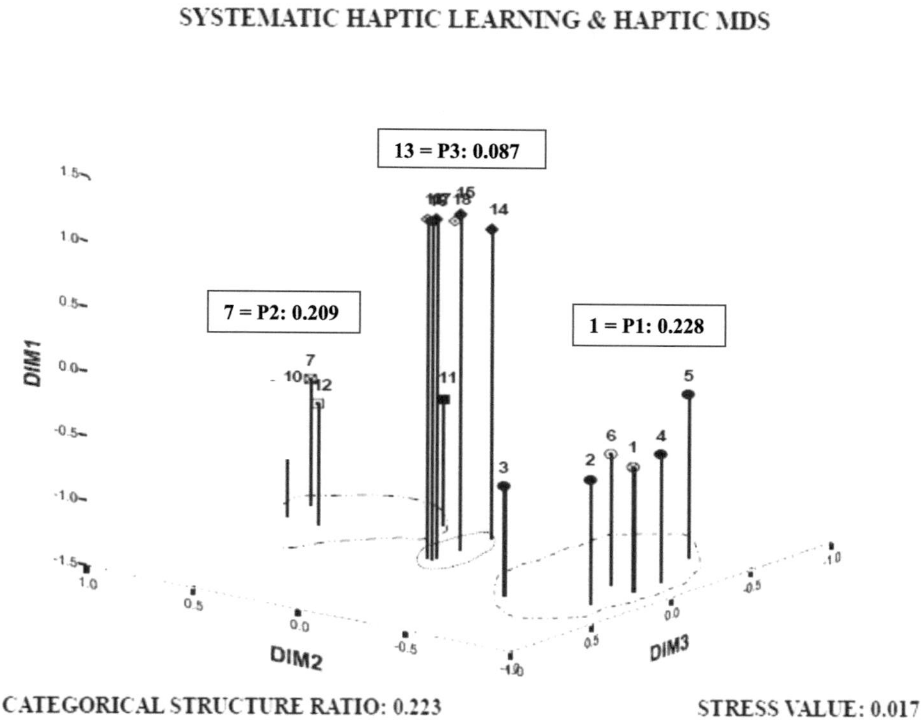

Fig. 10. Three dimensional MDS space following systematic learning in the haptic modality

6. General discussion

There exists ample evidence that vision and touch activate common neurological sites (Amedi *et al.*, 2001; Ernst & Banks, 2002) and that objects experienced visually or haptically can, with fair success, be recognized in the alternate modality (Klatzky, Lederman, & Metzger, 1985; Pensky *et al.*, 2008). However, almost nothing is known about the transfer of *categorical* information between these modalities. That is, can it be demonstrated that abstract categories, learned in one modality, maintain their categorical identity in an alternate modality? The answer, at least for the forms used here and considering only the visual and haptic modalities, is clearly yes.

We purposely selected fairly complex three dimensional objects that were comprised of continuous distortions from three prototypes that, informally at least, appeared to preclude simple naming of objects or even features. The major results of the three experiments that explored the learning, transfer, and retention of concepts acquired visually, haptically, or combined can be summarized: (a) Visual learning of categories, as expected, was more rapid than haptic learning, but haptic learning reached the same errorless criterion after only four study blocks; (b) When categories were learned in one modality, the classification of novel forms on a transfer test was virtually perfect, even when presented in the alternate modality; (c) The interposition of a week's delay had a statistically significant but minimal effect on classification accuracy.

The results for recognition were, however, less impressive: (a) Recognition accuracy was less accurate than classification, especially when learning occurred haptically and recognition occurred in the visual modality; (b) Transfer between the modalities was more accurate when the learning was visual rather than by touch; (c) Within-category, cross-modal conflict had no impact on learning and even appeared to enhance later recognition; and finally, (f) The psychological space for concepts acquired visually or haptically was virtually the same. We also found that presentation of the objects in a systematic, rather than random, order speeded learning and slightly improved overall transfer performance, and that the haptic space was somewhat better structured into the three categories than was the visual space.

Recognition following categorical learning was superior when the categories were formed visually and tested haptically rather than the reverse. This outcome could be explained most readily by assuming that two, distinct processes are involved in categorical recognition, an initial encoding of features relevant to the category, and a transfer of categorical information from one modality to another. A safe assumption is that the visual modality encodes more information than does the haptic modality. If the transfer from one modality to the other is not perfect, e.g., 50% of the information is transferred accurately and 50% is not, then the obtained ordering on the recognition test can be explained. That is, VV > HH = VH > HV. The multidimensional scaling of the category space, following either no learning or criterion learning, supports this interpretation, albeit indirectly. To see this, consider each object to be encoded with N-categorical features + K idiosyncratic features. Since classification transfer was accurate, with relatively few errors, we could assume that the two modalities encoded the categorical features to a similar degree. However, if the idiosyncratic features were more numerous following visual inspection, and if the idiosyncratic features are critical to later discrimination, then two outcomes would occur - recognition would be more accurate following visual training (more idiosyncratic features) and the similarity judgments, used to map the categorical spaces, would be more distinctive when objects were compared visually. Phillips et al. (2009) found that increasing object complexity influenced haptic judgments more than visual judgments, an outcome that would be consistent with the view suggested here. An alternative test would require that features more amenable to haptic than visual processing, such as texture and weight differences, be incorporated into a categorical paradigm. Under these circumstances, haptic recognition might improve overall and produce an MDS space that represented within-category objects as slightly less similar to each other.

Four other results are notable. First, systematic training had a small but consistently positive effect both in learning and later recognition, a result that replicates Zaki and Homa's (1999) study using two dimensional categorical stimuli. Second, the placement of the category prototypes in the multidimensionally-scaled space failed to preserve the prototype as an endpoint object of its category. Rather, the category prototype, especially following a learning phase, was found to gravitate more toward the center of its psychological category. Third, cross-modal conflict had a negligible effect in either learning or later transfer. In fact, this conflict seemed to enhance later recognition. Our impression is that most subjects failed to notice a conflict when the object explored visually and haptically were different, presumably because the objects were not namable, lacked dramatically different features, and belonged to the same category. It is less clear whether the subject integrated the slightly disparate sensations from the two different stimuli on each trial, formed a composite memory trace that included both visual and haptic features, or formed bi-modal concepts for each category. The last outcome seems least likely, since the learning of multiple categories should produce a slowing of category learning, an outcome not obtained. Regardless, additional research with categories composed of more distinctive features, e.g., texture differences, might permit separation of these competing explanations. Finally, the category prototype and midpoint objects were falsely recognized less often than other new objects. This occurred even though the midpoint objects were flanked by two similar training objects as were the new objects; the category prototypes similarly had two training objects that were similar as well. What seems likely is that exemplar similarity (e.g., Nosofsky, 1988) alone was not the sole determinate of recognition. Rather, categorical influences likely mitigated false recognition, since, for the midpoint objects, the two flanking training objects belonged to different prototypes. Why the category prototypes were not falsely recognized more often (or at least as often as the new objects) is less clear. However, the location of the prototypes, as an object at the vertex of two divergent paths, may have insulated the category prototype from false recognition because of extra-experimental knowledge, e.g., the subject might sense that the prototype is a generative pattern, not an old one. Regardless, there exists prior evidence that the category prototype may be treated as a novel ideal point rather than a familiar one based on object similarity alone (Homa *et al.*, 1993; Homa *et al.*, 2001).

Future research into multi-modal concepts, including situations where less than full stimulus information is available, is critical to a comprehensive theory of concepts. Creative paradigms that involve modalities other than visual and haptic processing is obviously needed, as are the criteria needed to address what is perhaps the most fundamental question of all in this domain - what evidence would suggest that our concepts become modality-free or modality-preserving?

7. References

Amedi, A., Malach, R., Hendler, T., Peled, S., & Zohary, E. (2001). Visuo-haptic object-related activation in the ventral visual pathway. *Nature Neuroscience, 4,* 324-330.

Bergmann-Tiest, W. M., & Kappers, A. M. L. (2006). Analysis of haptic perception of materials by multidimensional scaling and physical measurements of roughness and compressibility. *Acta Psychologica, 121,* 1-20.

Biederman, I. (1972). Perceiving real-world scenes. *Science, 177,* 77-80.

Busemeyer, J. R., & Pleskac, T. (2009). Theoretical tools for understanding and aiding dynamic decision making. *Journal of Mathematical Psychology, 53,* 126-138.

Castiello, U., Zucco, G. M., Parma, V., Ansuini, C., & Tirindelli, R. (2006). Cross-modal interactions between olfaction and vision when grasping. *Chemical Senses, 31,* 665-671.

Catherwood, D. (1993). The haptic processing of texture and shape by 7- to 9-month-old infants. *British Journal of Developmental Psychology, 11,* 299-306.

Cooke, T., Jakel, F., Wallraven, C., & Bulthoff, H. H. (2007). Multimodal similarity and categorization of novel, three-dimensional objects. *Neuropsychologia, 45,* 484-495.

Ernst, M. O. (2007). Learning to integrate arbitrary signals from vision and touch. *Journal of Vision, 7,* 1-14.

Ernst, M. O., & Banks, M. S. (2002). Humans integrate visual and haptic information in a statistically optimal fashion. *Nature, 415,* 429-433.

Ernst, M. O., & Bulthoff, H. H. (2004). Merging the senses into a robust percept. *Trends in Cognitive Sciences, 8,* 162-169.

Freides, D. (1974). Human information processing and sensory modality: Cross-modal functions, information complexity, memory, and deficit. *Psychological Bulletin, 81,* 284-310.

Freides, D. (1975). Information complexity and cross-modal functions. *British Journal of Psychology, 66,* 283-287.

Garbin, C. P. (1990). Visual-touch perceptual equivalence for shape information in children and adults. *Perception and Psychophysics, 48,* 271-279.

Garbin, C. P., & Bernstein, I. H. (1984). Visual and haptic perception of three-dimensional solid forms. *Perception & Psychophysics, 36,* 104-110.

Garrard, P., Lambon Ralph, M. A., Hodges, J. R., & Patterson, K. (2001). Prototypicality, distinctiveness and intercorrelation: Analyses of the semantic attributes of living and nonliving concepts. *Journal of Cognitive Neuroscience, 18,* 125–174.

Gentaz, E., & Hatwell, Y. (1995). The haptic "oblique effect" in children's and adults' perception of orientation. *Perception, 24,* 631-646.

Gentaz, E., & Hatwell, Y. (2003). Haptic processing of spatial and material object properties. In Y. Hatwell, A. Streri, & E. Gentaz (Eds.), *Touching for knowing: Cognitive psychology of haptic manual perception.* Amsterdam, PA: John Benjamins Publications, 123-160.

Gliner, C. R., Pick, A. D., Pick H. L., & Hales, J. J. (1969). A developmental investigation of visual and haptic preferences for shape and texture. *Monographs of the Society for Research in Child Development, 34,* 1-40.

Golledge, R. G. (1992). Do people understand spatial concepts? The case of first order primitives. In A. U. Frank, I. Campari, & U. Formentini (Eds.), *Theories and models of spatio-temporal reasoning in geographic space.* Berlin: Springer-Verlag, 1-21.

Golledge, R. G., Ruggles, A. J., Pellegrino, J. W., & Gale, N. D. (1993). Integrating route knowledge in an unfamiliar neighborhood: along and across route experiments. *Journal of Environmental Psychology, 13,* 293-307.

Hatwell, Y., Streri, A., & Gentaz, E. (2003), *Touching for knowing: Cognitive psychology of haptic manual perception.* Amsterdam, PA: John Benjamins Publications.

Hershberger, W. A., & Misceo, G. F. (1996). Touch dominates haptic estimates of discordant visual-haptic size. *Perception & Psychophysics, 58,* 1124-1132.

Homa, D. (1984). On the nature of categories. In G. H. Bower (Ed.), *The psychology of learning and motivation: Advances in research and theory.* San Diego, CA: Academic Press, 49-94.

Homa, D., Goldhardt, B., Burruel-Homa, L., & Smith, C. (1993). Influence of manipulated category knowledge on prototype classification and recognition. *Memory and Cognition, 21,* 529-538.

Homa, D., Kahol, K., Tripathi, P., Bratton, L., & Panchanathan, S. (2009). Haptic concepts in the blind. *Attention, Perception, & Psychophysics, 71,* 690-698.

Homa, D., Rhoads, D., Chambliss, D. (1979). Evolution of conceptual structure. *Journal of Experimental Psychology, 5,* 11-23.

Homa, D., Smith, C., Macak, C., Johovich, J., & Osorio, D. (2001). Recognition of facial prototypes: The importance of categorical structure and degree of learning. *Journal of Memory and Language, 44,* 443-474.

Kitchin, R. M., Blades, M., & Golledge, R. G. (1997). Understanding spatial concepts at the geographic scale without the use of vision. *Progress in Human Geography, 21*, 225-242.

Klatzky, R. L., & Lederman, S. J. (2003). The haptic identification of everyday life objects. In Y. Hatwell, A. Streri, & E. Gentaz (Eds.), *Touching for knowing: Cognitive psychology of haptic manual perception.* Amsterdam, PA: John Benjamins Publications, 105-122.

Klatzky, R. L., Lederman, S. J., & Metzger, V. A. (1985). Identifying objects by touch: An "expert system". *Perception & Psychophysics, 37*, 299-302.

Lederman, S. J., Klatzky, R., Tong, C., & Hamilton, C. (2006). The perceived roughness of resistive virtual textures: II. Effects of varying viscosity with a force-feedback device. *ACM Transactions on Applied Perception (TAP), 3*, 15-30.

Luck, S. J., & Vogel, E. K. (1997). The capacity of visual working memory for features and conjunctions. *Nature*, 390, 279-281.

Metcalfe, J., & Fisher, R. P. (1986). The relation between recognition memory and classification learning. *Memory and Cognition, 14*, 164-173.

Millar, S., & Al-Attar, Z. (2005). What aspects of vision facilitate haptic processing? *Brain and Cognition, 59*, 258-268.

Miller, E. A. (1972). Interaction of vision and touch in conflict and nonconflict form perception tasks. *Journal of Experimental Psychology, 96*, 114-123.

Moll, M., & Erdmann, M. A., (2003). Reconstructing the shape and motion of unknown objects with active tactile sensors. In J. D. Boissonnat, J. Burdick, K. Goldberg, & S. Hutchinson (Eds.), *Algorithmic and Computational Robotics: New Directions*, Springer Verlag, 293-310.

Norman, J. F., Norman, H. F., Clayton, A. M., Lianekhammy, J., & Zielke, G. (2004). The visual and haptic perception of natural object shape. *Perception & Psychophysics, 66*, 342-351.

Nosofsky, R. M. (1991). Tests of an exemplar model for relating perceptual classification and recognition memory. *Journal of Experimental Psychology: Human Perception and Performance, 17*, 3-27.

Osherson, D. N., Smith, E. E., Wilkie, O., & Lopez, A. (1990). Category-based induction. *Psychological Review, 97*, 185-200.

Pensky, A. E., Johnson, K. A., Haag, S., & Homa, D. (2008). Delayed memory for visual-haptic exploration of familiar objects. *Psychonomic Bulletin & Review, 15*, 574-580.

Phillips, F., Egan, E. J. L., & Perry, B. N. (2009). Perceptual equivalence between vision and touch is complexity dependent. *Acta Psychologica, 132*, 259-266.

Rosch, E., & Mervis, C. (1975). Family resemblances: Studies in the internal structures of categories. *Cognitive Psychology*, 7, 573-605.

Rumelhart, D. E., & Abrahamson, A. A. (1973). A model for analogical reasoning. *Cognitive Psychology, 5*, 1-28.

Salada, M. A., Colgate, J. E., Vishton, P. M., & Frankel, E. (2004). Two experiments on the perception of slip at the fingertip. In *12th Symposium on Haptic Interfaces for Virtual Environments and Teleoperator Systems*, 146-153.

Shin, H. J., Nosofsky, R. M. (1992). Similarity-scaling studies of dot-pattern classification and recognition. *Journal of Experimental Psychology: General, 121*, 278-304.

Stevens, S., & Harris, J. R. (1962). The scaling of subjective roughness and smoothness. *Journal of Experimental Psychology, 64*, 489-494.

Streri, A. (1987). Tactile discrimination of shape and intermodal transfer in 2- to 3-month old infants. *British Journal of Developmental Psychology, 2*, 287-294.

Volcic, R., Wijntjes, W. A., Kool, E. C., & Kappers, A. M. L. (2010). *Experimental Brain Research, 203*, 621-627.

Woodworth, R. S., & Schlosberg, H. (1954). *Experimental Psychology*. (2nd ed.). New York: Holt, Rinehart & Winston.

Zaki, S. R., & Homa, D. (1999). Concepts and transformational knowledge. *Cognitive Psychology, 39*, 69-115.

2

Computer Graphic and PHANToM Haptic Displays: Powerful Tools to Understand How Humans Perceive Heaviness

Satoru Kawai[1], Paul H. Faust, Jr.[1] and Christine L. MacKenzie[2]
[1]Tezukayama University,
[2]Simon Fraser University,
[1]Japan
[2]Canada

1. Introduction

The development of human/computer interfaces related to human haptics is subject to greater degrees of difficulty and complexity than those related to human visual and/or auditory senses. Such interfaces require direct contact and/or interaction with humans as opposed to visual and/or auditory devices that do not require such direct contact, manipulation and other force-related interactions. Therefore, without a deeper understanding of the mechanisms involved in haptics, such interfaces may be far from being user-centered or easy-to-use.

The focus of our research has been to understand the perceptual system of heaviness in humans. Heaviness perception, categorized as one aspect of haptic perception, is considered to be a vital ability in everyday life not only to recognize objects, but also to lift and manipulate them. Research in the field of experimental psychology, in particular psychophysics, has focused on identifying the properties and mechanisms of heaviness ever since Weber (1834, as translated by H. E. Ross & Murray, 1978) undertook his inquiries. Such properties and mechanisms have not yet been fully identified. Rather, the more experimental techniques and/or experimental environments have evolved, the more complex human perception of heaviness appears. This is because heaviness: (1) involves both perceptual systems and sensorimotor systems, such as the force programming system for lifting or holding objects, (2) is affected not only by object weight, but also by physical, functional and other properties of objects and (3) is affected by bottom-up processing by lower-order senses and by top-down processing by higher-order cognitive processes such as expectation and rationalization.

The purpose of this chapter is to overview human perception of heaviness to decipher its complexity. In addition, we introduce the usefulness of virtual reality systems to isolate and understand constraints on heaviness perception. One such system adopted for our research is the Virtual Hand Laboratory, creating virtual or augmented environments, in which humans interact with computer displayed objects or real physical objects. We illuminate mechanisms of heaviness perception with fundamental findings that might not have been obtained from the real world (i.e., Real Haptic + Real Vision). Also, we posit that superimposing computer-generated graphical objects precisely onto real, physical objects (i.e., Real Haptic + Virtual Vision) allows manipulation of visual properties of objects independently from physical properties. Finally, we introduce Virtual Haptic + Virtual Vision conditions, using a unique experimental augmented environment using both computer haptics AND computer graphics displays. This allows for selective experimental manipulations in which the haptic device affects haptic perception while computer generated graphics have an effect on visual perception, by superimposing computer-generated object forces precisely onto the graphical objects existing within the computer display. Presented are fresh findings regarding heaviness perception that enhance the knowledge base for the human perception of heaviness. These basic findings are expected to facilitate future research and development of haptic and graphic computer systems relating to human recognition, lifting, transport or manipulation of physical objects.

2. Factors influencing human perceptual system of heaviness

Figure 1 shows a schematic that provides an overview of three categories of factors influencing human perceived heaviness: (1) factors related to the sensorimotor system responsible for lifting and holding an object (Object Lifting Phase), (2) factors or physical properties relating to an object itself (Object), and (3) factors relating to perceiving or judging heaviness (Perceiving Heaviness Phase). These factors act not only individually but also interactively. It should be emphasized here that the human psychological unit of heaviness differs from the physical unit of measuring weight.

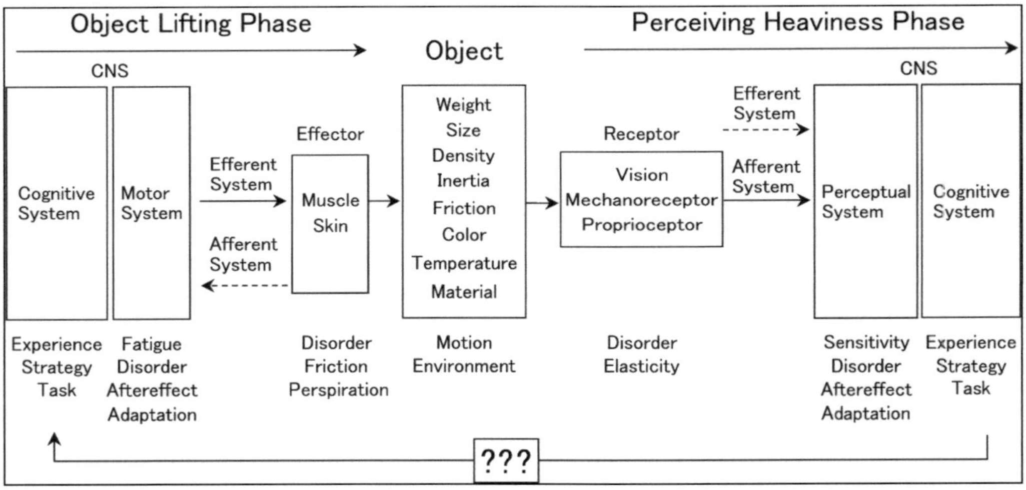

Fig. 1. Factors influencing human perceived heaviness. Question marks indicate whether or how humans use perceived heaviness for subsequent object lifting. This is controversial and requires further investigation (See Sec. 5.1).

2.1 Factors related to lifting and holding movements

Whenever a person attempts to perceive the heaviness of an object or to compare the difference in weight between two or more objects, grasping, lifting and holding movements must precede these behaviors (MacKenzie & Iberall, 1994). When an object is lifted by an adult, the sensorimotor system functions automatically, without any particular attention, to achieve a safe and effective grip to lift and hold, transport or manipulate the object, maintaining stability. This system is composed of two subsystems: a feedforward system and a feedback system.

A feedforward system works before the initiation of the grasping movement to predict object properties including weight and estimate the required motor commands, based on long-term memories (Gordon et al., 1993) and/or short-term memories if the lifts are repeated during a short period of time (Johansson, 1996). Finally, these programmed motor commands are sent to the related muscle groups to achieve stable lift of the target object. Interestingly, the motor commands are hypothesized to be sent not only to the effectors, i.e., related muscle groups for object lifts, but also for "efferent copies" to be sent to the CNS structures related to sensation, feedback processing or perception (Sperry, 1950; Holst, 1954; McCloskey, 1978).

Once the lift of an object has been initiated, the feedback system acts to optimize the output forces in the muscles through a local reflex feedback via Ia afferents in a muscle spindle (for muscle stretch) and Ib in a Golgi tendon organ (for muscle tension) (Crago et al., 1982; Rothwell, et al., 1982). These peripheral-origin signals ascend via the dorsal column through transcortical loops in the central nervous system (CNS) relating to motor control (S1, M1, basal ganglia, and cerebellum), and ongoing motor commands are probably modified via cortico-cerebellar connections with the CNS-origin signals "copied" to optimize subsequent discharge based on detected errors between the efferent copies and afferent information. The optimized signals, then, may contribute to achieving safer and more stable lift (Brodie & H.E. Ross, 1985). Grip forces applied at the object/digit interfaces are also automatically adjusted, based on the information from mechanoreceptors on glabrous skin, from the initiation of lifts according to frictional forces, object slipperiness (Johansson, 1996; Rinkenauer, et al., 1999) and object torque (Kinoshita et al., 1997).

The "copies" have been termed in such various ways as "sense of effort" (McCloskey, 1978), "collorary discharge" (Sperry, 1950) or "efferent copy" (Holst, 1954). Furthermore, in psychological research such as that for the size-weight illusion (SWI), (Charpentier, 1891 as cited in Murray, et al., 1999; See Sec. 3), efferent copy is replaced by the term "expectation" (H.E. Ross, 1969) or "ease with which could be lifted" (Müller & Schumann, 1889, as cited in Davis, 1973). These copies are thought to play an important role in object perception as well as for motor control. A well-known example is the ability to perceive an object and/or its surroundings as being at rest and clear without blurring when the eyes are moved. This is due to the copied signals relating to self-generated movement being compared with the signals obtained from vision (Holst, 1954). Without this system, we could not perceive an object accurately.

Interestingly, the forces generated when lifting an object correlate with object weight (Johansson, 1996) and that of heaviness perception (Harper & Stevens, 1948; Stevens, 1958). However, as to the correlation between the forces generated and perceived heaviness, researchers differ. Some researchers support their correlation (H.E. Ross, 1969; Davis & Roberts, 1976; Gordon et al., 1991) and others report their dissociation (Flanagan & Beltzner, 2000; Grandy & Westwood, 2006; Chang et al., 2008). What factors give rise to these opposing views and which view will eventually prevail remain matters to be resolved, noted by question marks in Fig. 1.

Yet, the motor-related commands for force generation and adaptation, at least partly or indirectly, relate to perceived heaviness. Evidence has shown involvement of the sensorimotor system in human perceptual system of heaviness (McCloskey, 1978). That is, the degree of perceived heaviness is reported to increase due to the effects of fatigue on related muscles (Jones & Hunter, 1983; Buckingham et al., 2009), to partial curarization or a peripheral anaesthesia effect on cutaneous or joint sensation (Gandevia & McCloskey, 1977a), and to muscle vibration on related muscle spindles (Brodie & H.E. Ross, 1984). Neural disorders relating to the sensorimotor system are also reported to affect perceived heaviness. In comparison to normal subjects, for example, it is reliable to be overestimated in patients with paresis (Gandevia & McCloskey, 1977b), in deafferented patients for muscle spindles and Golgi tendon organ (Rothwell et al., 1982), in those with cerebellum disorders (Holms, 1917; Cf. Rabe et al., 2009), and in those with Parkinson's disease (Maschke et al., 2006).

Furthermore, attention should be focused on the lifting conditions, i.e., how to discern the heaviness of an object as a higher order or more cognitive and strategic matter (Fig.1). The manner of lifting, for example, affects perceiving heaviness in various conditions: active lifting, such as jiggling an object (Brodie & H.E. Ross, 1985), tends to make more accurate weight discrimination than passive pressure (Weber, 1834, translated by H. E. Ross & Murray, 1978). In addition, the perceived heaviness when an object is lifted depends on which parts of the hand are in contact, with an increase of perceived heaviness being reported when an object is lifted distally, by the fingertips, compared to when lifted proximally, by the base of fingers or near the palm (Davis, 1974). Holway et al., (1938) reported that the same object is perceived as heavier in the second trial than that in the first. After repeated lifts of sets of heavier objects, the discriminative thresholds decreased in the sets of lighter objects compared to those without such preceding lifts of sets of heavier objects (Holway & Hurvich, 1937). Further, the degree of perceived heaviness changed when lifting two objects simultaneously using both hands compared to that when lifting two objects alternately using only one hand (Jones & Hunter, 1982).

2.2 Object properties and environmental surroundings influence perceived heaviness

Object weight is a vital factor for perceived heaviness (Harper & Stevens, 1948; Stevens, 1958). Heaviness is, however, not weight. Previous studies demonstrated that heaviness is affected by the input of information regarding size whether visually (H.E. Ross, 1969; Masin & Crestoni, 1988) or haptically (Ellis & Lederman, 1993). Input includes such factors as pressure on the contact-area of the skin (Charpentier, 1891, as cited in Murray et al. 1999), object surface slipperiness (Rinkenauer, et al., 1999), material (Ellis & Lederman, 1999; Buckingham et al., 2009), colour (De Camp, 1917; Payne, 1958), shape (Dresslar, 1894), temperature (Stevens & Green, 1978), inertia tensor whether perceived haptically (Amazeen, 1999) or visually (Streit et al., 2007), and density (J. Ross & Di Lollo, 1970; Grandy & Westwood, 2006). Regarding experimental surroundings (Fig. 1, bottom in middle), changes in gravity have been reported to affect perceived heaviness. Compared to a 1-G normal environment, zero-G reduces perceived heaviness and weight discrimination, while that of 1.8-G increases them (H. E. Ross & Reschike, 1982; H. E. Ross et al., 1984).

2.3 Bottom-up and top-down influences on heaviness perception

As peripheral or bottom-up processing issues related to perceptual system of heaviness, individual learning and sensitivity in weight discrimination are important factors. The Weber fraction, i.e., weight sensitivity, widely differs among individuals (0.02~0.16) (Holway et al., 1937; Raj et al., 1985). Age, especially, is a crucial factor leading to a decrease of sensitivity to weight or heaviness (Gandevia, 1996; Dijker, 2008). Serious deterioration is also reported for neural disorders including leprous neuropathy (Raj, et al., 1985), lesions to inferior-frontal cortex including PMv (Halstead, 1945), and left parietal and temporal lesions (Li et al., 2007).

As for higher level, cognitive-based or top-down processing, individual learning or experience is also an important factor to influence perception of heaviness (Fig. 1). An expectation that a larger object should be heavier than a smaller object, for example, is thought to affect perceived heaviness. Accordingly, when lifted, the larger of two objects of equal weight tends to be perceived as lighter than the smaller (H.E. Ross, 1969; Davis & Roberts, 1976; Gordon et al., 1991; Rabe et al., 2009; Buckingham & Goodale, 2010). This expectation factor is also experienced in relation to object colour (Payne, 1958), object material (Ellis & Lederman, 1999; Buckingham et al., 2009), and even the human conditions of gender and age (Dijker, 2008). For example, when viewed, darker or metallic objects are judged to be heavier than brighter or wooden ones, but are then perceived as lighter when actually lifted under same-weight conditions. When confronting conflicting issues, such as with the SWI, when two objects have different size but are of identical weight, subjects tend to rationalize that if the weight is the same, the larger object should be lighter, rather than depending on the current sensations of heaviness (Mon-Williams & Murray, 2000). This tendency seems to be more pronounced when subjects are subject to the forced-choice condition in which they must choose either Heavier or Lighter (Mon-Williams & Murray, 2000; Buckingham & Goodale, 2010). This raises the question, what is the best way to obtain accurate and natural responses from subjects: using the two category method "Heavier and Lighter", the three category method "Heavier, Lighter, and Similar", the bimanual or unilateral matching methods, or the magnitude estimation method? Other questions posed by experimenters such as, "Which is heavier?" or "Which is the heaviest" might cognitively bias perception of heaviness.

3. Effects of object "size" on perceived heaviness

Object size is the oldest, most-studied factor since Müller and Schuman (1889, as cited in Davis, 1973) and Charpentier (1891, as cited in Murray et al. 1999) reported the phenomenon of the size-weight illusion (SWI): the larger of two objects of equal weight is perceived as lighter than the smaller. The mechanism underlying the SWI has been continuously discussed with various interpretations: Expectation Theory (H.E. Ross, 1969), Information Integration Theory (Anderson, 1970; Masion & Crestoni, 1988), Density Theory (J. Ross & Di Lollo, 1970), Gain Adjustment Theory (Burgess & Jones, 1997), Inertia Tensor Theory (Amazeen, 1999), Bayesian Approach (Brayanov & Smith, 2010), and Throwing Affordance Theory (Zhu & Bingham, 2011). The reasons for these ongoing differences of opinion are that heaviness is affected by various factors (as noted in Sec. 2) and the difficulty of strictly manipulating object size as a single independent variable, uncontaminated by other object properties. As a result, object size remains a wide-open topic regarding perception of heaviness.

The next sections present our research on the effect of object size on perceived heaviness. The experimental environment must be set up in accordance with the objective of the experiment: objective first and methodology second. Therefore, note that totally different experimental environments were set up, based upon the questions asked and sensory modalities examined.

3.1 Effects of haptically perceived object size on perceived heaviness: Use of the Real Haptics – Real vision environment: First experiments

It is a common tendency to interpret object size to mean that which has been visually perceived rather than that which has been haptically acquired during grasping and lifting (MacKenzie & Iberall, 1994). Similarly, the majority of researchers on heaviness perception have focused specifically on the effects of visually perceived object size (Ellis & Lederman, 1993) despite the fact that object size affects heaviness perception both visually and haptically (Charpentier 1891, as cited in Murray et al. 1999). As a consequence, experimental environments have kept haptic size constant through the use of grip apparatus, a handle, or strings (Gordon et al., 1991; Mon-Williams & Murray 2000; Buckingham & Goodale, 2010). Surprisingly few studies specifically focused on the effects of haptic size on heaviness perception, in spite of the evidence that effects on heaviness were considerably stronger for haptic size than visual size (Ellis & Lederman, 1993).

Selecting an experimental environment to focus solely on the haptically perceived object size was quite simple. Where we normally interact with an object in the real world through both haptics and vision (left of Fig. 2), we had only to enclose the subject's working space with screens (right of Fig. 2), to remove the real world visual input. The next step was to determine the type of objects to be used. Since heaviness is affected by an object's physical properties as described in Fig. 1, it was decided to use cubes given the properties of distribution of mass, center of gravity, density, and inertia tensor. When grasping cubes it is possible to constantly maintain the center of gravity between the thumb and index finger. This keeps the points of action on the object surface where normal forces are applied along an opposition vector between the thumb and index finger pads, with the center of gravity on the same line. Spherical objects were also considered (Charpentier 1891, as cited in Murray et al. 1999; Zhu & Bingham, 2011), but it proved difficult to consistently grasp the exact center of gravity between the thumb and index finger in a precision grip, especially when visual input was not available.

The next experimental design decision was whether or not haptically perceived size should be treated as a single independent factor. Objects of equal size can vary in weight depending on their specific density (Harper & Stevens, 1948; Zhu & Bingham, 2011). On the other hand, objects of equal density can vary in weight depending on their specific size (J. Ross & Di Lollo, 1970; Zhu & Bingham, 2011). Logically then, objects of equal weight can vary in both size and density. Thus, all three factors of weight, size and density were considered. This led to the decision to use three sets of cubes with different densities, one set each of: copper (CP; 8.93 g/cm^3), aluminum (AL; 2.69 g/cm^3), and plastic (PL; 1.18 g/cm^3), with 10 cubes in each set having progressively varying weights ranging from 0.05 N to 0.98 N. The surfaces of all cubes were covered with smooth, black vinyl to standardize input related to texture, thermal conductivity, friction, compliance, and colour. As a result, subjects received no cues as to the underlying materials. Each subject performed weight discrimination trials between sets of two cubes of identical density, e.g., CP vs. CP. In addition, equal numbers of trials for each weight difference with identical combination of weights were presented for all density conditions.

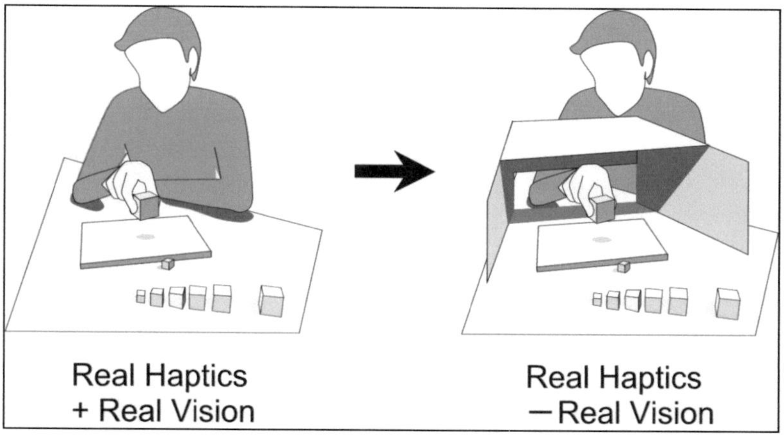

Fig. 2. A Real Haptics + Real Vision environment (Left) and a Real Haptics - Real Vision environment (Right). (Reproduced by permission from Kawai, 2002a. Copyright © 2002 Springer-Verlag.)

Figure 3A indicates, as an example, the differences between the 0.10 N-cube and the 0.20 N-cube among three different materials. By evaluating the accuracy of weight discrimination among three material conditions, it was possible to investigate whether or not haptic object size affected heaviness perception (Kawai, 2002a). As indicated in Fig. 3B, it was possible to investigate the accuracy of weight discrimination for all possible combinations by manipulating both weight (dotted arrows) and density (solid arrows) using these cubes. Surprisingly, this was the first published research attempt to study the psychological scales or discriminative abilities for weight or heaviness that covered all weight-density conditions (Kawai, 2003a). The probable reason for this is that researchers focusing on weight have concentrated on constant density conditions (D, E, and F in Fig. 3B) in which the psychological scale complemented physical weight. On the other hand, researchers focusing on the SWI have been interested primarily in equal-weight with different density conditions (B and H) believing that only in such conditions can object size affect heaviness perception. We believe that humans judge heaviness in the same manner for any combination of weight and density; our goal is to establish a heaviness model that explains heaviness perception for all weight-density conditions.

With these manipulations, new findings were obtained regarding the effect of haptic size on perceived heaviness: (1) Whenever we lift objects to compare heaviness, haptically perceived object size is significantly involved in heaviness perception (Kawai, 2002a), (2) The effect of haptic size is not limited to a specific situation such as Charpentier's SWI (Kawai, 2002a), (3) The effect of haptically perceived size was strong for some subjects but less for others (Kawai, 2002a), (4) Object density also contributes to perception of heaviness, with significant interaction with weight (Kawai, 2002b), (5) As no other forms of input were presented to subjects to detect object density, it is concluded that approximate, but not exact, information about density is derived possibly from the integration of haptic size information with weight (Kawai, 2002b), (6) The Weight/Aperture, the finger span formed during thumb-index finger grasp (the opposition vector), or the width of cube itself, can be derived as a heaviness model as it reflects subjective responses in any weight-density conditions (Kawai, 2003a, 2003b).

While it is clear that haptic object size is systematically involved in heaviness perception, the results of this study offer no neurological evidence about how, where and when in the nervous system this occurs (Flanagan et al., 2008; Chouinard et al., 2009).

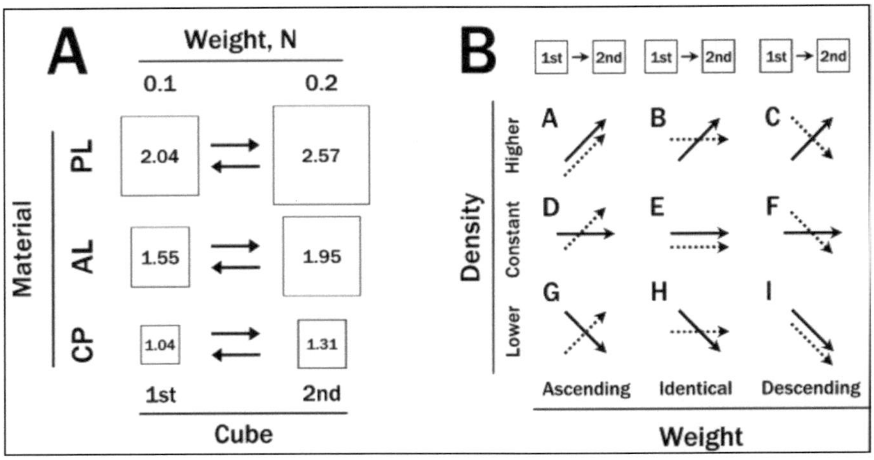

Fig. 3. A. Treatment of object size as a single independent factor. B. Weight-density conditions presented to the subjects (A: Reproduced with permission from Kawai, 2002a. Copyright © 2002 Springer-Verlag.)

3.2 Effects of visually perceived object size on heaviness perception: Use of the Real Haptics + Virtual Vision environment: Second experiments

In Sec. 3.1, investigation of the effect of haptic size was made possible by simply removing the Real Vision from the Real Haptics + Real Vision environment. Such a simple and inexpensive experimental set-up has a great advantage since it is easily reproduced and replicated by others. Now we turn to visually perceived size. In experimental paradigms for the role of visual size in heaviness perception, it has been conventional that two or more objects of equal weight but unequal sizes are alternatively or in parallel lifted by subjects using wires, handles, or grip apparatus, and then rated for heaviness (See left in Fig. 4A and 4B) (H.E. Ross, 1969; David & Roberts, 1976; Masin & Crestoni, 1988; Gordon et al., 1991; Mon-Williams & Murray, 2000; Chouinard, et al., 2009; Rabe et al., 2009). Thus the haptically perceived size is kept constant. All studies unanimously reported that visually perceived size affected perceived heaviness: the smaller object felt heavier than the larger object although they were identical in weight.

However, these experimental set-ups clearly involved the factor of inertia tensor (Amazeen, 1999) which has significant impact on perceived heaviness. When lifting objects of different length, width, volume, shape, and orientation, it is possible to haptically perceive the differences in heaviness, even without visual information (Turvey & Carello, 1995). Thus, strictly speaking, we cannot determine conclusively whether the SWI is derived from differences in visual size or inertia tensor, when we adhere to the conventional methodology of the Real Haptic + Real Vision environment (left in Fig.4A and Fig.4B). This is the limitation of the real physical world for experimental control.

We decided, therefore, that the only way to separate the factor of visual size cues completely from other factors such as inertial tensor was to use a combination of 3D motion analysis and 3D computer graphics techniques to create virtual objects for the SWI paradigm. This type of augmented environment was developed as the Virtual Hand Laboratory at Simon Fraser University in Burnaby, Canada, in which 3D graphics (and other displays) were driven by 3D motion and forces. Computer graphics were developed to ensure completely independent manipulation of visual size information by superimposing computer-created graphics of different sizes on a single object (Fig. 4A, top) or two physically identical objects (Fig.4B, bottom); thus, haptic information was kept constant. As seen in Fig. 4, two different experimental set-ups were designed: a single physical grip apparatus was used specifically to record grip and load forces applied on the grip handle (top in Fig 4A), while two physical cubes with identical physical properties were used to investigate the effects of visual size on heaviness (bottom in Fig. 4B). In both environments, visual size varied as a single independent parameter without changing the inertia tensor. As shown in the right of Fig. 4B, each subject wore Crystal Eyes goggles and viewed through a semi-silvered mirror the stereo images (dotted line) on a monitor.

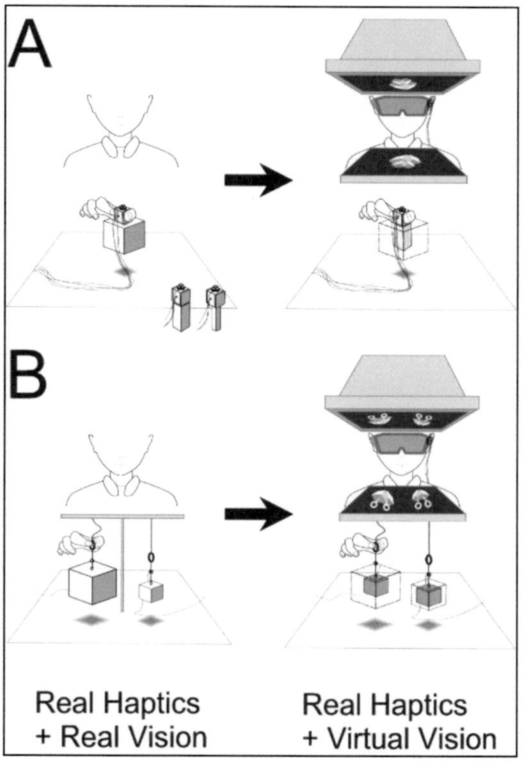

Fig. 4. From Real Haptics + Real Vision (left) to Real Haptics + Virtual Vision (right) environments. (A) a single stimulus presentation and (B) two stimuli presentation (Reproduced with permission from Kawai et al., 2007. Copyright © 2007 Springer-Verlag.)

An OPTOTRAK 3D Motion Analysis system tracked infrared emitting markers attached to the physical cubes and the goggles and these 3D position data were used to create the stereographic images of the cubes in real time and subsequently, to analyze the lifting motion of the cubes. The physical cubes of identical size (3.0 x 3.0 x 3.0 cm) and mass (30.0 g) were invisible to subjects. The graphical size of the standard cube placed on the left-hand side of each subject was constant (5.0 x 5.0 x 5.0 cm; indicated as triangles in Fig. 5), while the comparison cube presented on the right-hand side varied from 1.0 x 1.0 x 1.0 to 9.0 x 9.0 x 9.0 cm (See details in Fig. 5). After lifting each pair of cubes, subjects were asked to report whether the comparison cube presented was perceived as Heavier, Lighter, or Similar in heaviness as compared to the standard cube.

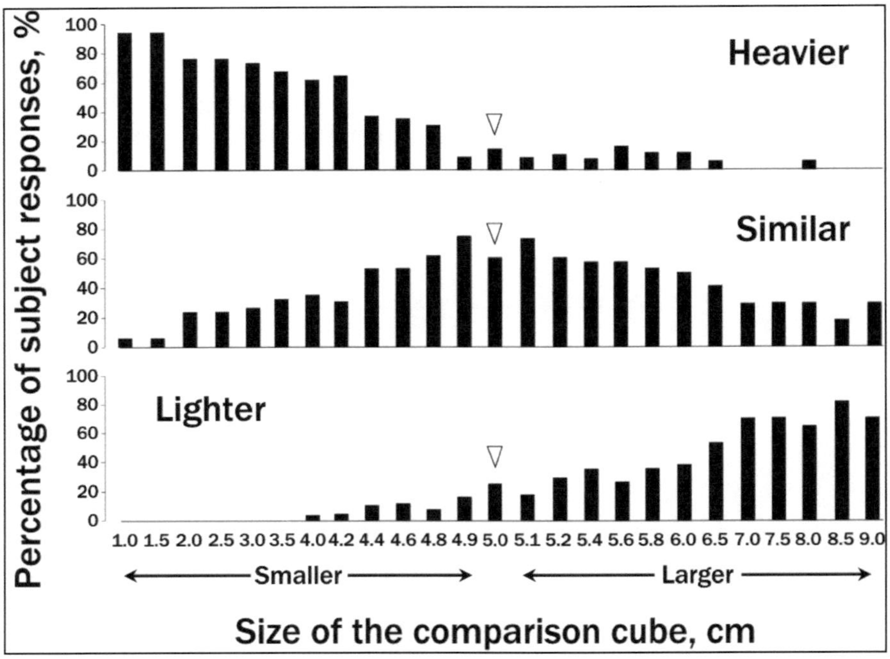

Fig. 5. Systematic contribution of visual size cues to human perceived heaviness. (Adapted from Kawai et al., 2007. Copyright © 2007 Springer-Verlag.)

Prior to undertaking trials, care was taken to accurately determine whether or not the augmented objects could produce for subjects a sense of reality, existence, or presence similar to real objects. Every participant had a strong sense of presence of the graphical objects and felt as if they were interacting with a physical object both in terms of force programming (Kawai, et al., 2002) and perceived heaviness (Kawai et al., 2007). It was concluded to be due to the characteristics of this augmented environment that the graphical objects moved without any noticeable delay (timing), in exactly the direction intended (direction), and synchronized with the subject's lifting movement (speed), developing a kind of personal relationship or ownership (Ehrsson, et al.,2004).

Findings indicated that: (1) visual size cues systematically affected heaviness; when the comparison cube was smaller in size than the standard cube, it was perceived to be heavier and vice versa (Fig. 5), (2) visual size cues influenced heaviness for all subjects under conditions with sufficient size differences between standard and comparison cubes of equal mass; that is, (3) when the comparison cube was smaller than 4.0 cm all the subjects perceived it to be heavier than the 5.0 cm standard cube (upper in Fig. 5), and when the comparison cube was larger than 7.0 cm all the subjects perceived it to be lighter (bottom in Fig. 5). (4) Interestingly, whether or not test subjects experienced the SWI was significantly correlated with their sensitivity to weight discrimination, but not their sensitivity to discriminate small differences in visual size, (5) Erroneously programmed motor commands were not systematically correlated to perceived heaviness or experience of the SWI (Kawai et al. 2007).

We emphasize that usage of the Real Haptic + Virtual Vision environment was the way to verify effects of only visual size cues on perception of heaviness, while presenting both visual and haptic cues "synchronously" to participants; it is impossible to obtain this evidence from any experimental set-ups in the real world (Real Haptic + Real Vision).

4. Pictorial depth cues of an object on perceived heaviness: Virtual Vision + Virtual Haptics environment: Third experiment

In Sec. 3.2, the Real Haptics + Virtual Vision environment ensured a strict manipulation of visual information independently from haptic information and suggested possibilities for presenting any type of visual/graphical stimulus with a range of intensities, unlike the Real Vision environment. Concerning vision, this suggested further study of visual components such as pictorial depth cues or stereopsis that may contribute to perceived object size and heaviness. For haptics, it suggested the development of a haptic display making possible the presentation of any type of haptic stimulus with a range of intensities. This led to the challenging experiment using a Virtual Haptic + Virtual Vision environment. Thus we demonstrate here an experiment using Virtual Vision + Virtual Haptics environment enabling us to address pictorial depth cues.

4.1 Volumetric information and pictorial depth cues in the size-weight illusion

Since volumetric information of objects has long been thought to be critical, numerous studies have focused on the volume of the object as the essential parameter for size in the size-weight illusion (SWI) (Scripture, 1897; H.E. Ross, 1969; Anderson, 1970; Ellis & Lederman, 1993). However, there is no direct evidence as to whether or not volumetric information is encoded in the process of size-weight integration in perceived heaviness. Further, although the dimensions of objects have been examined on reach-to-grasp movements (Westwood et al., 2002; Kwok & Braddick, 2003), no such research has been done on lifting movements or heaviness perception. This study investigated the effects of cues regarding pictorial depth and volumetric size cues on the size-weight integration in perceived heaviness. Weight displays were created using the PHANToM haptic stylus, synchronized and superimposed onto corresponding 2D graphic objects displayed on a 2D monitor, in accordance with manipulation of the stylus (virtual objects) by subjects. It was hypothesized that the degree of the SWI would be weakened, even to the point of disappearing, when the dimensions of pictorial depth cues were reduced from being a 3D cube to a 2D square.

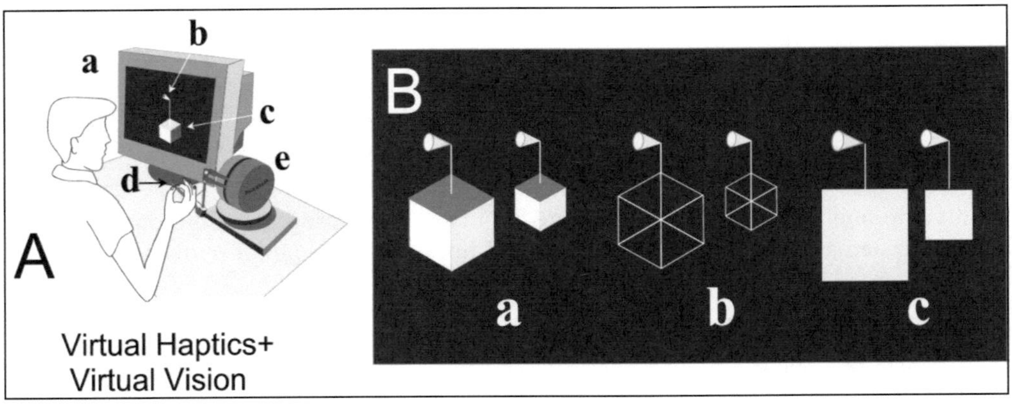

Fig. 6. A. Virtual Vision + Virtual Haptics, B. Visual stimuli with different sizes and pictorial depth cues.

4.2 Augmented environment created by computer graphics and computer haptics

Figure 6A is a schematic of the programmed augmented environment, (see Kuang, et al., 2004 for details). Software on a Silicon Graphics Inc. computer was developed to display on the monitor (a), a graphic hook (b), suspending a graphic object (c) by a graphic wire. A PHANToM haptic device (e) by SensAble Technologies Inc., integrated into the Virtual Hand Laboratory system, was programmed with forces (at 1000 Hz) to reflect the subject's manipulation of the PHANToM stylus (d), as the object was lifted with the haptic stylus/graphic hook. Either 0.5 or 0.75 N was programmed for virtual object weight. This weight was constant for the visual conditions in Fig. 6B. Thus, subjects grasped and lifted virtual objects with programmed haptic and graphic properties. They perceived the heaviness of the virtual objects based on the lift of the virtual object with the stylus/graphic hook. 3D position and acceleration of lifting were processed by the system at 200 Hz. Temporal lag for the system to sample human-generated forces acting on the system, calculate reflected force directions for the haptic device, and display the motion of the graphic object was 2-3 frames at 60 Hz, i.e., 50 ms max. Subjects did not notice any delay between their initial movement with the PHANToM stylus and initiation of movement of the graphic object.

Figure 6B shows three graphic stimuli with different sizes and pictorial depth cues (solid, wire-frame and square). Solid cubes (Fig. 6B-a) had 3D pictorial cues, with different colors on each of the three visible sides so that participants readily perceived them as solid or three-dimensional. Three different sizes of solid graphic cubes were used (large: 6.9 x 6.9 x 6.9 cm, medium: 5.0 x 5.0 x 5.0 cm and small: 3.0 x 3.0 x 3.0 cm, respectively). The large and small cubes were used to assess the frequency of the SWI, while the medium cubes were used for controls. The size ratios between the large and small solid cubes were approximately 12 : 1 in volume and 5.4 : 1 in planar area. Wire-frame graphic cubes (Fig. 6B-b) provided weaker 3D cues compared to solid cubes since colors were not added to any sides. As a result, the perception of depth or dimension was unstable like the Necker's cube; sometimes the graphic object was perceived with a cube shape and sometimes a plane hexagon. The ratios between the large and small frame cubes were identical to those for solid cubes. Graphic squares (Fig. 6B-c) had no 3D pictorial cues so that subjects perceived them as a two-dimensional plane. Three different sizes of squares (large: 10.4 x 10.4 cm, medium: 6.5 x 6.5 cm and small: 3.0 x 3.0 cm, respectively) were used. The ratio in size between the large and small squares was about 12 : 1 in planar area. For all graphic stimuli, the medium size was used for control purposes. All stimuli were experienced by all subjects. Subjects performed 4 trials in which the second object was larger in size than the first object (the Larger condition), 4 trials in which the second object was smaller in size than the first object (the Smaller condition), and 4 trials in which the size of the second object was identical to that of the first object (the Identical condition). Thus each subject performed 12 trials for each visual condition, and 36 trials in total. The trials were presented in random order across conditions and subjects.

Sixteen right-handed adults participated; none had any visual, muscular, or cutaneous problems. Further, none had previous experience with the experimental tasks or were familiar with the hypothesis being tested. Basically, subjects grasped and lifted virtual objects with programmed haptic and graphic properties, using the PHANToM stylus. They perceived weight of the virtual objects based on the reflected haptic 3D forces, and the graphic object motion viewed during the lift. Instructions were to grasp the stylus with the thumb and index finger of the dominant hand and to confirm that the stylus and graphic object motion were synchronously related to the lifting movement. At the outset, subjects were instructed to maintain the speed of the lift as constant as possible throughout the trials. To facilitate this, there were five to ten practice lifts to become accustomed to the Virtual Haptic and Virtual Vision environment, lifting each medium size stimulus. In addition, subjects were requested to view the object without the eyes being intentionally closed during the lifting process. Next for the test trials, each subject was instructed to grasp the stylus when the first of two graphic objects appeared on the monitor, to lift it vertically only once with a single smooth movement to a height of approximately 5 cm, and then to replace it after attempting to memorize their perception of its heaviness. Immediately after replacing the first graphic object, it disappeared. Following that, the second graphical object immediately appeared, to be maneuvered in exactly the same manner as the first. After completing the two lifts, each subject was requested to state whether the second object was perceived to be Heavier, Lighter, or Similar in comparison to the first object. Because cues related to visual size were very weak on perceived heaviness (Ellis & Lederman, 1993) and any cognitive bias is liable to affect judgment of heaviness in the final decision phase (Mon-Williams and Murray, 2000) or in the initial lifting phase in the form of expectation (H.E. Ross, 1969), the subject was requested to report perception of heaviness exactly and without hesitation, once the two lifts were completed in a given trial. These instructions, requests, and requirements were deemed essential to minimize such cognitive biases on perceived heaviness.

Similar to previous studies (Kawai, 2002a, 2002b), the percentage of subject responses were calculated as a function of the visual size of the second object and response categories (Heavier, Similar, and Lighter) for each individual subject. For example, if a subject's response was Heavier in two trials, Lighter in one trial, and Similar in one trial from among four trials for a particular visual condition, the percentage of responses for each category in this condition is 50 % for Heavier, 25 % for Lighter, and 25 % for Similar. The individual percentages were then averaged across subjects and visual conditions. To assess the effect of pictorial cues (3 levels), size (2 levels), and directions of size variation (2 levels) on perceived heaviness, a three-way within-subject ANOVA was performed on the individual means of frequency of subject responses. We summarize below the effects on the frequency of occurrence of the SWI.

4.3 Results: Effects of depth cues and size on perceived heaviness, and the size-weight illusion

Figure 7 indicates the mean values and standard errors of the percentages for the occurrence of the SWI obtained from each pictorial depth cue, i.e., solid cube (Cube), wire-frame cube (Frame) and square (Square). The white bars (A) indicate the Smaller condition in which the second object was smaller in size than the first. The smaller object was reported as heavier than the larger one. The gray bars indicate the Identical Condition in which sizes were identical between the first and second object. Although the graphical sizes remained constant in the Identical condition, for some reason, subjects accidentally reported a difference in heaviness between the first and the second lifts (See Sec. 2-1). The black bars (B) are those obtained from the Larger condition in which the second object was larger in size than the first. For these conditions, the larger object was reported as lighter than the smaller one. Again, the grey bars are those obtained from the Identical condition in which they reported the second object to be perceived as lighter.

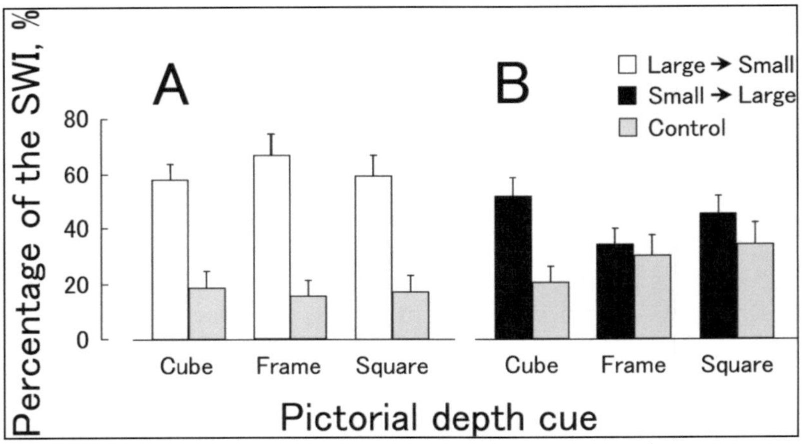

Fig. 7. Mean percentages (%) of the size-weight illusion (SWI) for each pictorial depth cue for each condition through which subjects compared the heaviness of the small size with that of the large (white bars), the large with the small (black bars), and the median with the equivalent median (gray bars).

There was a significant effect of change in size (F (1,15) =28.15, p< .001), indicating that the SWI occurred significantly for each pictorial depth cue when the size was changed compared to the conditions when the size was not changed. There were, however, no effects of pictorial depth cues (F(2, 30) =0.26) nor for the direction of size change (F(1, 15 = 0.46), suggesting pictorial depth cues do not affect the frequency or strength of the SWI. A significant interaction was observed only between pictorial depth cue and direction of size change (F(2, 30) = 31.53, p < .001). This is due to the fact that the SWI occurred more frequently in the Smaller condition (57.8% in Cube, 67.2% in Frame and 59.4 % in Square) than in the Larger condition (51.6% in Cube, 34.4 % in Frame and 45.3% in Square). There were no significant differences in probability in the Identical condition: the probability when the reports of test subjects regarding the small object being Heavier was similar to that of the large object being Lighter. This phenomenon has been described in detail and discussed previously, according to Weber's Law (Kawai, 2002a).

4.4 Discussion

All subjects experienced the SWI for all three visual stimuli in Fig. 6B without any significant differences, suggesting that, contrary to our hypothesis, the SWI occurs to the same degree with any pictorial depth cues! Volumetric information of an object has long been thought to be critical in bringing about the SWI (Jones, 1986). As a result, numerous studies have investigated the phenomenon of the SWI and discussed based on the volume of an object as the essential parameter for size (Scripture, 1897; H.E. Ross, 1969; Ellis & Lederman, 1993). Furthermore, in studies related to motor programming for the lifting of an object, information of volume has also been thought to be a critical factor in estimating weight of an object as part of the process for producing the required lift forces (H.E. Ross, 1969; Gordon et al., 1991). Thus, Westwood and his colleagues (2002) proposed the necessity of a volumetric object description in the process of specifying the grip force and the load force necessary for lifting and manipulation because such forces must be scaled to the anticipated mass of the object either by estimating its volume and density or by accessing stored knowledge related to the mass of the other object. It was, therefore, hypothesized at the beginning of this study that the SWI would decrease in frequency or even disappear when dimensional cues were reduced from 3D structure such as a cube to a 2D structure such as a square. The results, however, indicated that all the subjects equally experienced the SWI for all three visual stimuli with any cues of a 2D graphical object. This suggests that whatever the pictorial depth cues are, these factors are not critical for the occurrence of the SWI. The present results, therefore, conclude, contrary to commonly accepted theory, that pictorial depth cues responsible for 3D perception are not crucially necessary in the process of producing the SWI. In short, the perceptual system of heaviness may not be responsive to the dimension provided by pictorial depth cues, at least under the VIRTUAL VISION + VIRTUAL HAPTIC environment of this experiment.

5. Chapter conclusion

5.1 What is heaviness?

Various physical attributes are involved in the perception of heaviness of objects, leading to an understanding that psychological heaviness is not equal to physical weight. Heaviness perception is not simply a function for sensing object weight. Rather it functions as a form of recognition of the object. That is, all information obtained synchronously when humans grasp and lift an object may be gathered across modalities, integrated with or subtracted from each other, interpreted by object knowledge, and then formed as perceived heaviness.

Among physical properties influencing heaviness, rotational inertia can be considered vital for future investigation, given evidence rotational inertia firmly affects heaviness (Turvey & Carello, 1995; Amazeen, 1999; Streit et al., 2007; Cf. Zhu & Bingham, 2011). However, such evidence has not explained neurologically how it is obtained from lifting, holding and manipulating an object and how it contributes to forming its heaviness. Gaining an understanding of how humans process the information about the rotational inertia of objects will contribute to understanding how humans recognize an object as well as how humans dexterously manipulate an object or tool (MacKenzie & Iberall, 1994).

Another important issue for the future investigation is the connection between perceiving heaviness phase and the object lifting phase indicated in Fig. 1. How are heaviness perception and object manipulation interrelated? That is, what needs to be investigated is where heaviness ends and lifting begins (cf. Goodale, 1998) as well as whether or not humans make use of heaviness for object lifting in the sensorimotor system. The motor system for programming lifting forces is posited to operate independently of the perceptual system of heaviness (Goodale, 1998; Flanagan & Beltzner, 2000; Grandy & Westwood, 2006; Brayanov et al., 2010). This is based on the evidence that the load forces generated in the motor system quickly adapt to object weight while the heaviness perceptual system did not (Flanagan & Belzner, 2000; Grandy & Westwood, 2006; Flanagan et al., 2008). It seems, nevertheless, natural and reasonable to think that there should be some linkage enabling the exchange of some information, especially weight-related information, between the two systems (Maschke, et al., 2006), considering evidence related to the role of the sensorimotor system in heaviness perception (Sec. 2.1). It is believed that the solution of this action-perception matter will lead to the development of an optimal internal model in force programming to lift objects. These considerations, however, are not limited to heaviness, but probably hold true also for how human perceive movement and spatial orientation.

5.2 Computer graphics and haptic displays: Powerful tools to understand how humans perceive heaviness

Computer graphic and haptic displays have recently become more popular and widely used as experimental tools - or environments - in research related to heaviness (Heineken & Schulte, 2007; Haggard & Jundi, 2009; Mawase & Karmiel, 2010). The reason for this may be that researchers have noticed practical advantages of using such devices for experimental control even if reality or physical presence is slightly sacrificed. The spatial resolutions and temporal lags for these devices are also important; with high resolution, the objects and environments created can affect the human sensorimotor and perceptual systems in the same manner as real, physical objects. However, such superior technologies should not be depended upon haphazardly since they exhibit, in some cases, difficulties in experimental replication. Therefore, whether or not to adopt and/or adapt evolving technology is dependent on research goals (Sec. 3.2). The experimental set-up should always be objective-centered rather than technology-centered. Within this restriction, computer graphics and haptic displays have been incorporated into the experimental set-ups for this study. The resulting progress reveals the usefulness of such equipment and suggests many fundamental findings that can be expected from future experiments.

The perceived usefulness of these powerful tools includes:

1. The reality and presence of the environments and objects created by these computer displays depend on temporal and spatial precision, and on consistency of the timing, amplitude, and direction for forces/motions as humans interact with objects in the environments.
2. The created stimuli can functionally act on human perceptual and motor systems in a similar manner as real, physical stimuli.

3. These devices can accurately isolate or focus on only one single factor from all factors possible. Such a result is often impossible or exceptionally hard to accomplish with only physical objects.
4. These devices can present stimuli with a considerably wider range of intensity or even in smaller increments than physical stimuli. Thus, they can act on the sensorimotor and perceptual systems of individuals for whom sensitivities or discriminative abilities are quite different. In the physical world, individual variability in sensitivity sometimes prevents the uncovering of mechanisms underlying the perceptual system. That is, it is often the case that the intensities determined by the experimenters are sufficient for some humans to detect and discriminate, but not others. However, it is almost impossible to cover all the range of intensities of stimuli using hundreds of physical objects. In this sense, these devices are powerful tools for obtaining detailed assessments of the discriminative ability of human perception and for users of human/computer systems whose sensitivities are widely different.
5. These devices can quickly, in a timely, constant and invariant manner, vary or exchange a part or the whole of multimodal stimuli, for presentation to humans. This is also advantageous, compared to the physical environment, to the tasks in which subjects are required to compare two or more bits of sensory information among all the stimuli presented. This may elucidate the mechanisms of multimodal integration and unitary perception, e.g., object recognition.
6. These computer devices could possibly generate and present a stimulus possessing a weight-size relationship or an incredible density that humans are physically unable to experience on earth.
7. These devices enable accurate, precise and high resolution temporal and spatial perturbations to human vision, haptics, and goal-directed movement.

In the history of the development of haptic interfaces, little or no concern seems to have been paid to the human unit of heaviness. Instead, haptic devices - including robot hands and arms - have been developed based on the machine-centered unit of weight and reflected forces. This seems to hold true also for psychologists who have termed all psychological phenomena as illusions and have avoided interpreting them based on biological or physiological views. Of course, such weight-based devices have assisted humans to lift or manipulate a variety of objects in a smooth and safe manner. This success seems to depend, in large part, on efforts of users via their adaptation and/or learning systems, rather than via the engineered haptic systems. In the future, however, users of haptic devices will certainly include those lacking the abilities of adaptation and/or learning such as the elderly, the physically challenged, and medical patients who cannot easily adjust to such computer-centered systems. Thus, such systems developed in the future should be human-centered. Ideally such haptic devices should be suited for adaptation to the human haptic systems, to perceive and act in a manner similar to that of humans. We hope this chapter contributes to future development of human/computer interfaces, based on human haptics, that can contribute to quality of human life and human experience.

6. Acknowledgments

This research was supported by grants from the Japan Society for the Promotion of Science (JSPS), the Natural Sciences and Engineering Research Council of Canada (NSERC), and the Tezukayama Educational Institution. Thanks to Professor R. G. Marteniuk, staff and graduate students who collaborated in this project since 1996, including V. A. Summers, F. Henigman, and A. B. Kuang for systems integration, programming and setup of the experimental environments.

7. References

Amazeen, E. (1999). Perceptual independence of size and weight by dynamic touch. *Journal of Experimental Psychology, Human Perception and Performance,* Vol. 25, No.1, (February, 1999), pp. 102-119, ISSN 0096-1523

Anderson, N. (1970). Averaging model applied to the size-weight illusion. *Perception & Psychophysics,* Vol. 8, No.1, (January, 1970), pp. 1-4, ISSN 1943-3921

Brayanov, J. & Smith, M. (2010). Bayesian and "Anti-Bayesian" biases in sensory integration for action and perception in the size-weight illusion. *Journal of Neurophysiology,* Vol. 103, No.3, (March, 2010), pp. 1518-1531, ISSN 0022-3077

Brodie, E. & Ross, H. (1984). Sensorimotor mechanisms in weight discrimination. *Perception & Psychophysics,* Vol. 36, No.5, (September, 1984), pp. 477-481, ISSN 1943-3921

Brodie, E. & Ross, H. (1985). Jiggling a lifted weight does aid discrimination. AJP Forum, Vol. 98, pp. 469-471

Buckingham, G. & Goodale, M. (2010). Lifting without seeing: the role of vision in perceiving and acting upon the size weight illusion. *PLoS ONE,* Vol. 5, No.3, (March, 2010), e9709, pp.1-4

Buckingham, G.; Cant, J.; Goodale, M. (2009). Living in a material world: how visual cues to material properties affect the way that we lift objects and perceive their weight. *Journal of Neurophysilogy,* Vol. 102, No.6,(December, 2009), pp. 3111-3118, ISSN 0022-3077

Burgess, P. & Jones, L. (1997). Perceptions of effort and heaviness during fatigue and during the size-weight illusion. *Somatosensory and Motor Research,* Vol. 14, No.3, (n.d.), pp. 189-202. ISSN 0899-0220

Chang, E.; Flanagan, J. & Goodale, M. (2008). The intermanual transfer of anticipatory force control in precision grip lifting is not influenced by the perception of weight. *Experimental Brain Research,* Vol. 185, No.2, (February, 2008), pp. 319-329, ISSN 0014-4819

Chouinard, P.; Large, M-E.; Chang, E. & Goodale, M. (2009). Dissociable neural mechanisms for determining the perceived heaviness of objects and the predicted weight of objects during lifting: An fMRI investigation of the size-weight illusion. *NeuroImage,* Vol. 44, No.1, (January, 2009), pp. 200-212 ISSN 1053-8119

Crago, P.; Houk, H. & Rymer, W. (1982). Sampling of total muscle force by tendon organs. *Journal of Neurophysiology,* Vol. 47, No. 6, (June, 1982), pp. 1069-1083, ISSN 0022-3077

Davis, C. & Roberts, W. (1976). Lifting movements in the size-weight illusion. *Perception & Psychophysics,* Vol. 20, No.1, (January, 1976), pp.33-36. ISSN 1943-3921

Davis, C. (1974). The role of effective lever length in the perception of lifted weights. *Perception & Psychophysics,* Vol. 16, No.1, (January, 1974), pp. 67-69, ISSN 1943-3921

Davis, C. (1973). Mechanical advantage in the size-weight illusion. *Perception & Psychophysics,* Vol. 13, No.2, (June, 1973), pp. 238-240, ISSN 1943-3921

De Camp, J. (1917). The influence of color on apparent weight. A preliminary study. *Journal of Experimental Psychology*, Vol. 2, No. 5, (October, 1917), pp. 347-370, ISSN 0096-3445

Dijker, A. (2008). Why Barbie feels heavier than Ken: the influence of size-based expectancies and social cues on the illusory perception of weight. *Cognition*, Vol.106, No.3, (March, 2008), pp. 1109-1125, ISSN 0010-0277

Dresslar, F. (1894). Studies in the psychology of touch. *American Journal of Psychology*, Vol. 6, No.3,(June, 1984), pp. 313-368, ISSN 0002-9556

Ehrsson, H.; Spence, C. & Passingham, R. (2004). That's my hand! Activity in premotor cortex reflecting feeling of owenership of a limb. *Science*, Vol. 305, No. 5685, (August, 2004), pp. 875-877, ISSN 0036-8075

Ellis, R. & Lederman, S. (1993). The role of haptic versus visual volume cues in the size-weight illusion. *Perception & Psychophysics*, Vol. 53, No.3, (May, 1993), pp. 315-324, ISSN 1943-3921

Ellis, R. & Lederman, S. (1999). The material-weight illusion. *Perception & Psychophysics*, Vol. 61, No.8, (December, 1999), pp. 1564-1576, ISSN 1943-3921

Flanagan, J.; Bittner, J. & Johansson, R. (2008). Experience can change distinct size-weight priors engaged in lifting objects and judging their weights. *Current Biology*, Vol. 18, No.22, (November, 2008), pp. 1742-1747, ISSN 0960-9822

Flanagan, J. & Beltzner, M. (2000). Independence of perceptual and sensorimotor predictions in the size-weight illusion. *Nature Neuroscience*, Vol. 3, No.7, (July, 2000), pp. 737-740, ISSN 1097-6256

Gandevia, S. (1996). Roles for afferent signals and motor commands. In: *Handbook of Physiology: Section 12: Exercise: Regulation and Integration of Multiple Systems*, L. B. Rowell & J. T. Shepherd, (Eds.), pp. 128-172, American Physiological Society, Oxford Univ. Press, ISBN 0195091744, New York

Gandevia, S. & McCloskey, D. (1977a). Changes in motor commands as shown by changes in perceived heaviness, during partial curarization and peripheral anaesthesia in man. *The Journal of Physiology*, Vol. 272, No.3,(November, 1977), pp. 653-672, ISSN 0022-3751

Gandevia, S. & McCloskey, D. (1977b). Sensation of heaviness. *Brain*, Vol. 100, No.2, (n.d.), pp. 345-354, ISSN 0006-8950

Goodale, M. (1998). Visuomotor control: where does vision end and action begin? *Current Biology*, Vol. 8, No.14, (July, 1998), pp. R489-491.

Gordon, A.; Forssberg, H.; Johansson, R. & Westling, G. (1991). Visual size cues in the programming of manipulative forces during precision grip. *Experimental Brain Research*, Vol. 83, No.3, (February, 1991), pp. 477-482, ISSN 0014-4819

Gordon, A.; Westling, G.; Cole, K. & Johansson, R. (1993). Memory representations underlying motor commands used during manipulation of common and novel objects. *Journal of Neurophysiology*, Vol. 69, No.6, (June, 1993), pp. 1789-1796, ISSN 0022-3077

Grandy M. & Westwood, D. (2006). Opposite perceptual and sensorimotor responses to a size-weight illusion. *Journal of Neurophysiology*, Vol. 95, No.6, (June, 2006), pp. 3887-3892, ISSN 0022-3077

Haggard, P. & Jundi, S. (2009). Rubber hand illusions and size-weight illusions: Self-representation modulates representation of external objects. *Perception*, Vol. 38, No. 12, (n.d.), pp. 1796-1803, ISSN 0033-2909

Halstead, W. (1945). Brain injures and the higher levels of consciousness. Trauma of the central nervous system. Res. Publ. Assoc. Res. N. Williams and Wilkins, Baltimore

Harper, R. & Stevens, S. (1948). A psychological scale of weight and a formula for its derivation. *American Journal of Psychology*, Vol. 61, No.3, (July, 1948), pp. 343-351, ISSN 0002-9556

Hineken, E. & Schulte, F. (2007). Seeing size and feeling weight: The size-weight illusion in natural and virtual reality. *Human Factors*, Vol. 49, No.1, (February, 2007), pp. 136-144, ISSN 0018-7208

Holms, G. (1917). The symptoms of acute cerebellar injures due to gunshot injuries. *Brain*, Vol. 40, No.4, pp. 461-535, ISSN 0006-8950

Holst, von H. (1954). Relations between the central nervous system and the peripheral organs. *British Journal of Animal Behavior*, Vol. 2, No.3, (July, 1954), pp.89-94, ISSN 0950-5601

Holway, A.; Goldring, L. & Zigler, M. (1938). On the discrimination of minimal differences in weight: IV. Kinesthetic adaptation for exposure intensity as variant. *Journal of Experimental Psychology*, Vol. 23, No.5, (November, 1938), pp. 536-544, ISSN 0096-3445

Holway, A. & Hurvich, L. (1937). On the discrimination of minimal differences in weight: I. A theory of differential sensitivity. *The Journal of Psychology*, Vol. 4, No.2, (n.d.), pp. 309-332, ISSN 0022-3980

Holway, A.; Smith, J. & Zigler, H. (1937). On the discrimination of minimal differences in weight: II. Number of available elements as variant. *Journal of Experimental Psychology*, Vol. 20, No.4, (April, 1937), pp. 371-380, ISSN 0096-3445

Johansson, R. (1996). Sensory control of dexterous manipulation in humans. In : *Hand and Brain: The Neurophysiology and Psychology of Hand Movements*, A. M. Wing, P. Haggard, & J. R. Flanagan, (Eds.), pp.381-414, Academic, San Diego, CA, ISBN 012-759440X

Jones, L. (1986). Perception of force and weight: theory and research. *Psychological Bulletin*, Vol. 100, No.1, (July, 1986), pp. 29-42, ISSN 0033-2909

Jones, L. & Hunter, I. (1983). Effect of fatigue on force sensation. *Experimental Neurology*, Vol. 81, No. 3, (September, 1983), pp. 640-650, ISSN 0014-4886

Jones, L. & Hunter, I. (1982). Force sensation in isometric contractions. A relative force effect. *Brain Research*, Vol. 244, No.1, (July, 1982), pp. 186-189, ISSN 0006-8993

Kawai, S.; Kuang, A.; Henigman, F.; MacKenzie, C. & Faust, P. (2007). A reexamination of the size-weight illusion induced by visual size cues. *Experimental Brain Research*, Vol.179, No.3, (May, 2007), pp. 443-456, ISSN 0014-4819

Kawai, S. (2003a). Heaviness perception III. Weight/aperture in the discernment of heaviness in cubes haptically perceived by thumb-index finger grasp. *Experimental Brain Research*, Vol.153, No.3, (December, 2003), pp. 289-296, ISSN 0014-4819

Kawai, S. (2003b). Heaviness perception IV. Weight x aperture-1 as a heaviness model in finger-grasp perception. *Experimental Brain Research*, Vol.153, No.3, (December, 2003), pp. 297-301, ISSN 0014-4819

Kawai, S. (2002a). Heaviness perception I. Constant involvement of haptically perceived size in weight discrimination. *Experimental Brain Research,* Vol.147, No.1, (September, 2002), pp.16-22, ISSN 0014-4819

Kawai, S. (2002b). Heaviness perception II. Contributions of object weight, haptic size, and density to the accurate perception of heaviness or lightness. *Experimental Brain Research,* Vol. 147, No.1, (September, 2002), pp. 23-28, ISSN 0014-4819

Kawai, S.; Summers, V.; MacKenzie, C.; Ivens, C. & Yamamoto, T. (2002). Grasping an augmented object to analyse manipulative force control. *Ergonomics,* Vol. 45, No. 15, (n.d.), pp. 1091-1102, ISSN 0014-0139

Kinoshita, H.; Bäckström, L.; Flanagan, J. & Johansson, R. (1997). Tangential torque effects on the control of grip forces when holding objects with a precision grip. *Journal of Neurophysiology,* Vol. 78, No.3, (September, 1997), pp. 1619-1630, ISSN 0022-3077

Kuang, A.; Payandeh, S.; Zheng, B.; Henigman, F. & MacKenzie, C. (2004). Assembling virtual fixtures for guidance in training environments. *Proceedings of 12th International Symposium on Haptic Interfaces for Virtual Environment and Teleoperator Systems, IEEE Virtual Reality Conference,* pp. 367-374, Chicago, Illinois, USA, March 27-28, 2004

Kwok, R. & Braddick, O. (2003). When does the Titchener circles illusions exert an effect on grasping? Two- and three dimensional targets. *Neuropsychologia,* Vol. 41, No. 8, (n.d.), pp. 932-940, ISSN 0028-3932

Li, Y.; Randerath, J.; Goldenberg, G. & Hermsdörfer, J. (2007). Grip forces isolated from knowledge about object properties following a left parietal lesion. *Neuroscience Letters,* Vol. 426, No.3, (October, 2007), pp. 187-191, ISSN 0304-3940

MacKenzie, C. & Iberall, T. (1994). *The grasping hand,* Advanced in Psychology, Vol. 104, Elsevier Science, B. V. North-Holland, ISBN 0444817468, Amsterdam.

Masin, C. & Crestoni, L. (1988). Experimental demonstration of the sensory basis of the size-weight illusion. *Perception & Psychophysics,* Vol. 44, No.4, (July, 1988), pp. 309-312, ISSN 1943-3921

Maschke, M.; Tuite, P.; Krawczewski, K.; Pickett, K. & Konczak, J. (2006). Perception of heaviness in Parkinson's disease. *Movement Disorders,* Vol. 21, No. 7, (July, 2006), pp. 1013-1018, ISSN 1531-8257

Mawase, F. & Karmiel, A. (2010). Evidence for predictive control in lifting series of virtual object *Experimental Brain Research,* Vol. 203, No.2, pp. 447-452, ISSN 0014-4819

McCloskey, D. (1978). Kinesthetic sensibility. *Physiological Reviews,* Vol. 58, No.4, (October, 1978), pp. 763-820, ISSN 0031-9333

Mon-Williams M. & Murray, A. (2000). The size of visual size cue used for programming manipulative forces during precision grip. *Experimental Brain Research,* Vol. 135, No. , pp. 405-410. ISSN 0014-4819

Murray, D.; Ellis, R., & Bandmir, C. (1999). Charpentier (1891) on the size-weight illusion. *Perception & Psychophysics,* Vol. 61, No. 8), pp. 1681-1685, ISSN 1943-3921

Payne, M. (1958). Apparent weight as a function of colour. *American Journal of Psychology,* Vol. 71, No.4, (December, 1958), pp. 725-730, ISSN 0002-9556

Rabe, K.; Brandauer, B.; Li, Y.; Gizewski, E.; Timmann, D. & Hermsdorfer, J. (2009). Size-weight illusion, anticipation, and adaptation of fingertip forces in patients with cerebellar degeneration. *Journal of Neurophysiology,* Vol. 101, No.1, (January, 2009), pp. 569-579, ISSN 0022-3077

Raj, V.; Ingty, K. & Devananan, M. (1985). Weight appreciation in the hand in normal subjects and in patient with leprous neuropathy. *Brain*, Vol. 108, No.1, (n.d.), pp. 95-102, ISSN 0006-8950

Rinekenauer, G.; Mattes, S. & Ulrich, R. (1999). The surface-weight illusion: on the contribution of grip force to perceived heaviness. *Perception & Psychophysics*, Vol. 61, No. 1, (January, 1999), pp. 23-30, ISSN 1943-3921

Ross, H. (1969). When is a weight not illusory? *Quarterly Journal of Experimental Psychology*, Vol. 21, No.4, pp. 346-355, ISSN 1747-0218

Ross, H.; Brodie, E. & Benson, A. (1984). Mass discrimination during prolonged weightlessness. *Science*, Vol. 225, No.4658, (July, 1984), pp. 219-221, ISSN 0036-8075

Ross, H. & Rischike, M. (1982). Mass estimation and discrimination during brief periods of zero gravity. *Perception & Psychophysics*, Vol. 31, No. 5, (September, 1982), pp. 429-436, ISSN 1943-3921

Ross, H. & Murray, D. (1978). *The sense of touch* (Original work published by Weber, E. 1834), Academic Press, ISBN 012740550X, London

Ross, J. & Di Lollo, V. (1970). Differences in heaviness in relation to density and weight. *Perception & Psychophysics*, Vol. 7, No.3, (May, 1970), pp. 161-162, ISSN 1943-3921

Rothwell, J.; Traub, M.; Day, B.; Obeso, J.; Thomas, P. & Marsden, C. (1982). Manual motor performance in a deafferented man. *Brain*, Vol. 105, No.3, (n.d.), pp. 515-542, ISSN 0006-8950

Scripture, E. (1897). The law of size-weight suggestion. *Science*, Vol. 5, No.110, (February, 1897), p. 227, ISSN 0036-8075

Sperry, R. (1950). Neural basis of the spontaneous optokinetic response produced by visual neural inversion. *Journal of Comparative and Physiological Psychology*, Vol.43, No.6, (December, 1950), pp. 482-489, ISSN 0021-9940

Stevens, J. & Green, B. (1978). Temperature-touch interaction: Weber's phenomenon revisited. *Sensory processes*, Vol. 2, No.3, (Oct, 1978), pp. 206-209, ISSN 0363-3799

Stevens, S. (1958). Problems and methods of psychophysics. *Psychological Bulletin*, Vol. 55. No.4, (July, 1958), pp. 177-196, ISSN 0033-2909

Streit, M.; Shockley, K. & Riley, M. (2007). Rotational inertia and multimodal heaviness perception. *Psychonomic Bulletin & Review*, Vol. 14, No. 5, (October, 2007), pp. 1001-1006, ISSN 1069-9384

Turvey, M. & Carello, C. (1995). Dynamic touch. In: *Handbook of perception and cognition: perception of space and motion*. W. Epstein, & S. Rogers, (Eds.), pp. 401-490, Academic Press, San Diego, ISBN 0-12-240530-7 CA

Westwood, D.; Danckert, J.; Servos, P. & Goodale, M. (2002). Grasping two-dimensional images and three-dimensional objects in visual-form agnosia. *Experimental Brain Research*, Vol. 144, No.2, (May, 2002), pp. 262-267, ISSN 0014-4819

Zhu, Q. & Bingham, G. (2011). Human readiness to throw: the size-weight illusion is not an illusion when picking up the best objects to throw. *Evolution and Human Behavior*, Vol. 32, No. 4, (July, 2011), pp. 288-293, ISSN 1090-5138

3

On the Integration of Tactile and Force Feedback

Marco Fontana, Emanuele Ruffaldi,
Fabio Salasedo and Massimo Bergamasco
*PERCRO Laboratory - Scuola Superiore Sant'Anna,
Italy*

1. Introduction

Haptic interfaces promise to add a new channel to digital communication, through the exploitation of the sense of touch, beside the traditional sense of sight and of hearing. Nonetheless, even if they firstly appeared on the market in the early nineties, they haven't spread yet in the society as a consumer product. This is not due to the intrinsic nature of the sense of touch that is a very sophisticated sensorial system, able to perceive fine and complex time and spatial varying characteristics of the outer world, but to the limited capabilities of the nowadays available haptic systems. Indeed, if from one side they allow quite realistic rendering of "mediated contacts" (i.e. contact of an object mediated by a specific tool like a pen, scissors, screw driver etc.), on the other side they are less effective for the rendering of cases of interaction in which the human limbs contact directly the object (direct contact). The main limitation lays in the lack of a proper simultaneous elicitation of kinesthetic and tactile cues.

In this chapter we provide a review of the main problems and possible solutions for the realization of a complete hardware and software system that integrates kinaesthetic and tactile devices. We provide an analysis of the direct contact interaction and of possible HW/SW architectural solutions for the implementation of a haptic system.

We analyze the mechanical design aspects (Machine Haptics) and software computational issues (Computer Haptics) that arise when tactile and kinaesthetic device have to be integrated.

In the last section of this chapter we present a case study focussed on the realization of a complete integrated system for the simulation of haptic interaction with virtual textiles.

1.1 Integration of tactile and kinesthetic feedback toward direct contact simulation

Tasks that involve direct contact between hand and objects are the most complex manipulative actions that humans can perform. Human ability of exploring, grasping and manipulating tools and objects relies on superior morphological and physical properties of our hands. A sophisticated system of bone, joints and tendon allow our hands to perform complex movement and to control accurately interaction forces.

However, as many researches have demonstrated, those abilities are not only based on the high elaborated structural properties of our hands but the haptic sensory input is highly involved in such tasks and it plays a fundamental role.

Basically, there are two types of interaction mode with objects: Active Haptic Sensing and Grasping/Manipulation (Jones & Lederman, 2006). In both of them the multimodal sensing given by the simultaneous tactile and kinesthetic sensory input strongly come into play. It has been largely demonstrated that in Active Haptic Sensing the information gathered by tactile and kinesthetic channels are somehow integrated while performing explorations and recognition tasks. Lederman and Klatzky for example (Lederman & Klatzky, 1999) demonstrated that in absence of distributed tactile information the perceptual capabilities of our fingers are strongly impaired. In addition our ability in grasping/manipulation of objects strongly relies on both the sensory inputs. Several research works have demonstrated how the absence of tactile or kinesthetic sensory input makes our ability worse. Johansson and Flanagan for example in (Johansson & Flanagan, 2007) show how the distributed tactile information are deeply involved even in very simple manual tasks like grasping and lifting an object.

These considerations lead to conclude that a system that is asked to replicate with high level of realism the direct interaction of virtual objects with the human hands should include both tactile and kinaesthetic sensory inputs.

Unluckily, most of present day haptic feedback systems are able to stimulate only kinesthetic or tactile interactions separately. Traditional force feedback devices like Phantom® (Salisbury & Srinivasan, 1997) are typically only able to provide sensory input correlated with kinaesthetic information. Such device are usually employed for realistic rendering of "mediated contacts", however they can be connected to the user body through mechanical components like a thimble that guarantees a constant contact surface for the simulation of interaction with bare fingers. From the functional point of view these class of devices are able to provide as output a controlled force and/or torques and get as input the position and/or orientation of the interaction surface. The system is unable to transmit distributed and programmable sensory input on the skin surface and the exchanged information only relates with global force and/or torque and global position and/or orientation of a body.

The technical challenge of integrating tactile feedback on kinesthetic has been faced only in few research works. In this chapter we are going to summarize the issues that concern the Direct Contact simulation with the integration of tactile and kinesthetic feedback. The topic is treated on both the hardware and software perspective illustrating the basic problems found in mechanical and control electronics integration and in haptic rendering for efficient computation.

2. Hardware design of integrated devices

This section deals with the aspects that are related with the Machine Haptics issues of integrated tactile and kinesthetic devices. The scope is to provide a clear view of the problems that arise when these two type of feedback are closely integrated. In the first part of this section we briefly analyze the physics of contact with bare fingers. In the second part we give an overview of the general architecture of integrated kinesthetic and tactile systems and analyze typical issues related with mechanical design.

We decided not to include the topic of thermal display and feedback since it would require a special treatise.

2.1 Analysis of direct contact interaction: From perception to design of devices

Haptic interaction with objects can happen in two different ways. The first happens when a subject holds a special tool used for interacting with the surrounding environment. A pen, a joystick or a fork are examples of possible tools. The artificial creation of interaction with environment is then completely focused on replicating the information that is exchanged through the held object.

Alternatively the subject can directly interact with her/his bare fingers with the environment. In this case the artificial recreation of interaction is much more complex and is focused on reproducing the physical phenomena that occurs at the fingertip level.

We will refer to these two different cases respectively as Mediated Contact interaction and Direct Contact interaction. Hayward in (Hayward, 2008) provided a very clear theoretical description of the difference between these two modes.

2.1.1 Mediated contact interaction

During haptic interaction mediated by a tool the subject holds a tool in his hand and the haptic information regarding the interaction is practically contained in the motion and the forces that are acting on the tool. An ideal device able to perfectly reproduce the haptic interaction can be equipped with a toll moke-up that is a faithful reproduction of the real tool. The problem of perfectly reproducing the tactile and kinesthetic sensory input is then reduced to the problem of imposing to such moke-up the same static and dynamic behavior of the real tool.

For this kind of interaction kinesthetic haptic interface are theoretically very efficient but in many cases their mechanical performance in terms of frequency response, fidelity in force reproduction and force resolution are still insufficient for high fidelity reproduction of the real feelings.

A lot of research efforts has been applied for improving and optimizing kinesthetic haptic interfaces specifically developed for mediated tool interaction and many systems are already commercialized and available as an off the shelf product.

For example, in the field of surgical simulators for training of laparoscopic surgery, catheter insertion, phlebotomy, or, in the domain of Virtual Prototyping and Assembly, mediated contact device have been successfully employed.

2.1.2 Direct contact interaction

The analysis of the Direct Contact interaction requires looking with higher level of detail to the physics of the phenomena. The problem of perfectly reproducing the phenomena through artificial stimulus can be seen in a dual way. The first consists in defining the haptic interface as a device able to perfectly reproduce the shape and the spatial distributed mechanical impedance of the contact surface. Or, dually, the device can be seen as a generator of pressure field that perfectly reproduce the interaction pressure distribution that is generated at the contact surface. These two definitions are dual and functionally equivalent so we will assume this second perspective for defining the ideal haptic interface as a device able to perfectly reproduce the forces of interaction between finger and object i.e. able to generate a continuously distributed pressure field over the contact surface:

$$\vec{\rho}(\vec{x},t) = \begin{bmatrix} \rho_x(\vec{x},t) \\ \rho_y(\vec{x},t) \\ \rho_z(\vec{x},t) \end{bmatrix}$$

with: $\vec{x} \in \boldsymbol{S}_{(t)}$

Where $\vec{\rho}(\vec{x},t)$ is a pressure field made of three components: $\rho_z(\vec{x},t)$ is the normal component and $\rho_x(\vec{x},t)$and $\rho_y(\vec{x},t)$ the tangent components to the contact surface $\boldsymbol{S}_{(t)}$. Each component of such pressure distribution together with the contact surface changes independently with time over an infinite bandwidth with an infinite range of magnitude. Moreover the contact surface is also subject to large displacements and deformations that means the device should be able to exert such a pressure distribution in any wanted points of the space, e.g. when a soft object is grasped and lifted the contact area is subject to deformation during the prehension and to large displacement while lifting the object. The design of a system with such performances would require a tactile display with infinite resolution, infinite bandwidth and infinite force exertion capability. This is evidently far beyond what is currently feasible with present technologies.

The problem can be faced only through a simplification. A first reduction of complexity of the problem is achieved by reducing the requirements considering the limitations of the human tactile and kinesthetic senses. This means that the device has not to reproduce completely the physics of interaction but only the subset of components that can be perceived by the human tactile and kinesthetic senses i.e. components that are under perceptual thresholds in terms of intensity, spatial distribution and frequencies are neglected.

Unfortunately also under these hypotheses the problem remains technically unsolvable. Human tactile and kinesthetic senses are actually extremely efficient sensing systems (Jones & Lederman, 2004) with:

- very low sensitivity threshold of approximately some tens of milligrams;
- wide frequency range of sensing approximately 500-1000Hz
- high capacity of exerting and hold high forces up to several kilograms.
- high spatial acuity being able of discriminating two different contact point with a threshold of few millimeters (2-4mm depending on the stimulation frequency)

The ideal solution is then far from being implemented. However several simplified device have been realized and they are not able to simulate the whole interaction with fingers, but rather they are able to simulate a subset of features of the real interaction.

Basically these devices have been realized for purposely simulate a subset of the stimulus with fingertips that are strongly correlated with certain types of object properties or with certain scale of details.

Some devices are able to render roughness of object, other are able to render small details of the object shape, or global shape, or weight and friction etc. Of course one device can be able to render several of this characteristics but a device that is able to render the whole set of object properties has not been yet invented.

A rough classification of the type of device according to the type of details that are able to simulate can be done distinguishing the typical dimension and the scale that describe the geometry of the detail.

We can categorize the devices as:

- Kinesthetic devices: This type of devices are responsible of providing the net interaction force. These device are definitely the most popular type of haptic interface.
- Large Shape Displays: This type of device are able of generating the artificial stimulus that lead to the perception of curvature of surfaces. The perception of surface curvature with radius that are much greater that the typical dimension of the fingertip, is strongly correlated with the position and displacement of the contact area on our fingertips (Dostmohamed & Hayward, 2005). Large shape displays are thus device able to control the position of the contact surface around the user fingertip. Examples of portable large shape displays able to simulate also transition between non-contact to contact have been developed by Solazzi (Solazzi et al., 2010).
- Small Shape Displays: Surface details that have dimensions in that are smaller than the fingertip dimensions and are perceived through a distributed deformation of the skin of our fingertips. Small shape displays are devices that are able to locally replicate the shape of the surface. These devices are usually made of an array of transducer able to deform locally the skin of the fingertip. Basically two tyoe of working principle can be employed: the normal indentation as described in (Wagner et al., 2004) or lateral deformation (Wang & Hayward, 2010).
- Tactile Displays or Surface Properties Displays. This type of display are responsible of providing artificial stimulus that are related with very small details and textures whose dimensions are fraction of millimetres. Typically this kind of stimulus are distributed on the fingertip surface and they are characterized by a wide frequency content in the range of 10-500Hz. Such kind of the device are implemented through movable pin-array that can be actuated with very different technologies: piezo electric, electromagnetic, pneumatic and ultrasonic.

Of course research has been oriented also on other very specific device like (Bicchi et al., 2000) that is able to render the variation of the contact surface area on the fingertip. Actually the spreading of contact surface when contact occur has been demonstrated to be a fundamental input for perceiving the stiffness of deformable objects. The authors also integrated the device with a kinesthetic stage.

However we will mainly concentrate our analysis on the integration of tactile, shape and kinesthetic devices.

2.2 Mechanical architecture of integrated systems

As previously discussed the complexity of the general problem of creating the perfect illusion of touching a general object is still unsolved in the practice. However there are several device that are able to effectively reproduce a subset of fingertip physical interaction that generates artificial feeling of certain type of object properties.

A possible idea for implementing a more general and flexible interface consists in designing a device that integrates together devices conceived for different scales.

The mechanical architecture of this kind of integrated device can be visualized as in Fig. 1. The system is composed by different layers:

- A kinesthetic Device responsible of generating global force information.
- A Large Shape Display able to simulate large curvature of objects.
- A Small Shape display able to render details that generates variations in the pressure distribution on the fingertip.
- Tactile Display or (Surface Properties Display) able to render the micro textures of the surface of the virtual object.

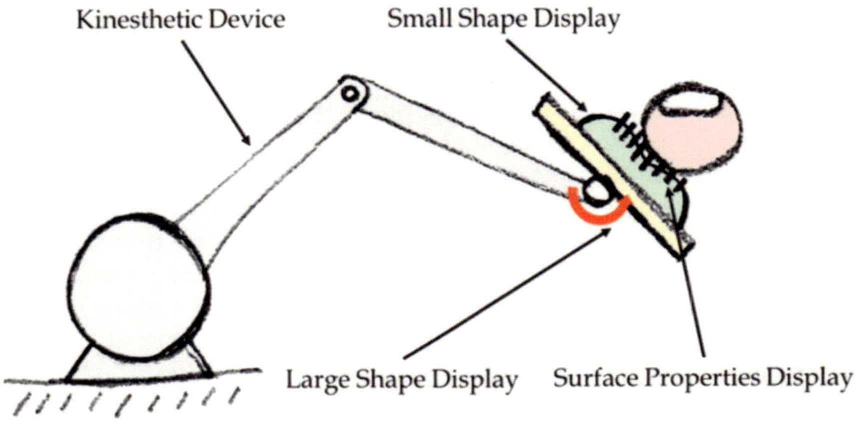

Fig. 1. Mechanical architecture of integrated haptic

This type of architecture can be found in many of the integrated haptic system that have been developed in (Frisoli et al., 2008), (Fontana et al., 2007),(Wagner et al., 2005) (Scilingo et al. 2010), (Sato et al.,2007).

2.3 General issues related with integration

Integration of haptic devices can generally raise several problems especially when both the tactile components and kinesthetic device are not conceived for the integration. Problems that may occur can be related to mechanics and electronics integration.

Mechanics:

- Miniaturization of tactile device

The tactile device must be lightweight as thin as possible and at the same time it has to be strong and must guarantee a sufficient array spatial density

When interaction requires more than one finger the encumbrance under the fingertip must be reduced in order to allow the fingers to get close together for grasping and manipulating virtual objects.

- Force transmission

The force that is exerted by the force feedback device to the user fingers have to be transmitted through a contact surface. In particular the way to transmit force has to take into account that the palmar side of the user finger surface is taken up by the tactile device. Such surface is than involved in the transmission of contact forces and the tactile array has to be capable of sustaining such efforts without compromising its functionalities.

- Force sensing:

Several kinesthetic devices are equipped with force sensors that measure the interaction force at the level of the fingers of the user. The force signal is generally employed to compensate friction and inertia effects. The integration of a tactile feedback with the force sensor is a trivial problem since the vibration generated by the tactile transducer may introduce a force noise reading (Fontana et al., 2007).

Electronics and wiring

- Wiring:
  Arrays with high density are desirable but as the number of transducers to be driven raises, the electrical cabling and the electronics get more and more complicated.
- Electronics
  Processing electronics for controlling independently each actuator of a tactile array can be complex. For example a 5x5 array requires to independently control 25 current or voltage signals (depending from the actuation technology) over a bandwidth of 1-2 kHz. Moreover if we want to simplify the cabling this control electronics must should be placed as close as possible to the tactile display thus its dimension and weight must be reduced in order to minimize additional weight and inertia compensation forces for the kinesthetic stage.

2.3.1 Scenario dependency

The global problem of artificial creation of touch experience is too complex and a simplification can be made developing specific devices that are able to simulate only certain types of scenario. Basically, according to scenario, the device can be simplified in order to be optimized for a certain kind of application. Scenarios can be classified according to the complexity of the interaction starting from one finger interaction on a planar surface getting to spatial interaction with multiple fingers of the same hand:

- One-Finger Planar: Haptic System for textile simulation 2D. This is the simplest scenario of integration of tactile and kinesthetic feedback.

The user can interact with an artificial surface moving on planar trajectories. According to the type of virtual surface, the speed and the forces exerted by the finger, the tactile display generates distributed stimulus. The kinaesthetic device can apply forces only on directions that are parallel to the plane and can simulate different macroscopic properties of the surface like friction or stiffness. Govindaraj in 2002 realize on planar system presenting a device able to simulate the interaction with a piece of fabric that is lying on a hard planar surface (Govindaraj et al., 2002). Another example of planar device has been realized by Yang(Yang & Zhang, 2009) that choose a cable-driven actuation system for the kinesthetic device.

In the case of planar devices the requirements for the integration of tactile and kinesthetic displays are less demanding. The weight and the encumbrance of the tactile display are less critical since there is no need of gravity compensation. Moreover the single finger interaction puts no strict limits to vertical encumbrance of the display.

- One Finger Spatial:

One finger device has a superior level of complexity since the weights of the display has to be compensated by the kinaesthetic device. There are various implemented solutions that differ from the type of tactile display that is employed.

Wagner in (Wagner, 2005) proposed the integration of kinaesthetic feedback with a shape display. Kheddar introduced the concept of a multilevel device for the different spatial level of details (Kheddar, 2004).

- Multiple Finger Spatial:

In the case of multi-finger interaction a major problem has to be considered. For allowing the simulation of grasping of reduced thickness the fingers have to be free to get close each other. This results in very though requirements for the thickness of the tactile display in the palmar area of the fingertip. The display has to be as flat as possible in order to allow the finger of user to get close together during grasps of small virtual objects. There are no experiments that exactly establish what is the exact tolerable thickness of a display for supporting multi-finger interaction, but simple tests can demonstrate that it must be kept in the range of few millimetres.

One possible way to get around this issue is to employ an electro-tactile display that can reach a very flat shape like in (Sato et al.,2007). However, electro-tactile displays show several disadvantages like large variation of perceived stimulus from subject to subject, dependence from wetness of the finger surface, employment of high voltage etc. Those unwanted feature made them hardly usable in the context of a virtual reality simulation.

Other attempts has been done for obtaining mechanical tactile displays with flat shape.

Benali-Khoudja in (Benali-Khoudja et al., 2003) developed a pin-array display based on a multilayer approach that has been conceived for integration with kinesthetic feedback. In the European Project HAPTEX a system composed by a desktop haptic device and a piezo-electric pin-array display have been adapted for the integration and tested (Fontana et al., 2007).

Recently a novel pin-array display based on a customized solenoid transducer has been purposely developed by authors for the integration with a hand exoskeleton (Salsedo et al.,2011).

3. Software for integrated haptic rendering

This section deals with the Computer Haptics aspects of the integrated force and tactile feedback, addressing, from one side, the physical and geometrical model of interaction, from the other, the computational challenges of the integrated rendering. The first part of this section is dedicated to a review of the models of contact, taking into account friction, soft finger representation and multiple finger interaction, both for kinesthetic and tactile feedback. The second part deals with architectural configurations of simulation and haptic rendering engines taking into account multi-rate and multi-resolution techniques.

The haptic rendering for object manipulation and exploration has the characteristic of combining the techniques from physics simulation with the principles of control and knowledge about human perception. Without losing generality haptic interaction scenarios can be represented by a physics simulation in which one or more virtual entities have the special role of exchanging haptic information with the user. These entities are called *proxies*. In some scenarios these virtual entities represent a user body part that directly interacts with other objects in the environment. A different type of representation is the one happening when the user interacts by means of a virtual tool as a stylus or a more complex tool. Examples of applications in the former type are exploration of surfaces, grasping, haptic rehabilitation and scenarios in which an avatar is employed. Examples of the latter type are drilling, simulation and even driving simulation. Clearly, the type of proxy depends on the type of haptic interface and the specific attachment to the user body part. For direct contact, like virtual finger exploration, the robotic end-effector applies forces on the fingers of the user using a rigid attachment to the user, or, following an encountered haptic approach. Instead devices in which the user holds a stylus or a handle are more suited for tool based proxies.

The type of proxy has effects, for the purpose of our discussion, in terms of the geometry and physical modeling of contact having to simulate, in one case, the contact between the finger or a body part with virtual objects, while in the other the contact of a virtual rigid object that transmits the contact to the user.

The general aim of the proxy is to be respectful of the physical properties of the virtual world, meaning that its behavior will avoid penetration with other objects. There is anyway a caveat. In real world the user moves the haptic interface end-effector specifying in this way a requested virtual position for the proxy. This requested position and orientation is a virtual entity called *haptic handle*. When the proxy touches an object like a virtual wall, the haptic interface produces a force to represent the opposition of the wall to penetration but this force is not always able to prevent the motion of the user in real space into the space where the virtual object is located. The discrepancy between proxy position and haptic handle position is a key element of haptic rendering. The common to rendering approach is to simulate the presence of a virtual spring between the proxy and the handle with a factor proportional to the stiffness of the object in contact. This approach is called penalty based because force is proportional to the penalty of entering with the handle into the object. This spring can introduce some instability and for this reason it can be replaced by a damped spring. Please note how, in this discussion, we have not taken into account the effect of the force produced by the spring on the proxy.

Moreover, we have not made distinctions between impedance and admittance interfaces. In the formers the low level controller receives forces to be applied to the user at the end-effector, and in most of the cases such force is computed on the side of the computer performing simulation and collision. In the latters the low level controller specifies a position to be held with a given stiffness, up to the maximal force of the device.

3.1 Geometric and physical modeling of contact

Contact is a fundamental element of haptic interaction with virtual objects. At large it can be considered as the result of two modeling aspects, first the geometrical aspect then the physical one. The former describes the geometrical representation of the shape of the proxy and the objects touched, while the latter comprises the effects of deformation and material properties like friction. In terms of temporal scale it is possible to organize contact distinguishing between first impact and then continuous contact, having two different time scales and physical modeling.

At beginning of haptic rendering research, contact has been modeled by representing the proxy as a single point like in the reference god-object algorithm (Zilles & J. Salisbury, 1995) or as a rigid sphere (Ruspini et al., 1997). In both cases the interaction between the proxy and the objects is based on geometrical considerations with the objective of avoiding penetration. The proxy is mass-less, and it produces a force on the handle proportional to the material's stiffness without being affected by such force. This model is effective for rendering tool proxies that are rigid, with the advantage of high performance, requiring only point or sphere contact with object geometry. This model contains several simplifications that allow discussing the later improvements. First, both the proxy and the object are considered rigid in geometrical terms, while for realistic contact it will be necessary to represent soft fingers and deformable bodies. Second, the contact has no friction, an aspect that can be integrated with or without a complete physic simulation of the proxy. Third, the feedback has only a force component, while contact for grasping requires a torsion component. Fourth, contact is quasi static because there is low frequency contact transient.

There is anyway a general result that has been applied by later approaches with different geometry models and physical properties: the proxy is constrained to move over the surface of the object without penetration while the haptic handle pulls it around. The other general result is the importance of a collision detection method that allows to identify or to predict the intersection of the proxy with the object. For a review on the topic see (Teschner et al., 2005). As in this case it is not necessary that both proxy and object have the same geometrical representation, it is instead more usual the case of adopting an asymmetric scheme, knowing that the proxy object is under the control of the user.

3.1.1 Contact model

Contacts between objects can be represented with few entities that do not depend on the geometrical representation and the collision detection algorithm. For two contacting objects A and B we identify the two points P and Q that are computed as the innermost points of collision respectively on the two objects. The normal of contacting surfaces can be a general n vector not necessarily directed along QP, and assumed to be toward the inner part of A. In addition, the velocities of the two points are provided, all in world coordinates. The Signorini law of contact expresses the contact of two generic objects by means of two functions: the first is the stress exerted on an object at a given point, and the second is the gap, or penetration depth, that is the projection of the QP vector on the normal. For the assumptions before a positive gap means that the two objects are penetrating. The Signorini model states that, when the contact is resolved, the gap is zero and the object B exerts a pressure toward the object A at point P, or the gap is negative and there is no pressure. When pressure is exerted it can be represented by a force directed along the normal n.

In general, contact is characterized by an impulsive phase and later by a contact force. The impulsive phase takes into account Signorini law and restitution coefficient of the material, providing an impulsive force that separates the two objects. Later, the contact has to be taken into account during the evolution of the system. In literature this is addressed in two ways. The first way is a penalty function that applies a force directed along the contact direction and proportional to the computed penetration, expressed in terms of penetration depth or volume. Its simplicity is balanced by the fact of reduction of realism. The second way transforms the collision into a constraint equation that prevents the two objects to penetrate. This model is formulated as an additional equation in the Linear Complementarity Problem (LCP) that is used to describe the body dynamics.

3.1.2 Rigid objects

Objects for haptic interaction can be represented in several ways like implicit functions describing the surface (K Salisbury & Tar, 1997), volumetric objects based on voxels, or distance fields, but the most common are triangulated meshes that allow to rely on proven techniques from the fields of simulation and computer graphics. Due to the timing constraints of haptic rendering these representations can take advantage of boundary representation for collision detection or hierarchical representation of the object for reducing the computational effort. An interesting example is the technique of sensation preserving simplification by Otaduy (Otaduy & Lin, 2003) in which an object is represented by a hierarchy of variations of the object, each more detailed than the parent. Every level is represented by an aggregation of convex parts. In this approach the proxy is also an aggregate of convex parts, while collision detection is performed at a given level by comparing pairs of convex elements using the effective GJK algorithm (Gilbert, Johnson, & Keerthi, 1988). The sensation preservation is taken into account when the algorithm has to decide if it is necessary to descend into the hierarchy or to compute the force feedback at the current level. Surface properties of the pair are used to evaluate if the additional details can provide more sensation information or they are not influent.

3.1.3 Deformable objects

The interaction with deformable objects raises the computational requirements of haptic rendering and it requires adapting the deformable representations coming from other domains (Nealen, M"uller, Keiser, Boxerman, & Carlson, 2006) to the specific characteristics of haptics. The fact that the object is deformable means that it has smaller stiffness, reducing the required update rate. Several models have been explored in literature mostly based on Finite Element Models (FEM) depending on the linearization approach and the entity of supported deformations.

The key point of deformable haptics is the management of the potential collision. When the collision between the proxy and the object is identified at a given point in space and time, it is being handled by the collision response. The first stage of the response deals with handling the spatial overlapping that is typically managed by moving the deformable surface outside the proxy, as an extension of the impulsive phase discussed above. The second stage has the role of preventing future penetration and it can be solved using the general methods discussed above: penalty or motion constraints. In cloth simulation, for example, the constraint model is applied using filtering of the motion inside a Conjugate Gradient method (Baraff & Witkin, 1998). Duriez et al. (Duriez, Andriot, & Kheddar, 2004), instead, adopted a contact model that employs Signorini's law for quite convincing FEM model supporting contacts between deformable objects. In particular the contact is resolved by equating the gap with a combination of a post contact gap and the projection of the two displacements along the contact normal. This equation is then expressed in terms of the exchanged contact forces and resolved in the general deformable FEM framework.

3.1.4 Modeling friction

Friction is important for providing surface information during object exploration, and it is fundamental in the context of grasping. Friction is modeled by means of the Coulomb's friction law that is based on two states: stick and slip. In stick state the norm of the tangential component of the force between two objects is less than the product of the norm of the normal force by the static friction coefficient. In this case there is no relative motion. When the tangent component has a norm larger than the proportional normal force the slip occurs. In this case the effective tangential force is directed against relative motion and proportional to the normal component of the force by the dynamic friction coefficient.

In the basic case of mass-less rigid proxy, as in the god-object algorithm, Coulomb friction can be implemented by means of the friction cone algorithm (Melder & Harwin, 2004). In this case the force is obtained by a spring connected between proxy and handle. Without friction the force is directed along the normal of the surface based on the position of the proxy. In the friction cone model the stick state keeps the proxy in the previous position producing a tangential force up to the level of tangential force that makes the proxy enter the slip state.

The friction model in rigid body simulation can be performed with reduced precision by means of a sequential resolution of frictional contacts. In this case the friction force is applied as an external force that is added to other methods for contact resolution. More sophisticated models take into account the friction model in the integration step extending the LCP model. Specifically the friction cone is represented in the equation as a k-sided polygonal cone, at the cost of increased complexity of the system to be solved. Alternatively Durez et al. integrated friction cone in deformable haptics using Gauss-Seidel algorithm improving performance and precision of the friction model.

3.1.5 Soft fingers

Deformable bodies for contact allow us to introduce an important aspect for the rendering of direct interaction: the soft modeling of fingertips. Barbagli et. al (F Barbagli, A Frisoli, K Salisbury, & M Bergamasco, 2004) discussed fingertip contact deformation models and measured several in-vivo characteristics for comparing them with the models. In particular the indentation displacement, contact area and friction coefficient. These measurements allowed them to design a soft-finger 4 DOF proxy algorithm that took into account torsional friction based on applied pressure (Antonio Frisoli, Federico Barbagli, Ruffaldi, Massimo Bergamasco, & Ken Salisbury, 2006). The investigation on the model of human fingertip can be applied on the haptic rendering of soft fingers when they interact with rigid and deformable objects. In particular Ciocarlie et al. (Ciocarlie, Lackner, & Allen, 2007) presented a method for computing the soft finger contacts based on local geometries and object curvatures.

3.1.6 High frequency contact

The position control approach for rendering first contact is not able to represent high frequency transients that characterize stiff materials. A possible solution to this problem has been addressed by event-based haptics (Kuchenbecker, Fiene, & Niemeyer, 2005) in which the first instants of contact are performed in open loop by superimposing a previously recorded force profile.

3.2 Haptic rendering architecture

The above contact models and contact resolution techniques have to be implemented in a framework that manages the interfaces with the haptic interface control module under the limitations of computational resources. Each module has a different target rate connected to the perceptual field namely: 1 kHz for kinesthetic, 300Hz for tactile and 60Hz for visual. The computational resources pose strong limitations to the achievable update rates. Modularization allows not only to manage correctly different rates but also to keep the software flexible against changes, for design exploration and management. The result of such modularization is a multi-rate architecture (F Barbagli, Prattichizzo, & K Salisbury, 2005) in which modules at different rates exchange data at synchronization points. In particular we can identify several elements:

- Simulation: performs a relatively slow simulation of the object in the environment. Depending on the contact model it consider the proxy object as part of the simulation
- Collision detection: evaluates the collision between entities in the environment, and in particular the proxy
- Haptic Rendering: transforms the state and forces acting on the proxy into commands for the control of the kinesthetic part
- Tactile Rendering: transforms the proxy into information for the tactile part

The collision detection module is typically the slowest part because it has to take into account the overall geometry of the virtual objects, although some techniques can be applied to limit the area of search based on speed and space boundaries. In addition, some GPU techniques can improve the rate, although it is difficult to reach the rate of the other components, in particular the haptic one. The connection between the collision detection and the simulation models is based on the notification of the contacts that are then used in the simulation block. Depending on the quality of the simulation in some cases it is worth clustering the contacts aggregating them based on their distance as performed by Otaduy (Miguel A. Otaduy, 2005).

An additional technique that can be employed for guaranteeing haptic rates in the simulation is the adoption of a multi level approach in the simulation, in particular when dealing with deformable models. A coarse representation of the objects is used in a slow simulation, slow in the sense that the time step of the simulation advances at large steps, while a finer representation localized around the contact point with the user is computed at faster rates. The complexity of this approach is in the transfer of the effects from the fast model to the slow one. An example of application of this approach to textile simulation is provided by Bottcher et al. (Böttcher, Dennis Allerkamp, & F.E. Wolter, 2010).

Timing is very important in real-time interaction and in particular it is interesting to discuss how time behaves in simulation. The simulation takes some real computational time to perform an integration step, and if the simulation is based on iterative methods then this computation can take a variable amount of time. The desired behavior of the simulation is to be synchronous with the real timing allowing presenting a realistic behavior. Due to the computational time required by the integration step this means that the simulation has to perform a larger time step than the simulation, eventually estimating in advance the final computational time. There is anyway an issue in the selection of the integration time step, that depends on the integration method and the material parameters: a too large time step is not able to express the propagation of deformation waves inside the material, and, at the same time, a too large time step can produce numerical issues when part of the matrix depends on time and others are constant. This issue is well represented by the Courant condition that, for implicit integration, states how the squared maximum integration step should be of the order of a ratio between the mass of each element and the stiffness factors. This condition together with the computational time function can express how a given material and a simulation implementation are not suitable for real-time computation.

3.3 Integrated rendering

The integrated rendering deals with the combination of kinesthetic and tactile rendering based on the overall interaction of the proxy with the virtual environment. Such integration is realized by the communication between the kinesthetic haptic rendering module and the tactile rendering module running at different rates. In such communication the tactile rendering should receive sufficient information for actuating the haptic interface. Although there is not a reference approach for tactile devices, such information can be identified as a distribution of contact points over the fingertip expressing for each of them the amount of pressure and the relative velocity against the contacting object. The surface properties of the material together with this piece of information can be then used for generating the vibrations that allow simulating the tactile feedback. An example of approach is discussed in Böttcher et al. (Böttcher, D Allerkamp, & F. E. Wolter, 2010).

4. Case study: Haptic display of textile properties

In this section we discuss an integrated system for kinesthetic and tactile simulation applied to the interaction with virtual textiles. In the first part we introduce the scope of the system and its main characteristics. Then we proceed with the presentation of the integrated haptic interfaces. The section is closed by a discussion about the haptic rendering strategy that supports the discussed haptic interface, taking into account the models and the approaches presented in the previous sections.

4.1 Introduction

Textiles are deformable objects characterized by very fine surface and bulk physical properties, indicated with terms such as stiffness, smoothness, softness, fullness, crispness, thickness, weight, etc. Taken as a whole they constitute the so called Fabric Hand (Behery, 2005) of a specific fabric, which is the basis for assessing its quality in relation to a given use. These properties can be well distinguished and quantitatively evaluated by the human haptic sensorial system, with an important contribution given by the sense of sight. There is experimental evidence that the highly sophisticated mechanoreceptors located in the human skin are combined in the brain with those generated by the kinesthetic sensors located in the physiological articulations and in the muscles providing the so-called Tactile Picture of the fabric. For example, when gently stroking the fingertip on a fabric to evaluate its smoothness, the kinesthetic sensors give to the brain information about the fingertip speed and the global force exerted on the fabric while the mechanoreceptors sense the small local fluctuation of the tangential force due to friction.

Due to the limitations of the present technology, since the beginning it has been decided to focus the system simulation capability on the interactions that can be attained using only two fingertips: the ones of the index and the thumb (see Fig. 2).

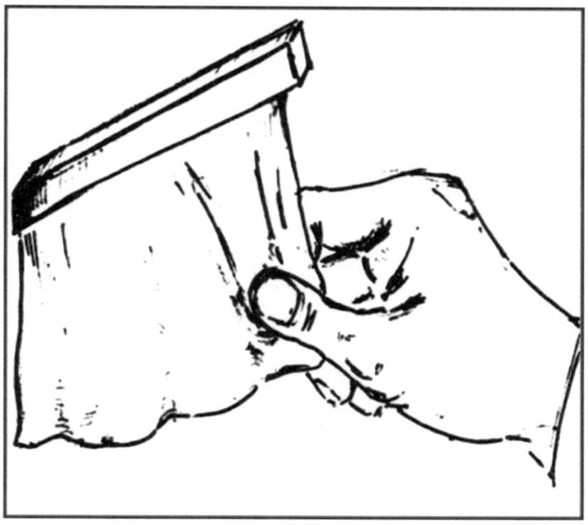

Fig. 2. Scenario of the interaction in which the user can use thumb and index finger for rubbing and stretching a standing piece of virtual textile.

Taking into account the above considerations, the reference configuration for the development of the device responsible for generating the artificial mechanical stimuli to be delivered on the fingertips, has been conceived as the combination of two independent force-controlled manipulators (Force Feedback Device, FFD), and two arrays of independently actuated pins (Tactile Actuator, TA).

Each FFD is able to track the movements of the index and thumb fingertips and to convey the global force of arbitrary direction on it, and each TA mounted on the end-effector of the corresponding FFD is able to deliver to the surface of the fingertip skin specified spatial and temporal sensory input patterns, (see Figure 2).

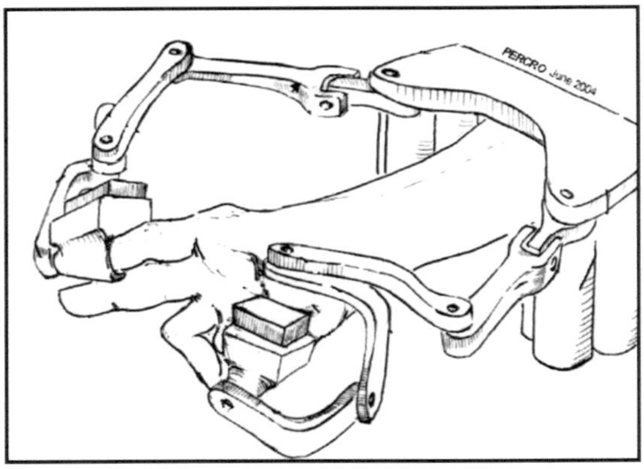

Fig. 3. General architecture of the mechanical interface

4.2 Hand exos and custom tactile array

4.2.1 Kinesthetic and tactile stages conceived for integration

As briefly analyzed in the previous section multi-finger interaction is the most demanding and complex scenario. However it is also the most versatile application of haptics and the potential application fields are extremely wide. One of the most relevant aspects of the design of an integrated tactile/kinaesthetic display is to guarantee at the same time:

- Reduced thickness of the display under the fingertip;
- High spatial resolution of the display
- Force transmission through the display must be considered.

In the present case study we introduce an example of design for integration where both tactile display and kinaesthetic devices were conceived for the integration. In particular a new transducer for the realization of a tactile display was purposely developed for the integration with an dual finger hand-exoskeleton.

The exoskeleton device is a dual arm serial manipulator able to deliver accurate forces in the range of 5N on the fingertip of the index and thumb fingers the device is shown in Fig. 4 and presented in detail in (Fontana et al., 2009). The architecture and the mechanical solutions for the exoskeleton have been studied in order to enhance performances and allow the hosting of a tactile display. The main characteristics can be summarized in table 1. The HE has been integrated in the work described in (Fontana et al., 2007) with tactile display based on piezo-electric beam that was purposely developed for the integration by Univeristy of Exeter. The system was integrated system was successfully tested on a scenario for virtual textile haptic simulation.

Despite of the effort applied for realizing a compact tactile display the system shows limitations in usability. Bulky shape of the display and wiring were determined by the basic principle. The piezo-beam actuators require a minimum length of few centimetres for each beam to guarantee a sufficient displacement of the contact pin.

A second tactile display has been studied focusing on compact electromagnetic actuators. The system described in (Salsedo et al., 2011) is based on a solenoid transducer that was designed for optimal force-displacement versus encumbrance performances.

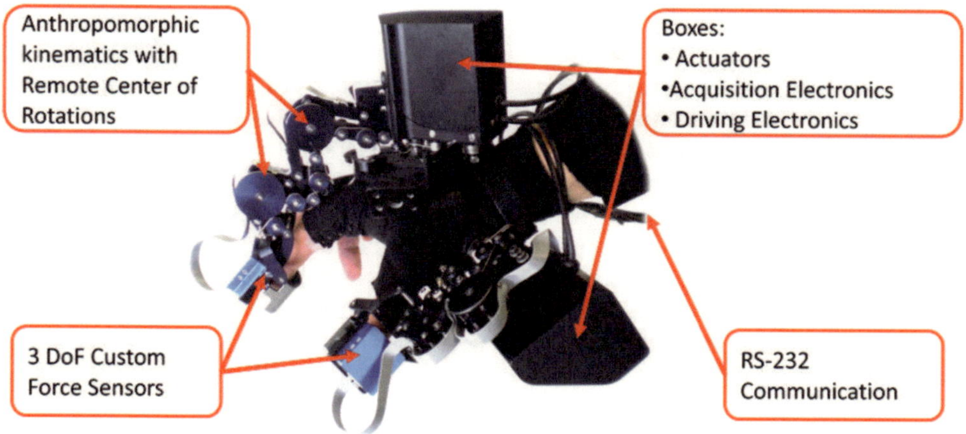

Fig. 4. PERCRO Dual finger Exoskeleton with 3 DoF for each finger able to deliver 5N on the fingertip of index and thumb. The device was purposely developed for the haptic interaction with textiles and for the integration with a tactile display.

HAND EXOSKELETON Mechanical Performances		
Symbol	QUANTITY	Value
DoF	Degrees of Freedom for each finger	3
F_{max}	Maximum continuous force	5N
W	Weight of the whole device	1.1 kg
w_a	Weight of one finger mechanism	0.51 kg
B_w	Mechanical Bandwidth (expected)	25 Hz

Table 1. Mechanical performances of the hand-exoskelton

The transducers were arranged in an array of 5x6 with a spacing of 2.4 mm with 4mm of thickness (Fig. 5).

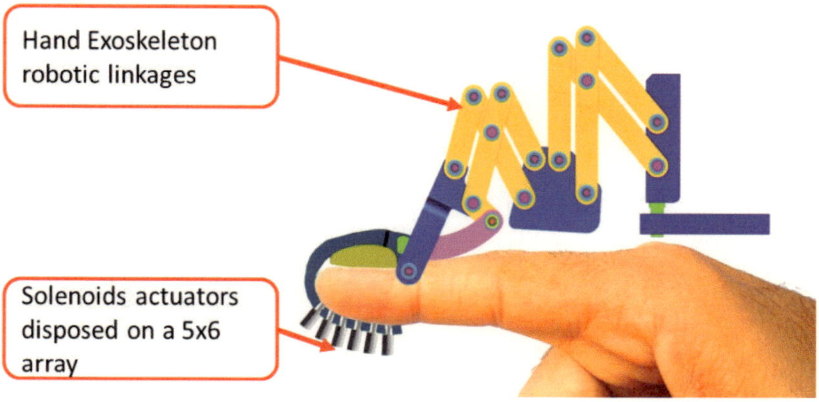

Fig. 5. Scheme of the integration of tactile display with the hand exoskeleton

4.2.2 Electronics and control

One of the issues regarding the integration of a tactile array on a force feedback device is the bulkiness and disturbances introduced by the large number of connectors and signals that are needed for the independent control of each transducer of the tactile array. For getting around this issue the control electronic board should be integrated on the robotic structure as near as possible to the transducers. This solution is necessary for reducing the impact of the cabling on the robotic structure, but also it imposes constraints on the encumbrance of the electronic. For this reason specific customized solutions have to be adopted for the control of each transducer. Here we present a possible approach based on the strategy for controlling the status of the pixels in a LCD display called active matrix addressing. This strategy can be implemented in any *n by m* array of actuators but we show an implementation that is referred to the solenoid array described in the previous section.

4.3 Control of a single tactile transducer

For the sake of clarity we firstly present a method for the control of one transducer and extend the concept to multiple transducers in the following section. The scheme for controlling the current applied to a single transducer is shown in Fig. 6. The solution is based on current Pulse Width Modulation (PWM) technique. The represented circuit allows applying a pulsed current that can assume any wanted average value programmed by a PWM output of a microcontroller (named as uP in the figure).

Referring to the scheme in Fig. 6, the coil is schematized by an RL series circuit. The PWM output of the microcontroller modulates the current by mean of a the signal S through a MOSFET. When the MOSFET is turned on (ON phase), the current flows into the coil and also into the capacitor. When the MOSFET is turned off (OFF phase), the coil current is supplied by the capacitor. The capacitor is introduced in order to limit the current ripple.

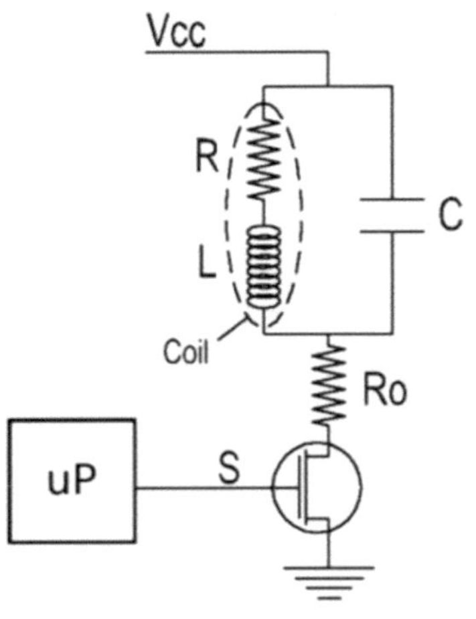

Parameter	Value	Unit
R	1	Ω
L	$0.56 \cdot 10^{-4}$	H
V_{CC}	3.3	Volt
R_0	4.5	Ω
C	100, 33	μF

Fig. 6. Scheme for the PWM control of a single tactile transducer

During the OFF phase, the function of the coil current is given by transient behavior of the RLC-series circuit, characterized by the natural frequency, damping ratio and time constant

$$\omega_{n,OFF} = \frac{1}{\sqrt{LC}}; \quad \chi_{OFF} = \frac{R}{2}\sqrt{\frac{C}{L}}; \quad \tau_{OFF} = \frac{2L}{R}.$$

During the ON phase, the transfer function which expresses the coil current respect to the supply voltage is the following

$$\frac{I_L}{V_{CC}} = \frac{1}{R_0 LCs^2 + (R_0 RC + L)s + R_0 + R}$$

in which the typical MOSFET on-resistance is considered inside the term R_0. The natural frequency, the damping ratio and the time constant are:

$$\omega_{n,ON} = \omega_{n,OFF} \cdot \sqrt{\frac{1 + R/R_0}{1}}; \chi_{ON} = \chi_{OFF} \cdot \frac{1 + L/R_0 RC}{\sqrt{1 + R/R_0}};$$

$$\tau_{ON} = \tau_{OFF} \cdot \frac{1}{1 + L/R_0 RC};$$

A necessary condition for limiting the variation of current through the coil during a PWM cycle is to dimension the capacitor C and the resistor R_0 imposing a time constants of the OFF phase circuits larger enough than the period of the PWM cycle.

Assuming that this requirement is satisfied, it's possible to find a simplified relation between the coil current and the duty cycle of the PWM signal. Making the assumption that V_C is a constant voltage applied to the capacitor, the current i_C flowing into the capacitor during the ON phase is given by

$$i_{C,ON} = \frac{V_{CC} - V_C}{R_0} - \frac{V_C}{R}$$

The supplied electrical charge can be written as:

$$Q_{ON} = T_{ON} \frac{1}{C}\left(\frac{V_{CC} - V_C}{R_0} - \frac{V_C}{R}\right)$$

During the OFF phase, the above quantities can be expressed as follow

$$i_{C,OFF} = \frac{V_C}{R}; Q_{OFF} = T_{OFF} \frac{1}{C}\frac{V_C}{R};$$

Indicating with α and T_{PWM} respectively the duty cycle and the period of the PWM signal,

$$\begin{cases} T_{ON} = \alpha \cdot T_{PWM} \\ T_{OFF} = (1-\alpha) \cdot T_{PWM} \end{cases}$$

When the frequency content of variation of the imposed average current is much lower than the PWM frequency we can assume that the charge during the two phases are identical. We can than calculate the duty cycle for obtaining an average coil current i_L :

$$\alpha = \frac{R_0 \cdot i_L}{V_{CC} - R \cdot i_L}$$

Supposing that the supply voltage V_{CC} is fixed, by the previous equation it's also possible to define the relation between the resistance R_0 and the maximum coil current $i_{L,max}$:

$$i_{L,\max} = V_{CC} \frac{\alpha_{\max}}{\alpha_{\max} \cdot R + R_0}$$

Where a_{max} is the maximum duty cycle of the PWM signal. In particular, if $a_{max} = 1$, we obtain

$$i_{L,\max} = V_{CC} \frac{1}{R + R_0}$$

4.3.1 Design and simulation

For testing the current modulation performances of the proposed technique, the circuit shown in Fig. 6 has been simulated using Simulink (Matlab). The adopted system parameters for the simulation are reported in the same figure. The PWM switching frequency is fixed at 10kHz. A sine wave with frequency of 100Hz, amplitude of 0.6A and an offset of 0.3A is chosen as the average current to be imposed. The resistance R_0 has been dimensioned for obtaining the maximum current of 0.6A with a duty cycle $a_{max} = 1$. In Fig. 7, the currents flowing through the coil by using three different capacitors of 100μF and 33μF are reported.

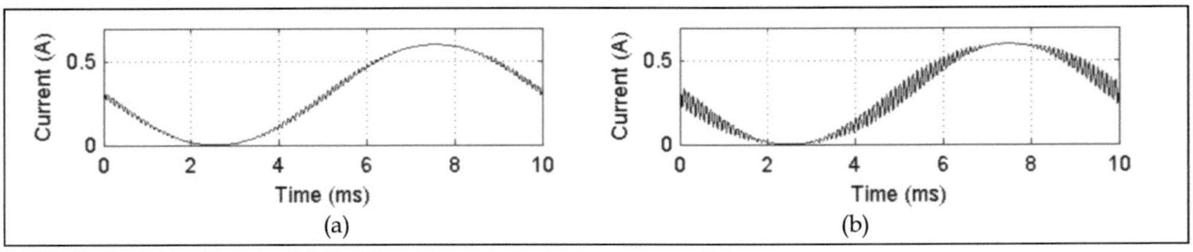

Fig. 7. Current with cap of C of 100μF (a) and 33μF (b).

4.4 Control of the complete tactile array

The extension of the single actuation scheme proposed in the previous section to an m x n array of transducers imposes the use of a microcontroller able to generate m x n independent PWM signals and m x n wired connections.

In order to obtain simple hardware architecture, an actuation solution base on matrix addressing technique has been analyzed. In this case, only $m + n$ control signals are required. The PWM signals are divided in into row signals and column signal. The row signals determine the row that is addressed: all of the m transducers on the selected row are addressed simultaneously. When a row is selected, each signal of the n columns should be individually controlled for modulating the respective coil current.

This type of addressing is similar to the strategy for controlling the status of the pixels in a LCD display called *active matrix addressing*. In Fig. 8, a scheme for controlling three rows and three columns of the tactile array is shown. For controlling the current of the generic element B_{ij} (that indicates the *ij*-esim solenoid) it is sufficient to activate the row *i* by powering the gates of the associated miniature p-MOSFETs (digital output R_i is set to logic 1) and to modulate the current by setting the correspondent duty cycle of the PWM signal which control the column *j*.

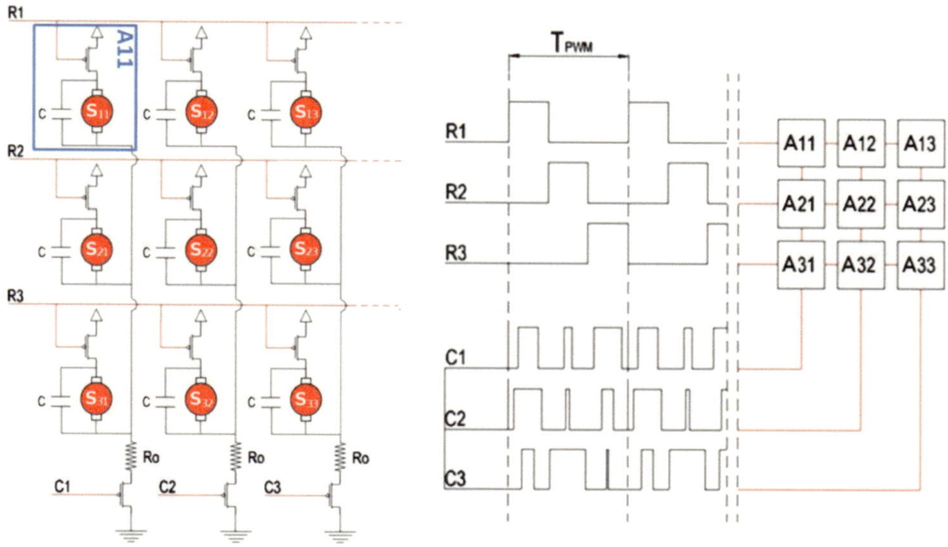

Fig. 8. Scheme of the control electronics of a 3 x 3 array of pins.

Referring to Figure 8, the algorithm for controlling the *m+n* digital signal in order to apply the required current values for the all transducers of the tactile array is the following:

- the rows are sequentially activated: indicating with T_H the period of time required for a whole refresh of the array and with *m* the number of its rows, the selection time for each row is $T_R = T_H/m$;
- when the row *i* is active, the digital signals of the columns are used for modulating the current of the coils which are placed on the row *i*: the period of time which is available for realizing the modulation is limited to T_R; this means that the maximum duty cycle indicate in formula (3) is equal to $a_{max} = 1/m$.

The limitation of the maximum duty cycle for each coil (due to the limited period of time for the modulation) requires a higher impulse of the supplied current (approximately *m* time higher in comparison to the case of a single transducer). This produces higher disturbances in the coil current, as shown in 0 where the coil current are estimated as described in section 4.1 but limiting the maximum duty cycle to 0.2 (that is, considering the case of our array of 5 row).

According to a first set of preliminary tests, despite the fact that the current ripple seems to be quite large (Fig. 9), its effect on the output of the tactile transducer is not so relevant. Probably the mass and the friction of the electromechanical solenoid acts as a filter for frequencies of 10kHz and the resulting displacement of the plunger is extremely reduced.

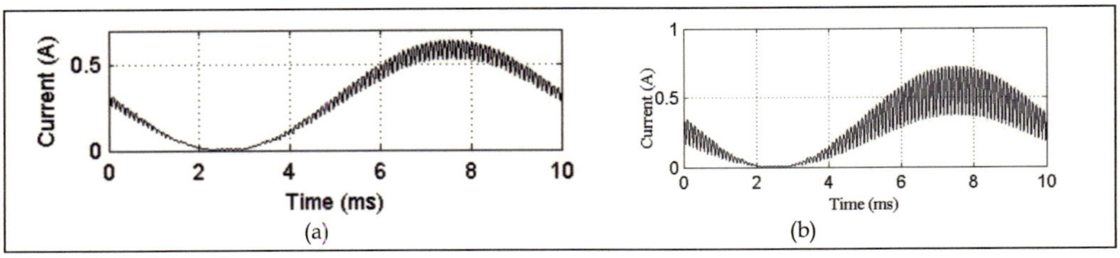

Fig. 9. Coil current of a matrix with 5 row and with capacitance C of 100μF (a) and 33μF (b).

4.5 Haptic rendering

In this case study the target task is the simulation of interaction with a textile of a relatively small size, namely 20x20 cm, whose physical parameters have been taken from Kawabata measurements (Kawabata & Niwa, 1993). This textile is simulated by means of a multi-rate approach that decouples simulation, haptic rendering and tactile rendering. The discussion starts with the description of the simulation, then the haptic rendering and finally the integration part. The overall architecture of the system is shown in Fig. 10.

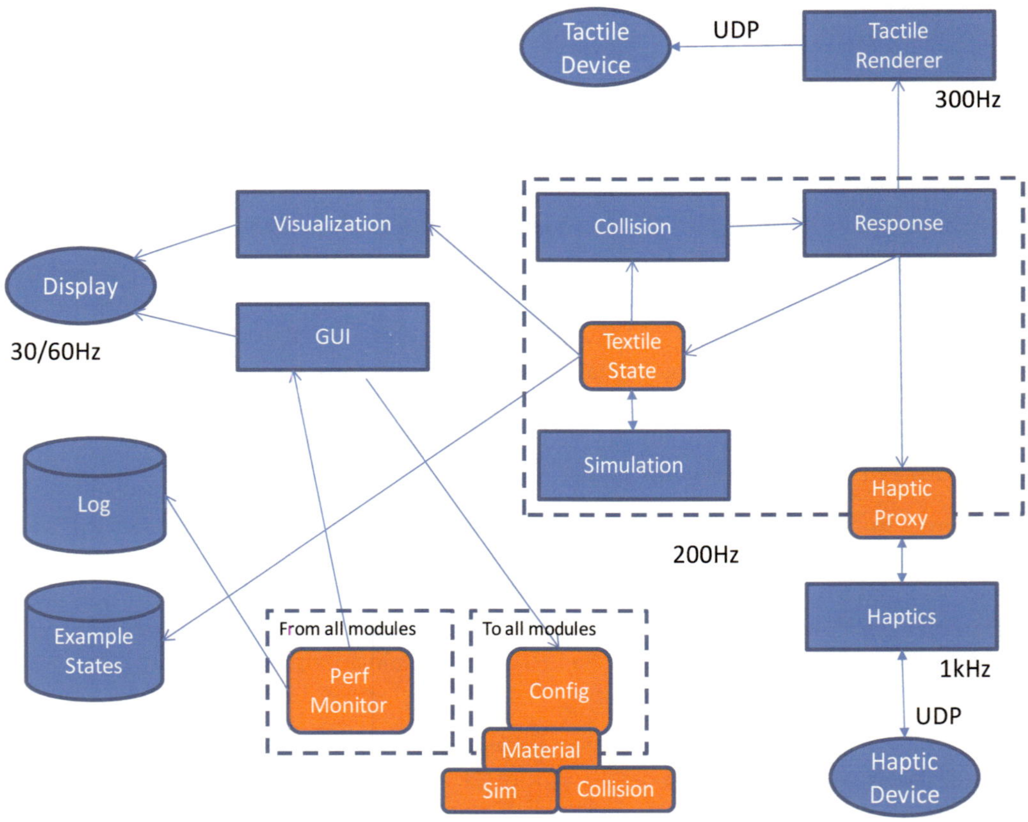

Fig. 10. Architecture of the software highlighting rates and components

4.5.1 Simulation

The geometrical model adopted is based on FEM because they have been proved to be able to map and represent physical properties of material in a better way. In particular the textile is represented by thin triangular shells along the application to cloth simulation by Etzmuss (Etzmuss, Keckeisen, & Strasser, 2003). The physical forces employed are the stretch and bend as expressed by the elastic tensor. These forces are computed from the deformation of the triangle against its original condition but such computation is quite expensive. For this reason we employed co-rotated triangles in which the triangle deformation is expressed by a combination of a rotation and a deformation of the planar version of the triangle. The overall equation of motion of the nodes of the triangles takes into account these forces in addition to external forces like gravity. The node equation is then integrated using implicit Euler that provides more precise simulation at the cost of resolution of a system of equations. This system of equation is solved using a preconditioned conjugate gradient in which the preconditioning is the block diagonal.

4.5.2 Collision

The collision method employed is based on the contact between two spherical proxies of the subject fingers and the vertices of the textile. Each collision makes the textile instantly to move to avoid the collision and then the collision is implemented as a constraint that blocks the motion of the node toward the proxy sphere. This constraint on the node is taken into account in the system resolution by means of a modified preconditioned conjugate model using the filtering approach introduced by Baraff (Baraff & Witkin, 1998). This representation of constraints allows implementing also generic constrained nodes to hang the textile in a given position.

4.5.3 Proxy and haptic feedback

The haptic feedback module runs in a separate thread and it has two objectives: provide feedback of interaction among the finger proxies, and the interaction with the textiles. The finger feedback is provided by means of a damped virtual spring that is activated when the two proxies are below a given threshold. This spring is necessary to compensate the effective size of the gimble that surround the fingers. When each proxy sphere collides with the nodes of the textile it moves the node outside the sphere. The overall force on the proxy is made by two components one impulsive that accounts for the instantaneous motion of the textile, while the other is the pressure applied by the node on the sphere. This pressure of the node on the proxy can be measured as the action performed by the node over the constraint that is effectively the residual of the iterative resolution of the system. This approach is different with respect the previous work (Fontana et al., 2007) the haptic force was based on a penalty method.

The model described so far does not take into account two related aspects of the interaction: friction and textile compression. Without introducing textile compression friction emerges from the forces exchanged between the proxy and the nodes due to the work of the constraints of the contacting nodes. Effectively this model produces small exchanged forces due to the small work of these constraints. An additional contribution to the normal component is caused by the compression of the textile. The FEM model does not take into account these forces because it is a thin shell, but we can use them for the haptic computation. In particular when two proxies are both contacting the same region of the textile they can squeeze the material increasing the normal force on the contacting node, hence raising the effect of friction. The effect of the friction force on the nodes of the textile is integrated in the simulation with a stick slip model. A node subject to static friction is sticked to the surface of the sphere by means of a full constraint.

4.5.4 Tactile integration

The tactile rederer receives information from the contact response module, in particular the position of the contact points, relative velocities and pressures. This information is then used to control the tactile device, in which the 30 pins can be controlled using a single frequency of a sinusoid, whose intensity and phase can be changed for every pin. The rendering is performed by following the approach proposed in (D Allerkamp et al., 2007) and later integrated in (Fontana et al., 2007) although with a different device and with multiple degree of freedom in control. The idea is to start from a geometrical representation of the local feature of the textiles obtained from edge extraction of high resolution photos. Then the local height field is repeated over the textile surface and the position of the tactile actuators in real space is mapped to the surface of the textile. Taking into account the motion of the actuator over the surface the height local information is transformed into a profile of heights along the line of motion that can be transformed into a frequency signal. This signal is the one used for controlling the distinct pins. Differently from the cited work in which two frequencies where selected, this work uses a single sinusoidal frequency but different intensities and phases of the pins.

This model has to be extended for taking into account pressure over the textile and relative velocity. These two featured have indeed the effect of modifying the height of the surface and alter the frequencies of generated signal. Multiple contact points on the surface nearby the tactile actuator have the effect of cumulating the alteration on the surface due to pressure and velocity.

4.5.5 Implementation

The system discussed here has been implemented in C++ using the Eigen template library for optimized matrix manipulation and Qt for visualization and user interface. For exploiting parallel computing on modern hardware multiple versions of the core software have been implemented. In particular we started from a C++ version that has been extended with OpenMP commands for portable parallelization on the CPU although the advantage was quite limited. The reason is that the most computational intensive element is the conjugate method that, being iterative, it is inherently sequential. A second version has been created implementing the same functionalities in OpenCL for portable parallelism among CPU and GPU. This solution improved CPU performance while GPU one was reduced due to the many data structures of the topology.

4.5.6 Dimensions and performance

This system runs at a satisfactory rate with a configuration of 32 x 32 nodes in the FEM models obtaining around 200 frames per second on an Intel Core i750 3GHz with a tolerance of 0.05.

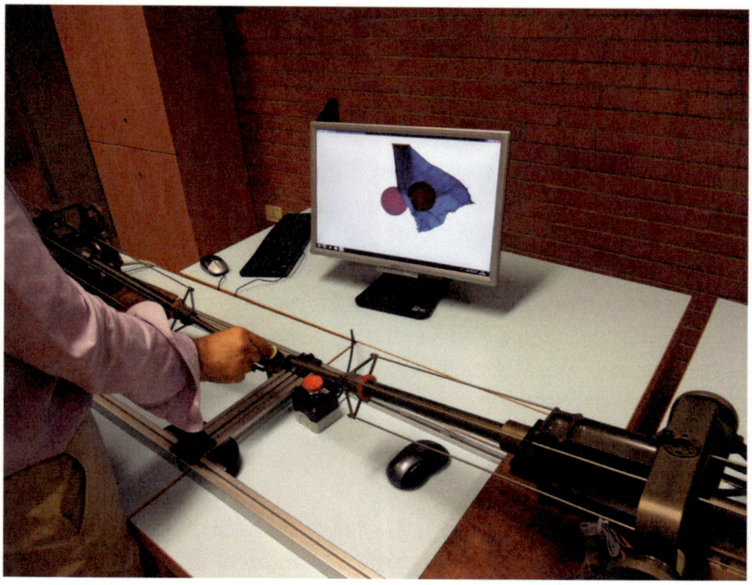

Fig. 11. Photo of the Haptic device and textile simulation

These parameters have been selected for balancing frame-rate with precision of the system. Fig. 11 shows a snapshot of the execution of the execution of the system: the two fingers are the big spheres. On the top line there are the constrained vertices. The small light circles near the fingers are the contacting points.

5. Conclusions

Haptic interface technology has started in the late fifties with first teleoperation applications. After sixty years of research there have been strong improvements each of the field of Machine Haptics, Computer Haptics and Human Haptics knowledge. The haptic systems that are now available have been employed in many fields like medicine, industry and education. However, while current technology has demonstrated to be quite effective for the simulation of Mediated Contact scenarios, there is still a lack in the simulation of Direct Contact. At the same time, the implementation of a system able to effectively simulated interaction with bare finger could be a real breakthrough. Many researches are currently working on integration of tactile and kinesthetic devices and rendering toward this objective.

In this chapter we introduced the main issues that concern with integration of tactile and kinesthetic feedback considering both Machine Haptics and Computer Haptics aspects.

An example of case study that includes the integration of a hand-exoskeleton with a pin-array device is presented. A possible approach for the real-time rendering of both tactile and kinesthetic components is shown.

6. Acknowledgments

Part of the work described in this chapter was partially funded by the RTD national project MANTES financed by the Regione Toscana.

7. References

Allerkamp, D.; Bottcher, G.; Wolter, F.E.; Brady, A.C.; Qu, J & Summers, I R. (2007). A vibrotactile approach to tactile rendering, *The Visual Computer*, Vol. 23(2), pp 97-108. Springer.

Baraff, D. & Witkin, A. (1998). Large steps in cloth simulation, *Proceedings of the 25th annual conference on Computer graphics and interactive techniques - SIGGRAPH '98*, pp 43-54. New York, New York, USA: ACM Press. doi: 10.1145/280814.280821.

Barbagli, F.; Frisoli, A.; Salisbury, K. & Bergamasco, M. (2004). Simulating human fingers: a soft finger proxy model and algorithm. *Proceedings of Conference on Haptic Interfaces for Virtual Environment and Teleoperator Systems, HAPTICS'04*, pp. 9-17.

Barbagli, F.; Prattichizzo, D. & Salisbury, K. (2005). A multirate approach to haptic interaction with deformable objects single and multipoint contacts, *The International Journal of Robotics Research*, 24(9), p.703-728. SAGE Publications.

Behery, H. (2005); *Effect of Mechanical and Physical Properties on Fabric Hand*, Publisher: Taylor & Francis Ltd, 2005.

Benali-Khoudja, M.; Hafez, M.; Alexandre, J.-M. & Kheddar, A. (2003) , Electromagnetically driven high-density tactile interface based on a multi-layer approach, *Micromechatronics and Human Science,*. MHS 2003. Proceedings of 2003 International Symposium on, pp. 147- 152, 19-22 Oct. 2003.

Bicchi, A.; De Rossi, D. E.; Scilingo, E. P.(2000). The role of the contact area spread rate in haptic discrimination of softness, *IEEE trans. On Robotics and Automation vol. 16*, no. 5, pp. 496–504, 2000.

Bottcher, G.; Allerkamp, D. & Wolter, F.E. (2010). Multi-rate coupling of physical simulations for haptic interaction with deformable objects, *The Visual Computer*, 26(6), 903-914. Springer.

Böttcher, G.; Allerkamp, D. & Wolter, F.E. (2010). Multi-rate coupling of physical simulations for haptic interaction with deformable objects, *The Visual Computer*, 26(6-8), 903-914.

Ciocarlie, M.; Lackner, C.; & Allen, P. (2007). Soft finger model with adaptive contact geometry for grasping and manipulation tasks. *IEEE Computer Society*.

Dostmohamed, H. & Hayward, V. (2005). Trajectory of contact region on the fingerpad gives the illusion of haptic shape. *Experimental Brain Research* 164(3) 387–394

Duriez, C.; Andriot, C. & Kheddar, A. (2004). Signorini's contact model for deformable objects in haptic simulations. *Intelligent Robots and Systems*, 2004.(IROS 2004). Proceedings. 2004 IEEE/RSJ International Conference on (Vol. 4, pp. 3232-3237).

Etzmuss, O.; Keckeisen, M. & Strasser, W. (2003). A fast finite element solution for cloth modelling. *11th Pacific Conference on Computer Graphics and Applications*, 2003. Proceedings., 244-251. IEEE Comput. Soc. doi: 10.1109/PCCGA.2003.1238266.

Fontana, M.; Dettori, A.; Salsedo, F. & Bergamasco, M. (2009), Mechanical design of a novel Hand Exoskeleton for accurate force displaying., *Proceedings of ICRA 2009 Conference*, pp. 1704-1709.

Fontana, M.; Marcheschi, S.; Tarri, F.; Salsedo, F.; Bergamasco, M.; Allerkamp, D.; Bottcher, G.; Wolter, F.-E.; Brady, C. A.; Qu, J. & Summers, I. R.; (2007). Integrating Force and Tactile Rendering Into a Single VR System. *Proceedings of Cyberworlds, International Conference on*, pp. 277-284.

Frisoli, A.; Barbagli, F.; Ruffaldi, E.; Bergamasco, M. & Salisbury, K. (2006). A Limit-Curve Based Soft Finger god-object Algorithm. *Haptic Symposium.*

Frisoli, A.; Solazzi, M.; Salsedo, F. & Bergamasco, M. (2008). A Fingertip Haptic Display for Improving Curvature Discrimination, *Presence: Teleoperators & Virtual Environments* - 17 : 1 - 12 (2008)

Gilbert, E. G., Johnson, D. W. & Keerthi, S. S. (1988). A fast procedure for computing the distance between complex objects in three dimensional space. *IEEE J. Robotics and Automation*, 4(2), 193-203.

Govindaraj, M.; Raheja, A. & Garg, A.(2002); Haptic Simulation of Fabric Hand, *Proceedings of the 31st Textile Research Symposium*, Mt. Fuji, Japan.

Hayward, V. (2004). Display of Haptic Shape at Different Scales. *Proceedings of Eurohaptics Conference.* Munich, Germany, June 5-7, pp. 20-27.

Hayward, V. (2008). Haptic Shape Cues, Invariants, Priors, and Interface Design. *Human Haptic Perception - Basics and Applications*, Grunwald, M., Birkhauser Verlag, pp. 381-392.

Jansson, G. & Monaci, L.; (2006). Identification of real objects under conditions similar to those in haptic displays: providing spatially distributed information at the contact areas is more important than increasing the number of areas. *Virtual Reality*, Vol. 9, No. 4, pp243-249. Springer-Verlag London, UK, ISSN: 1359-4338.

Johansson, R.S. & Flanagan, J.R.; (2007). Tactile sensory control of object manipulation in humans, *Handbook of the Senses.* Vol.: *Somatosensation.* Edited by Kaas J. and Gardner E. Elsevier.

Johansson, R.S. & Westling, G.; Tactile afferent signals in the control of precision grip. *In Attention and Performance*, vol XIII Edited by Jeannerod M. 1990 pp 677-713. Erlbaum, Hilldale, NJ.

Jones, L.A. & Lederman, S. (2006). Human hand functions, *Oxford University Press*, ISBN 0195173155.

Kawabata, S. & Niwa, M. (1993). Objective measurement of fabric mechanical property and quality:: its application to textile and clothing manufacturing. *International Journal of Clothing Science and Technology*, 3(1), 7-18. MCB UP Ltd.

Kheddar, A.; Drif, A.; Citérin, J. & Le Mercier, B. (2004). A multi-level haptic rendering concept. *Proceedigns of Eurohaptics Conference*, Munich, Germany, June 5-7., pp. 147- 154.

Kron, A. & Schmidt, G. (2003). Multi-Fingered Tactile Feedback from Virtual and Remote Environments. *Proceedings of 11th Symposium on Haptic Interfaces for Virtual Environment and Teleoperator Systems*, p. 16-24.

Kuchenbecker, K. J.; Fiene, J. & Niemeyer, G. (2005). Event-based haptics and acceleration matching: Portraying and assessing the realism of contact. *Proc. World Haptics Conference.*

Lederman, S. & Klatzky, R. (1999). Sensing and displaying spatially distributed fingertip forces in haptic interfaces for teleoperator and virtual environment systems, *Presence*, Vol.8, No. 1, pp. 86–103, ISSN 1054-7460

Li, B.; Xu, Y. & Choi, J. (1996). Applying Machine Learning Techniques, *Proceedings of ASME 2010 4th International Conference on Energy Sustainability*, pp. 14-17, ISBN 842-6508-23-3, Phoenix, Arizona, USA, May 17-22, 2010

Lima, P.; Bonarini, A. & Mataric, M. (2004). *Application of Machine Learning*, InTech, ISBN 978-953-7619-34-3, Vienna, Austria

Melder, N. & Harwin, W. S. (2004). Extending the friction cone algorithm for arbitrary polygon based haptic objects. *12th International Symposium on Haptic Interfaces for Virtual Environment and Teleoperator Systems*, (HAPTICS 04) (pp. 234-241).

Miguel, A. & Otaduy, M. C. L. (2005). Stable and Responsive Six-Degree-of-Freedom Haptic Manipulation Using Implicit Integration. *Proceedings of IEEE Worldhaptics05*.

Nealen, A.; Muller, M.; Keiser, R.; Boxerman, E. & Carlson, M. (2006). Physically based deformable models in computer graphics. *Computer Graphics Forum*, Vol. 25, pp. 809-836.

Otaduy, M. & Lin, M. (2003). Sensation preserving simplification for haptic rendering. *Proc. of ACM SIGGRAPH*.

Ruspini, D.C.; Kolarov, K. & Khatib, K. (1997). The Haptic Display of Complex Graphical Environments. *Proceedings of SIGGRAPH*.

Salisbury, K. & Srinivasan, M.A. (1997). Phantom-based haptic interaction with virtual objects. *Computer Graphics and Applications, IEEE* , vol.17, no.5, pp. 6- 10, Sept.-Oct.

Salisbury, K & Tar, C. (1997). Haptic rendering of surfaces defined by implicit functions. *ASME Dyn. Sys. and Control Div.* (Vol. 61, pp. 61-67).

Salsedo, F.; Marcheschi, S.; Fontana, M. & Bergamasco, M. (2011). Tactile Transducer Based on Electromechanical Solenoids. *Proceedings of Worldhaptics Conference 2011*, pp.220-226.

Sato, K.; Kajimoto, H.; Kawakami, N. & Tachi, S. (2007). Improvement of Shape Distinction by Kinesthetic-Tactile Integration. World Haptics Conference, pp. 391-396, *Second Joint EuroHaptics Conference and Symposium on Haptic Interfaces for Virtual Environment and Teleoperator Systems*, pp. 391-396.

Solazzi, M.; Frisoli, A. & Bergamasco, M. (2010). "Design of a novel finger haptic interface for contact and orientation display," *Haptics Symposium, 2010 IEEE* , pp.129-132, 25-26.

Scilingo, E.P.; Bianchi, M.; Grioli, G. & A. Bicchi (2010). Rendering Softness: Integration of kinaesthetic and cutaneous information in a haptic device. *Transactions on Haptics*, 3(2):109 - 118, 2010.

Teschner, M.; Kimmerle, S.; Heidelberger, B.; Zachmann, G.; Raghupathi, L. & Fuhrmann, A. (2005). *Collision Detection for Deformable Objects. Computer Graphics Forum*, 24(1), 61-81.

Wagner, C.R.; Lederman, S.J. & Howe, V R. D. (2004). Design and Performance of a Tactile Shape Display Using RC Servomotors. *Haptics-e*, 3(4), Aug 2004.

Wagner, C. R.; Perrin, D. P.; Feller, R. L.; Howe, R. D.; Clatz, O.; Delingette, H. & Ayache, N. (2005). Integrating Tactile and Force Feedback with Finite Element Models. *Proceedings of IEEE International Conference on Robotics and Automation*, Barcelona, Spain, pp. 1–10.

Wang, Q. & Hayward, V. (2010). Biomechanically Optimized Distributed Tactile Transducer Based on Lateral Skin Deformation. *International Journal of Robotics Research.* 29(4):323-335.

Yang, Y. & Zhang, Y. (2009) A New Cable-driven Haptic Device for Integrating Kinesthetic and Cutaneous Display, *Proceedings of ASME/IFToMM International Conference on Reconfigurable Mechanisms and Robots*, London, United Kingdom, June 22-24, 2009, pp. 386 – 391.

Zilles, C. & Salisbury, J. (1995). A ConstraintBased God-Object Method For Haptic Display. *Proc. IEE/RSJ International Conference on Intelligent Robots and Systems, Human Robot Interaction, and Cooperative Robots*, Vol. 3, pp. 146-151.

4

Spatial Biases and the Haptic Experience of Surface Orientation

Frank H. Durgin and Zhi Li
Swarthmore College,
USA

1. Introduction

The two main purposes of this chapter are to review past evidence for a systematic spatial bias in the perception of surface orientation (geographical slant), and to report two new experiments documenting this bias in the manual haptic system. Orientation is a fundamental perceptual property of surfaces that is relevant both for planning and implementing actions. Geographical slant refers to the orientation (inclination or pitch along its main axis) of a surface relative to the gravitationally-defined horizontal. It has long been known that hills appear visually steeper than they are (e.g., Ross, 1974). Only recently has it been documented that (1) there is also bias in the haptic perception of surface orientation (Hajnal et al., 2011), and that (2) similar visual and haptic biases even exist for small surfaces within reach (Durgin, Li & Hajnal, 2010).

To provide a context for understanding the present experiments, we will first provide an overview of the prior experimental evidence concerning bias in the perception of geographical slant. First we will discuss findings from both vision and haptic perception that have documented perceptual bias for surfaces in reach. We will then review the literature on the visual and haptic biases in the perception of the greographical slant of locomotor surfaces such as hills and ramps. At the intersection of these two literatures is the historical use of haptic measures of perceived geographical slant, and we will therefore review these measures with particular attention to understanding some pitfalls in the use of haptic measures of perception. We next contrast these haptic measures with proprioceptive measures of perceived orientation and discuss the problem in interpreting calibrated actions as measures of perception.

Having laid out these various past findings we will then report two novel experiments that demonstrate spatial biases in the haptic experience of real surfaces. The experiments include both verbal and non-verbal methods modelled on similar findings we have reported in the visual domain. Following the presentation of the experimental results we will discuss issues of measurement in perception - especially pertaining to the interpretation of verbal reports, and conclude with a discussion of functional theories of perceptual bias in the perception of surface orientation.

2. Spatial bias in the perception of orientation: Surfaces within manual reach

What is meant by a spatial bias in the perception of surface orientation? Durgin, Li and Hajnal (2010) reported a series of studies of a bias they called the "vertical tendency" in slant perception. Specifically, they found that small, irregularly-shaped wooden surfaces appeared steeper than they actually were both when viewed visually and when experienced haptically while blindfolded. The term "vertical tendency" was used to distinguish the observed effect from what has been called "frontal tendency" in the literature (Gibson, 1950). For many years it has been argued that surfaces viewed visually, appear compressed along the depth axis of visual regard and thus appear more frontal to gaze than they are. However, when Durgin, Li and Hajnal asked participants to make estimates of the geographical slants of wooden surfaces within reach, they found that that they got approximately the same bias function whether the surfaces were at eye level (so that "frontal" and vertical coincided) or viewed with gaze declined by about 40°. Moreover, the same kinds of bias were found when surfaces were experienced haptically by placing the palm of the hand on them, though their measurements of this were limited to the angle of 0-45°. The typical bias function for vision is shown in Figure 1.

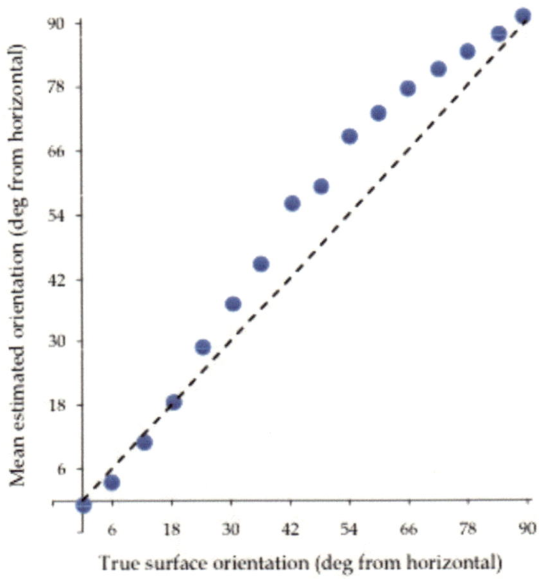

Fig. 1. Surface orientation estimates for near visual surfaces presented within reach of the hand (Durgin, Li & Hajnal, 2010, Experiment 1). Symbol size approximates SEM.

The estimates shown in Figure 1 are based on verbal/numeric estimates of orientation relative to horizontal, but the bias observed cannot be due to verbal coding. Essentially the same spatial function was found if participants instead estimated orientation relative to vertical and their responses were then subtracted from 90° in order to express them relative to horizontal. Thus for example, a surface that was actually at a 42° orientation from horizontal (and thus 48° from vertical), was estimated as being about 60° from horizontal by one group of participants and about 30° from vertical by another. Clearly both groups saw it as much steeper than its actual slant. When the same 42° surface was explored, haptically, by a third group of participants by each placing the palm of the right hand against it while blindfolded, it was also judged to be 60° from horizontal (Durgin, Li & Hajnal, 2010, Experiment 4).

Moreover, to emphasize that these biases did not depend on generating verbal estimates, Durgin, Li and Hajnal (2010) asked a fourth set of participants to judge whether various oriented planar surfaces were closer to horizontal or to vertical. They fit a psychometric function to the resulting choice data and found that a surface slanted by only 34.3° from horizontal was, on average, visually perceived to be equidistant from vertical and horizontal.

This spatial bias function for near surfaces closely matches the observed proprioceptive function for the perceived declination of gaze. That is, when people are asked to report the pitch of their gaze, verbal reports provide evidence of an exaggerated deviation from horizontal that closely matches the bias function shown above for perceived surface slant (Durgin & Li, 2011a; Li & Durgin, 2009). Thus, it appears that several different perceptual representations of pitch contain a bias that expands the scale of differences near horizontal while compressing the scale near vertical.

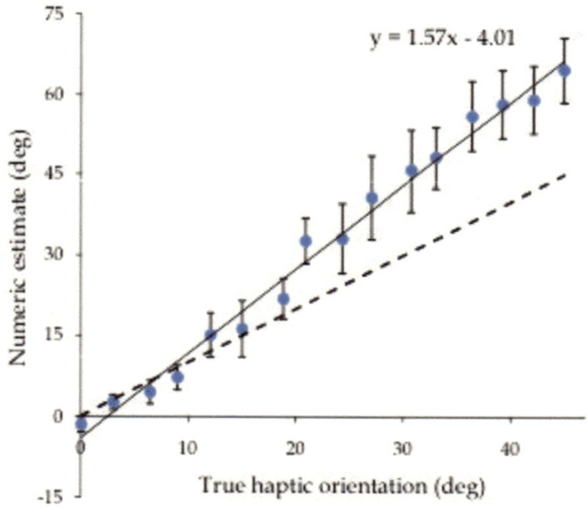

Fig. 2. Surface orientation estimates for surfaces (0-48°) felt with the palm of the hand (Durgin, Li & Hajnal, 2010, Experiment 4). Error bars indicate ±1 SEM.

In the haptic domain and in the proprioception of gaze, the perceptual scale of the bias function for perceived pitch has mostly only been measured for orientations within about 50° from horizontal (e.g., Durgin, Li & Hajnal, 2010). In this range the scaling of pitch tends to closely approximate a linear scale with a gain of 1.5 (Durgin & Li, 2011a). For example the haptic data of Durgin, Li and Hajnal are shown in Figure 2. These data are based on numeric estimates of orientation in deg (relative to horizontal) made based on placing the palm of the hand on various real slanted surfaces while blindfolded. Durgin and Li have reported a very similar function for explicit estimates of the pitch of gaze over a similar range. Durgin and Li (like Durgin, Li & Hajnal) supplemented their verbal estimation data with a horizontal-vertical bisection task and again found that a rather shallow gaze declination of about 30° from horizontal was perceived as the bisection point between vertical and horizontal gaze.

These observations are particularly relevant to the present discussion because they emphasize that the form of the perceptual bias may not be a "vertical tendency." Rather, the linear gain of about 1.5 found in various measurements of perceived pitch between 0° and 45° from horizontal suggests that deviations from horizontal are being exaggerated and therefore that it is the horizontal that is special. Durgin and Li (2011a) have hypothesized that the expanded scaling (near horizontal) of the perceived pitch of gaze direction serves to expand the most highly utilized portion of the angular range for purpose of maintaining greater cognitive precision. Across a variety of contexts, they proposed that a gain of about 1.5 may provide efficient scaling for retaining greater precision in this lower half of the range when sending neural pitch signals upstream to cognitive and motor areas.

3. Bias in the perceived orientation of locomotor surfaces: Hills and ramps

While there are clear and consistent visual and spatial biases in the perception of surfaces within reach of the hands, visual biases measured in the perception of locomotor surfaces have tended to be seem even more exaggerated. These exaggerations were initially documented by Kammann (1967) who proposed that they might reflect the heightened energetics of the gravitational vertical, and by Ross (1974), but were most extensively documented by Proffitt et al. (1995). Although many of the theoretical conclusions of Proffitt et al. have been called into question by more recent work, their basic documentation of the judged orientation of 8 distinct hills on their campus remains a useful basic source regarding the overestimation of hills. In particular, Proffitt et al. reported that paths with physical slants of 4°, 5° or 6° were typically perceived as being about 20° in orientation when viewed with gaze forward, as shown in Figure 3.

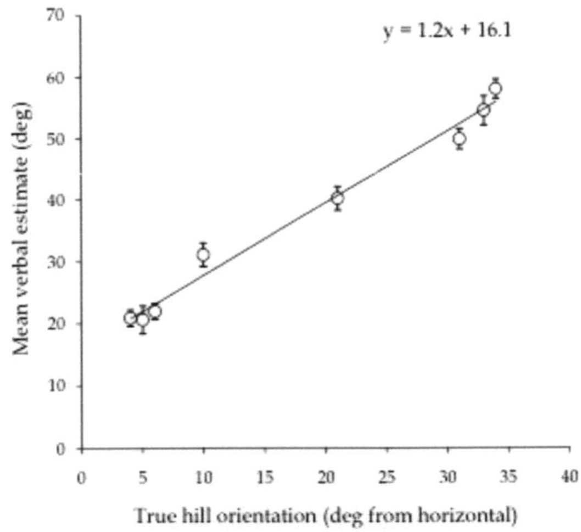

Fig. 3. Verbal estimates of the (visual) slants of eight hills from Proffitt et al. (1995), ± 1 SEM. Hills were viewed from the base with gaze forward.

Because the range of orientations in most locomotor settings is no more than ± 10° from horizontal, and physical/biomechanical limitations restrict bipedal locomotion to surfaces of less than about 35°, Proffitt et al. (1995) proposed that the exaggerated perception of hill orientation was an adaptive strategy to represent the range of human behavioural potential and energetic costs and thus to inform decisions about route selection during locomotion in the wild. A difficulty with this view is that perceived hill orientation decreases as one approaches a hill (Li & Durgin, 2010), and nearer portions of hills appear shallower than farther portions (Bridgeman & Hoover, 2008). In fact, as we will discuss below, there is continuity between orientation biases we have measured for small, near surfaces and those measured by Proffitt et al. for hills (Li & Durgin, 2010).

Proffitt further proposed that physical actions, such as stepping, were controlled by an *unbiased* perceptual representation (vision for action) that was contrasted with the exaggerated representation available for long-range cognitive planning. This view has since been challenged by studies of the haptic perception of locomotor inclines.

3.1 Haptic bias in the perceived orientation of locomotor surfaces

Hajnal et al. (2011) asked participants to step onto ramps that they could not see. (They were either wearing a blindfold or an occluding collar that blocked their view of the floor.) The ramps varied in orientation from 4° to 16°. Participants were asked to provide either verbal estimates of the surface orientation or to gesture the orientation with the their hand, which was measured using digital photography. The data are reproduced in Figure 4, along with a photograph of the experimental situation. Both forms of measurement documented surprisingly-large perceptual exaggerations of haptic slant. For somewhat steep ramps, the haptic exaggeration of perceived slant was even greater than the visual exaggeration observed when the same participants judged the orientations of the ramps when looking at them afterward. For example, Hajnal et al. found that participants standing on a 16° ramp judged it to be about 35-40° (both verbally, and as measured by hand gesture) based on their haptic experience, whereas when looking down at a 16° ramp (while standing on a level surface at the base of the ramp) they judged it to be only about 22-24°. The same pattern (higher estimates based on haptic perception) was found for a 14.5° ramp by Durgin et al. (2009) who collected visual estimates before having people step onto the ramp.

Haptic evaluations of the surface under one's feet are more valuable for immediate motor planning than for distal route planning. Hajnal et al. (2011) therefore suggested that these distortions might be the perceptual consequence of dense coding of orientations near horizontal that led to functionally exaggerated perceived orientation for the more precise control of action.

Kinsella-Shaw et al. (1992) had previously reported that participants were good at matching haptic inclines underfoot to visual inclines. To rule out the possibility that the haptic exaggerations were learned from calibrating haptic experience to visual experience, Hajnal et al. (2011) also tested a population of four congenitally blind individuals using verbal report. The blind individuals' estimates were quite similar to those of the sighted participants, though they were slightly higher. This indicates that the haptic exaggeration of the apparent inclination of surfaces on which one stands exists even in the absence of visual experience.

3.2 Proprioceptive bias in the perceived orientation of locomotor surfaces

Proprioceptive error in the perceived declination of gaze was first reported in a study of downhill slant perception: Li and Durgin (2009) observed that standing back from the edge of an outdoor downhill surface made it appear steeper than when standing closer to the edge. Indeed, for a steep hill, the maximum perceived orientation seemed to occur when standing far enough back from the edge of the hill that one's line of gaze was nearly coincident with the surface of the hill. Using a virtual environment in which viewing position was manipulated orthogonally to the steepness of the incline, Li and Durgin found that the functions relating simulated optical slant to perceived optical slant only lined up with one another at the two viewpoints if it was assumed that the change in perceived declination of gaze was exaggerated with a gain of about 1.5.

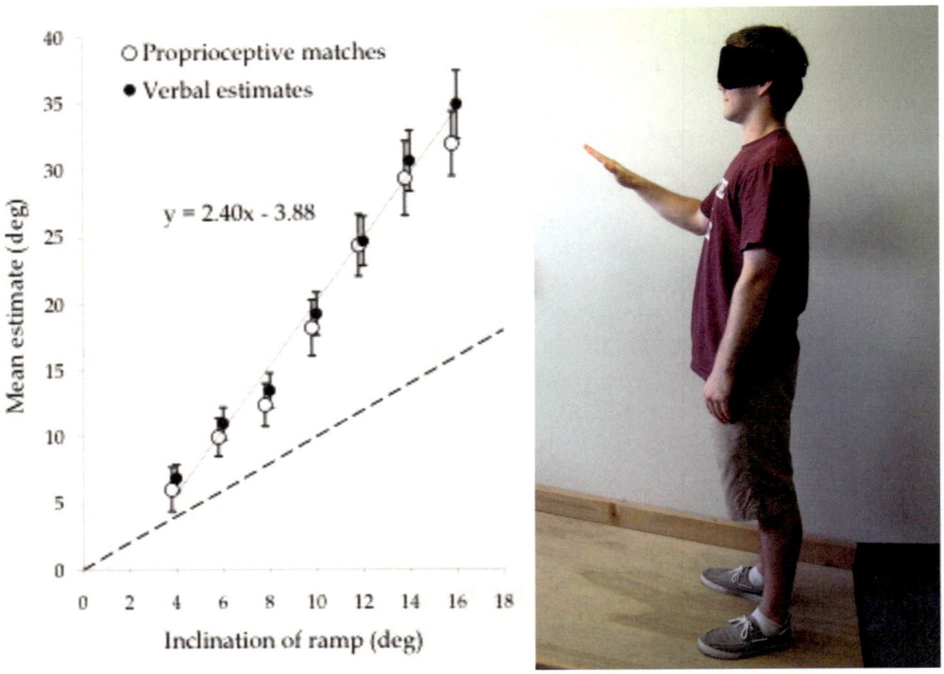

Fig. 4. Verbal and proprioceptive (hand gesture) estimates of the haptically-perceived orientation of a ramp while standing on it, blindfolded (from Hajnal et al., 2011). Hand gesture data has been recomputed to represent the main orientation of the hand rather than the orientation of the palm, which is about 6.5° steeper (see Durgin, Li & Hajnal, 2010). Proprioceptive points are displaced to show the SEMs. Fit line is to verbal data.

Deducing from these observations that the perceived direction of gaze might itself be distorted Li and Durgin (2009) tested this directly by asking people to look at targets at various declinations out of upper-floor windows and estimate the downward pitch of their gaze. Again, a gain of 1.5 was found. Later studies confirmed that the gain of perceived gaze declination is about 1.5 even for objects in near space and along a locomotor surface (Durgin et al., 2011), as discussed in Section 2.

3.3 Continuity between visual biases for near and far surfaces

Across a number of studies, Li and Durgin (2009, 2010; Durgin & Li, 2011a) have found systematic evidence suggesting that the visual perception of slant also has a gain of 1.5 in the low end of the geographical slant range. But this led to a puzzle. If perceived slant has a gain of only 1.5, then why does a hill of 5° appear to be 20° rather than, say, 7.5°? And why is the perceptual gain for outdoor hills, as illustrated in Figure 3, limited to a factor of about 1.2? Following up on the observations of Bridgeman and Hoover (2008), Li and Durgin (2010) noted that viewing outdoor hills from the base of the hill with gaze forward means that geographical slant is confounded with viewing distance to the hill surface. For example, for a typical eye-height of 1.6 m, a 5° hill is viewed at a horizontal distance of 18 m, whereas a 30° embankment would be viewed at a horizontal distance of less than 3 m.

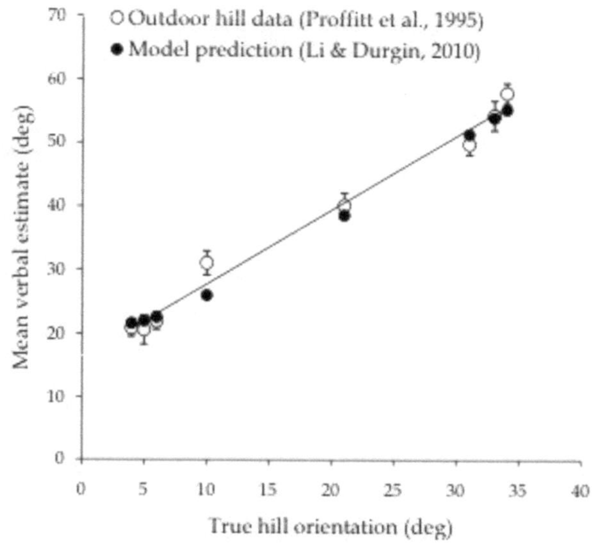

Fig. 5. Predictions of outdoor visual data from Proffitt et al. (1995) based on a model with only one free parameter. With the overall intercept set to 0°, and the slant gain fixed at 1.5, the perceived slant model depicted here is simply $\beta_p = 1.5 \cdot \beta + k \cdot \log(D)$, where D denotes the horizontal viewing distance from the base of the hill (assuming an eye height of 1.6 m), β denotes actual slant and β_p denotes perceived slant; the one free parameter, k, equals 5.

Using a high quality virtual environment, Li and Durgin (2010) decoupled viewing distance and geographical slant by presenting large full-cue binocular surfaces at 6 orientations in the linear range of 6-36° at 5 distances in the logarithmic range of 1 to 16 m. Viewing was horizontal. They found that at each viewing distance the gain of perceived slant was about 1.5, but that the intercept of the slant function increased with the log of distance. Thus, the 30 combinations of orientation and distance could be fit with a three-parameter model including an overall intercept, a constant multiplied by log distance and a slant gain of about 1.5). Despite the many potential differences between virtual environments and real ones, Li and Durgin showed that a 3-parameter model derived from their verbal report data in the virtual environment provided an excellent fit to Proffitt et al.'s (1995) outdoor hill data when the viewing distance required for each hill was taken into account. By setting the slant gain to 1.5 and assuming an overall intercept of 0°, we can reduce the model to a single free parameter, based on the multiplier of log viewing distance. The predictions of such a model are shown in Figure 5 alongside each of the observed mean estimates from Proffitt et al. The success of this model in fitting the outdoor data shows that, once viewing distance is taken into account, the underlying slant gain for outdoor hills as for small surfaces seems to be 1.5.

This analysis provided by Li and Durgin (2010) shows how the apparent discrepancy between the perceived slants of hills and of near surfaces may be due to differences in viewing distance. However, the model does not explain why haptic slant perception of ramps underfoot has such a high gain. The most intriguing observation we can make about this concerns the discrepancy between the haptically perceived slant of the 16° ramp (~35°) and the visually perceived slant of that same ramp (~23°). Because the ramp was viewed at a near viewing distance, with head declined, the resulting exaggerated scaling in vision ought to be by about 1.5 times, and it was. In contrast, if a 16° hill were viewed with gaze forward, the horizontal distance to the surface would be 5.6 m away, and the model prediction would be a perceived slant of 32.6°, which is quite close to the haptically-perceived slant of the 16° ramp. In contrast, for a 6° ramp, the estimates given haptically and from visual estimates of the ramp were in close agreement with one another (~11°, Hajnal et al., 2011). Although these were both far lower than (i.e., about half) what would be expected for forward viewing of a 6° hill, a value of ~11° is consistent with predictions of the one-parameter model for the actual viewing distance of about 1.8 m. Thus, the data of Hajnal et al. suggest that there is indeed *some* calibration between pedal and visual estimates of slant for common slants (of 10° or less) of near surfaces, as Kinsella-Shaw et al. (1992) suggested. However, Hajnal et al. (2011) have emphasized that the biomechanics of placing the foot upon a locomotor surface allow for rapid accommodation of the foot to the surface and may not require a very precise visual estimate of surface orientation in order for stepping to be successful. It is probably surprising to many that using hand gestures to try to match the slant of the surface on which one stands produces as much error as it does. This seems strong confirmation that the perceptual experience of the slants underfoot really is quite exaggerated. Because of the limited range of upward flexion of the foot, the extreme scaling of pedal slant is consistent with the idea of sensory scaling of perceived ramp orientation partly representing the biomechanical range of flexion. The evidence that a similar magnitude of perceptual exaggeration is present in participants who are congenitally blind lends support to this interpretation, by indicating that calibration is not the source of the haptic distortion. It seems unlikely that the visual distortion derives from the haptic.

4. Problems with measuring perceived slant with haptic matching tasks

One current controversy in the study of slant perception concerns a popular method of assessing perceived slant. Proffitt et al. (1995) developed a method of assessing perceived slant that they initially referred to as a haptic measure, but also (e.g., Bhalla & Proffitt, 1999) described as an action measure. The measure consists of using one's hand to adjust the orientation of a "palm board" so as to match the perceived slant of a surface. The palm board was originally developed by Gibson (1950) as a non-verbal measure of perceived slant. In their studies of hills, Proffitt et al. (1995) placed the palm board at waist level so that it was at the edge of the field of view of the observer. They found that unlike verbal measures, which overestimated hill orientations, the palm board measure was relatively accurate. Bhalla and Proffitt interpreted the relative accuracy of the palm board measure as evidence of an accurate underlying perceptual representation "for action." However, some simple control experiments carried out by Durgin, Hajnal, Li, Tonge and Stigliani (2010) suggested that that palm boards were only accidentally accurate.

Durgin, Hajnal, Li, Tonge and Stigliani (2010) reasoned that if palm boards were assessing accurate motor representations of space, then they ought to be particularly accurate for matching near surfaces with which the hand could actually interact. That is, Durgin et al. presented full-cue wooden surfaces within reach and had people try to match their orientations using a palm board. Rather than being accurate, as the action theory predicted, palm board settings were much too low. Durgin et al. interpreted this as a haptic/proprioceptive error due to inaccurate scaling of wrist flexion. Durgin et al. showed that people overestimated the flexion of their wrist with about the same gain as they overestimated far surfaces. Li and Durgin (2011a) showed that when verbal estimates of near surfaces (similar to those shown in Figure 1) were used to predict palm board matches to those surfaces the function relating the two measures was identical to the function that related verbal estimates of hills to palm board matches to those hills. In other words, the perceived orientation of the palm board was exaggerated in a way that (imperfectly) approximated the exaggeration of hills viewed at a distance. Palm board measures were not tapping into a separate motor representation, but rather were differently-scaled outputs tapping into the same distorted representation as verbal reports. When the distortion in vision was approximately cancelled by the distortions in proprioception/haptics, the illusion of accuracy resulted.

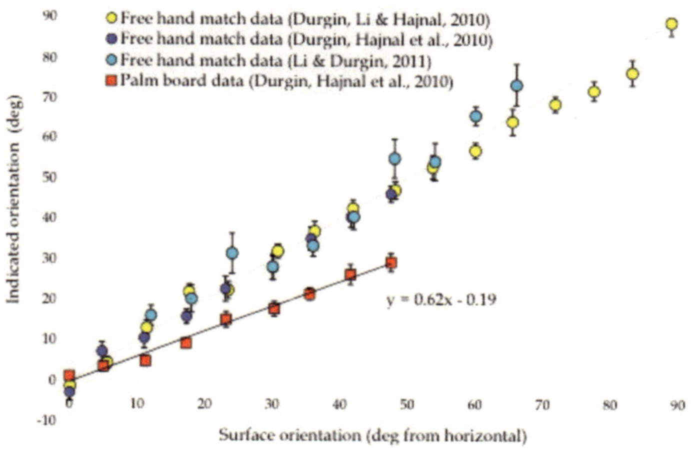

Fig. 6. Contrasting the gain of a palm board measure (i.e. 0.62) with the gain of a free-hand gesture for matching full-cue surfaces within reach (i.e., ~1.0). The hand was occluded from vision in all cases. The visual surfaces were wooden surfaces within reach of the hand.

Strikingly, Durgin, Hajnal, Li, Tonge and Stigliani (2010, 2011) also showed that proprioceptive performance for near surfaces was greatly improved if the palm board were simply removed and people were allowed to gesture freely with their hand (with the hand hidden behind an occluding barrier). Some of their data are shown in Figure 6. As in the study of the haptic perception of ramps underfoot, free-hand gestures for far hills were found to grossly overestimate the slants of those hills (roughly consistent with verbal reports), but free-hand gestures for surfaces in near space were quite precise and accurate. The main difference between free-hand gestures and palm board matches were that palm boards prevented the use of the elbow as a primary axis of hand rotation. Because the axis of the palm board was near the wrist, the wrist had to be the principal joint for adjusting the palm board. Moreover, Durgin, Li and Hajnal (2010) showed that the perceived orientation of a fairly steep palm board was even higher than haptic perception of a rigid surface of the same orientation – perhaps because of the additional forces used to maintain the tilted orientation of the palm board.

In summary, haptic matching tasks have proven to be very difficult to interpret for at least three reasons. First, evidence of surprising accuracy between palm board matches and hills has turned out to be spurious. Palm boards simply feel much steeper than they are because they require flexing the wrist more than is customary in normal circumstances. Second, the perceptual gain of haptic surface perception is generally unknown. If people see a visual surface as 45° when it is only 34° and they feel that a haptic surface is 45° when it is only 34°, they may seem to be correctly matching a 34° surface when they think they are matching a 45° surface. Finally, the fact that passive contact with a rigid surface dissociates from active rotation of a palm board suggests that haptic measures can be contaminated by active control of the surface's orientation.

4.1 Calibration between proprioception and the visual experience of slant

The function shown in Figure 6 for free-hand manual gestures was obtained with the same set of surfaces used to obtain the function in Figure 1 for verbal estimates of slant. Nonetheless the verbal estimates show a great deal of bias (exaggeration of the deviation from horizontal), whereas the manual gestures appear to be well-calibrated. One possibility is that proprioception is calibrated to vision. That is, the perceived orientation of the hand ought to match the perceived orientation of the surface. In support of this view, Li and Durgin (submitted) have found that perceived hand orientation during free-hand gestures follows the same function as the verbal pattern shown in Figure 1.

4.2 An apparent discrepancy in the calibration account

So far we have suggested that hand gestures are calibrated to near surfaces, but are not calibrated for far surfaces (which seem steeper). We have argued that palm board measures, which have been described by some as calibrated for hills, aren't really calibrated to visual surfaces at all. And we have suggested that the haptic experience of slants underfoot may be partly calibrated to the visual experience of hills, but needn't be. The guiding rule might be that calibration occurs when there is some real possibility for action with immediate spatial feedback from more than one modality. Underfoot surface calibration may be unnecessary because the foot is biomechanically adaptive and people tend not to look at their own feet when walking. Touching surfaces manually provides haptic and visual feedback.

However, there is one apparent exception to this proposed guiding rule. Hajnal et al. (2011) used a force feedback robotic arm (Phantom) to allow participants to feel a virtual surface. With this (carefully calibrated) device, they collected verbal estimates of perceived slant. Given the calibration account (based on the potential for shared visual and haptic experience in normal life) we should expect that haptic exploration of a surface by dynamic touch would reveal the same kind of spatial bias that is evident in vision (Figure 1) and in static haptic contact (Figure 2). In fact, although Hajnal et al. did observe overestimation of slant in their procedure, they applied a linear fit to their data that they interpreted as suggesting a fairly constant overestimation across all orientations. Their fit line is shown in the left panel of Figure 7. In fact, most of their data can be captured by a curved bias function such as we have seen in other data. As shown in the right panel of Figure 7, only the lowest three plot points deviate from the typical curvature we have observed elsewhere. We therefore sought to replicate their dynamic touch result. We chose to use a real physical surface instead of a virtual one.

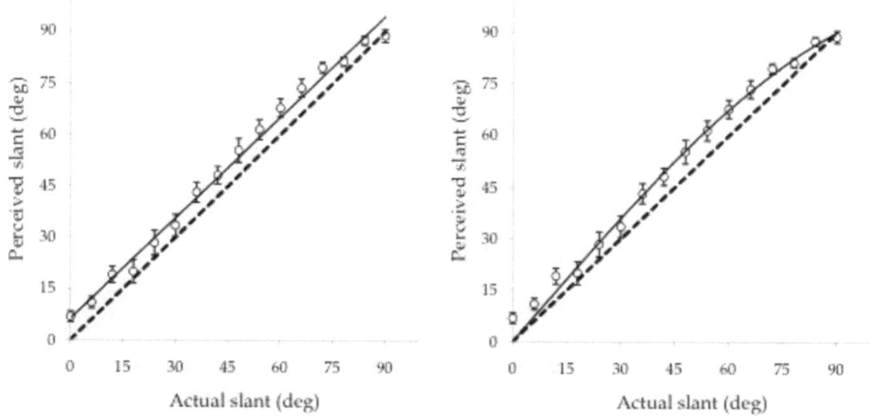

Fig. 7. Hajnal et al.'s (2011) dynamic touch data with two different fit lines. In the left panel, the linear fit line originally plotted by Hajnal et al. is shown. In the right panel, a cubic function with an intercept of (0, 0) was fit to the data.

5. Experiment 1: Numeric estimation of real surface orientation in depth assessed by dynamic touch with the tip of the index finger

The main question of the present experiment is whether the haptic perception of surface orientation (geographical slant in the pitch axis relative to the observer) by dynamic touch will show the same kinds of spatial bias documented in vision by Durgin, Li and Hajnal (2010). Whereas Durgin, Li and Hajnal reported evidence of similar bias in perceived surface orientation based on static contact with the palm of the hand, Hajnal et al. (2011) have argued that there is very little bias evident in dynamic touch. However, as noted above, it is not clear that the linear fit they plotted is better justified by their data than a cubic fit, like that shown in Figure 7. Moreover, examination of the raw data of Hajnal et al. suggested that participants relied nearly exclusively on angular estimates that were multiples of 5. This may have contributed to distorting the lower end of the range. Finally, because Hajnal et al. did not constrain their participants' exploratory strategies, it is possible that the observed function was less exaggerated in some places because of a tendency for oblique paths of travel along the slanted surface. In the present study we used real surfaces and provided a ridge along the main axis of the surface to ensure that the steepest direction of inclination was felt. In addition we asked that participants be as precise as possible in their responses.

5.1 Method

All experimental procedures were conducted in accord with the ethical standards of the American Psychological Association and approved by a local institutional review board. The general method is similar to those employed by Hajnal et al. (2011) and by Durgin, Li and Hajnal (2010). Participants made numeric estimates of the slant of surfaces explored haptically.

5.1.1 Participants

The participants were 20 Swarthmore College undergraduate students (13 female) who participated in partial fulfilment of a course requirement. Half were assigned to the horizontal coding condition and half to the vertical coding condition.

5.1.2 Apparatus

The haptic surface was a varnished wooden board mounted on a mechanical adjustable slant device (see Li & Durgin, 2009). The center of the surface was about 113 cm from the floor. A metal ridge was attached to the surface perpendicular to the axis of rotation as a guide. Participants stood in front of the apparatus wearing a blindfold (a plush sleep mask) throughout the experiment. The set-up is shown in Figure 8.

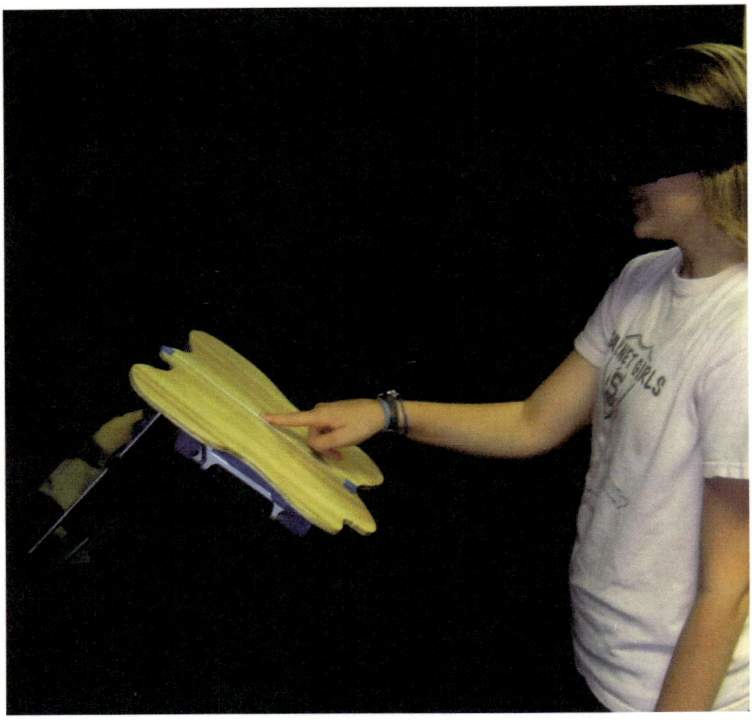

Fig. 8. The experimental set up. The orientation of the board could be rapidly adjusted to one of 16 orientations from 0° to 90°.

5.1.3 Design

Participants were assigned in alternation to the vertical or horizontal coding condition. Following the practice of Durgin, Li and Hajnal (2010), half the participants gave verbal estimates relative to horizontal and half gave estimates relative to vertical so that spatial biases could be distinguished from verbal biases. In each condition the same set of 16 orientations from 0 to 90° (by 6° increments) were presented in random order in each of two blocks of trials for a total of 32 trials. Random orders were generated in advance for each participant.

5.1.4 Procedure

Participants were shown the apparatus with the surface in the horizontal position and the procedure was explained to them prior to signing an informed consent form. Participants were shown where to stand (directly in front of the apparatus) and then asked put on the blindfold. Before each trial, the surfaces were set to the intended orientation manually using pre-set positions by the experimenter who then told the participant to explore the surface. The participants were to run the tip of their right index finger alongside the elevated ridge formed by a wire attached to the surface. No time limit was specified for exploration. When satisfied with their haptic observation the participant was to indicate the orientation of the surface in deg. Half were instructed that vertical was 0° and horizontal was 90°. The other half were told to consider horizontal to be 0° and vertical to be 90°. Participants were encouraged to be as precise as possible in their estimates by estimating orientation to the nearest 1° (even with such instruction, there is a strong bias toward values divisible by 5).

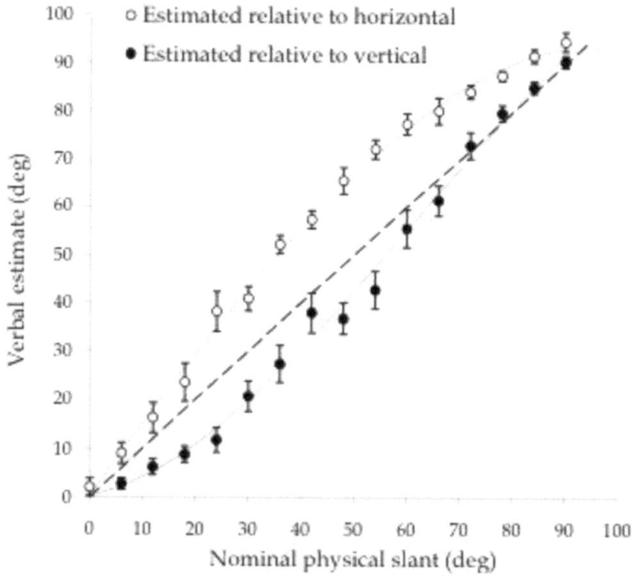

Fig. 9. Mean haptic slant estimates by reference condition in Experiment 1 with error bars representing ± 1 SEM. Trend lines are best fitting cubic polynomials.

5.2 Results

Mean estimates were computed for each presented orientation by condition. Figure 9 shows the estimates for each condition. It can be seen that the spatial bias was in the same direction in each condition inasmuch as participants overestimated deviations from horizontal and underestimated deviations from vertical.

To represent the spatial bias function, we recalculated each estimate in the vertical referent condition with respect to horizontal and then averaged all estimates with respect to horizontal. The resulting function is plotted in Figure 10, superimposed on the similarly-derived spatial function for visual slant perception from Durgin, Li and Hajnal (2010, Experiment 1), plotted earlier in Figure 1. The functions are strikingly similar, as predicted by the calibration hypothesis. Both functions seem to reflect a common underlying spatial coding bias.

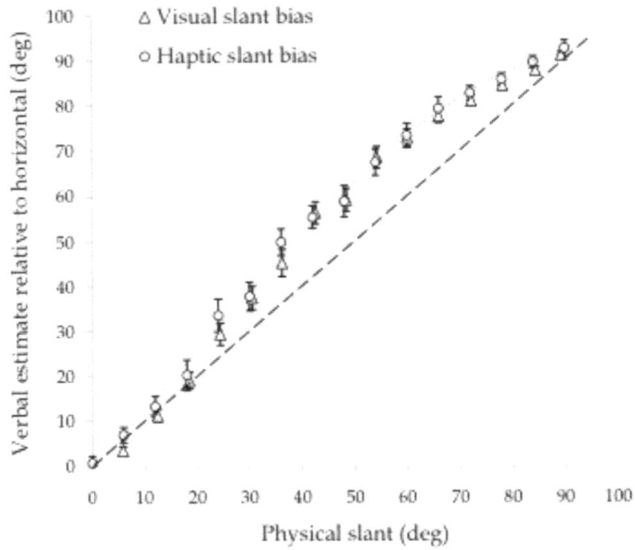

Fig. 10. Overall spatial bias in haptic perception of slant (Experiment 1) superimposed on the visual slant bias function from Durgin, Li and Hajnal (2010).

5.3 Discussion

Using real surfaces with a demarcated axis of haptic exploration, we sought to extend the methods used by Durgin, Li and Hajnal (2010) to the haptic domain. Our results indicate a close correspondence between visual and haptic spatial biases in the peception of orientation. Our results are somewhat at variance with those of Hajnal et al. (2011). Because Hajnal et al. did not constrain the path of digital exploration, it is possible that participants tended to explore their surfaces along a somewhat oblique (and therefore less steep) axis. Our data are consistent with the proposal that there is a trend for there to be calibration between visual and haptic representations of 3D surface orientation.

6. Experiment 2: Horizontal/vertical bisection point for surface orientation in depth assessed by dynamic touch with the tip of the index finger

To avoid verbal biases, Durgin, Li and Hajnal (2010) used a bisection task in which they presented surface visually and asked participants to indicate whether the surface was closer to vertical or to horizontal. They reported a mean visual bisection of point of 34° from horizontal. That is, a surface of 34° was equally likely to be judged closer to vertical as it was to be judged closer to horizontal. In fact the cubic fit to their verbal data predicted that the 45° point would have been at 36.3° in the visual case, and it seems likely that verbal reports tend to slightly underestimate the magnitude of the actual spatial bias (see also Durgin & Li, 2011a, 2011b). The present experiment simply replicated the bisection procedure of Durgin, Li and Hajnal for the haptic case.

6.1 Method

The haptic horizontal/vertical bisection point was measured.

6.1.1 Participants

The participants were 12 Swarthmore College undergraduate students who either participated in partial fulfilment of a course requirement or were paid to participate.

6.1.2 Apparatus

The apparatus was the same as in Experiment 1, except that a computer program was used to dynamically choose stimuli for presentation based on a staircase procedure designed to sample densely in the range surrounding each participant's subjective bisection point.

6.1.3 Design

Each participant gave responses to individual stimuli selected from an up-down staircase procedure. There were 10 blocks of 6 trials each in which two trials from each of three staircases were randomly interleaved. The starting values for the three staircases were either approximately 12°, 42°, and 72° (N=6) or 18°, 48° and 78° (N=6). The step size of each staircase was 18°. That is, if the presented orientation was deemed closer to vertical, the next orientation presented by that staircase was 18° lower, and if the presented orientation was judged closer to horizontal, the next presented orientation was 18° higher. The three staircases together sampled orientation space with a resolution of 6° and approximated a method of constant stimuli that was centered on the apparent bisection point.

6.1.4 Procedure

Participants were shown the apparatus with the surface in the horizontal position and the procedure was explained to them prior to signing an informed consent form. Participants were shown where to stand (directly in front of the apparatus) and then asked put on the blindfold. Before each trial, the surfaces were set to the required orientation manually by the experimenter according to a computer instruction. The participant then explored the surface as in Experiment 1. When the participant gave the forced choice response ("closer to vertical" or "closer to horizontal"), the experimenter pressed either the up-arrow key or the down arrow key on a keyboard, causing the computer to record the trial and update the staircase. The computer then gave instruction to the experimenter concerning the orientation of the next stimulus.

6.2 Results

The responses for each participant were fitted with a logistic function and the subjective bisection point was calculated for each psychometric function as the point at which participants were equally likely to respond that the surface was closer to vertical and that it was closer to horizontal. The average subjective horizontal/vertical bisection point was 31.2° (SEM = 2.0°) from horizontal. Although numerically lower than the 34° average reported for visual slant by Durgin, Li and Hajnal (2010), this difference was not statistically reliable. The subjective bisection point did not differ reliably from 30°, $t(11) < 1$, but did differ reliably from 45°, $t(11) = 6.89$, $p < .0001$.

6.3 Discussion

Using real surfaces with a clearly-demarcated axis of haptic exploration, we sought to extend the bisection method used by Durgin, Li and Hajnal (2010) to the haptic domain. Our results are consistent with a close correspondence between visual and haptic spatial biases in the perception of orientation. The haptic results are also quite similar to the average perceived horizontal/vertical bisection point (31°) measured by Durgin and Li (2011a) for perceived gaze declination. In other words, across a variety of modalities (proprioception of gaze declination, visual perception of 3D surface orientation in depth and haptic perception of 3D surface orientation in depth) the perceived bisection point between horizontal and vertical is very close to 30° from horizontal.

7. A descriptive model of the slant bias function for manual reaching space

The main purpose of our present study has been to clear up an apparent discrepancy in the coding of near-space orientation. That is, for manual reaching space, there had seemed to be a discrepancy between the dynamic touch results of Hajnal et al. (2011) and the static haptic results of Durgin, Li and Hajnal (2010). The present results support the idea that the same bias exists for dynamic touch as has been found for visual slant perception and static haptic slant perception. The bias function found previously for the evaluation of visual slants and for haptic slants experienced by static contact has now been replicated for dynamic touch by fingertip. In combination with recent evidence that the proprioceptively-perceived orientation of a freely-extended hand shows a very similar bias function (Li & Durgin, submitted), the present results seem to point to a stable and systematic bias in the perception of 3D orientation in reachable space.

7.1 A family of biases

Our description is intentionally limited to 3D slant in manual reaching space because it is fairly clear that the underfoot haptic perception of ramp orientation, for example, follows a rather steeper function than the one for manually reachable surfaces (Hajnal et al., 2011). The shape of that function has only been explored over a limited range, however. Similarly, the bias function for the perceived orientation of palm boards (Bhalla & Proffitt, 1999) has been shown to differ (especially at steeper orientations) from the haptic perception of stable surfaces (Durgin, Li & Hajnal, 2010). There seems to be some continuity between the near-space bias function and biases shown in hill perception, once distance is taken into account. That is, Li and Durgin (2010) argue that there is a perceptual gain of about 1.5 in the lower range of slants at all distances they tested, but a shift in the overall intercept. Durgin and Li (2011a) have argued that the 1.5 gain also applies to perceived gaze declination in the relevant range of declinations (i.e. out to about 45°).

With so many similar bias functions developed by recording verbal estimates of slant it is natural to wonder whether the bias might actually be in the numeric production system, but three important facts argue against this. First, non-numeric horizontal/vertical bisection tasks seem to provide converging evidence that a 3D slant or orientation of about 30° appears to be equidistant between horizontal and vertical. This is consistent with the gain of 1.5 for the low range of angles. Second, in the present study, the bias function was very similar in shape when a very different set of numbers was required to produce it as a result of labelling vertical as 0°. Finally, the third important fact that argues against a purely numeric bias is that a very different bias function emerges when 2D orientation (of lines on a plane) is studied using similar numeric methods (Durgin and Li, 2011b). In this case, there is still a bias function that exaggerates deviations from horizontal, but absolute signed error peaks at 30° rather than at 60° as for the 3D function.

7.2 Sine function scaling predicts the gain of 1.5

The characteristic shape of the error functions we have observed somewhat resembles the first quarter cycle of a sine function. Such a function is plotted in Figure 11, scaled to 90°. Here we will first consider the features of the sine function that render it a promising model.

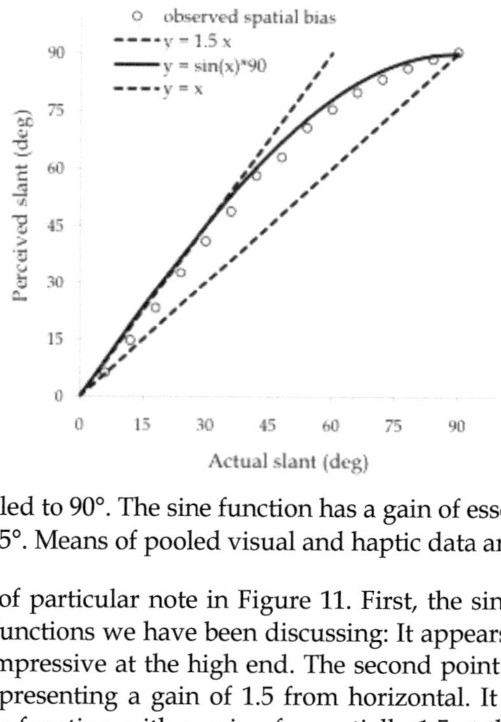

Fig. 11. Sine of slant, scaled to 90°. The sine function has a gain of essentially 1.5 over the range from 0 to nearly 45°. Means of pooled visual and haptic data are shown.

There are two features of particular note in Figure 11. First, the sine function captures the main shape of the bias functions we have been discussing: It appears fairly linear at the low end of the scale and compressive at the high end. The second point is made graphically by the line in Figure 11 representing a gain of 1.5 from horizontal. It turns out that the sine function produces a bias function with a gain of essentially 1.5 at the low end of the scale. Given the variety of empirically observed angular bias functions that have proven to have nearly exactly that gain near horizontal (e.g., visually perceived optical slant, haptically and visually perceived geographical slant, perceived gaze declination), this seems like either a striking coincidence or an impressive quantitative match.

A sine function represents the ratio between the surface length and the vertical extent of the surface. Unlike grade, which corresponds to the tangent function (rise over run), the sine function would seem to place priority on surface length, which has the virtue of being an ecologically relevant variable. For perceived gaze declination along a ground plane, where the relevant vertical extent is normally the observer's eye height, the sine of gaze declination corresponds to the reciprocal of the optical distance from the observer's eye to the point at the center of regard along the ground. If the optical distance from the eye to a target is held fixed, then the sine function is proportional to the frontal vertical extent created between the target and the horizontal plane at eye level. It remains unclear why these specific ratios might be used as a scale of angle. It is possible that the sine function only incidentally matches the underlying bias function. Durgin and Li (2011a; see also Hajnal et al., 2011; Li & Durgin, 2009) have proposed that the shape of the bias function is driven by the utility of expanding the portion of the range used most frequently. At present we only propose that the sine function appears to capture the shape of the 3D angular bias function remarkably well.

7.3 An implied direction of calibration?

The idea that haptic scaling of perceived orientation during dynamic touch might be based on the ratio between the vertical extent of (finger-tip) travel and the total extent of (finger-tip) travel is intriguing. Gravitational forces are highly relevant to haptics. The coding of orientation in this form would serve to express a useful ratio. When there is no vertical movement, the surface is horizontal. When the vertical component equals the total extent of travel, the surface is vertical. When the vertical extent is half the total extent of travel (i.e., sin(30°) = 0.5), the surface is "half-way" between horizontal and vertical (i.e., the perceived bisection point). These facts fit our data well and seem appropriate for manual haptics. It is much less clear why the visual perception of the slant of manually-reachable surfaces should be similarly coded, given that neither the vertical extent of orientation change nor the overall surface extent are directly given in vision. However, if vision is calibrated to haptic experience, this would be sufficient to suggest why the visual and haptic codings are aligned, but also why the haptic experience of individuals who are congenitally blind are distorted in a similar manner. Insofar as it depends on manual haptic exploration, this hypothesis would apply specifically to manually-reachable surfaces. An implied direction of calibration does not require that calibration always go in this direction, but only supposes that there is a natural basis for sinusoidal scaling of manual haptic slant perception and that this basis could then drive the visual scaling.

7.4 Scale expansion theory

For large scale (locomotor) space, Durgin and Li (2011a) have proposed that the special role of proprioception of gaze direction in estimating distance (e.g., Wallach & O'Leary, 1982) may encourage scale expansion near horizontal with a gain of 1.5. Because their model provides impressive quantitative predictions of perceptual matching tasks (Li, Phillips & Durgin, 2011), it seems to capture an important feature of locomotor space perception. Durgin and Li have proposed that the 1.5 gain in the scaling of perceived slant may be driven by the 1.5 gain in gaze proprioception. That is, for horizontal ground surfaces to look flat requires a 1.5 gain in the optical slant. Thus, it might be argued that the expanded scale of perceived gaze declination also creates pressure for an expanded scale of visual slant.

8. Conclusion

In this chapter we reviewed basic knowledge concerning spatial biases in the perception of slant and then presented novel experimental results. Our experiments tested whether the perceived 3D orientation bias function for surfaces explored by dynamic touch was similar to that for visually perceived slant and static haptic touch. We found evidence that supports the view that the spatial bias for the perceived 3D orientation of surfaces in manual reaching space is similar across visual and haptic modalities whether measured numerically with respect to vertical or with respect to horizontal or even when measured non-verbally using a horizontal-vertical bisection task. We have further suggested that the orientation bias function in manual reaching space resembles the first quarter cycle of a sine function.

9. Acknowledgments

This research was supported by Award Number R15 EY021026-01 from the National Eye Institute. The content is solely the responsibility of the authors and does not necessarily represent the official views of the National Eye Institute or the National Institutes of Health. This work was also supported by a Swarthmore College Faculty Research Grant.

10. References

Bhalla, M. & Proffitt, R.D. (1999). Visual-motor recalibration in geographical slant perception. Journal of Experimental Psychology: *Human Perception and Performance,* Vol. 25, No. 4, pp. 1076-1096

Bridgeman, B. & Hoover, M. (2008). Processing spatial layout by perception and sensorimotor interaction. *Quarterly Journal of Experimental Psychology,* Vol. 61, pp. 851-859, Available from doi: 10.1080/1747021070162371

Durgin, F. H.; Baird, J. A.; Greenburg, M.; Russell, R.; Shaughnessy, K. & Waymouth, S. (2009). Who is being deceived? The experimental demands of wearing a backpack. *Psychonomic Bulletin & Review,* Vol. 16, No. 5, pp. 964-969, Available from doi: 10.3758/PBR.16.5.964

Durgin, F. H.; Hajnal, A.; Li, Z.; Tonge, N. & Stigliani, A. (2010). Palm boards are not action measures: An alternative to the two-systems theory of geographical slant perception. *Acta Psychologica,* Vol. 134, No. 2, pp. 182-197, Available from http://dx.doi.org/10.1016/j.actpsy.2010.01.009

Durgin, F. H.; Hajnal, A.; Li, Z.; Tonge, N. & Stigliani, A. (2011). An imputed dissociation might be an artifact: Further evidence for the generalizability of the observations of Durgin et al. 2010. *Acta Psychologica,* Vol. 138, No. 2, pp. 281-284. Available from http://dx.doi.org/10.1016/j.actpsy.2010.09.002

Durgin, F. H. & Li, Z. (2011a). Percepual scale expansion: An efficient angular coding strategy for locomotor space. *Attention, Perception & Psychophysics,* Vol. 73, No. 6, pp. 1856-1870. Available from doi: 10.3758/s13414-011-0143-5

Durgin, F. H. & Li, Z. (2011b). The perception of 2D orientation is categorically biased. *Journal of Vision,* Vol. 11, No. 8, Art. 13, pp. 1-10, Available from http://www.journalofvision.org/content/11/8/13

Durgin, F. H.; Li, Z. & Hajnal, A. (2010). Slant perception in near space is categorically biased: Evidence for a vertical tendency. *Attention, Perception & Psychophysics,* Vol. 72, No. 7, pp. 1875-1889, Available from doi: 10.3758/APP.72.7.1875

Feresin, C.; Agostini, T. & Negrin-Saviolo, N. (1998). Testing the validity of the paddle method for the kinesthetic and visual-kinesthetic perception of inclination, *BehaviorResearch Methods, Instruments & Computers,* Vol. 30, No. 4, pp. 637-642, Available from doi: 10.3758/BF03209481

Gibson, J. J. (1950). The perception of visual surfaces. *The American Journal of Psychology,* Vol. 63, No. 3, pp. 367-384

Hajnal, A.; Abdul-Malak, D. T. & Durgin, F. H. (2011). The perceptual experience of slope by foot and by finger. *Journal of Experimental Psychology: Human Perception and Performance*, Vol. 37, No. 3, pp. 709-719. Available from doi: 10.1037/a0019950

Kammann, R. (1967). Overestimation of vertical distance and slope and its role in moon illusion. *Perception & Psychophysics*, Vol. 2, No. 12, pp. 585-589, Available from doi: 10.3758/BF03210273

Kinsella-Shaw, J. M.; Shaw, B. & Turvey, M. T. (1992). Perceiving "Walk-on-able" slopes. *Ecological Psychology*, Vol. 4, No., pp. 223-239.

Li, Z. & Durgin, F. H. (2009). Downhill slopes look shallower from the edge. Journal of Vision, Vol. 9, No. 11, Art. 6, pp. 1-15. Available from http://journalofvision.org/9/11/6

Li, Z. & Durgin, F. H. (2010). Perceived slant of binocularly viewed large-scale surfaces: A common model from explicit and implicit measures. Journal of Vision, Vol 10, No. 14, Art. 13, pp. 1-16. http://journalofvision.org/content/10/14/13

Li, Z. & Durgin, F. H. (2011). Design, data and theory regarding a digital hand inclinometer: A portable device for studying slant perception. *Behavior Research Methods*, Vol. 43, No. 2, pp. 363-371, Available from doi: 10.3758/s13428-010-0047-7

Li, Z. & Durgin, F. H. (submitted). *Manual matching of perceived surface orientation is affected by arm posture: Evidence of calibration between hand action and visual experience in near space.*

Li, Z.; Phillips, J. & Durgin, F. H. (2011). The underestimation of egocentric distance: Evidence from frontal matching tasks. *Attention, Perception & Psychophysics*, Vol. 73, No. 7, pp. 2205-2217, Available from doi: 10.3758/s13414-011-0170-2

Proffitt, D. R.; Bhalla, M.; Gossweiler, R. & Midgett, J. (1995). Perceiving geographical slant. *Psychonomic Bulletin & Review*, Vol. 2, No. 4, pp. 409-428

Ross, H. E. (1974). *Behaviour and perception in strange environments*, Allen & Unwin, ISBN 0041500474, London

Wallach, H. & O'Leary, A. (1982). Slope of regard as a distance cue. *Perception & Psychophysics*, Vol. 31, No. 2, pp. 145-148, Available from doi: 10.3758/BF03206214

Part 2

Haptic Rendering

5

Abstract Feelings Emerging from Haptic Stimulation

Kohske Takahashi[1], Hideo Mitsuhashi[2], Kazuhito Murata[2], Shin Norieda[2] and Katsumi Watanabe[3]
[1]*Research Center for Advanced Science and Technology, The University of Tokyo*
Japan Society for the Promotion of Science
[2]*NEC System Jisso Research Labs.*
[3]*Research Center for Advanced Science and Technology, The University of Tokyo*
Japan Science and Technology Agency
Japan

1. Introduction

Haptic stimulation yields diverse sensations such as pressure, softness and hardness, vibration, and roughness of surface (Katz, 1989). These sensations originate from the sensory process through mechanoreceptors on the skin, such as Pacinian corpuscles, Meissner's corpuscles, Merkel's discs, and Ruffini corpuscles (Fig. 1.). The mechanoreceptors work interactively to build up haptics as an elaborate sensory system. Thus far, a number of studies have investigated the characteristics of the mechanoreceptors, yet the mechanisms have not been fully understood. Instead, these studies have exposed the complexity of the haptic sensory process.

Apart from the mechanoreceptors and the sensory system, cognitive scientists have investigated perceptual processing for haptic stimulation. They have revealed how haptic

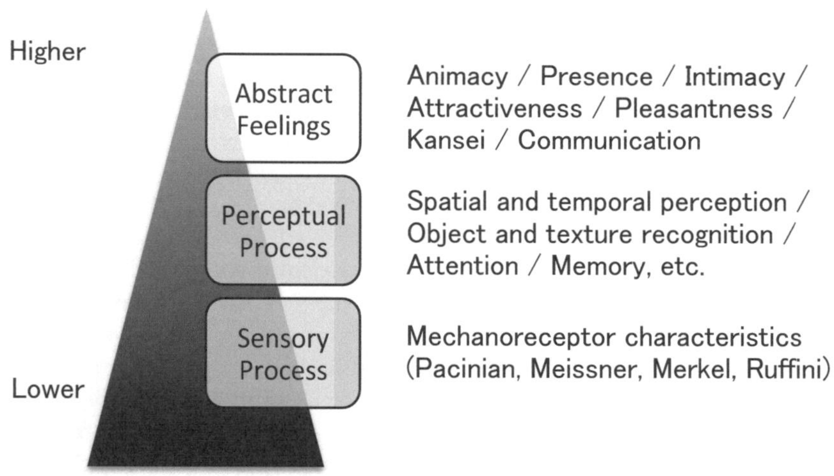

Fig. 1. Schematic illustration of 3 levels of haptic information process.

inputs are processed in the perceptual system for spatial and temporal perception, object and texture recognition, attention, and memory (Fig. 1.). Here again, haptic perception was revealed to be complex since the haptic perception is built on interaction with other cognitive functions such as action (e.g., active touch) (Gibson, 1962), and other sensory modalities (e.g., proprioceptive, vision and audition).

In addition to these sensory and perceptual systems, and although this aspect is often downplayed, we experience abstract feelings from haptic stimulation, such as feelings of animacy, pleasantness, presence, and intimacy (Fig. 1.). For example, a fisherman can sense the movement of an animate object on his rod when a fish is caught on the hook without seeing or hearing the fish. When we hold hands with a lover, we sense her or his presence through the hands and develop a feeling of pleasure. Hence, there is no doubt that haptic stimulation and these abstract feelings (i.e., feelings of animacy, pleasantness, or presence) are strongly related (Knapp & Hall, 1992; Morris, 1971; Richmond et al., 2007). Since the haptic system has no receptor that is directly associated with animacy or pleasantness, however, these abstract feelings would emerge from dynamic spatial-temporal patterns of haptic stimulation to the mechanoreceptors and from the perceptual process thereof.

In daily experience, the abstract feelings emerging from haptic stimulation seem not to be trivial. Rather, most haptic experience seems to involve these kinds of abstract feelings to some degree. In fact, haptic sensation is one of the essential channels of interpersonal communication (Richmond et al., 2007). When we communicate with others in daily life, physical contact involving haptic sensation is the most primitive communication channel, as may be widely observed in human infants and animals (Knapp & Hall, 1992; Richmond et al., 2007). Certainly, the purpose of haptic communication is not to inspect, for example, the stiffness or texture of another person's skin. The purpose of haptic communication would be to feel animacy or the presence of the other and to develop a feeling of pleasure.

The abstract feelings emerging from haptic stimulation are not limited to situations of interpersonal communication. As in the case of the fisherman, we sometimes feel strong and vivid animacy from haptic stimulation. Although the vivid animacy of haptic stimulation would originate from the sensory and perceptual system, we are not usually conscious of the perceptual aspects of haptic stimulation (e.g., stiffness, softness, and frequency). Rather, in most cases we cannot explicitly describe the perceptual aspects of haptic stimulation that lead to animacy. We directly feel the animacy of the object. In other words, such abstract feelings seem to be dominant in our consciousness.

Although the abstract feelings emerging from haptic stimulation can be widely seen and, hence, would be worthwhile to examine empirically, our knowledge thereof is very poor. What types of haptic stimulation yield which kinds of abstract feelings? How do such abstract feelings affect our experience, for example, in interpersonal communication? Do abstract feelings emerging from haptic stimulation interact with the process in the sensory modalities other than with regard to haptics? All these questions are still open.

In this chapter, we review 3 psychological studies recently conducted in our laboratory. All these studies were aimed at understanding how abstract feelings emerge from haptics sensation and, at the same time, how such feelings affect our behavior and experience. The first study investigated the characteristics of haptic stimulation associated with abstract feelings, especially focusing on the animacy of haptic stimulation. The second study investigated the effect of abstract feelings on experience and behavior in interpersonal haptic communication. The third study investigated haptic modulation on abstract feeling in the sensory modalities other than haptics.

Although we developed a simple haptic display (Fig. 2.) that is suitable for examining abstract feeling emerging from haptic stimulation, the purpose of these studies **was not** to develop a haptic device to enable users to experience abstract feelings. Instead, we aimed at understanding the human cognitive process in relation to the abstract feelings emerging from haptic stimulation and their impact on human behavior and experience, and also providing useful and basic insights to design a user-friendly haptic device that is able to present abstract feelings efficiently.

2. Feelings of animacy for vibratory haptic stimulation

Humans can perceive animacy even from inanimate visual objects. This feeling of the animacy of inanimate objects has been well investigated in the context of animacy perception (Blakemore et al., 2003; Gao et al., 2010; Gao & Scholl, 2011; Heider & Simmel, 1944; Scholl & Tremoulet, 2000). In animacy perception, given the mutually interactive motion of multiple visual objects, human observers sense intention or sociality in artificial visual objects (Fukuda & Ueda, 2010; Gao et al., 2009; Santos et al., 2008). Furthermore, recent studies have reported that a particular motion pattern of a single visual object could induce animacy perception (Tremoulet & Feldman, 2000), which implies that apparently higher cognitive appreciation of complex properties such as animacy may originate from low-level sensory processes. Along with these studies, cognitive neuroscientific studies using functional magnetic resonance imaging (fMRI) have shown that the neural activities in primary visual areas, as well as in higher brain areas that are related to the cognitive function (Santos et al., 2010), such as the mirror system (Rizzolatti, 2005) or the theory of mind (Gallese & Goldman, 1998), might be related to animacy perception (Morito et al., 2009). Thus, the emergence of animacy perception of inanimate objects may originate not only from the top-down cognitive processes of intention or sociality but also partially from the bottom-up processes of primitive sensations such as vibration, softness, and warmth.

As in the fisherman's case, haptic stimulation that induces feelings of animacy in daily life is composed of dynamic and complex patterns. However, given the possibility that primitive sensations might induce feelings of animacy in a bottom-up manner, one challenging question concerns what the lower limit of haptic stimulation is that induces feelings of animacy. To answer this question, Takahashi et al. (2011a) developed a haptic display device and investigated whether simple and cyclic haptic vibratory stimulation can induce feelings of animacy and pleasantness, and if so, what would determine the strength of these feelings.

2.1 Haptic device

In order to investigate the abstract feelings for haptic sensation, we developed a haptic display device that is suitable for presenting a soft haptic sensation (Takahashi et al., 2011a) (Fig. 2.). The device can present only vibratory pressure stimulation. However, since the pressure was determined by impressed voltage, and because the impressed voltage was programmable, the device could present arbitrary pressure changes.

The device was composed of an operator personal computer, an amplifier, and a stimulator. The amplifier was attached to a digital-to-analog converter connected to the operator PC. The stimulator comprised (a) an actuator, (b) a medium, (c) a chassis, and (d) a contact plate (Fig. 2B.). The actuator can be one that changes in size by impressed voltage. Any incompressible fluid may work as the medium. The chassis must be a rigid body, be filled with liquid, and be completely enclosed. We chose a piezoelectric vibrator for the actuator (diameter was 54.5 mm), water for the medium, an acrylic resin and polyurethane-tube (inner and outer

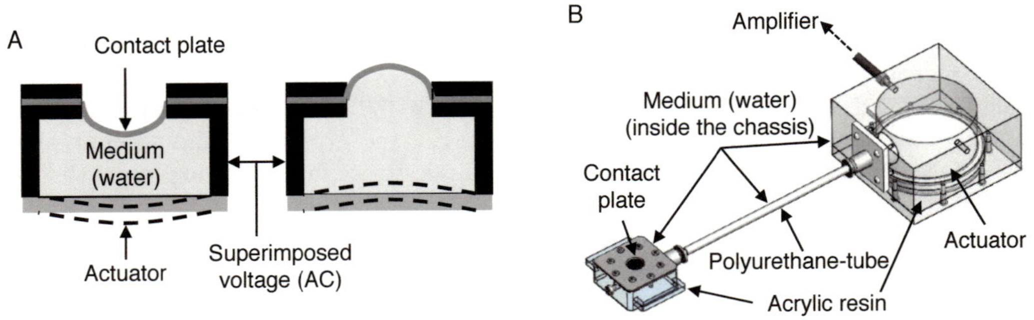

Fig. 2. Haptic device. **A**. Working principle of the device. **B**. Appearance and structure of the haptic stimulator used in the experiment. The figures were modified from Takahashi et al. (2011a).

diameters were 4 mm and 6 mm, respectively) for the chassis, and silicon rubber for the contact plate (the diameter was 16 mm, and the size of the box, including contact plate, was 30 mm × 30 mm × 12 mm).

The working principle of the stimulator was as follows (Fig. 2.). The waveform of pressure change was defined using the operator PC and sent to the stimulator through the DA converter and the amplifier. The input terminal of the actuator of the stimulator was attached to the output terminal of the amplifier. After a start signal was sent to the DA converter, actual voltage was conveyed to the stimulator through the amplifier, which induced the vibration of the actuator. The actuator and contact plate parts were connected with a polyurethane-tube, which was also water-filled. The vibration of the actuator was conveyed to the contact plate through the medium, leading to the production of haptic stimulation at the contact plate.

A significant feature of the device we developed is as follows:

1. **Flexibility of the material of the contact plate**
   Although we chose silicon rubber for the contact plate because we wanted to create a limp sensation, one can choose a hard or textured material (e.g., harsh, scratchy) as required.
2. **Flexibility of the placement of the contact plate**
   In our device, the actuator and contact plate were not solidly attached but were connected by a flexible material (i.e., the polyurethane-tube), and the component, including the contact plate, was small and lightweight. The mobility of the components enables the stimulation of any part of the body surface, and hence enables one to compare the haptic stimulation among the different body parts using identical stimuli.
3. **Dynamic range of pressure displacement**
   The device can present a wide range of pressure displacement. The ratio of the size of the actuator and contact plate determines the amplitude of the displacement of the contact plate; a smaller contact plate and a larger actuator lead to a larger amplitude. The larger amplitudes of the displacement lead to a larger pressure change in the haptic sensation.
4. **Programmable pressure change**
   Since the pressure change is defined as the change of impressed voltage and because the impressed voltage is fully programmable, the device can present any temporal profile of pressure change.

2.2 Animacy and pleasantness emerges from haptic sensation

Using the haptic display device, Takahashi et al. (2011a) conducted a psychological experiment to investigate the effects of the frequency of vibratory stimulation on felt animacy and pleasantness.

Six volunteers participated in the experiment. In each trial, haptic stimuli were presented for 3 s after a 1 s blank period, which was followed by an evaluation display on a touch panel screen. The participants were instructed to evaluate the strength of felt animacy and the pleasantness of the haptic stimuli on a 7-point scale.

They conducted two conditions according to the body parts where the haptic stimuli were presented—finger condition and wrist condition. In the finger condition, the haptic stimuli were presented to the pad of the right index finger. The participants were instructed to softly touch the contact plate by their right index finger. In the wrist condition, the haptic stimuli were presented to the inner side of the right wrist. The component, including the contact plate, was fixed to the right wrist using a band. A haptic stimulus was sinusoidal vibratory stimulation with variable frequency. The frequency was randomly chosen from 0.5, 1, 2, 5, 10, 25, and 50 Hz.

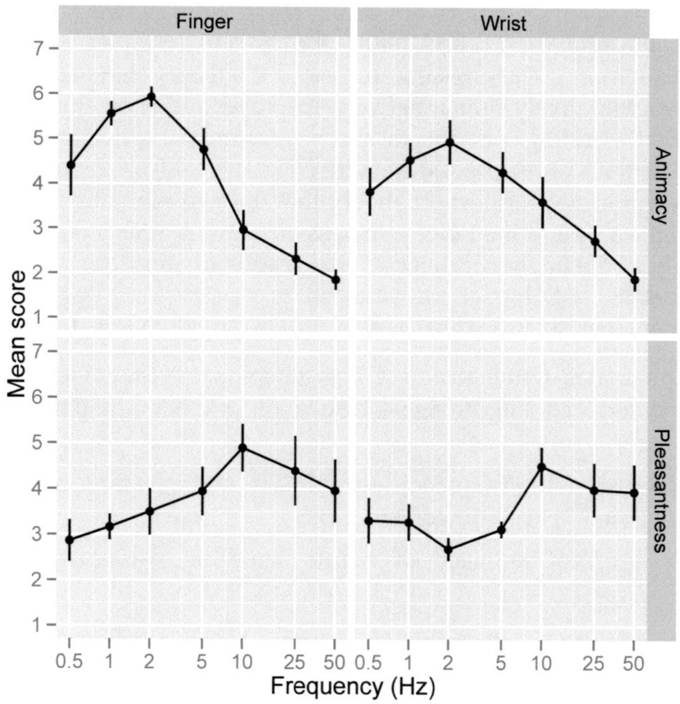

Fig. 3. Mean scores of feelings of animacy (top) and pleasantness (bottom) as a function of stimulus frequency and sensed body part. Error bars indicate the standard errors of means. The figures were modified from Takahashi et al. (2011a).

Fig. 3. shows the felt animacy and pleasantness as a function of the stimulus frequency and body parts. A statistical test (two-way repeated measures ANOVA) revealed that the stimulus frequency significantly affects felt animacy ($F(6,30) = 13.1, p < .01$), whereas the body parts did not significantly affect felt animacy ($F(1,5) = 2.98, p = .15$). Thus, the effects of the stimulus frequency on animacy perception were qualitatively similar between finger and wrist stimulation, although they were quantitatively different. At first glance, the low-frequency stimulation (from 0.5 to 5 Hz) appeared to induce stronger feelings of animacy than the high-frequency stimulation (from 10 to 50 Hz) in both the finger and wrist conditions. The peak rating of animacy was around 1 to 2 Hz in both conditions, but the peak looked more prominent in the finger condition than in the wrist condition. The felt animacy in the finger condition was significantly, or marginally significantly, stronger at 1 Hz ($F(1,5) = 7.08$, $p < .05$) and 2 Hz ($F(1,5) = 4.27$, $p < .10$) and significantly weaker at 25 Hz ($F(1,5) = 7.79$, $p < .05$) than that in the wrist condition. These results imply that the finger was more sensitive to the frequency difference of haptic stimulation than the wrist in feeling animacy. Note that the patterns of frequency dependence were consistent among different participants.

With regard to the feeling of pleasantness, neither the stimulus frequency nor the body parts affected the pleasantness of the haptic stimuli, although a visual inspection of the data would suggest that the high-frequency stimulation induced stronger feelings of pleasantness than the low-frequency stimulation.

Fig. 4. shows the scatter plot of the finger condition vs. wrist condition (top) and that of the animacy rating vs. pleasantness rating (bottom). Each data point indicates the data from individual participants. There were strong correlations between the finger and wrist sensations in both the animacy ($r = 0.83$, $t(40) = 9.40$, $p < .01$) and pleasantness ($r = 0.71$, $t(40) = 6.34$, $p < .01$) evaluations. These results supported the theory that feelings of pleasantness and animacy were qualitatively similar between the finger and wrist stimulation.

On the other hand, the feelings of animacy and pleasantness did not correlate in both finger conditions ($r = -0.13$, $t(40) = 0.80$, $p = .43$) and wrist ($r = 0.04$, $t(40) = 0.25$, $p = .80$). However, the pattern of results would not support the theory that the two evaluations were independent. A visual inspection, as well as the Lowess regression of the scatter plot, exhibited an inverse V shape, especially in the finger condition. These results suggest that the moderate strength of animacy is associated with higher pleasantness.

Thus, the experimental study in Takahashi et al. (2011a) suggested the following:

1. The stimulus frequency systematically affects felt animacy. The lower stimulus frequency around 1–2 Hz induced the strongest feeling of animacy compared with the higher stimulus frequency.
2. The effect of the stimulus frequency on animacy and pleasantness were comparable between different body parts—finger and wrist.
3. The moderate level of animacy of haptic sensation was associated with higher pleasantness.

In another series of studies, Takahashi, Mitsuhashi, Norieda, Murata & Watanabe (2010) showed that the patterns of frequency dependence were partially different between finger and wrist stimulation. Takahashi, Mitsuhashi, Norieda, Murata & Watanabe (2010) showed a V-shaped curve for animacy evaluation as a function of the stimulus frequency in the wrist stimulation: the felt animacy was stronger for 1–2 Hz stimulus frequency, weak for 5–10 Hz frequency, and stronger again for 25 Hz frequency. The main difference between Takahashi, Mitsuhashi, Norieda, Murata & Watanabe (2010) and Takahashi et al. (2011a) was the pressure of water inside the haptic stimulator (Fig. 2A.). In Takahashi et al. (2011a), the chassis was filled with water to the maximum, while this was not the case in Takahashi, Mitsuhashi, Norieda, Murata & Watanabe (2010). Although further examinations are warranted, this difference in pressure might lead to the different patterns of frequency dependence. Perhaps

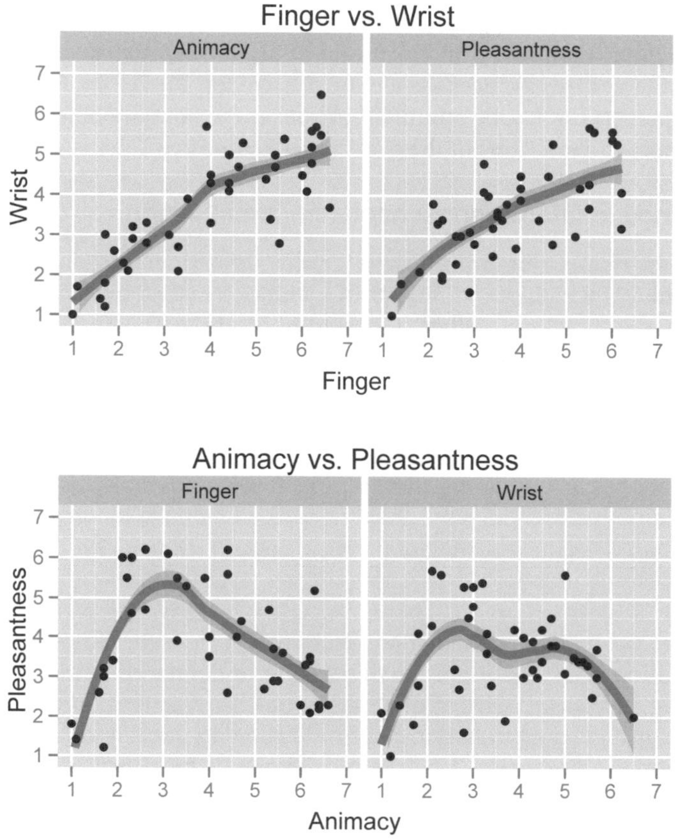

Fig. 4. **Top:** Scatter plot of finger and wrist sensations of animacy and pleasantness. **Bottom:** Scatter plot of feeling of animacy and pleasantness in the finger and wrist conditions. In both panels, each point indicates individual participants. The dark gray curve indicates the Lowess (locally weighted scatter plot smoothing) regression curve (degree of smoothing = 0.75, degree of polynomials = 2). The light gray area indicates the standard error of the Lowess regression. The figures were modified from Takahashi et al. (2011a).

the feeling of animacy for haptic stimulation was susceptible to the pressure as well as to the stimulus frequency.

2.3 Summary

Takahashi et al. (2011a) showed that the stimulus frequency strongly influenced the feeling of animacy vibratory stimulation, with the lower frequency (1–2 Hz) inducing stronger feelings of animacy than the higher frequency (25–50 Hz). The frequency dependence was consistent among different participants. The animacy for haptic stimulation would partially but intrinsically originate from temporal patterns of haptic stimulation.

How do human observers come to feel animacy from the simple vibratory stimulation of an inanimate object? Two accounts, which are not mutually exclusive, would be possible. First, humans may intrinsically feel animacy from low-frequency haptic stimulation. Second, animacy perception may emerge as a result of the frequent experience of touching animate objects such as animals. While the stimulation from these animate objects would involve more complex patterns than those noted in Takahashi et al. (2011a), the frequency of stimulation might be the major factor that induces the feeling of animacy. Therefore, it would be intriguing to survey the frequencies of haptic stimulation from these animate objects in the real world and to compare them to the results of the experimental study in Takahashi et al. (2011a).

3. Abstract feelings in interpersonal haptic communication

In social life, nonverbal communication is crucial for conveying abstract feelings (i.e., "Kansei" information), which is too ambiguous and abstract to be described verbally, and for sharing them with others. When we communicate with others in our daily lives, we use various nonverbal channels such as gestures, facial expressions, or gaze. Among them, haptic communication is the most primitive channel, and it is widely seen in human infants and animals (Knapp & Hall, 1992). In particular, haptic communication plays a dominant role in directly conveying abstract feelings such as emotions (Richmond et al., 2007). Although nonverbal haptic communication has been less understood as compared to verbal communication, some researchers have challenged the kinetic taxonomy of physical contact or categorization based on the meaning of physical contact (Morris, 1971).

The sense of touch or haptics is complex (Katz, 1989), bidirectional, and interactive (e.g., active touch (Gibson, 1962)). Therefore, what is conveyed in interpersonal haptic communication cannot be determined straightforwardly. Instead, the perceptual process for haptic communication itself, the cognitive process for understanding the intention of others, and the context (e.g., the social position of others) would interactively affect what is conveyed. The abstract feelings conveyed in haptic communication are loosely categorized on the basis of the types of motion. For example, stroking someone's head may express affection, and shaking hands may express amity. However, the abstract feeling in haptic communication is also subject to the context of the communication (Richmond et al., 2007). Let us consider a handshake between politicians, that between a mother and a baby, and that between close friends at the time of farewell. It is almost certain that the feelings of the people are not identical in these contexts, although the motions involved in the haptic communication are rather similar.

Given the importance of haptic communication in conveying and sharing abstract feelings, we expect that the quality of experience shared with others could be altered by adding haptic communication. Some innovative studies have already tried to develop haptic devices enabling interpersonal communication and have empirically examined their effect on task performance and subjective impressions (Fujita & Hashimoto, 1999; Reiner, 2004; Sallnäs et al., 2000; Wang et al., 2004). For example, Fujita & Hashimoto (1999) showed that users could feel the presence of another person through haptic bidirectional communication even without seeing each other. Sallnäs et al. (2000) also reported that those who were performing collaborative tasks in a virtual environment felt increased reality or presence and showed an improvement in their task performance due to the force feedback from the virtual environment.

In this chapter, we discuss abstract feelings in interpersonal haptic communication. One question concerns how people experience interpersonal haptic communication in their daily activity. Takahashi, Mitsuhashi, Norieda, Sendoda, Murata & Watanabe (2010) and Takahashi et al. (2011c) conducted a psychological survey to investigate this question. Another question is whether haptic communication could change the subjective quality of an experience, and if so, how. To examine this question, Takahashi et al. (2011b) conducted an experimental study investigating the effects of haptic communication on the quality of participants' experiences, as well as on their impression of the person with whom they communicated.

3.1 Psychological survey on interpersonal haptic communication

In a series of psychological surveys, Takahashi, Mitsuhashi, Norieda, Sendoda, Murata & Watanabe (2010) and Takahashi et al. (2011c) investigated how people experience interpersonal haptic communication in their daily activity.

Takahashi, Mitsuhashi, Norieda, Sendoda, Murata & Watanabe (2010) presented observers with pictures depicting two persons performing either positive (e.g., hugging, shaking hands) or negative (e.g., grappling) haptic communication. The observers were asked to make a subjective evaluation of the depicted communication concerning its desirability, frequency of experience, and impressiveness. All these evaluations had a positive correlation ($R > 0.59$, $p < .001$), suggesting that the haptic communication that was more frequently experienced and that made a stronger impression tended to be evaluated as more desirable. Although these correlations cannot reveal a causal relationship, one possibility may be related to the widely known psychological phenomenon of "mere exposure effect" (Zajonc, 1968), and the other is related to "directional forgetting" (Golding & Macleod, 1998).

The observers were also asked to identify the person who was imagined to be involved in the communication depicted in the picture. The persons associated with the desirable communication were a spouse, a child, a mother, a son or a daughter, a father, and a grandparent. Thus, haptic communications that recall family members are more desirable.

Takahashi et al. (2011c) asked their observers to evaluate two types of haptic communication, tapping and padding, by using adjectives, and examined what factors reside in haptic communication. Table 1 shows the results of the factorial analysis. The results suggested that two factors represent interpersonal haptic communication. One factor affected the evaluation of lightsome, pleasant, comfortable, and warm feelings, and the other factor affected the evaluation of strong, rough, and active feelings. Thus, the first factor was associated with the abstract feelings of haptic communication, while the second factor was relevant to the characteristics of motion. These structures were common between the two types of haptic communications. Furthermore, the first factor strongly affected the desirability of the haptic communications when compared with the second factor, suggesting that the abstract feeling emerging from the communication, not the motion itself, strongly influenced the desirability of the haptic communication.

	Tapping		Patting	
Adjective	Factor 1	Factor 2	Factor 1	Factor 2
Lightsome	0.87	0.01	0.80	0.07
Pleasant	0.86	0.05	0.83	0.09
Comfortable	0.86	-0.07	0.70	-0.26
Warm	0.83	-0.13	0.79	-0.25
Soft	0.46	-0.51	0.59	-0.44
Strong	-0.06	0.90	0.19	0.67
Rough	-0.22	0.80	-0.18	0.73
Active	0.47	0.61	0.69	0.35

Table 1. First and second component score of each adjective for describing two types (tapping and patting) of haptic interpersonal communication. Data were from Takahashi et al. (2011c).

These psychological surveys in Takahashi, Mitsuhashi, Norieda, Sendoda, Murata & Watanabe (2010) and Takahashi et al. (2011c) suggested that desirable haptic communication is experienced with closer persons in daily life (Knapp & Hall, 1992; Morris, 1971; Richmond et al., 2007), and that the abstract feelings emerging from the haptic communication are essential for determining the desirability of the communication.

3.2 Experimental study on shared experience via interpersonal haptic telecommunication

Takahashi et al. (2011b) conducted an experimental study to investigate how interpersonal haptic communication affects shared experience and found that haptic communication could improve the quality of experience as well as the impression of the other person. They examined the effects of haptic communication on the quality of the experience shared with another person along with the impression of the other person with whom they communicated. In the experiment, two persons watched a movie at the same time. All forms of communication except haptic communication were completely removed. The persons could communicate by triggering a haptic stimulation in the other person.

Forty graduate and undergraduate students participated in the experiment in 20 pairs, which were divided into two groups of 10 pairs each. Each pair in the groups was assigned to one of two experimental conditions. In the experiment, two LCD TVs were placed on two desks. The participants were seated at the desks and simultaneously watched a movie on the TV with headphones. The desks were separated by a partition; hence, the participants could not see or hear each other. Each participant held a push button with his or her left hand and touched the haptic device (Fig. 2.) with his or her right hand. The button sent a signal to the operator PC when it was pressed and released. The haptic stimulator generated 2-Hz of vibratory pressure stimulation when receiving a signal from the operator PC. The operator PC sent a signal to the haptic stimulator of one person when the other person pressed his or her button. The timing of the button press/release was recorded by the operator PC. Takahashi et al. (2011b) chose a Japanese comedy movie clip of approximately 220 s duration as the visual stimulus. The movie was played on two temporally synchronized screens.

In an experimental session, the participants were instructed to watch the movie and to press the button while they found it hilarious. They were also told explicitly that pressing their button sent a haptic stimulation to the other person and that the other person's button press triggered a haptic stimulation in their sensor. They experienced this haptic communication prior to the experimental session. Thus, the participants were aware that they could perceive the other person's response through the haptic stimulation. The participants were explicitly instructed to decide on their own whether to press the button and to avoid following the lead of the other person.

One of the two experimental groups was an uninterrupted group, in which the button press always triggered the haptic stimulation to the other person throughout the experimental session. The other experimental group was an interrupted group, wherein the haptic stimulation was interrupted for 90 s, between 75 s and 165 s after the movie started. The participants in the interruption group were not told of the interruption of the haptic stimulation prior to the experimental session; hence, they believed that the absence of haptic stimulation indicated that the other person did not find the movie hilarious. After watching the movie, the participants answered a questionnaire consisting of 8 questions and using a 7-point scale (Table 2).

Using a post-experiment questionnaire survey, Takahashi et al. (2011b) found that the interruption of haptic communication affected the subjective evaluation of the quality of the

Q1	The movie was hilarious.
Q2	It felt as if the movie was more hilarious due to watching it with the other.
Q3	It seemed as if I wanted to convey the hilarious feeling to the other.
Q4	It seemed as if I could convey the hilarious feeling to the other.
Q5	I was concerned about the other.
Q6	It seemed as if the other's hilarious feeling could be convey to me.
Q7	It felt as if I agreed with the other's hilarious feeling.
Q8	It felt as if I wanted to watch the movie again with the other.

Table 2. Questions on the questionnaire. Each question was rated on a 7-point scale (1: strongly disagree–7: strongly agree).

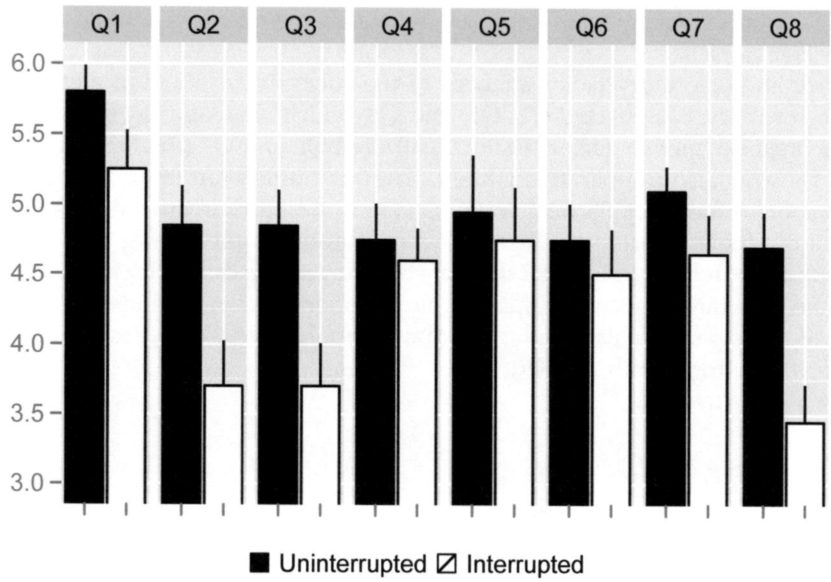

Fig. 5. Mean rating score for each question of the questionnaire. Error bars indicate the standard errors of means. The figure was modified from Takahashi et al. (2011b).

experience and the impression of the other person. Fig. 5 shows the ratings for each question (Table 2). A higher score indicates a stronger agreement with the question. The statistical test (t-test) showed that the rating scores of three questions (Q2, Q3, and Q8) were significantly higher in the uninterrupted group than in the interrupted group (all $t(38) > 2.66$, $p < .05$).
Q2 asked whether the participants felt that the experience with the other person made the movie more hilarious. The participants' impressions may be attributed more to the sharing of the experience with the other person if the haptic communication was uninterrupted. Q3 asked if the participants felt eager to convey their feelings to the other person, and Q8 asked if the participants felt they would like to watch a movie with the other person again in the future. These questions concerned the participants' feelings toward the other person, and the interruption of haptic communication decreased such responses toward the other person.
On the other hand, as for Q1, where the participants were asked to rate the hilariousness of the movie itself, the rating score of the uninterrupted group was slightly higher than that

of the interrupted group, but the difference was not statistically significant ($t(38) = 1.64$, $p = 0.11$). It seemed that the subjective evaluation of the quality of the experience itself was less susceptible to the absence or presence of haptic communication.

As for the other questions, Q4, Q5, Q6, and Q7, the rating scores were comparable between the two experimental groups. Q4 and Q6 asked whether feelings were conveyed efficiently between the participants during the experiment. Q5 and Q7 asked about their involvement and agreement with the other person during the experiment. These questions were partially similar to Q3 and Q8 in that all the questions were related to the communication with the other person. However, while Q4, Q5, Q6, and Q7 focused on the feelings of the other person during the experiment, Q3 and Q8 referred to the strength of the intentions toward the other person in present and future communication. In summary, the interruption of haptic communication had little effect on the subjective evaluation of the shared experience with others. However, it modulated the impression of the other person, especially the intention to build a relationship with him or her.

The results of an exploratory factor analysis of the subjective evaluation were interesting, since one factor (Factor 1) affected Q2, Q3, and Q8, which showed the group difference in the rating score, and another factor (Factor 2) affected Q6 and Q7 (the loadings of Factor 2 for Q1 and Q4 were also comparatively high). The straightforward interpretation would be that the questions affected by Factor 1 were relevant to the attitude toward the other person, and that the questions affected by Factor 2 were relevant to the feeling of the experience itself. The questions related to Factor 2 did not show any group difference in the rating score. Taken together, the interruption of haptic communication did not degrade the retrospective impression of the experience itself but did reduce the participants' concern toward the other person with whom they communicated.

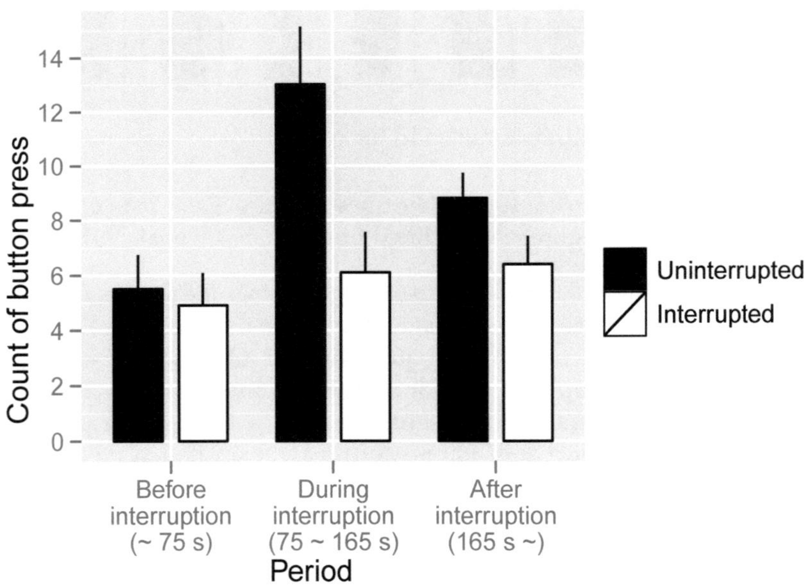

Fig. 6. Number of button presses. Error bars indicate the standard errors of means. The figure was modified from Takahashi et al. (2011b).

In addition to the subjective evaluation using the post-experiment questionnaire survey, the interruption of haptic communication affected the participants' behavior while watching the movie—namely, the number of button presses during the movie presentation. Fig. 6. shows the total number of button presses for three different periods. The first one was the period before the interruption of haptic stimulation; hence, there was inherently no difference between the two groups. The numbers of button presses did not differ between the two groups in the first period ($t(18) = 0.62$, $p = 0.54$). In the second period, the haptic stimulation was cut off between 75 and 165 s for the interrupted group. In this period, the number of button presses in the uninterrupted group was significantly larger than that in the interrupted group ($t(18) = 2.65$, $p < 0.05$). The third period was the one after the interruption. Although the number of actions was slightly larger in the uninterrupted group, the difference was not significant ($t(18) = 1.59$, $p = 0.13$).

In the questionnaire survey, we found that the retrospective evaluation of how hilarious the movie was did not significantly differ between the two groups (Q1). In contrast, the behavioral performance clearly showed that the number of button presses—namely, how often the participants felt the movie was hilarious—was decreased by the interruption of the haptic communication. These results suggest that the haptic communication implicitly modulated the quality of the experience, although the participants could not be explicitly aware of that.

3.3 Summary

Both psychological surveys (Takahashi et al., 2011c; Takahashi, Mitsuhashi, Norieda, Sendoda, Murata & Watanabe, 2010) and the experimental study (Takahashi et al., 2011b) showed the importance of haptic stimulation in interpersonal communication. The desirability of haptic communication was associated with the factor relevant to abstract feelings (lightsome, pleasant, comfortable, and warm) (Takahashi et al., 2011c; Takahashi, Mitsuhashi, Norieda, Sendoda, Murata & Watanabe, 2010). The presence of haptic communication improved the quality of experience and the impression of the other person as well (Takahashi et al., 2011b). As the vibratory haptic stimulation could affect the quality of experience, the presence of haptic communication, not the contents of the stimulation, may be essential for influencing the quality of experience. Abstract feelings emerging from the haptic stimulation in interpersonal communication would be important for persons who share a high-quality experience and have a good impression of each other (Morris, 1971).

4. Cross-modal effect of haptic stimulation in abstract feelings

Humans have multiple sensory modalities for accessing the external world, such as vision, audition, and, of course, haptics. Although inputs into different sensory modalities are processed in different brain regions at early sensory levels, different sensory modalities are no doubt interactively processed at the perceptual level to build up unified perceptions of the external world, which is referred to as cross-modal interaction (Shams & Kim, 2010; Shimojo & Shams, 2001). For example, the ventriloquism effect (Alais & Burr, 2004) and McGurk effect McGurk & MacDonald (1976) are well known phenomena demonstrating visual modulation on auditory perception.

Although cross-modal interaction has mainly been examined using vision and audition, cross-modal interaction at the perceptual level is not limited between them. Inputs into haptics can affect perceptual processes in the sensory modalities other than haptics. For example, the dominant interpretation for an ambiguous visual figure (e.g., the Necker cube) is biased by haptic inputs to make visual and haptic perception consistent (Blake et al., 2004; Bruno et al., 2007). Furthermore, inputs into haptics and vision are integrated in a statistically optimal fashion (Ernst & Banks, 2002; Ernst & Bülthoff, 2004). Thus, a good amount of experimental evidence has shown that inputs into haptic modality can affect perceptual processes in the modalities other than haptics beyond the boundary of sensory modalities.

Consequently, can abstract feelings emerging from different sensory modalities also interact with or modulate from each other? Recent experimental studies suggest that cross-modal interaction takes place at quite high levels of the perceptual process, such as emotion recognition (Bertelson & de Gelder, 2005; Tanaka et al., 2010). For example, face emotion and voice emotion are strongly related. Emotion recognition of facial expression is biased when the voice expresses emotion different from that of the face, and vice versa (Bertelson & de Gelder, 2005).

Although it is true that perceptual and emotional processes interact with each other between different sensory modalities, it is still open if abstract feelings such as animacy can be shared among multiple sensory modalities. However, in daily experience, it seems that such abstract feelings simultaneously emerge from multiple sensory modalities. For example, a mother and a baby communicate through eyes, ears, and hands to feel presence or animacy from each other. Therefore, it would be possible to expect that cross-modal interaction also appears for the abstract feelings. In the following section, we introduce an original research recently conducted in our laboratory, which examined if haptic stimulation can modulate abstract feelings for voice stimuli.

4.1 Voice perception modified by haptic sensation

In order to investigate if the abstract feeling emerging from haptic sensation can affect the cognitive process of sensory modalities other than haptics, we conducted an experiment wherein observers evaluated abstract feelings for another person's voice. In the experiment, the voice stimuli either were or were not accompanied by haptic stimulation.

Twenty-four paid volunteers took part in the experiment. All of the participants reported normal hearing and haptic sensitivity. They were naive as to the purpose of the experiment.

The haptic stimulus was 2Hz sinusoidal vibratory stimulation presented by the custom-made haptic display device shown in Fig. 2. Voice stimuli were presented though headphones. The voice stimuli were 5 Japanese greeting phrases from daily conversation ("Ohayou," "Irasshai-mase," "Arigatou-gozaimashita," "Oyasumi-nasai," and "Otsukare-sama-deshita," which correspond to "Good morning," "Can I help you?" "Thank you," "Good night," and "That's wrap," respectively). The voices were spoken by 5 professional voice actors and were emotionally-neutral.

In a trial, the participants touched the haptic device with their right index fingers. After the participants pressed the space bar of an operator PC, the voice stimulus was presented. In half of the trials, the voice stimuli were accompanied by the haptic vibratory stimulation. The haptic stimulus was presented for 3 s and the voice stimuli were presented during the haptic stimulation. In the other half of the trials, the haptic stimulation was not presented and only the voice stimuli were presented.

After the stimulus presentation, the participants were asked to rate how strongly the voice yielded various abstract feelings—animate, pleasant, warm, familiar, or attractive—on a 7-point scale. They were explicitly told to ignore the contents of the conversation as well as the haptic stimulation. One practical trial was followed by two trials with haptic stimulus and two trials without haptic stimulus. The order of trials and the contents of the conversation were randomized.

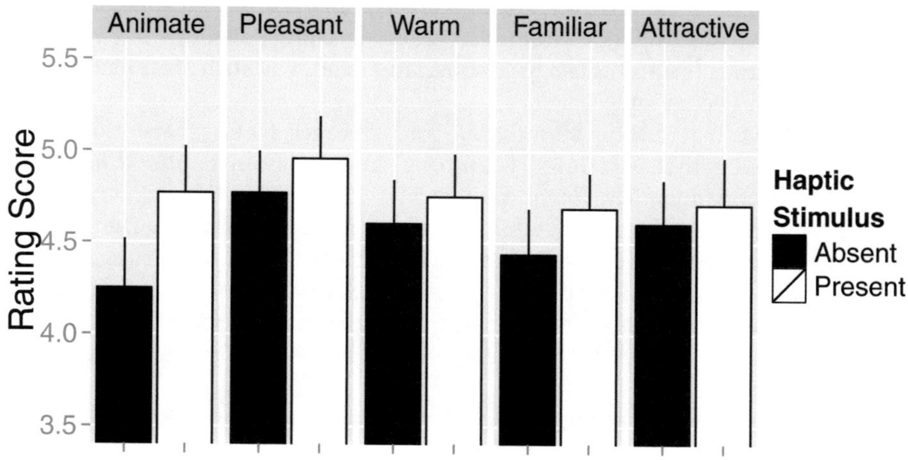

Fig. 7. Rating scores of abstract feelings for voice with and without haptic stimulus. The error bars indicate standard errors of means.

Fig. 7. shows the mean rating scores of 5 questions. The feeling of animacy was significantly stronger when the voice was accompanied by the haptic stimulus than when the voice was presented alone (one-tailed paired t-test, $t(23) = 1.87$, $p < .05$). As for the other questions, although the means rating score was slightly higher when the haptic stimulus was present, the difference between the haptic-present and the haptic-absent trial was not statistically significant (Pleasant: $t(23) = 0.85$, $p = .20$, Warm: $t(23) = 0.50$, $p = .31$, Familiar: $t(23) = 0.82$, $p = .21$, Attractive: $t(23) = 0.33$, $p = .37$).

Thus, the results of the experiment clearly showed that the feeling of voice animacy increased when haptic vibratory stimulation was added to the voice stimuli. Even when the haptic stimulation was task irrelevant and the observers were explicitly told to ignore it, the haptic stimulation modulated the abstract feelings for voice stimuli. As described in Section 2, Takahashi et al. (2011a) and Takahashi, Mitsuhashi, Norieda, Murata & Watanabe (2010) showed that a strong feeling of animacy emerged from 1–2Hz of haptic vibratory stimulation. The fact that only the feeling of animacy, that was expected to emerge from haptic stimulatin, was manifest, out of 5 abstract feelings, seems to demonstrate that the effect was not due to general bias in rating higher when the voice was accompanied by haptic stimulus.

4.2 Summary

We investigated if haptic stimulation can modulate abstract feelings for voice stimuli. The results showed that haptic stimulation that is associated with feelings of animacy can increase the felt animacy for voice stimuli. Perhaps the abstract feeling emerging from haptic stimulation interacts with inputs into sensory modalities other than haptics.

These results suggested that the processes concerning abstract feelings, as well as perceptual (Shams & Kim, 2010; Shimojo & Shams, 2001) and emotional (Bertelson & de Gelder, 2005; Tanaka et al., 2010) processes, work interactively among different sensory modalities. It may be plausible to argue that higher levels of cognitive processes have vaguer boundaries between different sensory modalities (Fig. 1.).

5. Overall summary and future direction

In this chapter, we introduced a series of psychological studies recently conducted in our laboratory and discussed the abstract feelings emerging from haptic stimulation. These studies aimed at investigating how humans conceive abstract feelings such as animacy, presence, or pleasantness from simple haptic stimulation and how such abstract feelings affect human experience and behavior.

In sum, we showed that haptic stimulation and abstract feelings are closely related. The first study showed that a feeling of animacy emerges from haptic stimulation in a frequency-dependent manner. The lower frequency (1–2 Hz) of haptic vibratory stimulation yielded the stronger feeling of animacy, while the higher frequency did not. The second study showed the importance of haptic stimulation in interpersonal communication. The presence of haptic communication in particular improved the quality of experience and the impression of the other person, even from a simple vibratory stimulation. The third study showed that haptic stimulation can modulate abstract feelings emerging in sensory modalities other than haptics.

Although all these studies have suggested the potential impact of haptic stimulation on abstract feelings, the empirical evidence of abstract feelings' emerging from haptic stimulation is much less than for the perceptual and sensory processes. The first reason may be that abstract feelings are too vague to examine empirically. Another reason relates to the difficulty of controlling haptic stimulation. However, at least with regard to the second reason, we have shown that simple vibratory haptic stimulation can be associated with abstract feelings. Therefore, it would be possible to investigate abstract feelings using simple haptic stimulation, which would accelerate the research concerning haptic stimulation associated with abstract feelings.

Future research directions regarding haptic stimulation and abstract feelings could include the following:

- Compare abstract feelings emerging from simple haptic stimulation and the real object.
- Examine the relation between haptic stimulation and abstract feelings other than animacy.
- Test factors other than frequency of haptic stimulation on abstract feelings.
- Measure the indices other than subjective evaluation, such as physiological responses to haptic stimulation.
- Relate controlled experimental studies to uncontrolled daily experience (e.g., patterns of frequency dependence for animacy and the frequencies of real-world animals).

All these studies could provide further insights into how humans conceive abstract feelings in response to haptic stimulation, and more generally, what abstract feelings emerge from haptic stimulation.

Finally, it would be worthwhile to state the potential applications of the results of the study of abstract feelings emerging from haptic stimulation. In the past decade, implementation of a sense of touch in communication devices has been advancing rapidly (e.g., humanoid and pet robots, mobile phones, and video games). Strong feelings of animacy might enhance the quality of communication through these devices. Furthermore, if other abstract feelings such as presence or intimacy were implemented in a future haptic device, the device should appreciate in value and would be expected to be widely used in real society. While the research discussed in this chapter is positioned as basic research on humans' cognitive process with regard to haptics, the results may help in designing and developing user-friendly devices by implementing the emergence of abstract feelings.

6. References

Alais, D. & Burr, D. (2004). The ventriloquist effect results from near-optimal bimodal integration, *Current biology* 14(3): 257–262.

Bertelson, P. & de Gelder, B. (2005). Psychology of multimodal perception, *in* C. Spence & J. Driver (eds), *Crossmodal space and crossmodal attention*, Oxford University Press, pp. 151–177.

Blake, R., Sobel, K. V. & James, T. W. (2004). Neural synergy between kinetic vision and touch, *Psychological science* 15(6): 397–402.

Blakemore, S.-J., Boyer, P., Pachot-Clouard, M., Meltzoff, A., Segebarth, C. & Decety, J. (2003). The detection of contingency and animacy from simple animations in the human brain, *Cerebral cortex (New York, NY : 1991)* 13(8): 837–844.

Bruno, N., Jacomuzzi, A., Bertamini, M. & Meyer, G. (2007). A visual-haptic Necker cube reveals temporal constraints on intersensory merging during perceptual exploration, *Neuropsychologia* 45(3): 469–475.

Ernst, M. O. & Banks, M. S. (2002). Humans integrate visual and haptic information in a statistically optimal fashion, *Nature* 415(6870): 429–433.

Ernst, M. O. & Bülthoff, H. H. (2004). Merging the senses into a robust percept, *Trends in cognitive sciences* 8(4): 162–169.

Fujita, Y. & Hashimoto, S. (1999). Experiments of haptic and tactile display for human telecommunication, *8th IEEE International Workshop on Robot and Human Interaction*, pp. 334–337.

Fukuda, H. & Ueda, K. (2010). Interaction with a Moving Object Affects One's Perception of Its Animacy, *International Journal of Social Robotics* 2(2): 187–193.

Gallese, V. & Goldman, A. (1998). Mirror neurons and the simulation theory of mind-reading, *Trends in cognitive sciences* 2(12): 493–501.

Gao, T., McCarthy, G. & Scholl, B. J. (2010). The wolfpack effect. Perception of animacy irresistibly influences interactive behavior., *Psychological science* 21(12): 1845–1853.

Gao, T., Newman, G. E. & Scholl, B. J. (2009). The psychophysics of chasing: A case study in the perception of animacy, *Cognitive psychology* 59(2): 154–179.

Gao, T. & Scholl, B. J. (2011). Chasing vs. stalking: Interrupting the perception of animacy., *Journal of experimental psychology: Human perception and performance* 37(3): 669–684.

Gibson, J. J. (1962). Observations on active touch., *Psychological Review* 69: 477–491.

Golding, J. & Macleod, C. (1998). Intentional Forgetting: Interdisciplinary Approaches, Lawrence Erlbaum Assoc Inc.

Heider, F. & Simmel, M. (1944). An Experimental Study of Apparent Behavior, *The American Journal of Psychology* 57(2): 243–259.

Katz, D. (1989). *The World of Touch*, Psychology Press.

Knapp, L. M. & Hall, A. J. (1992). *Nonverbal communication in human interaction*, Holt Rinehart and Winston.

McGurk, H. & MacDonald, J. (1976). Hearing lips and seeing voices, *Nature* 264(5588): 746–748.

Morito, Y., Tanabe, H. C., Kochiyama, T. & Sadato, N. (2009). Neural representation of animacy in the early visual areas: a functional MRI study, *Brain research bulletin* 79(5): 271–280.

Morris, D. (1971). *Intimate Behavior*, 1st us edition edn, Triad Books.

Reiner, M. (2004). The role of haptics in immersive telecommunication environments, *IEEE Transactions on Circuits and Systems for Video Technology* 14(3): 392–401.

Richmond, V. P., McCroskey, J. C. & Hickson, M. L. (2007). *Nonverbal Behavior in Interpersonal Relations*, 6 edn, Allyn & Bacon.

Rizzolatti, G. (2005). The mirror neuron system and its function in humans, *Anatomy and embryology* 210(5-6): 419–421.

Sallnäs, E.-L., Rassmus-Gröhn, K. & Sjöström, C. (2000). Supporting presence in collaborative environments by haptic force feedback, *ACM Transactions on Computer-Human Interaction* 7(4): 461–476.

Santos, N. S., David, N., Bente, G. & Vogeley, K. (2008). Parametric induction of animacy experience, *Consciousness and cognition* 17(2): 425–437.

Santos, N. S., Kuzmanovic, B., David, N., Rotarska-Jagiela, A., Eickhoff, S. B., Shah, J. N., Fink, G. R., Bente, G. & Vogeley, K. (2010). Animated brain: a functional neuroimaging study on animacy experience, *NeuroImage* 53(1): 291–302.

Scholl, B. & Tremoulet, P. (2000). Perceptual causality and animacy., *Trends in cognitive sciences* 4(8): 299–309.

Shams, L. & Kim, R. (2010). Crossmodal influences on visual perception, *Physics of life reviews* 7(3): 269–284.

Shimojo, S. & Shams, L. (2001). Sensory modalities are not separate modalities: plasticity and interactions, *Current opinion in neurobiology* 11(4): 505–509.

Takahashi, K., Mitsuhashi, H., Murata, K., Norieda, S. & Watanabe, K. (2011a). Feelings of Animacy and Pleasantness from Tactile Stimulation: Effect of Stimulus Frequency and Stimulated Body Part, *IEEE Int. Conf. on Systems, Man, and Cybernetics (SMC2011)*.

Takahashi, K., Mitsuhashi, H., Murata, K., Norieda, S. & Watanabe, K. (2011b). Improving Shared Experiences by Haptic Telecommunication, *International Conference on Biometrics and Kansei Engineering*.

Takahashi, K., Mitsuhashi, H., Murata, K., Norieda, S. & Watanabe, K. (2011c). Kansei Information and Factor Space of Nonverbal Interpersonal Communicaion – Psychological Investigation on Physical Contacts Modified by Japanese Onomatopoieas –, *Transactions of Japan Society of Kansei Engineering* 10(2): 261–268.

Takahashi, K., Mitsuhashi, H., Norieda, S., Murata, K. & Watanabe, K. (2010). Frequency-dependence in haptic, visual, and auditory animacy perception, *IEICE Human Communication Group Symposium 2010*, pp. 331–336.

Takahashi, K., Mitsuhashi, H., Norieda, S., Sendoda, M., Murata, K. & Watanabe, K. (2010). Japanese Onomatopoeias and Sound Symbolic Words in Describing Interpersonal Communication., *The Proceedings of the International Conference on Kansei Engineering and Emotion Research 2010*, pp. 2162–2171.

Tanaka, A., Koizumi, A., Imai, H., Hiramatsu, S., Hiramoto, E. & de Gelder, B. (2010). I feel your voice. Cultural differences in the multisensory perception of emotion., *Psychological science* 21(9): 1259–1262.

Tremoulet, P. D. & Feldman, J. (2000). Perception of animacy from the motion of a single object, *Perception* 29(8): 943–951.

Wang, D., Tuer, K. & Ni, L. (2004). Conducting a real-time remote handshake with haptics, *Proceedings of the 12th international conference on Haptic interfaces for virtual environment and teleoperator systems*.

Zajonc, R. B. (1968). Attitudinal effects of mere exposure., *Journal of personality and social psychology* 9(2): 1–27.

6

Effective Haptic Rendering Method for Complex Interactions

Josune Hernantes, Iñaki Díaz, Diego Borro and Jorge Juan Gil
CEIT and TECNUN (University of Navarra)
Spain

1. Introduction

The development of haptic technology is allowing the introduction of Virtual Reality systems as teaching and working tools into many fields such as engineering (Howard & Vance, 2007; Savall et al., 2002) or surgery (Basdogan et al., 2004; Li & Liu, 2006).
Haptic devices allow users to interact with a certain environment, either remote or virtual, through the sense of touch, considerably enhancing interactivity. A haptic device is a mechanism that allows users to control the movements of a virtual tool or a real robot and receive tactile and kinesthetic information from the working environment (Fig. 1).
The usability of these systems is conditioned by the quality of the haptic feedback applied to the user. Technologically, the computation of appropriate and realistic haptic stimuli continues to be a complicated issue. The human sensory-motor system demands a fast update rate (at least 1 kHz) for the haptic stimuli applied to the user in order to avoid instabilities in

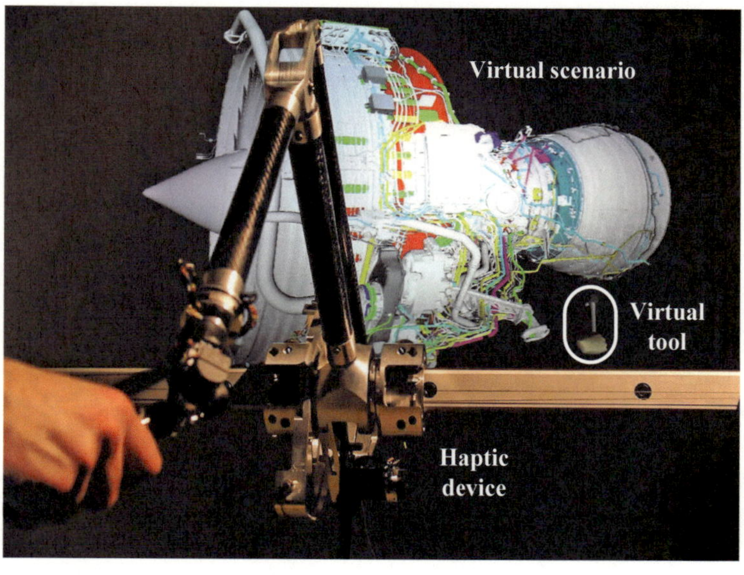

Fig. 1. Haptic interaction with a virtual environment

the system and to present rigid objects with reasonable stiffness (Shimoga, 1992). However, this update rate is often difficult to reach by haptic rendering methods, especially when working in complex environments. One possible solution is to reduce the computational cost of calculating the haptic response by decreasing the accuracy of the method. However, this can result in the emergence of discontinuities in the response. This leads to find a trade-off between the accuracy of the method, which guarantees a smooth and stable haptic response, and the computational cost.

This chapter describes a haptic rendering method to properly compute interacting forces and torques in complex environments, ensuring improved feedback by seeking a compromise between continuity and computational cost. In addition, the proposed method pays particular attention to provide users with comfortable interaction. The method is valid for applications in which the virtual environment is composed of rigid and static objects, excluding deformable objects.

The remainder of this chapter is organized as follows: Section 2 presents an overview of the related research on the area. Afterwards, Section 3 describes the haptic rendering method proposed by the authors, describing in detail all algorithms necessary to render appropriate and stable forces and torques to the user. The proposed method is then evaluated in Section 4 within two different virtual scenarios simulating common collisions during aeronautic maintainability tasks. Aeronautic virtual mock-ups have been selected for algorithms testing due to their high interaction complexity. Finally, conclusions and future directions are drawn in Section 5.

2. Related research

The process of computing and generating forces in response to user interactions with virtual objects is known as haptic rendering (Salisbury et al., 1995). The application of haptic rendering algorithms to complex contact scenarios becomes a challenging issue, due to the inherent cost of collision detection that induces slow force updates. The haptic display of virtual objects has been an active area of research throughout the last decade. Previous research in haptic rendering can be mainly classified within two groups: penalty and constraint-based methods.

When it comes to penalty methods, collision response is computed as a function of object separation or penetration depth. McNeely et al. (1999) proposed point-voxel sampling, a discretized approximation technique for contact queries that generates points on moving objects and voxels on static geometry. This approximation algorithm offers run-time performance independent of the environment's input size by sampling the object geometry at a resolution that the given processor can handle. Renz et al. (2001) adapted this method with several modifications for smoother and more stable haptic feedback. In another research project, Gregory et al. (2000) presented a 6-DOF haptic rendering system that combined collision detection based on convex decomposition of polygonal models, predictive estimation of penetration depth and force and torque interpolation. Kim et al. (2003) attempted to increase the stability of force feedback by using contact clustering, but their algorithm for contact queries suffers from the same computational complexity.

Otaduy and Lin (2003) have presented a sensation preserving simplification technique for 6-DOF haptic rendering of complex polygonal models by adaptively selecting contact resolutions. Later, they have also presented a modular algorithm for 6-DOF haptic rendering, that provides transparent manipulation of rigid models with a high polygon count (Otaduy & Lin, 2006).

Unlike penalty methods, constraint-based methods do not use the interpenetration between rigid objects to calculate collision response. These methods use virtual coupling techniques (Colgate et al., 1995) and restrict the movement of virtual objects on the surface of obstacles.

Zilles and Salisbury (1995) proposed a constraint-based method for 3-DOF haptic rendering of generic polygonal objects. They introduced the "god-object", an idealized representation of the position of the haptic device that is constrained on the surface of obstacles. At each time step, the location of the god-object minimizes the distance to the haptic device and the difference between the two positions provides the force direction. Ruspini et al. (1997) extended this approach by replacing the god-object with a small sphere as well as proposing methods to smooth the object surface and add friction. Later, Ortega (2006) extended the 3-DOF constraint-based method of Zilles and Salisbury by employing a 6-DOF god-object.

The different haptic rendering methods described above have contributed extensively to a better representation of contact events between virtual objects. However, haptic interactions with multiple contacts, which also include geometrical discontinuities, have not yet been adequately accomplished computing unrealistic or unstable haptic feedback in these cases. These type of situations are very common in real scenarios and therefore it is necessary to compute properly a stable haptic response in order to improve the usability of these systems. The proposed haptic rendering method overcomes limitations from previous approaches in this type of collisions.

3. Proposed haptic rendering method

The haptic rendering method outlined in this chapter computes the force and torque that result when a collision between two type of objects occurs: a virtual tool (mobile object) manipulated by the user of the haptic device and any object in the simulation (static object).

Three main modules can be identified in the haptic rendering method proposed (Fig. 2): collision detection, collision response and control module.

The complete haptic rendering sequence could be described as follows: firstly, the control module acquires the position ($\boldsymbol{U}_h$) and orientation ($\boldsymbol{R}_h$) of the haptic device and sends it to the collision detection module. With this information, the module checks for collisions between the mobile object and the static environment. If no collisions occur, it waits for new information from the control module. Otherwise, when a collision event occurs, the contact information of both static and mobile objects ($\mathbf{C}_s$, $\mathbf{C}_m$) is sent to the collision response module which calculates the interaction force and torque. This haptic feedback approximates the contact force and torque that would arise during contact between real objects ($\boldsymbol{F}_r$, $\boldsymbol{T}_r$). Finally, the collision response module sends this information to the control module, which applies it to the haptic device ($\boldsymbol{F}_h$, $\boldsymbol{T}_h$), maintaining a stable system behaviour.

A more complete description of each module can be found in the following sections.

3.1 Collision detection

The collision detection method presented in this chapter can handle non-convex objects without modifying the original mesh. A technique based on a spatial partition (voxels) has been chosen. Hierarchical methods like octrees have also been tested since they require less

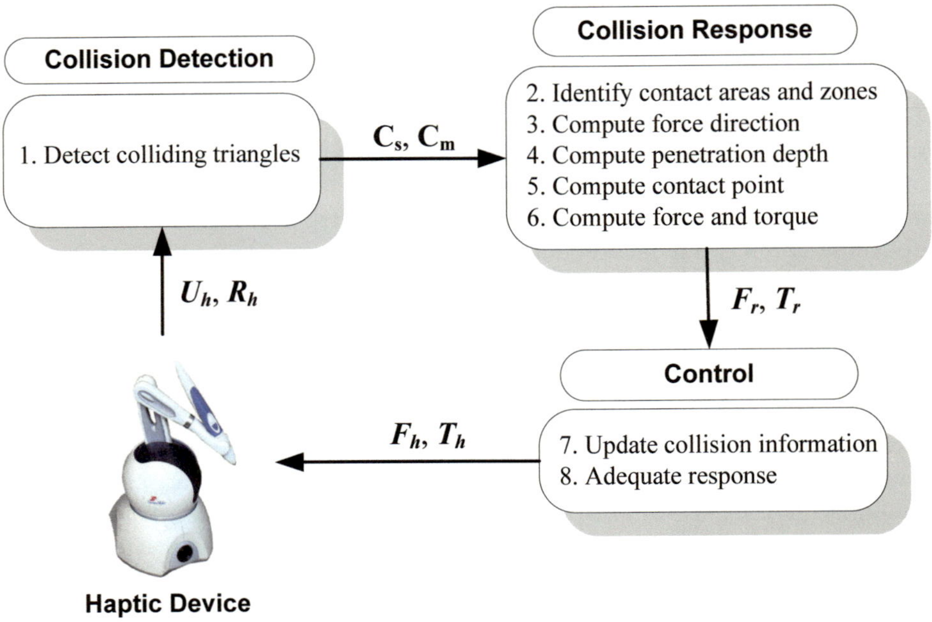

Fig. 2. Diagram of haptic rendering algorithm

memory storage. However, their computation time is higher than that needed for direct access voxel techniques.

It is well-known that algorithms based on voxel techniques have several disadvantages, such as high memory storage requirements and the selection of voxel size. According to previous experiments (Borro et al., 2004), hashing techniques can solve the first problem by reducing memory storage up to 60 % without performance loss, and the choice of an optimal voxel size can be solved by means of an analytical solution based on the algorithm cost function.

The method, in a pre-process, computes a voxel partition from the virtual scene and assigns each triangle of the static environment to its corresponding voxel. This voxel partition is used only for the static object. In addition, each voxel will have a flag identifying it as internal (V_{int}), external (V_{ext}) or boundary (V_{bnd}). The last ones contain the triangles that define the surface of the static object.

Next, at runtime, the partition model is used to detect the set of voxels in collision with the mobile object and to carry out interference checks between triangles.

Fig. 3a shows an example of colliding static triangles (***CST***) and colliding mobile triangles (***CMT***) detected by the method in a virtual collision of a tool with an obstacle. As it can be seen colliding triangles do not provide enough information to delimit the volume that defines the intersection between the objects. Therefore, unlike other existing methods in the literature, the proposed algorithm detects additional triangles in order to calculate the intersection volume correctly (Fig. 3b). The union of the colliding triangles and these additional triangles are referred to as *contact triangles*.

The additional triangles can be classified within three groups: internal mobile (***IMT***), boundary mobile (***BMT***) and boundary static (***BST***). With regard to the mobile object, (***IMT***) are those in contact with V_{int} whereas (***BMT***) are those in contact with V_{bnd}, but that do not intersect with static triangles (***CST***) (Fig. 4).

Regarding the static object, ***BST*** set of triangles are those in contact with V_{bnd} (Fig. 5), but that do not intersect with mobile triangles. These triangles are usually in the centre of the contact area surrounded by colliding static triangles.

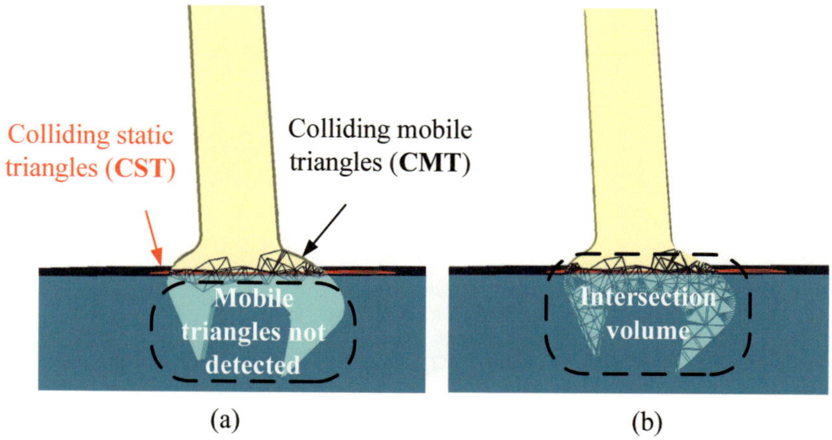

Fig. 3. Colliding triangles detected (a) and additional triangles that define the intersection volume (b)

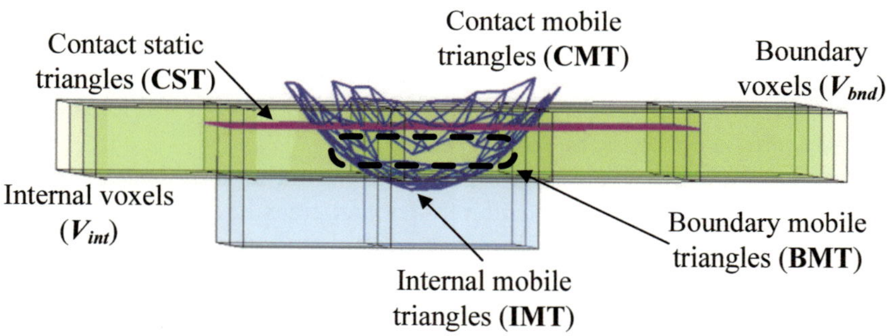

Fig. 4. Internal and boundary mobile triangles

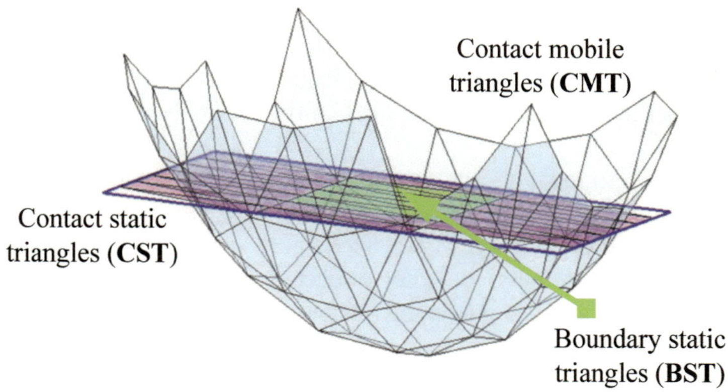

Fig. 5. Static boundary triangles

At the end, the collision detection module yields two sets of contact triangles, one belonging to the static object ($\mathbf{C}_s$) and the other to the mobile object ($\mathbf{C}_m$).

$$C_s = \{CST \bigcup BST\} \quad (1)$$

$$C_m = \{CMT \bigcup BMT \bigcup IMT\} \quad (2)$$

3.2 Collision response

The algorithm proposed follows the well-known penalty methods based on elastic model, thus the haptic response that users feel as a consequence of a collision in the virtual environment is determined by a direction and a penetration value. Both factors have substantial influence on user perception.
The force ($\boldsymbol{F_r}$) and torque ($\boldsymbol{T_r}$) are calculated as follows:

$$\begin{aligned} \boldsymbol{F_r} &= Kd\boldsymbol{n} \\ \boldsymbol{T_r} &= (\boldsymbol{cp} - \boldsymbol{gc}) \times \boldsymbol{F_r} \end{aligned} \quad (3)$$

where K is virtual stiffness, d is penetration depth, $\boldsymbol{n}$ force direction, $\boldsymbol{cp}$ the contact point and $\boldsymbol{gc}$ the centre of mass of the virtual tool.
In complex scenarios, it is common to encounter multiple contacts. The lists of triangles ($\mathbf{C}_s$ and $\mathbf{C}_m$) obtained by the collision detection module do not give a priory information about the number of different contacts. Therefore, the method divides these sets of triangles into different contact areas considering their spatial proximity. The forces and torques of each area are then added up to compute the net force and torque.
A certain amount of static triangles form a contact area when they are adjacent. In other words, they share at least one edge. Once the different contact areas have been calculated from $\mathbf{C}_s$, it is necessary to identify the mobile triangles in contact that are associated with those areas. To facilitate this process, a sphere is created in each contact area that covers the bounding box defined by its triangles. Finally, each triangle of $\mathbf{C}_m$ is associated with the contact area depending on the sphere which contains it. Fig. 6 shows an example of the division of contact areas.
The difficulty in calculating an appropriate and stable haptic response increases when the geometry has sharp edges, since haptic instabilities often appear due to abrupt force direction or penetration depth changes. In order to detect these cases, each contact area is sub-divided into different contact zones that provide information about the nature of the geometry in collision.
The collision response module subdivides a collision area into different contact zones taking surface C^1 discontinuities into account. When two triangles share an edge and the angle between their normal vectors is lower than a fixed value, the edge is designated as "smooth". Triangles in a contact zone must be interconnected and all the shared edges must be smooth. There will be as many contact zones as necessary to satisfy the condition of smooth connectivity (Fig. 7).
Once the contact areas and zones have been detected, the method computes the contact normal vector (force direction) of each area ($\mathbf{n_c}$). If the contact area has a unique contact zone, the contact normal is computed as the normalized sum of all normal vectors of the static triangles of that zone. Otherwise, when a contact area has two or more contact zones, the

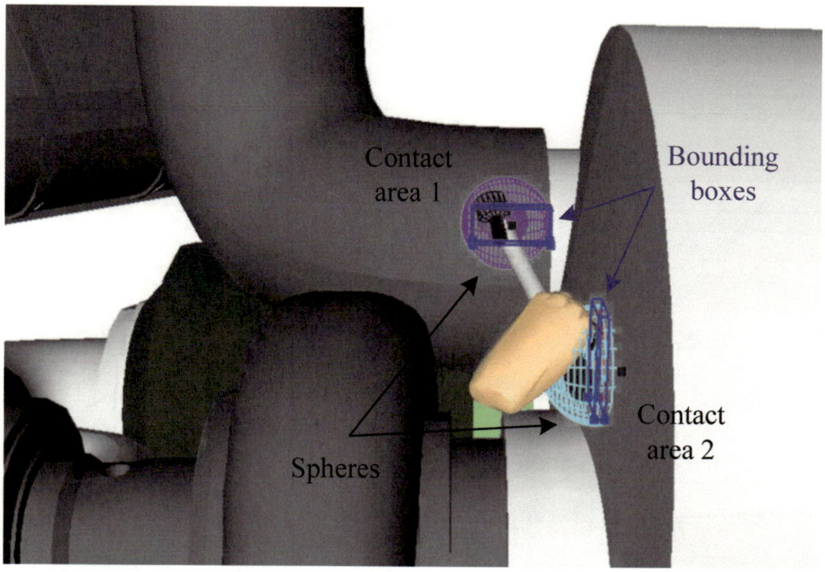

Fig. 6. Example of two contact areas

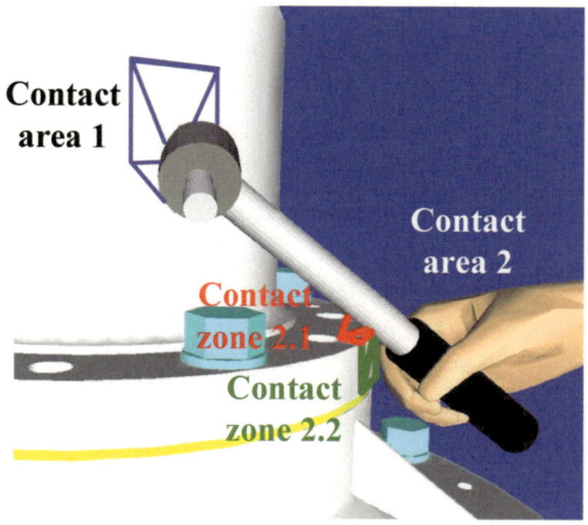

Fig. 7. Example of two contact areas. The second one has two contact zones

contact has occurred in an area of the static object that is not a continuous surface. In this case, static triangles do not provide enough information to obtain a suitable force direction. Therefore, $\mathbf{n_c}$ is computed as the normalized sum of all normal vectors of the mobile triangles of that area. This solution enables smoother direction transitions when interacting with sharp edges.

After computing the force direction in each area, the following step is the calculation of the minimum distance required to separate the two objects, known as penetration depth (d). For that purpose, the method samples the volume of intersection measuring heights throughout this volume to determine the penetration between two objects. These heights are determined by tracing a ray from the centroid of each static triangle in $\mathbf{n_c}$ direction (Fig. 8). If this ray intersects with a mobile triangle (Möller & Trumbore, 1997), the height is defined as the distance between the centroid and the intersection point. The final value of penetration for each area is computed as an average of all the computed heights.

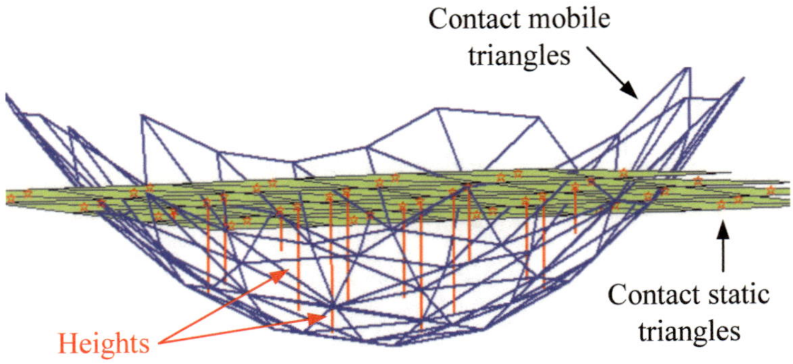

Fig. 8. Rays traced to compute penetration depth

The last parameter necessary to compute collision torque is the contact point (**cp**). Selecting an inappropriate point such as the most penetrating one for each contact area might lead to non-continuous changes in the haptic feedback (Hasegawa & Sato, 2004). To avoid this effect, the proposed solution is to choose a representative contact point for each contact area. This point is calculated as the average of the midpoints of the boundary voxels associated with each contact area.

3.3 Control module

The control module receives the ideal interaction force and torque calculated by the collision response method, adapts them to the device's capabilities and applies them to the user at a 1 kHz sampling rate. Since the control loop runs faster than the collision module, several strategies must be implemented in order to avoid abrupt changes in contact force and torque when collision information is not available (Savall et al. (2002)).

There are two main problems that should be taken into account. The first one is the delay that exists in the collision-related information. This information, calculated by the response module, is valid for a previous user position, but not the actual one. The second problem resides in the existence of some control loops without collision-related information, since the response module is slower than the control loop. In order to deal with these problems, a strategy based on intermediate representations (Adachi et al. (1995)) is implemented.

Let $\boldsymbol{M}_h$=($\boldsymbol{F}_h$, $\boldsymbol{T}_h$) be the six-dimensional vector of the force and torque that we want to apply to the user and $\boldsymbol{X}_h$=($\boldsymbol{U}_h$, $\boldsymbol{R}_h$) be the six-dimensional configuration of the haptic device ($\boldsymbol{U}_h$ represents the position, and $\boldsymbol{R}_h$ the axis angle representation of the rotation). First, the control method updates the force and torque ($\boldsymbol{M}_r$) computed by the response module at a previous sampling period j, to the current one i (K represents virtual stiffness):

$$\boldsymbol{M}_h(i) = \boldsymbol{M}_r(i-j) - K(\boldsymbol{U}_h(i) - \boldsymbol{U}_h(i-j)) \quad (4)$$

These forces and torques might vary quite abruptly if they are applied to the user every time they are updated by the collision response method. Therefore, the control module restores

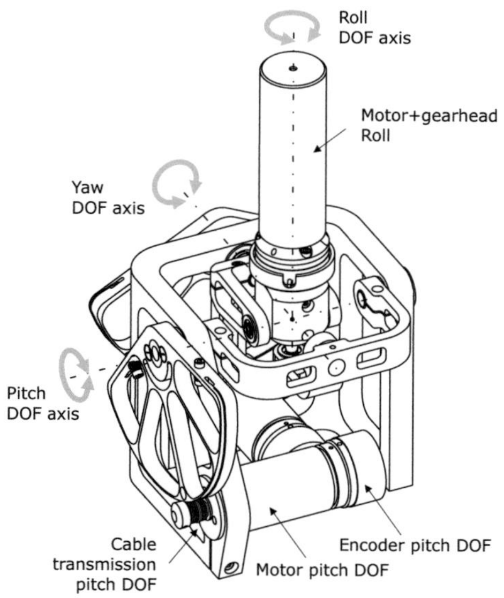

Degrees of freedom	
Sensing input	3 DOF (Pitch-Yaw-Roll)
Feedback output	3 DOF (Pitch-Yaw-Roll)
Workspace	
Pitch-Yaw	±70 °
Roll	Unlimited
Continuous output level	
Pitch-Yaw	0.7 Nm
Roll	0.2 Nm
Peak output level	
Pitch-Yaw	1.6 Nm
Roll	0.9 Nm
Actuators	
Pitch-Yaw	DC MaxonRE35, 90 W + Cable Transmissions 13.5:1
Roll	DC MaxonRE-max21, 6 W + Maxon Planetary GP22C 29:1
Encoders	
Pitch-Yaw	Quantum Devices QD145, 5000 ppr
Roll	MaxonMR TypeM, 512 ppr

Fig. 9. 3-DOF torque feedback device used for the experiments

them in n subsequent sampling periods:

$$\begin{aligned} \Delta \boldsymbol{M}_h(i) &= \frac{\boldsymbol{M}_r(i-j) - K(\boldsymbol{U}_h(i) - \boldsymbol{U}_h(i-j)) - \boldsymbol{M}_h(i-1)}{n} \\ \boldsymbol{M}_h(i) &= \boldsymbol{M}_h(i-1) + \Delta \boldsymbol{M}_h(i) \end{aligned} \tag{5}$$

In the next sampling period $(i+1)$, the method also takes the new movements performed by the user into account:

$$\boldsymbol{M}_h(i+1) = \boldsymbol{M}_h(i) + \Delta \boldsymbol{M}_h(i) - K(\boldsymbol{U}_h(i+1) - \boldsymbol{U}_h(i)) \tag{6}$$

This will continue until the collision response method updates the collision-related information. To determine n, the optimal value should approximate the number of control sampling periods that the collision module needs to compute the response. Since this number can vary significantly depending on the number of triangles in collision, a conservative number can be set. However, if n is very high, the method may excessively filter the signal. Moreover, n can have a fixed value during the entire task or can be modified by means of the average collision response delay in previous sampling periods.

4. Implementation and results

Two different virtual scenarios have been designed to test the effectiveness and stability of the proposed haptic rendering algorithm on complex interactions. A 3-DOF torque feedback device has been used for the experiments. The mechanism was designed and built at CEIT and inspired by past research (Angerilli et al., 2001). Fig. 9 shows the device and its main specifications.

The system is controlled by a dSPACE DS1104 board that reads encoder information, processes the haptic control loop and outputs torque commands to the motors. Graphic rendering and collision detection are performed on a PC running the Windows XP operating system with a Pentium Dual Core 6600, 2GB memory and an NVIDIA GeForce 8600 GT.

4.1 Analysis of multiple contacts and geometrical discontinuities

The first scenario is composed of two parallelepipeds, one central cylinder and a virtual tool similar to a clamp (see top of Fig. 10). The virtual scenario consists of 25,000 triangles while the clamp is composed of 1,500 triangles. The aim is to analyze the behavior of the method when multiple contacts and geometrical discontinuities are involved. For that purpose, a sequence of different collisions has been simulated:

1. Collision with the central cylinder in which two contact areas are involved.
2. Collision with the corners of the two parallelepipeds (C^1 discontinuities).
3. Collision with four contacts simultaneously, combining the previous cases.

Fig. 10 shows the torque feedback computed in all three axis by the collision response method during the sequence. The figure also shows the number of contact triangles detected and the computational cost in each frame.
Notice in the figure that the torque feedback applied to the user during collision is quite smooth and does not offer abrupt changes or discontinuities that may degrade the user's perception of contact. The last figure shows that the collision response method computes the haptic feedback at an average of 2.5 ms, which is not far from the optimal computation time (1 ms) necessary for a realisic haptic experience. This allows the control module to compute the real forces and torques at 1 kHz using a low number of n transitions (described in Section 3.3), and thereby maintaining a stable system behaviour. Specifically, for this experiment, the number of transitions n for the control algorithm was set to 5.

4.2 Simulation of a disassembly task

The task designed for the second experiment is similar to the extraction of a clamp from a pipe, which frequently appears in engine disassembly tasks in aeronautics maintenance. Once the clamp is unfastened, the exit path is established by following the spatial trajectory laid out by the pipe itself. Along said path, the curves and bends of the pipe and other obstacles force the clamp to rotate in space. Therefore, in order to accomplish this task properly, it is important that the haptic feedback restored to the user is realistic. The virtual engine mock-up is defined by 100,000 triangles while the clamp is composed of 2,000 triangles.
The torque feedback device used in the previous experiment does not allow any translation. Thus, to be able to displace the clamp within the virtual environment, it is necessary to provide the mechanism with a translational DOF. For that purpose, a linear actuator designed and built at CEIT (Savall et al., 2008) is used. The displacement along this linear DOF is mapped into a displacement of the clamp along the axial direction of the pipe, and forces along this DOF are also displayed when collisions occur. Fig. 11 shows both the designed virtual environment and the haptic device used for the experiments.
A virtual path from right to left along the route of extraction was performed. During this process, different types of collisions occurred between the clamp and the environment. Fig. 12 shows an example of the main possible stages during the extraction:

1. Initial position.

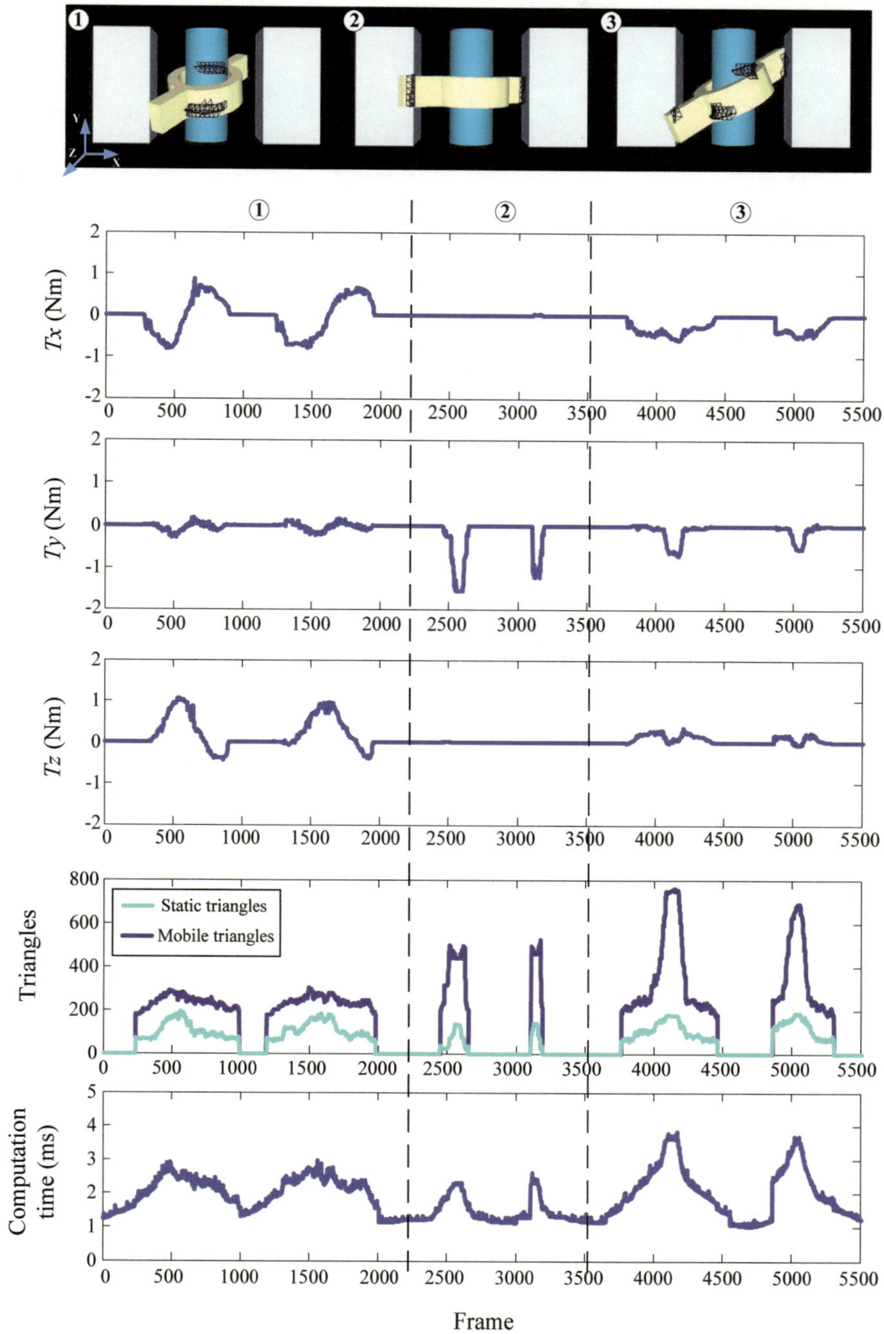

Fig. 10. Performance of our approach in multiple contacts and geometrical discontinuities

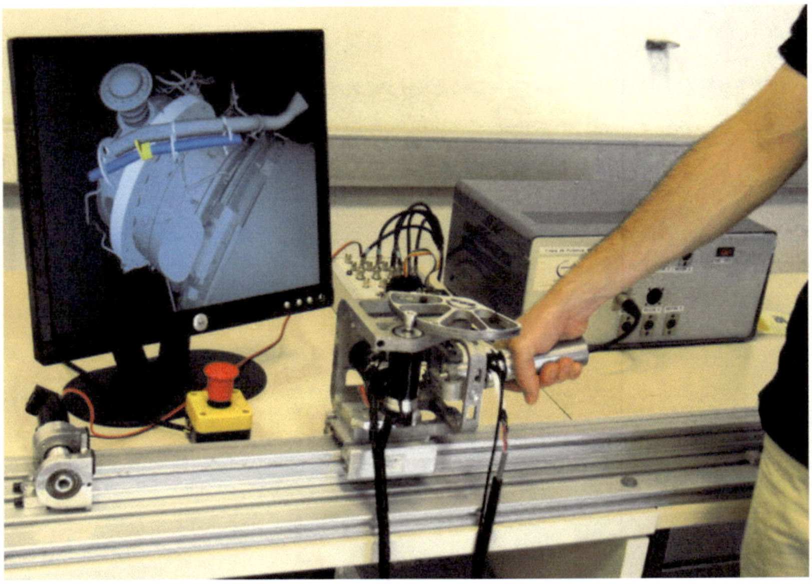

Fig. 11. Haptic system used for the experiment

2. Collision of the clamp with the first obstacle. In this case, the linear actuator restores a force in the X axis to avoid translational movement.

3. The clamp is inside the obstacle and, when rotating along the X axis, it collides with the upper part of the obstacle.

4. Collision of the clamp with the pipe when rotating along the Z axis.

5. Collision of the clamp with the pipe resulting in complex multi-axis torque.

6. Final position. The clamp is disassembled.

Fig. 12 shows the torque applied to the user in each axis (T_{r_x}, T_{r_y} and T_{r_z}) and the force exerted by the linear actuator (F_{r_x}) computed by the collision response method. It also indicates the number of triangles in collision, in addition to the computational cost at each frame. Notice that in this figure data are shown from right to left according to the movement of the tool.

Haptic feedback obtained gives a realistic perception of collision events and allows to perform the task properly. Unlike the previous scenario, designed to study the behavior of the method in situations with multiple collisions, in this case the aim is to simulate a real task. For this reason, although the complexity of the environment is higher, the number of simultaneous contacts decreases because the user corrects trajectory when a collision is detected.

Fig. 13 is an augmentation of the third collision stage of Fig. 12 (frames 3450–3650) for torque feedback in the x axis, with and without applying the control algorithms. It can be seen that torque computed by the collision response is smooth and avoids abrupt changes. In addition, control algorithms improve the continuity of the feedback signal and apply it to the user at a sampling rate of 1 kHz. As in the previous example, in this case the number of transitions for the control algorithms is also 5.

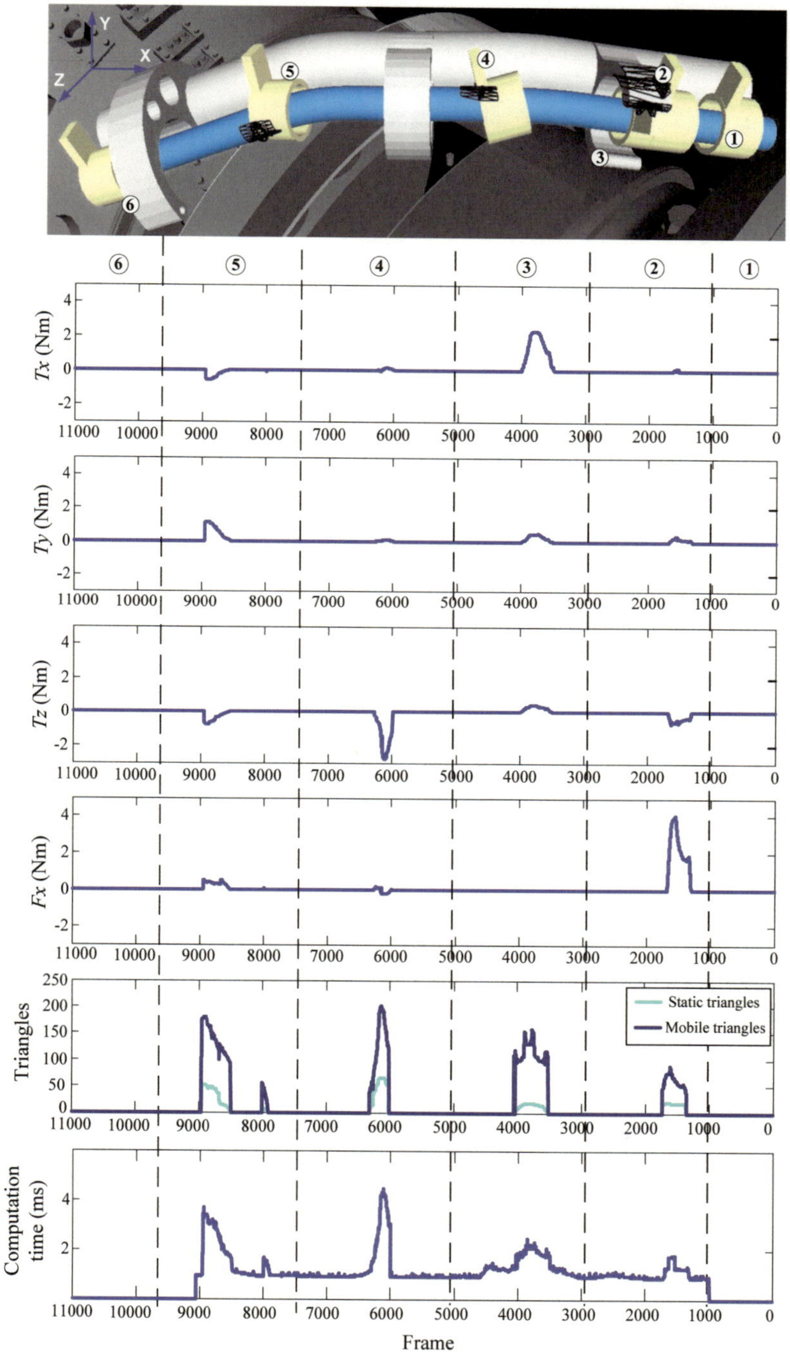

Fig. 12. Extraction of a clamp from a pipe

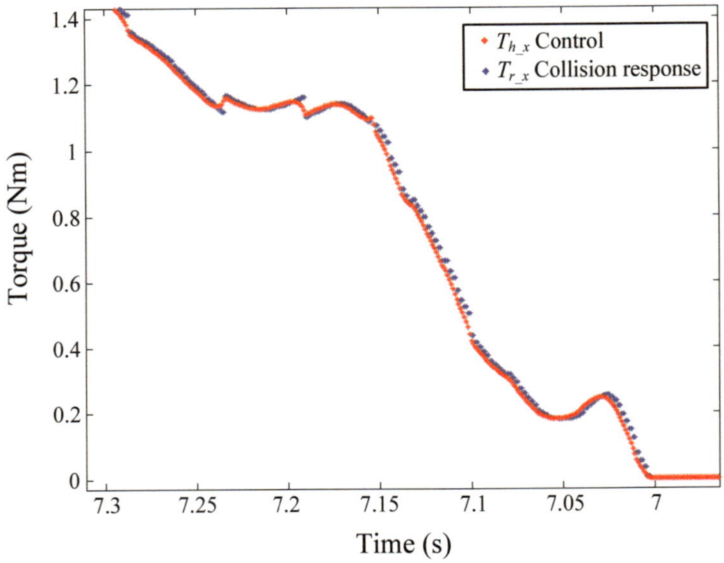

Fig. 13. An augmentation of the third collision stage for torque feedback in the X axis, with and without applying the control algorithms

5. Conclusions and future research

The real-time computation of the forces and torques in a virtual environment is a complicated task but a key point for the effectiveness of haptic systems. It is known that non-realistic or inappropriate haptic feedback has negative effects on the usability and leads to frustration when manipulating haptic systems. Therefore, it is very important to guarantee smooth and realistic haptic feedback.

This chapter outlines a haptic rendering method that computes a proper haptic response in complex environments. It ensures improved feedback by seeking a compromise between continuity and computational cost. The method avoids abrupt changes in the haptic force direction and magnitude, thereby improving the overall stability of the haptic system.

In order to validate the proposed method, two different scenarios containing complex collision examples, such as multiple contacts and geometrical discontinuities, have been used. The yielded results validate the applicability of the method in these types of interactions.

In terms of future research, the authors plan to analyze the performance of the method from a perceptual perspective carrying out studies of human factors to improve the responsiveness. The authors also hope that the research included in this chapter will provide a better understanding of the many phenomena that challenge the development of improved haptic rendering methods able to display adequate force and torque feedback while preserving stability, and thereby improve performance of current haptic interfaces.

6. Appendix: List of notation

- x, y, z : Reference displacement axis
- $\mathbf{U}_h$: User displacement of the haptic handle
- $\mathbf{R}_h$: User rotation of the haptic handle in angle-axis notation

- $\mathbf{X}_h$: User displacement and rotation of the haptic handle
- $\mathbf{F}_r$: Collision force computed by the collision response method
- $\mathbf{T}_r$: Collision torque computed by the collision response method
- $\mathbf{M}_r$: Collision force and torque computed by the collision response method
- $\mathbf{F}_h$: Force feedback applied to the user
- $\mathbf{T}_h$: Torque feedback applied to the user
- $\mathbf{M}_h$: Force and torque feedback applied to the user
- $\mathbf{V}_{int}$: Internal voxels
- $\mathbf{V}_{ext}$: External voxels
- $\mathbf{V}_{bnd}$: Boundary voxels
- $\mathbf{C}_s$: List of static triangles in collision
- $\mathbf{C}_m$: List of mobile triangles in collision
- $\mathbf{cp}$: Collision contact point
- $\mathbf{gc}$: Centre of mass of the virtual tool
- K : Virtual object stiffness
- d : Penetration of the mobile tool within a static object
- $\mathbf{n}$: Force direction
- $\mathbf{n}_c$: Force direction of each contact ares
- n : Number of transitions for the control algorithm

7. References

Adachi, Y., Kumano, T. & Ogino, K. (1995). Intermediate representation for stiff virtual objects, *IEEE Virtual Reality Annual International Symposium* pp. 203–210.

Angerilli, M., Frisoli, A., Salsedo, F., Marcheschi, S. & Bergamasco, M. (2001). Haptic simulation of an automotive manual gearshift, *10th IEEE International Workshop on Robot and Human Interactive Communication*, pp. 170–175.

Basdogan, C., De, S., Kim, J., Muniyandi, M., Kim, H. & Srinivasan, M. (2004). Haptics in minimally invasive surgical simulation and training, *IEEE Computer Graphics and Applications* 24(2): 56–64.

Borro, D., García-Alonso, A. & Matey, L. (2004). Approximation of optimal voxel size for collision detection in maintainability simulations within massive virtual environments, *Computer Graphics Forum* 23(1): 13–23.

Colgate, J., Stanley, M. & Brown, J. (1995). Issues in the haptic display of tool use, *IEEE International Conference on Intelligent Robot and Systems*, Vol. 3, Pittsburgh, PA, USA, pp. 140–145.

Gregory, A., Mascarenhas, A., Ehmann, S., Lin, M. & Manocha, D. (2000). Six degree-of-freedom haptic display of polygonal models, *IEEE Conference on Visualization*, Salt Lake City, Utah, United States, pp. 139–146.

Hasegawa, S. & Sato, M. (2004). Real-time rigid body simulation for haptic interactions based on contact volume of polygonal objects, *Computer Graphics Forum* 23(3): 529–538.

Howard, B. M. & Vance, J. M. (2007). Desktop haptic virtual assembly using physically based modelling, *Virtual Reality* 11(4): 207–215.

Kim, Y. J., Otaduy, M. A., Lin, M. C. & Manocha, D. (2003). Six-degree-of-freedom haptic rendering using incremental and localized computations, *Presence: Teleoperators and Virtual Environments* 12(3): 277–295.

Li, M. & Liu, Y.-H. (2006). Haptic modeling and experimental validation for interactive endodontic simulation, *IEEE International Conference on Robotics and Automation*, Orlando, Florida, USA, pp. 3292–3297.

McNeely, W. A., Puterbaugh, K. D. & Troy, J. J. (1999). Six degree-of-freedom haptic rendering using voxel sampling, *ACM SIGGRAPH - Computer Graphics*, Los Angeles, California, USA, pp. 401–408.

Möller, T. & Trumbore, B. (1997). Fast, minimum storage ray-triangle intersection, *Journal of Graphics Tools (JGT)* 2(1): 21–28.

Ortega, M., Redon, S. & Coquillart, S. (2006). A six degree-of-freedom god-object method for haptic display of rigid bodies, *IEEE Virtual Reality Conference*, pp. 191–198.

Otaduy, M. A. & Lin, M. (2006). A modular haptic rendering algorithm for stable and transparent 6-dof manipulation, *IEEE Transactions on Robotics* 22(4): 751–762.

Otaduy, M. A. & Lin, M. C. (2003). Sensation preserving simplification for haptic rendering, *ACM Transactions on Graphics* 22(3): 543–553.

Renz, M., Preusche, C., Pötke, M., Kriegel, H.-P. & Hirzinger, G. (2001). Stable haptic interaction with virtual environments using an adapted voxmap-pointshell algorithm, *Eurohaptics*, Birmingham, UK, pp. 149–154.

Ruspini, D. C., Kolarov, K. & Khatib, O. (1997). Haptic interaction in virtual environments, *IEEE International Conference on Intelligent Robots and Systems*, Vol. 1, Grenoble, France, pp. 128–133.

Salisbury, J. K., Brock, D. L., Massie, T., Swarup, N. & Zilles, C. (1995). Haptic rendering: Programming touch interaction with virtual objects, *ACM Symposium on Interactive 3D Graphics*, Monterey, California, USA, pp. 123–130.

Savall, J., Borro, D., Gil, J. J. & Matey, L. (2002). Description of a haptic system for virtual maintainability in aeronautics, *IEEE International Conference on Intelligent Robots and Systems*, Lausanne, Switzerland, pp. 2887–2892.

Savall, J., Martín, J. & Avello, A. (2008). High performance linear cable transmission, *Journal of Mechanical Design* 130(6).

Shimoga, K. B. (1992). Finger force and touch feedback issues in dextrous telemanipulation, *Fourth Annual Conference on Intelligent Robotic Systems for Space Exploration*, pp. 159–178.

Zilles, C. & Salisbury, J. (1995). A constraint-based god-object method for haptic display, *International Conference on Intelligent Robots and Systems, Human Robot Interaction, and Cooperative Robots*, Vol. 3, pp. 146–151.

Part 3

Haptic Medical Modelling and Applications

7

Sensorized Tools for Haptic Force Feedback in Computer Assisted Surgery

Arne Sieber[1,2,3], Keith Houston[1,3], Christian Woegerer[3], Peter Enoksson[4], Arianna Menciassi[1] and Paolo Dario[1]
[1]The Bio Robotics Institute, Scuola Superiore Sant'Anna, Pisa,
[2]Imego AB, Gothenburg,
[3]Profactor GmbH, Steyr,
[4]MC2, Chalmers University of Technology, Gothenburg,
[1]Italy
[2,4]Sweden
[3]Austria

1. Introduction

For centuries, open surgery was the usual way of performing an operation on a patient. Usually large incisions were required, thus this technique was traumatic for the patient and resulted in large scars and long and expensive recovery time. One paradigmatic example is cardiac surgery, where for an open surgery procedure a sternotomy is required, where the surgeon has to open with a saw the patient's sternum to access the heart and create an adequate workspace. Minimally invasive surgery (MIS) has revolutionized the way surgeries are performed in the last few decades. Here endoscopes and specialized instruments that fit in natural openings in the body or through keyhole incisions (typically 5-12 mm in diameter) are used and meet the patients demand for smaller incisions and shorter recovery times.

MIS techniques have numerous benefits for patients over open techniques, but unfortunately there are several drawbacks: images are usually captured from a 2D endoscopic camera and displayed on a monitor, thus the surgeon has no stereoscopic view and looses depth perception in the operating field. Another drawback is that holding rigid and long shafted instruments and controlling them at a distance leads to higher fatigue and extremely limited tactile perception. Another severe disadvantage is that mirrored motions from that of the operating field are required, as instruments are pivoting about the incision point.

1.1 Robotic assisted minimal invasive surgery

An alternative to traditional minimal invasive surgery is robot assisted minimal invasive surgery. Many disadvantages of manual MIS are overcome with robotics:

- robot systems can emulate human hand motions without mirrored movements;
- additional degrees of freedom in the wrists are added increasing dexterity and improving instrument control;
- motion can be scaled and filtered enabling more precise motions within the patient;
- magnified 3D enhanced computer vision system provides a view of the operating site with greater clarity than open surgery (Camarillo et al., 2004).

State of the art robotic assisted surgery systems like the Da Vinci System (Intuitive Surgical, (California, USA) enable minimal invasive incisions thus offering a more conservative alternative to standard open surgery. Unfortunately, due to the lack of haptic force feedback, these systems can only be used in cases where the visual information is enough and haptic sensing is not needed (Wagner et al., 2002). Often surgeons and robotic researchers point out this fact as major limitation of robotic aided surgery (Mohr et al., 2001) (Cavasoglu et al., 2003).

A key element for enabling haptic force feedback robotic or computer assisted surgery are force sensorized tools:

"Smart medical tools" often stands for sensorized devices (Dario et al., 2003). One example are catheters with integrated pressure sensors (Strandman et al., 1997, Kalvesten et al., 1998, Melvås et al., 2002) which are mainly for diagnostic purposes, but not for surgical interventions except in the combination with so called balloon dilation for cardiac vessel expansion.

Sensorized microgrippers are described in (Houston et al., 2007). In these grippers micro strain gauges are integrated into the polymer arms, thus an accurate and precise gripping force monitoring and control is possible. On the basis of this gripper, an endoscopic tool for robotic aided surgery was developed (Houston et al., 2008) where a wire driven joint (Harada et al., 2005) allows rotation of the gripper.

Robotic aided surgical interventions where precise cutting tasks have to be performed are quite difficult - one main reason is again the lack of haptic force feedback. One approach to deal with this problem is to equip tools with Micro Electrical Mechanical Systems (MEMS) (Rebello, 2004). A force sensorized microsurgical tip is detailed in (Berkelman et al., 2003). A first prototype of a cutting blade based on a triaxial MEMS force sensor (Beccai et al., 2005) was presented in (Valdastri et al., 2005). With the help of an advanced assembly process (Sieber et al., 2007) the MEMS sensor could be directly mounted on a flexible substrate - which allowed a further miniaturization of the sensorized cutting device as detailed in (Valdastri et al., 2007).

1.2 Sensorized catheters

Another topic addressed in this chapter is the development of sensorized tools for catheter based minimal invasive surgery. One example of a smart catheter is the recently developed TactiCath® [Endosense, Switzerland]. It is an ablation catheter, that is equipped with a force sensor to provides real time contact force measures (Vijaykumar et al., 2011).

Especially during catheter navigation through thin vessels, that can easily be damaged, haptic force feedback can improve largely the safety of such interventions. A recent approach of a "smart tool", developed especially for treatment of pulmonary atresia

(Daubeney et al., 2005) using fetoscopy (Sydorak and Albanese, 2003), consists of a steerable and flexible catheter equipped with a fiber optic reflectance sensor for color detection, 4 electrodes for bio-impedance spectroscopy and a patented washing system (patent Sieber et al., 2007) to enable optical measurements in the presence of blood.

1.3 Haptic force feedback input devices

Next to force sensorized tools, haptic force feedback input devices are a key element for future computer aided surgery. One approach is to use visual force feeback. A study (Reiley et al., 2008) was carried out demonstrating that visual force feedback offers benefits like reduced suture breakage, lower forces, and decreased force inconsistencies; however it was concluded, that these benefits are mainly an advantage for novice robot-assisted surgeons and diminishing benefits among experienced surgeons.

Song et al. (2006) have developed a laboratory set up for haptic force feedback tele-operation consisting of a 6-DOF robot and a commercially available haptic force feedback input device (PHANTOM Omni). Forces on a tool (like a blade) were acquired with a 3DOF force sensor. A different group proposed to incorporate haptic force feedback into the ZEUS system by integrating a PHANTOM input device (Ortmaier et al., 2001). Another PHANTOM based system was discussed in (Tavakoli et al., 2003). In the PHANTOM haptic force feedback system, force feedback is generated with DC motors that apply a torque on the joints. Similar, but very simplified, technology is used in haptic force feedback joysticks for gaming, where the position of the joystick is acquired with 2 potentiometers and force feedback is generated by the torque of a DC motor.

For our work with the sensorized microgripper (Houston et al, 2011) we have developed a force feedback haptic tweezer. In contrast to the operating principle of the PHANTOM and haptic force feedback joysticks, the haptic tweezer is an active servo actuated tool, where the force on the tweezer is measured with a strain gauge and the tweezer is moved actively in a closed control loop. Advantages are precise movement control and low manufacturing costs. In the third part of this chapter a novel haptic force feedback joystick is described which derives from the haptic tweezer. The force on the joystick is measured with strain gauges and the joystick is actuated with servos in a control loop. The same principle can be used for designing low cost haptic input devices with 3 or more DOFs.

2. Methods

The methods section comprises three of our latest developments: a force sensorized cutting tool (described in Section 2.1), a steerable force sensorized catheter with haptic force feedback for fetoscopy (described in Section 2.2), and a novel joystick with haptic force feedback (described in Section 2.3) which can be used as haptic force feedback input device for the control of the sensorized cutting tool as well as the sensorized catheter.

2.1 Force sensorized cutting tool

Typical cutting forces in surgical interventions can reach values of up to ±3N for tangential and 10N for normal loadings. The device described in (Valdastri et al., 2005) uses a silicon-based MEMS sensor to measure forces on a cutting blade. The MEMS sensor deployed in the final prototype was designed for about one tenth of these forces, thus a kinematical chain was introduced to scale down the forces on the cutting blade to the MEMS force range.

Unfortunately the viscoelastic behavior of the polyurethane kinematical chain allowed repeatable results only for alternating loadings, but not for static ones. Moreover the limited force resolution of 50mN was not sufficient for a precise haptic force feedback. Additionally the tool turned out to be quite fragile: Applying strong tangential forces to the blade often resulted in a detachment of the blade support and breakage of the silicon structure. While further developments of that prototype are still ongoing, in parallel to that, a complete redesign of the force sensorized cutting tool was initiated with focus on:

- accurate and precise force readings;
- linear force readings over a wide force range;
- at least 10 times higher force resolution;
- high mechanical robustness.

The main idea behind the development of the novel tool is to design a mechanical structure from a strong and tough material (stainless steel) that deflects linearly when a normal or tangential force is applied in the required force range. On the support micro strain gauges are bonded, which allows the direct measurement of the elastic deflections of the structure thus simplifying the whole device. Thus a kinematical chain as in (Valdastri et al., 2005) can be avoided (the viscoelastic behavior of the kinematical chain was the main reason for inaccurate readings for static forces).

Figure 1a details the first design of the cutting tool. Mechanical simulations were carried out in Comsol Multyphysics (figure 1a) to calculate optimum dimensions, whilst keeping the overall size to a minimum and mechanical performance to a maximum. The most important criteria are that the sensor can function to a maximum load of ±3N tangential and ±20 N normal and that the force readings are linear and have low hysteresis. The first structure prototype parts were fabricated using micro-Wire-EDM from a plate of 400μm thick stainless steel.

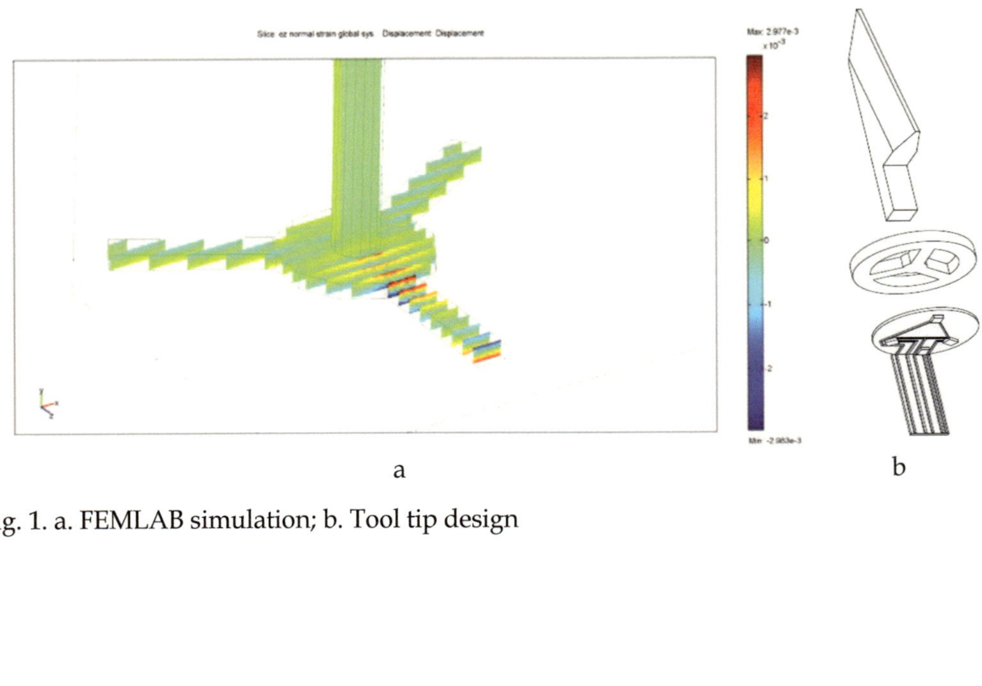

a b

Fig. 1. a. FEMLAB simulation; b. Tool tip design

After these parts were cut out and prepared the cutting blade is brazed to the stainless steel structure using a special holding fixture. The cutting blade used was a conventional scalpel blade cut with wire EDM to smaller dimensions, both to reduce the size of the overall tool and also to allow a proper fit to the other parts of the sensor. To measure the deflection of the 3 support arms, micro fabricated strain gauges from Vishay on a flexible substrate were then bonded to the structure with M-600 epoxy from Vishay. For assembly of the first prototype separate micro strain gauges were used to simplify the construction. These strain gauges were of an overall area of approximately 2mm x 2mm (contact pads included, foil grid of 380μm x 500 μm) and excess material was cut out to leave a strain gauge of approximately 450μm x 1000μm. In reality mass production requires an automatized industrial assembly process but for the first prototype the manual steps are sufficient. In the final design the three micro strain gauges are incorporated with the necessary connections on a common flexible substrate, which would make assembly much easier (figure 1b).

Once the strain gauges were mounted (Fig 2a) , the next step was to bond wires to the strain gauges by soldering and then set the wires so that they can be easily taken out of the tool for connection to a suitable connector. To house the sensor an aluminum tube of diameter 4mm was chosen. Recesses were machined into the top part of the tube to allow mounting of the sensor tip. The sensor tip is then carefully placed into the tube with all wires and then set into a fixture. The final step is to form the top lip of the aluminum tube over the sensor, thus partially closing the sensor and mechanically clamping it to the tube. For the prototype a manual fixture was used to close the structure but for a more automated approach with higher tolerances and overall quality a customized press would be necessary. A Polyoxymethylene (POM) support was developed for a first characterisation of the device (Fig 2b).

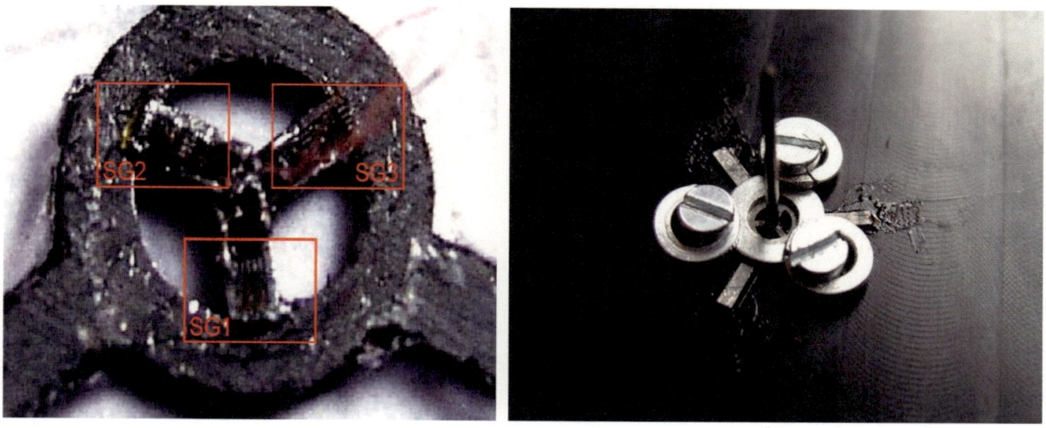

a b

Fig. 2. a. Micro strain gauges mounted on the steel structure; b. Demonstrator ready for characterisation

Figure 3 details the processing of the strain gauges (Rsg1, Rsg2 and Rsg3) in ¼ Wheatstone bridge configuration. A reference voltage of 2.5 V is generated with the two resistors Rref1 and Rref 2 with 10 kΩ each. Three potentiometers are integrated for offset removal.

For processing of the three analog channels a 24bit sigma delta AD converters [AD7730, Analog Devices] are used, which are with their programmable input range from 10mV to +-80 mV especially designed for sensor signal processing. Reference voltages as low as 1V are possible. Moreover a programmable digital filter can be used to suppress noise.

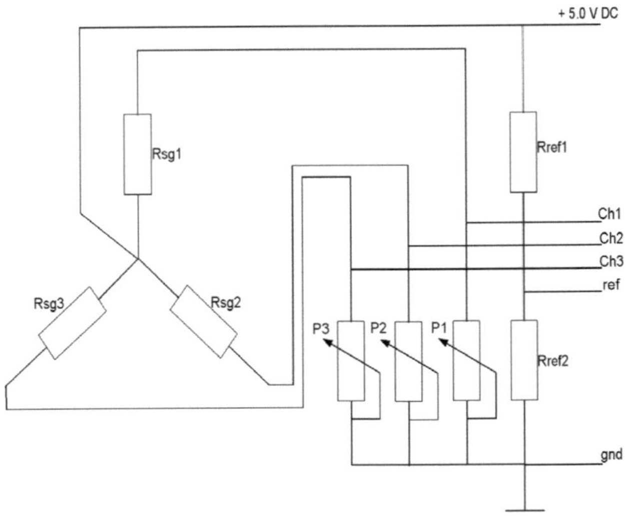

Fig. 3. Strain gauges in ¼ Wheatstone Bridge configuration

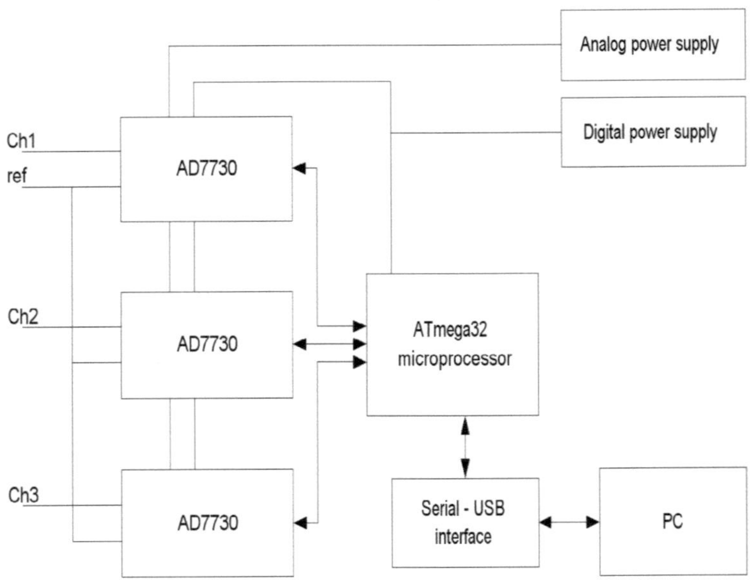

Fig. 4. Interfacing the AD converters

In a first prototype of the electronics the AD converters were directly connected to the parallel port of a PC and then interfaced with software developed in LabView 8.5 [National Instruments]. The software emulated serial peripheral interface did not perform flawlessly, thus in the final version (Fig 4) the three analog AD converters are interfaced to a 8 bit RISC microcontroller [Atmel, ATmega32] and then connected to the PC via a serial to USB interface [FT232, Future Technology Devices International Limited, United Kingdom]. The firmware for the microcontroller was developed in AVR Studio [Atmel] and the WinAVR GNU C Compiler. Measurement data are then processed and visualized with a GUI under LabView.

Several prototypes with various lengths (figure 5a, b and 6 a, b) were manufactured and characterized. In the following the main technical data of the prototypes are listed:

Length: 16mm (including support):
Diameter of the device: 4mm
Tangential forces: max ±3N, 4 mN resolution
Normal forces: max 20 N, 50 mN resolution

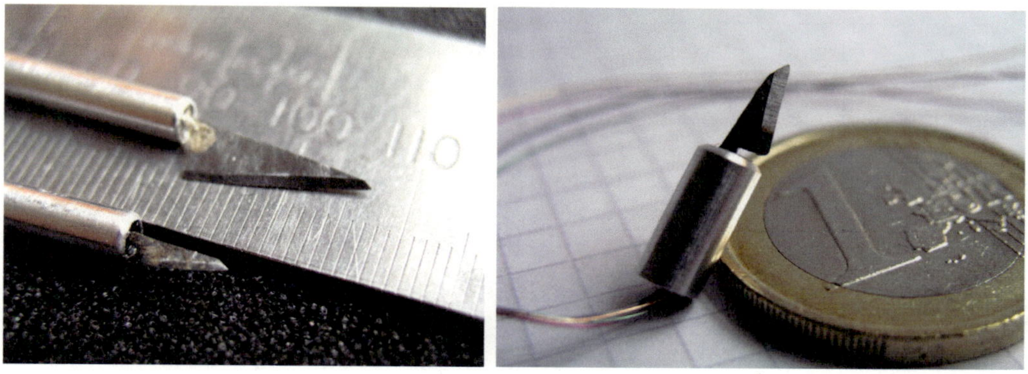

a b

Fig. 5. a. Prototypes with an overall length of 25 and 50mm including the support structure; b. Prototype of total length 20 mm

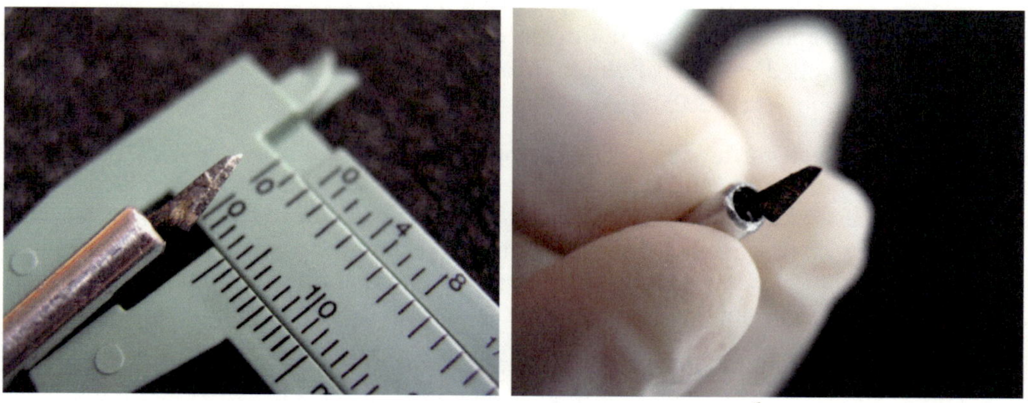

a b

Fig. 6. Final prototype has an outer diameter of 4 mm

In a first characterisation of the device the output signals were compared to the ones of a commercial available load cell in a setup similar to (Valdastri et al., 2007). The sensor gives linear readings of strain gauge output versus load. The sensor is also robust which is necessary for surgical applications. Its small size (4mm diameter) makes it suitable for robotic aided surgery.

2.2 Sensorized catheter

2.2.1 Introduction to fetoscopy

For a recently aborted fetus with diagnosed congenital malformation, continuation of the pregnancy until termination with a Cesarean delivery, change in timing mode, or place of delivery are the only three options available. Fetal surgery may provide a further solution in these cases. Open fetal surgery is state of the art (Harrison, 2003) (Berris and Shoham, 2006) and is already available in over a dozen clinical centers worldwide. Endoscopic fetal surgery, which is commonly referred as Fetoscopy (Sydorak and Albanese, 2003) is however a medical discipline that is still in its early development stages. Fetal surgery has given the possibility to treat some fetal congenital malformation in utero (diaphragmatic hernia, myelomeningocele, lower urinary tract obstruction).

The R&D of a surgical tool for interventions on the fetus during pregnancy requires highly advanced micro/nanotechnologies from the system integration point of view and a close collaboration with medical doctors to develop it according to their real needs. At present fetal surgery lacks purposely developed micro instrumentations because paediatric surgeons are trying to apply standard minimal invasive instruments to fetal surgery applications. These instruments are far too large for interventions like treatment of pulmonary atresia in such early stage and also do not offer capabilities such as tissue classification.

2.2.2 Pulmonary atresia

During pregnancy the oxygen necessary is not supplied through the fetal lungs but by the placenta. The Foramen Ovale is an opening between the right and the left atrium, that allows blood to pass by the ventricles. After birth this opening is usually closed. Pulmonary Atresia is a malfunction that may appear during pregnancy: it is an incorrectly developed pulmonary valve. Instead of a valve there is just a membrane. Thus no blood supply to the lungs is possible, and this causes the death of newborns when oxygen supplied by the placenta is not supplied anymore. Pulmonary atresia occurs in about one out of every 20,000 live births. (Daubeney et al., 2005) (Litovsky et al., 2005)

Anatomic obstruction to the right or left ventricular outflow tract may cause ventricular dysfunction, can divert fetal blood flow in the uterus and result in cardiac chamber hyperplasia. Thus severe aortic or pulmonary stenosis can result in a hypoplastic left or right ventricle with an inability for the ventricular chambers to support the systemic or pulmonary circulation. Theoretically early relief of the fetal aortic or pulmonary stenosis may prevent such occurrence and might preserve the right or left ventricular function .

Pulmonary atresia can be diagnosed in the 12-14th week of gestation. The surgical intervention should be performed as soon as possible. In the 14th week the fetus size is about 9-14cm and has a weight in the range of 60 - 200g. In this development stage the pulmonary membrane has a diameter of approximately 1mm.

In the case of pulmonary atresia an early surgical intervention is the only alternative to abortion and could allow normal development of the pulmonary valve and the right ventricle. A suitable surgical procedure for the treatment of pulmonary atresia is by accessing the right ventricle with a steerable micro catheter, identifying the pulmonary valve/membrane and then perforating it. However one must consider that tissues in this early development state are very fragile and can be damaged easily, thus haptic force feedback is a important safety feature in order to avoid to damage to the vessels or the heart when navigation the catheter, which would be life threatening for the fetus.

2.2.3 Catheter design

The catheter prototype is fabricated from polyurethane with a flexible end of 40 mm length and an outer diameter of 3,5 mm. The diameter of the main inner lumen is 2,5 mm . Four 380 µm thin lumen are integrated in the wall (thickness: 550 µm) and serve as guidance for four Bowden cables. A micromachined tip (Fig 7a and 7b) fabricated from Polyether Ether Ketone (PEEK) is bonded to the flexible end of the catheter and mainly acts as a support for four impedance measurement electrodes and two optical fibers. Furthermore it offers a main channel leading to the inner lumen of the catheter. This inner lumen serves as a supply of washing solution (physiological saline solution).

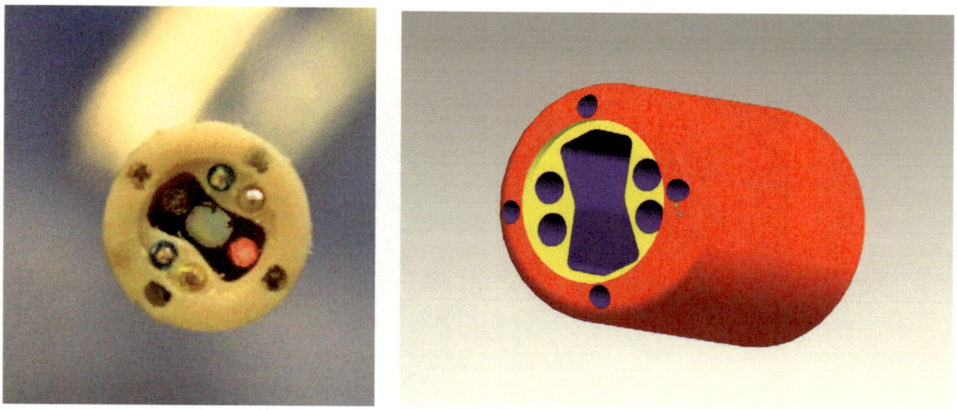

a b

Fig. 7. a. Catheter tip prototype; b. Catheter tip 3D model

To be able to reach the point of interest, the catheter needs to be equipped with steering capabilities. The multi lumen catheter consists of a very flexible ending and a less flexible part. In the walls of the catheter four lumen are integrated, each one for one steering wire. Such wires are usually referred as Bowden cables. Pulling on these four wires and releasing at the same time the wire which is on the opposite side in the catheter will primarily result in a bending movement of the flexible end part of the catheter. Two microcontroller driven servo drives are used to pull and release the wires. This microcontroller is then connected to a personal computer, which is equipped with a haptic force feedback joystick allowing a precise control of the catheter. A third degree of freedom is realized by either manually or servo supported driving the catheter forward and backwards. The arm on the servo controller, which is actuating the Bowden wire is equipped with a strain gauge, which allows measurement of the actuation forces on the Bowden wire. As the actuation force reflects the force required to bend the catheter tip, it also reflects a force on the catheter tip itself, thus it can be used for haptic force feedback. For the readout of the strain gauges a similar circuit, but just with two AD converters, like described in 2.1, figure 4 was used. Figure 8 shows the first prototype of the catheter controlled by a commercial joystick.

For electrical characterisation of tissues in front of the sensors an electrical impedance sensor was integrated. Bio-impedance spectroscopy allows tissue classification and identification by recording and analyzing the electrical impedance at different frequencies. From the electrical point of view cell membranes behave like capacitors. In comparison to low frequency electrical current where the current path is leading mainly through extra cellular fluid, high frequency electrical current is able to penetrate the cells. Thus impedance over frequency and phase over frequency plots (or both combined in "Wessel plots") are characteristics of tissues as they reflect the electrical characteristics of the cells and the tissue composition. Principle Component Analysis can then be used to classify a tissue by a recorded data set. For impedance spectroscopy two or four electrodes configuration are state of the art. Four electrodes impedance measurement allows higher accuracy, as two electrodes are used to drive in the electrical current and the other two, which are normally arranged in between the first two ones, are used for measuring the voltage drop, so called four probe measurements. The electrical contact impedance (usually current dependent) of the two voltage sensing electrodes can when be neglected, as the sensing input of impedance meter is high - so there is almost no current flowing.

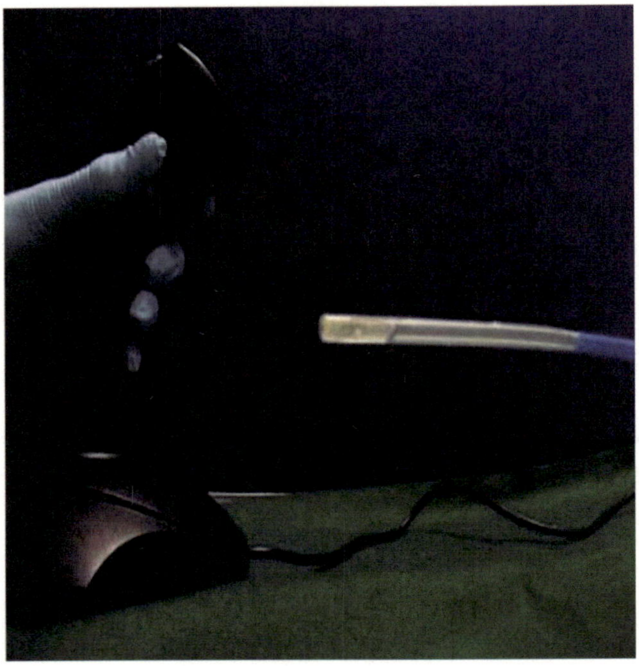

Fig. 8. Operation of the steerable catheter tip

In comparison to the four electrodes measurement technique the two electrodes configuration has the disadvantage of sensing the voltage through the same electrodes which are used to drive the electrical current. The recordings therefore show tissue impedance in serial with the electrode impedances. A two electrode configuration has the advantage of needing less space, which is an important aspect in designing a miniaturized catheter. Furthermore the two electrodes configuration can be divided into a small electrode on the tip of the catheter and a large area counter electrode which is attached to the body.

The recorded impedance spectrum is then mainly defined by the electrical impedance characteristics of the tissue exactly in front of the small sensing electrode. This electrode configuration is especially interesting from the miniaturisation point of view, as the centre electrode could then also be used for radio frequency cutting needed for the perforation of the pulmonary membrane.

It must be kept in mind that for tissue classification it is not necessary to record accurate impedance data from the electrical point of view. It is important that the training data sets are recorded with the same electrode configuration to give comparable recordings.

Even if a two electrode configuration may be suitable for tissue classification, four electrodes are integrated in the peek tip of this first catheter prototype so that two and four electrodes configurations can be compared to each other. In the test setup a TEGAM 3550 LCR Meter is used to record impedance data. It is connected to a Personal Computer through a GPIB link.

Another way of characterisation of tissues is optical spectroscopy. Therefore two optical fibers were integrated in the front of the catheters tip. A suitable light source illuminates the tissue with light guided to the point of interest through an optical fiber. Reflected light is then received with a second fiber leading to an optical spectrophotometer. The spectral range must be chosen according to the ranges where the tissues have characteristic reflectance spectra.

In normal conditions the heart is filled with blood. Haemoglobin is a strong light absorber, where the wavelength dependent light absorption is furthermore dependent on the oxygenation status of haemoglobin. Measuring tissue characteristics in such an environment with a spectrophotometric method is not possible. The solution for this problem was solved with the integration of another lumen in the catheter to provide washing solution. With a small amount of physiological saline solution blood in front of the catheters tip can be washed away. Blood in the measuring zone is thus substituted with the optical clear washing solution, which enables spectrophotometric reflectance measurement.

Impedance spectrum recording and spectrophotometric spectrum recording requires steady state conditions - the tissue in front of the catheter should not move relatively to the catheter, which is difficult to realize in a beating heart environment. To solve this problem the washing system describes above can be used in a second way: After the blood is washed away with a small amount of physiological washing solution, the washing solution pump will be used to suck in washing solution thus creating suction in front of the catheter which will suck the tissue in front of the catheter to the tip thus establishing a reliable electrical connection to the electrode(s) and steady conditions for the measurements. A differential pressure sensor is integrated to allow precise suction force control.

Once tissue is classified as "pulmonary valve tissue" the perforation of the membrane is the next step. In this case an electrode is used for RF cutting. This electrode can either be a separate electrode or one of the impedance electrodes on the catheters tip. For this task a tissue fixation as described above is also a great advantage, as it allows a safe and controlled perforation in a quasi-static environment. Figure 9 shows the principle function of the catheter for electrical and optical tissue characterisation

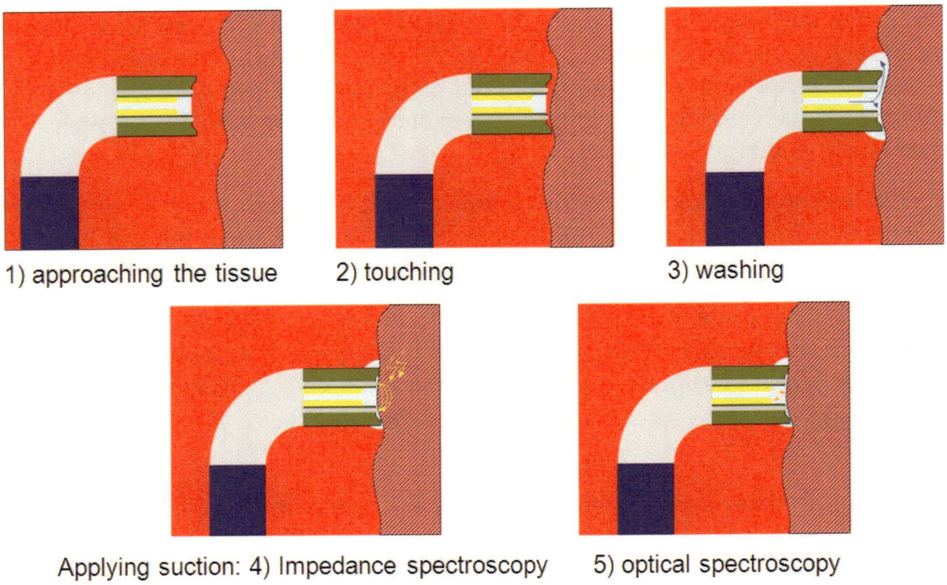

Fig. 9. Multifunctional catheter tip for impedance and optical spectroscopy with integrated suction fixature

2.3 Research and development of a haptic force feedback joystick

In the first instance, the steerable catheter described in 2.2. was actuated with a commercial available low cost force feedback joystick. This kind of joysticks is typically used for playing computer games like flight simulators to achieve a more realistic gaming experience. The position of the joystick is sensed with potentiometers and haptic force feedback is generated by DC motors. An interface was developed under National Instruments Labview to read in the joystick coordinates and to apply forces with the DC motors. First tests revealed that the precision of the force feedback motors is rather insufficient and cannot be precisely controlled and the maximum torque is rather low. A precise force feedback comparable to operator experiences when using an expensive haptic input device like the Phantom is not possible with this kind of joystick.

For the control of the catheter a device is necessary that allows:

- precise control of the force feedback
- force feedback torques up to 1 Nm
- fast control to allow smooth force feedback to the operator
- smooth movement without binding
- "intelligent" control of feedback to give the right "feel"

2.3.1 Sensor / actuator design approach

Previously we have developed a haptic tweezer for force feedback microgripping. Different from devices like the PHANTOM of the previously tested commercial force feedback joysticks, where the position of the inpout device is sensed and then a torque/force is applied with a motor, forces on the microgripper are sensed with strain gauges and the tweezer arms are actively moved with a microservo. The closed loop control does not only allow a precise control of the forces excerted by the haptic tweezer to the fingers, but also the behavior of the device can be programmed. In the easiest form, the "virtual" spring constants of the tweezer can be set.

The main idea for the R&D of our force feedback joystick was to use the same sensing/actuation principle we used for the haptic tweezer for a device with more DOFs. A first 1DOF demonstrator was built consisting of a high torque servo and a 12 cm PEEK handle mounted on the servo actuator. The diameter of the handle was 12mm, but reduced to a square profile of 5x5 mm^2 in a 15mm long section close to the *axis of rotation of the handle* in the high strain area. Here 2 strain gauges were positioned in this area.

A microcontroller (Atmel ATmega32L) was used to read out the strain gauges and control the servo. A closed loop control was implemented allowing to

- read in the signal on the strain gauges
- calculate the actuation torque
- compare the actuation torque with the position and the force feedback model (like for example a spring model)
- set the servo position

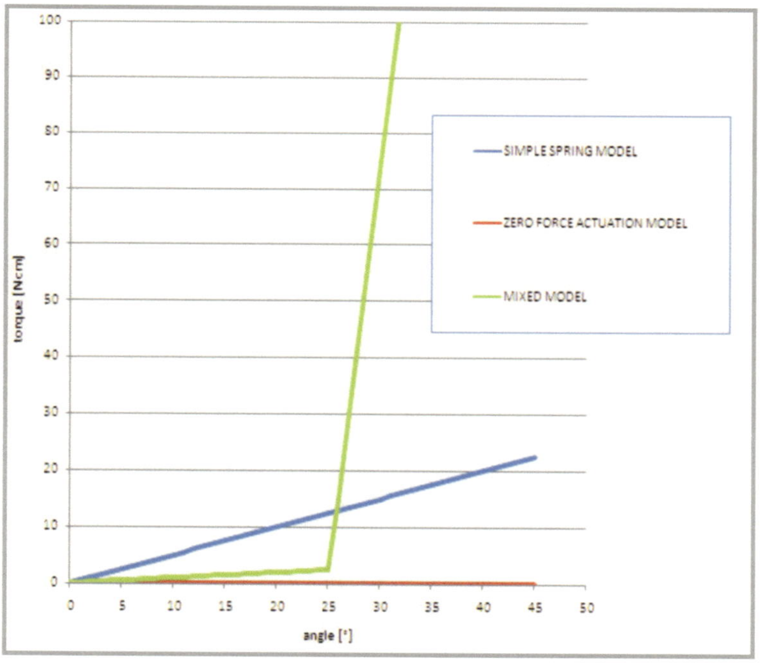

Fig. 10. Torque on the handle of the actuator

Simple scenarios were successfully tested, including the simple spring model (the torque on the handle increases with the angle), zero force actuation (a minimum force is required to move the handle) and mixtures of both. The latter was especially important as it reflects the requirements for the catheter control. When the catheter tip is freely moving without touching, zero actuation force is used. Alternatively, one might consider to program a low spring constant to move the joystick back to central position when released. When at a certain angle the catheter touches for instance a wall, a force is sensed in the bowden wires. This force signal is then used to generate a force feedback signal. Figure 10 shows the torques applied by the servo motor in these 3 scenarios. In the simple spring model the torque is directly dependent on the angle (0.5 N cm/°). In the zero actuation force model practically no force is required to move the handle. If the handle is released, it stays at the last position. In the mixed model, a low spring constant was programmed for 0-25°, above that a spring constant of 10Ncm/° was implemented to simulate touching. If the handle is released, it returns to the central position.

2.3.2 Design of the force feedback joystick

Fig.11 shows a CAD plot of the original prototype design. Principal design objectives were that the device should be low cost therefore plastics were extensively used, only the actual control stick (#5) is made of (metal) aluminium. The other parts shown in Fig.11 (support brackets #2,3,6 , base plate #3) are made of POM. Parts 1 & 6 are digital servo motors (GRAUPNER DS8311) and were specifically chosen for their durability (metal bearings), precision (13 bit), compactness and high torque output (112 Ncm @ 6V supply) values.

To enable force sensing and closed loop force feedback 4 strain gauges are placed at the base of the control stick (Part #8) which will allow the force felt by the user in the X & Y axes to be measured. Screws and bearings as well as the electronic control board (integrated into the base plate) are not shown. The base plate has dimensions 140mm x 140mm.

The idea of the haptic force feedback joystick was now to add another pair of strain gauges and add a second servo actuator for force feedback on the second axis.

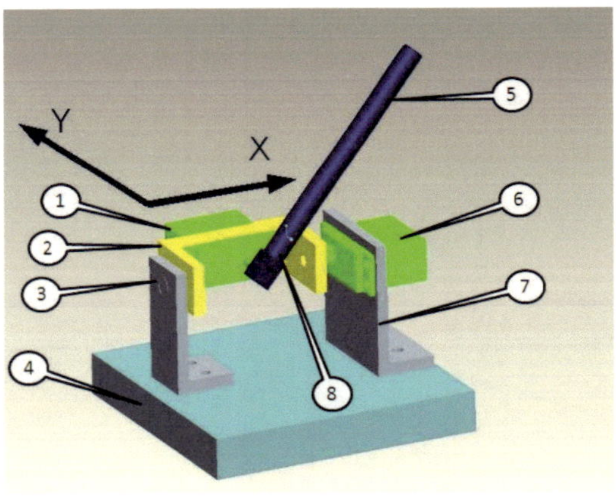

Fig. 11. CAD design of prototype joystick

Fig. 12a shows the fabricated prototype being tested by a user. All plastic parts were milled from stock POM material while the control stick was turned and then the surfaces for the strain gauges were milled flat. The strain gauges are protected from damage by a rigid plastic cover (#2). Note the servo control cables leading from the servos to the control board under the base plate (#1). Fig. 12b shows a larger view of the sensorized control stick (plastic cover removed) with the 4 strain gauges (#1-4) and the electrical connector (#5).

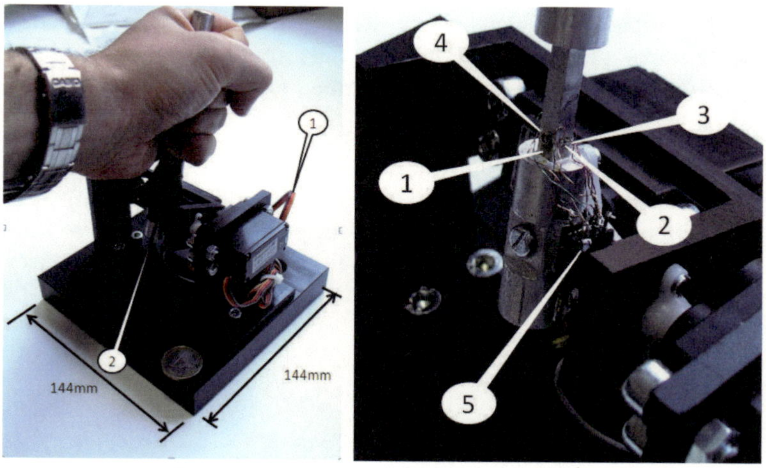

a b

Fig. 12. a. Fabricated joystick prototype; b. Strain gauges and connector on control stick

Fig.13a shows the electronic control board which is fixed in a cavity under the base plate. This cavity was milled out of the bottom of the base plate. The control system purpose is to control the servo motors to give a resistive force to the user which is determined by the hand movements of the user and the control algorithms used by the microcontroller to vary the user experience. The strain gauges are in a Wheatstone bridge configuration and the differential voltages are fed to the voltage amplifiers (2 x AD623, #3). The amplified voltages (which represent the resistive force felt by the user) are processed by the ATMEL ATmega32 microcontroller (#2) which through a specific algorithm then send digital commands to the servo motors (#4) to continually adjust this force. The force sensed by the user and the position of the control stick in both X & Y axes can be communicated to a PC by the microcontroller. The microcontroller transmits the data to the RS232 chip (#1) which communicates to the external device connected to #6 with the RS232 protocol. The board is powered with a regulated 6V supply connected at #5.

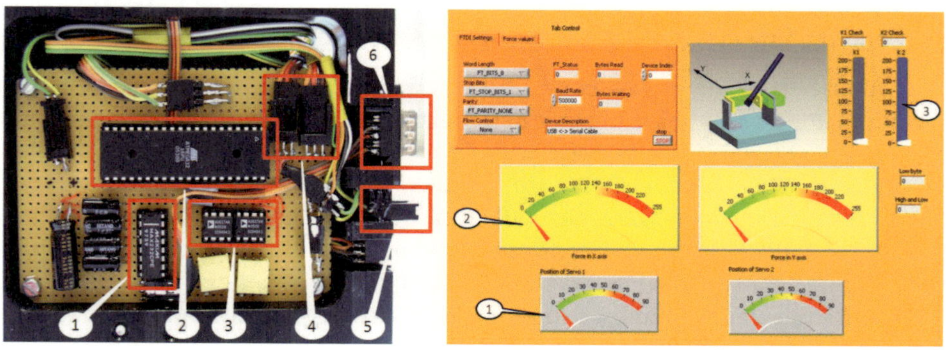

a b

Fig. 13. a. Electronic control board; b. Graphical User Interface

Fig.13b shows a PC user interface developed using Labview which was used to test the performance of the input device in registering both control stick position (#1) and force (#2) and also using the PC interface to change the stiffness (resistance) of the control stick sensed by the user. Only simple trials were performed with linear spring constants to vary the stiffness of the control stick but for future trials more advanced algorithms will be programmed to also feedback non-linear and damped forces to the user.

A second prototype was designed with the aim of further reducing the size of the input device. Fig.14 shows the CAD design of the second prototype which has a base plate dimension reduced from 140 x 140 mm^2 to 84 x 84 mm^2 (40% reduction). The same servos will be used in a different configuration and the supporting brackets have been modified to make more efficient use of space. The material for all load bearing parts (base plate, brackets, control stick) will be aluminium to make the design more robust but will also slightly increase the manufacturing costs.

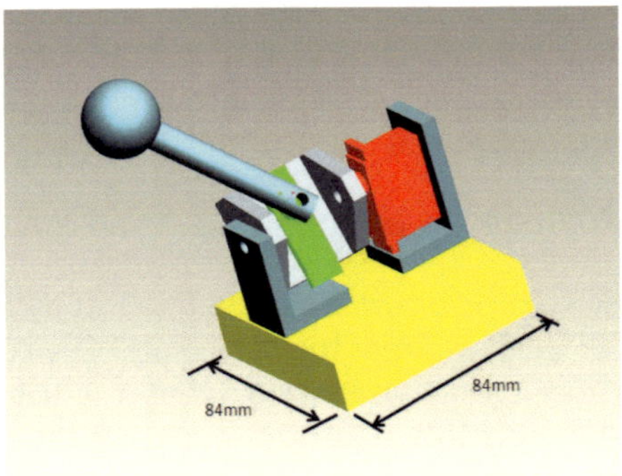

Fig. 14. CAD model of second prototype with 40% size reduction

3. Conclusion

The sensorized surgical blade, with its large force range and high resolution, is perfectly suitable for minimal invasive surgery and has the potential to lead to a new generation of endoscopic tools for robotic aided surgery capable also of providing precise and accurate haptic force feedback. The tool can withstand a normal load of 20N and a tangential load of 3N without damage to the structure. At the same time, it is possible to perform sensitive touching and probing movements with high force sensitivity down to the mN range.

In applications where the crucial point of the surgical intervention is not accessible with rigid manipulators, a steerable catheter can be helpful. A novel device was developed that is equipped with a steerable tip, but also with an electrical and an optical sensor system for tissue characterisation. The catheter tip is steered by a joystick. First insertion and navigation tests in phantoms were successfully carried out. The current catheter diameter is 3.5mm, but for applications in severe cases like pulmonary atresia, a further miniaturisation to an outer diameter of 0.8mm is necessary and still feasible. Forces on the bowden wires are detected with strain gauges and used to generate haptic force feedback.

Commercial available force feedback joysticks turned out not to be precise enough for haptic sensing, thus a prototype device was developed to satisfy these additional requirements. Differently from existing force feedback input devices, where the position is sensed and then a torque is applied by a motor, in this device the force is first sensed and then the position of the joystick is set according to the programmed force/angle model within a closed loop control. A design for a second prototype joystick with reduced dimensions and improved electronics was also presented. Based on the same force sensing/control approach a further development of an haptic input device with 3 or more DOF is possible, which can be a low cost alternative to devices like the Phantom.

Force sensorized tool and haptic force feedback input devices for surgical interventions are still in early development stages and only few devices are already used in surgical interventions, but latest developments are promising. These novel devices have the potential to revolutionize robotic aided surgery, as the can be considered as key elements to regain the sensation of feeling tissues in a robot dominated surgical scenario.

4. Acknowledgment

The work described in this paper was supported by the ASSEMIC project, Marie Curie Research & Training Network (MRTN-CT- 2003-504826). Currently Arne Sieber is funded through the Marie Curie Project Lifeloop (EU FP7-People-IEF-2008, project nr. 237128). A special mention to Mr. C. Filippeschi for his continuous and invaluable help.

5. References

Beccai, L., Roccella, S., Arena, A., Valvo, F., Valdastri, P., Menciassi, A., Carrozza, M.C., Dario, P. (2005) Design and fabrication of a hybrid silicon three-axial force sensor for biomechanical applications. Sensors and Actuators A, 120, 2005, pp. 370–382.

Berkelman, P.J., Whitcomb, L.L., Taylor, R.H., Jensen, P. (2003) A miniature microsurgical instrument tip force sensor for enhanced force feedback during robotassisted manipulation, 2003, pp. 917–922.

Berris, M., Shoham, M. (2006). Febotics - a marriage of fetal surgery and robotics, Computer Aided Surgery, July 2006; 11(4): 175–180

Camarillo, D.B., Krummel, T.M., Salisbury, L.K. (2004). Robotic technology in surgery: past, present, and future. Am. J. Surg., 188(4A):2S–15S, 2004.

Cavusoglu, M.C., Williams, W., Tendick, F., Sastry, S.S. (2003) Robotics for telesurgery: Second generation berkeley/ucsf laparoscopic telesurgical workstation and looking towards the future applications. Ind. Rob., 30(1):22–29, 2003.

Dario, P., Hannaford, B., Menciassi, A. (2003). Smart surgical tools and augmenting devices. IEEE Trans. Robot. Automat., 19(5), 2003., pp. 782–792.

Daubeney, P.E.F., Wang, D., Delany, D.J., Keeton, B.R., Anderson, R.H., Slavik, Z., Flather, M., Webber, S.A. (2005), Pulmonary atresia with intact ventricular septum: predictors of early and medium-term outcome in a population-based study. J Thorac Cardiovasc Surg 2005; 130:1071.

Harada, K., Tsubouchi, K., Fujie, M.G., Chiba, T. (2005). Micro Manipulators for Intrauterine Fetal Surgery in an Open MRI, Proceedings of the 2005 IEEE International Conference on Robotics and Automation Barcelona, Spain, 2005

Harrison, M.R. (2003). Fetal Surgery: Trials, Tribulations, and Turf, Journal of Pediatrics Surgery, 2003, Vol. 38, pp. 275-282.

Houston, K., Sieber, A., Eder, C., Menciassi, A., Dario, P. (2008). Novel Haptic Tool and Input Device for Bilateral Biomanipulation addressing Endoscopic Surgery, Biodevices 2008, Funchal, Portugal, 2008

Houston, K., Sieber, A., Eder, C., Tonet, O., Menciassi, A., Dario, P. (2007). Novel Haptic Tool and Input Device for Real Time Bilateral Biomanipulation addressing Endoscopic Surgery, EMBC 2007, Lyon, France, 2007

Houston, K., Sieber, A., Eder, C., Vittorio, O., Menciassi, A., Darion, P., (2011), A Teleoperation System with Novel Haptic Device for Micro-Manipulation, International Journal of Robotics & Automation, Vol. 26, No. 3, 2011

Kalvesten, E., Smith, L., Tenerz, L., Stemme, G.,. The first surface micromachined pressure sensor for cardiovascular pressure measurements, MEMS 98. Proceedings., The Eleventh Annual International Workshop on Micro Electro Mechanical Systems, 1998, Page(s): 574 - 579

Litovsky, S., Choy, M., Park, J., Parrish, M., Waters, B., Nagashima, M., Praagh, R.V., Praag, S.V. (2000), Absent pulmonary valve with tricuspid atresia or severe tricuspid stenosis: report of three cases and review of the literature., Pediatr Dev Pathol 3(4), 353--366.

Melvås, P., Kälvesten, E., Enoksson, P.,Stemme, G. A free-hanging strain-gauge for ultraminiaturized pressure sensors, Sensors and Actuators A: Physical, Volumes 97-98, 1 April 2002, Pages 75-82

Mohr, F.W., Falk, V., Diegeler, A., Walther, T., Gummert, J.F., Bucerius, J., Jacobs, S., Autschbach, R. (2001). Computer-enhanced "robotic" cardiac surgery: Experience in 148 patients. J. Thor. Cardio. Surg., 121(5):842–853, 2001.

Ortmaier, T., Reintsema, D., Seibold, U., Hagn, U., Hirzinger, G. (2001) The DLR minimally invasive robotivs surgery scenario. Workshop on Advances in Interactive Multimodal Telepresence Systems, Munich, Germany, March 2001

Rebello K. (2004). Applications of MEMS in surgery. Proc. IEEE, 92(1), 2004., pp. 43–55

Reiley, C.E., Akinbiyi, T., Burschka, D., Chang, D.C., Okamura, A.M., Yuh, D.D. (2008) Effects of visual force feedback on robot-assisted surgical task performance. Thorac Cardiovasc Surg 2008;135:196-202

Sieber, A., Valdastri, P., Houston, K., Menciassi, A., Dario, P. (2007) Flip Chip Microassembly of a Triaxial Force Sensor on Flexible Substrates, Journal of Sensors and Actuators, 2007

Song, G., Guo, S., Wang, Q. (2006), A Tele-operation system based on haptic feedback. Proceedings of the 2006 IEEE International Conference on Information Acquisition August 20 - 23, 2006, Weihai, Shandong, China

Strandman, C., Smith, L., Tenerez, L., Hoek, B. (1997). A production process of silicon sensor elements for a fibre- optic pressure sensor. Sensors and Actuators A, 63(1), 1997., pp. 69–74

Sydorak, R.M., Albanese, C.T. (2003). Minimal access techniques for fetal surgery, World J Surg, 2003, Vol. 27, pp. 95–102.

Tavakoli, M., Patel, R.V., Moallem, M. (2003) A Force Reflective Master- Slave System for Minimally Invasive Surgery. Proceedings of the 2003 IEEE/RSJ Intl. Conference on Intelligent Robots and Systems, Las Vegas, Nevada, 2003.

Valdastri, P., Sieber, A., Houston, K., Menciassi, A., Dario, P., Ynangihara, M., Fujie, M. (2007) Miniaturized Cutting Tool With Triaxial Force Sensing Capabilities for Minimally Invasive Surgery. ASME Journal of Medical Devices, Sept. 2007

Valdastri, P., Harada, K., Menciassi, A., Beccai, L., Stefanini, C., Fujie, M., Dario, P. (2005) Integration of a miniaturised three axial force sensor in a minimally invasive surgical tool, IEEE Trans. Biomed. Eng, 2005

Vijaykumar, R., Locke, A.H., Kralovec, S., Neuzil, P., Fonck, E., Harari, D., Reddy, VZ.(2011) Spatiotemporal Distribution of Catheter-Tissue Contact Force across the Left Atrium during Pulmonary Vein solation, Heart Rhythm Society, San Fransisco, CA, PO6-85, May 2011

Wagner C.R., Stylopoulos, N., Howe, R.D. (2002). Proc. of the tenth symposium on haptic interfaces for virtual environment and teleopertator systems, 2002, pp73-79

8

Haptic Device System for Upper Limb and Cognitive Rehabilitation – Application for Development Disorder Children

Yoshiyuki Takahashi[1] et al.*
Toyo University, Tokyo, Japan

1. Introduction

A rehabilitation system using mechatronics, virtual reality can provide interactive therapy that engages the user's interest. It can also offer a simple and flexible environmental setup with precise recursive training and can gather training data at the same time. Several kinds of virtual reality applications are currently available in this field. For example, MIT-MANUS, MIME (Mirror Image Movement Enabler), Assisted Rehabilitation and Measurement (ARM) Guide, and a rehabilitation training system using an electrorheological actuator. Current research is primarily focused on providing effective rehabilitation of adult users. However, users of rehabilitation systems also include children. According to occupational therapists, therapy for developmentally disabled children should include a variety of training and typically requires hand-eye coordination because this is an important skill for school.

Currently, most conventional rehabilitation programs tend to be repetitive. Therefore, children are difficult for users to stay motivated while improving impaired functions. Nevertheless, several methods are available to evaluate the level of disability. These assessments are largely based on the therapist's subjective observations. Moreover, sometimes the result depends on the quality of therapy and the experience of the therapist. Therefore, it is necessary to measure, analyze, and evaluate the user's performance in objective and quantitative terms.

To solve these problems and meet specific requirements, we developed a rehabilitation system using a haptic device that integrates both motion and sensory therapy. The system is designed to maintain the user's interest during the rehabilitation activity. To evaluate the

* Yuko Ito[2], Kaoru Inoue[2], Yumi Ikeda[2], Tasuku Miyoshi[3], Takafumi Terada[4], Ho kyoo Lee[5], and Takashi Komeda[6]
[2] *Tokyo Metropolitan University, Japan*
[3] *Iwate University, Japan*
[4] *Mitsubishi Precision Co., Ltd., Japan*
[5] *Hyogo Institute of Assistive Technology, Japan*
[6] *Shibaura Institute of Technology, Japan*

system and gather basic data for quantitative evaluation of the levels of disorders, we carried out experiments with healthy child subjects.

In this paper, an outline of our developed haptic device system is introduced and experiments on the interactions of kindergarten children with this system are described. It was found that the proposed system effectively performed hand-eye coordination training.

2. Research background

For children with a development disorder, occupational therapy is usually performed. Occupational therapy for such children includes a variety of different therapies with many evaluation methods either proposed or existing. A suitable therapy provides individual therapy to treat the level of the disorder and the age of the child.

In the therapy for young children, the goal is to prepare them for elementary school. Of course, preparation requires many different actions. Occupational therapy is mainly focused on obtaining handwriting skills and self-reliance in daily life. Thus, the goals of therapy are enabling development of dexterous hand and visual perception. This means that hand-eye coordination is important.

In occupational therapy, many different tools are used, for example, toys, musical instruments, paper projects, mazes, and puzzles. Most of these tools are readily available in retail markets. Also, some are handmade by the therapist. These tools are used not only for therapy but also for evaluation the level of disorder. However, the evaluation of the effects are mostly based on the therapist's subjective observations and conventional pen-paper tests. At the present time, evidence-based occupational therapy is desirable. Therefore, establishment of quantitative evaluation methods are required. To meet this need, we apply computer technology and virtual reality to conventional therapy.

Additionally, therapists are interested in how to motivate patients and maintain the motivation for both children and adults. Virtual reality devices offering visual and sound experiences provide tactile and haptic sensations, which are interesting for patients, especially young patients. Therefore, we developed an effective haptic device system with training software that provides a haptic sensation on a hand grip held by the user. The sensation generated depends on the visual program.

3. Haptic device system

3.1 Hardware system

Our haptic device system is intended for upper-limb rehabilitation. Fig. 1 shows a photograph of the proposed haptic device system. The system consists of a haptic device, a display, and a computer. The haptic device consists of two servomotors with reduction gears, link rods, a hand grip, and a flat panel. The grip and servomotors are connected by link rods. Patients can move the grip on the surface of the flat panel and train their upper-limb movements in horizontal.

The haptic device and the computer are connected by a USB interface. The moving range is 400 mm in the lateral direction and 250 mm in the longitudinal direction. The servomotors can apply a maximum force of 30 N to the grip. Optical encoders are attached to the servomotors. The position of the grip is calculated by the encoder pulse count and the length of the link rods. The LCD display shows the visual symbols of the training programs. The aspect ratio of the work field on the display is proportional to the actual flat panel. Advantages of the haptic device are ease of handling and portability in a hospital or a home. In this model, the user only needs to plug in the USB connector to a PC and run the training program. The computer executes the following functions:

- Controlling the haptic device
- Displaying the training program
- Acquiring the training data
- Evaluating the training result

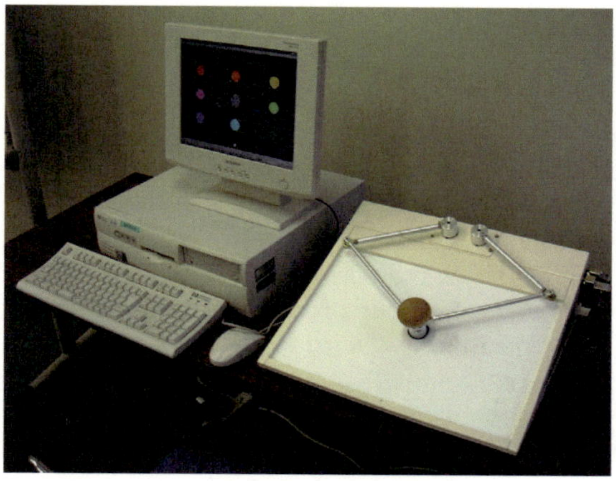

Fig. 1. Haptic device system

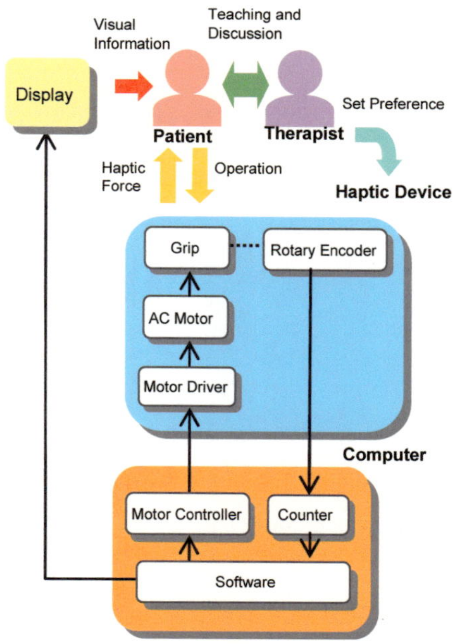

Fig. 2. Flow of the haptic device system

3.2 Haptic force generation

Six types of haptic forces can be provided on the rehabilitation system: load, assistance, spring, viscosity, friction, and special effects. The therapist can change the type and magnitude of the haptic force according to the user's level of disorder. The details of each force are described as follows.

1. Load: The load force is generated in the opposite direction of the grip velocity vector. The magnitude of the force increases in proportion to the distance between the current grip position and the target position. Load force F_l is shown in (1). When the grip position is (x, y), the target position is (x_0, y_0) and the gain is K_1.

$$F_l = \begin{bmatrix} F_{lx} \\ F_{ly} \end{bmatrix} = K_l \left(\begin{bmatrix} x_0 \\ y_0 \end{bmatrix} - \begin{bmatrix} x \\ y \end{bmatrix} \right) \qquad (1)$$

2. Assistance: The assistance force is generated in the same direction as the grip velocity vector. The magnitude of the force increases in proportion to the distance between the current grip position and the target position. The assistance force F_a is the same as the force in (1), except the gain is replaced by K_a.
3. Spring: The spring force is generated in the direction of the initial grip position. The magnitude of the force increases in proportion to the distance between the current position and the initial position of the grip. The spring force F_s is the same as the force in (1), except the gain is replaced by K_s.
4. Viscosity: The viscosity force is generated in the opposite direction of the grip velocity vector. The magnitude of the force increases in proportion to the velocity of the grip. The viscosity force F_v is shown in (2). The gain is K_v.

$$F_v = \begin{bmatrix} F_{vx} \\ F_{vy} \end{bmatrix} = K_v \begin{bmatrix} \dot{x} \\ \dot{y} \end{bmatrix} \qquad (2)$$

5. Friction: The friction force is generated in the opposite direction of the grip velocity vector. The magnitude of the force is constant. The friction force F_f is given as shown in (3). The gain is K_f.

$$F_f = \begin{bmatrix} F_{fx} \\ F_{fy} \end{bmatrix} = K_f \begin{bmatrix} \dfrac{\dot{x}}{|\dot{x}|} \\ \dfrac{\dot{y}}{|\dot{y}|} \end{bmatrix} \qquad (3)$$

6. Special effect: The special effect force F_e is generated especially in game programs (e.g., the contact force of the pieces of the puzzle and the reaction force when hitting some object).

Therefore, the total haptic force on grip F is the sum of the above six forces, as shown in (4).

$$F = F_l + F_a + F_s + F_v + F_f + F_e \qquad (4)$$

A haptic force other than the above can be generated by easy modification of a program.

4. Software for rehabilitation and evaluation

The software has two functionalities: training and evaluation. The training program consists of six different programs. The evaluation program consists of four different programs. When moving the grip, the cursor on the display simultaneously moves with the grip, and the haptic device provides a force that can either assist the movement of the arm or work against it. The level and the direction of the force are also adjustable. Moreover, the user can sense haptic perceptions such as contact force, viscosity, and surface friction. The data acquisition program runs with both programs and stores training data such as the time and the grip position. This data can be used in the quantitative analysis for motor control as well as cognitive function rehabilitation. Fig. 3 shows the program selection menu. The four icons on the left side are evaluation programs and the six icons on the right side are training programs.

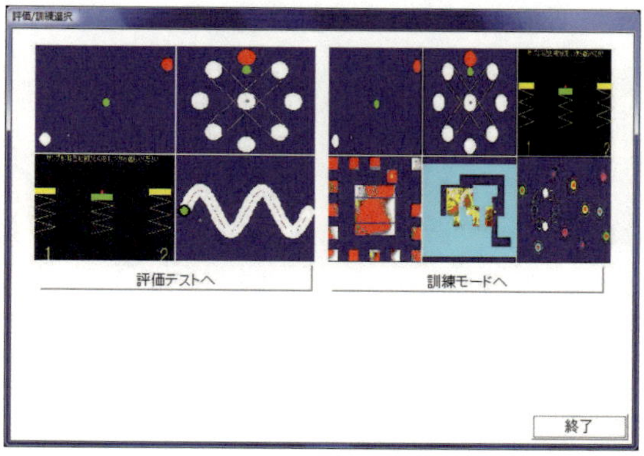

Fig. 3. Program selection menu

4.1 Training program

In the training programs, the user is urged to move her or his arms along diagonal, straight, and voluntary paths. The user can work a puzzle and play other game-like programs. These programs also help the user to develop concentration during training. Screenshots of the programs are shown in Figs. 4 to 7. Details of the programs are presented in the following.

1. Following the dot in the diagonal direction: White circles are positioned in the display in a diagonal position. A green target dot moves between two circles, and the user follows the target green dot by using the cursor. The color of the circles changes from white to red when the user attains the goal. The radius of the circles and the velocity of the target dot can be changed.
2. Following the dot in the radial direction: Nine circles and nine line sets, which connect the circle in the center, are shown on the display. The user tries to move the cursor from circle to circle while staying on the lines by following the target dot. The displacement and radius of the circles can be changed.
3. Feeling the haptic force: Three subprograms to feel the difference of haptic sensations are prepared (Fig. 4). The sensations are spring force, viscosity force, and load (weight). Three different objects appear on the display and each object provides a haptic force. The user tries to touch and move the virtual objects and feel the haptic forces. The right

or left objects have the same magnitude and texture haptic force of the center object. The user tries to check which side object has same of center one. The subprograms, types and magnitude of the haptic forces can be selected from the pop-up menu.

4. Puzzle: The puzzle frame is shown in the center and the puzzle pieces are shown around the frame (Fig. 5). The user tries to pick and move each piece to the appropriate position in the frame and complete the puzzle to show the original image. When moving the piece, the user can feel the weight of the piece. The original puzzle image can be generated from uploaded pictures. The user or therapist can select and use a favorite or suitable picture for training. The number and the weight of pieces can be changed to adjust the level of difficulty.

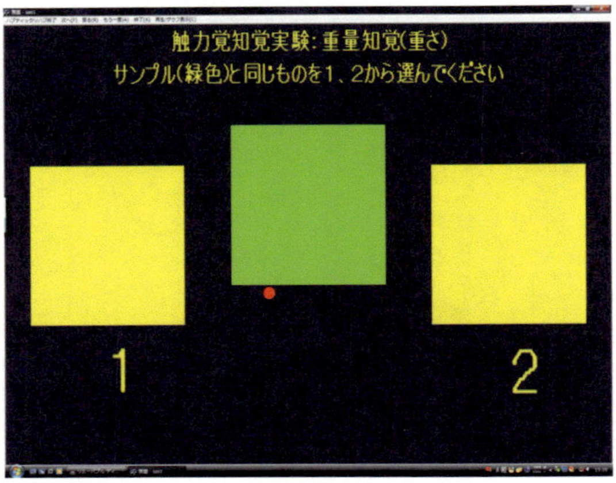

Fig. 4. Comparing the load (weight) of the objects

Fig. 5. Puzzle

5. Sweeping tiles: Square-shaped colored tiles are shown in the display (Fig. 6). The user tries to move the cursor over all of the tiles. When the cursor is located over a tile, the color of the tile is replaced with a hidden picture. Pictures interesting to the user can be displayed to keep his or her concentration during the training. Prepared arbitrary picture files can be used as the hidden pictures. The number of tiles and the magnitude and direction of the virtual force in the training are adjustable.

6. Balloon operation: Colorful circular rings are shown in the center of the display and ringed solid circles are randomly located around the rings (Fig. 7). The user tries to move the ringed solid circles to the same color rings at the center of the display. Each ringed circle has a different a virtual weight and vulnerability. When pushing the ringed solid circle by using the cursor, if the user pushes hard (by moving quickly), the ring and circle will be broken. The goal of this program is to move the all ringed circles to appropriate colors.

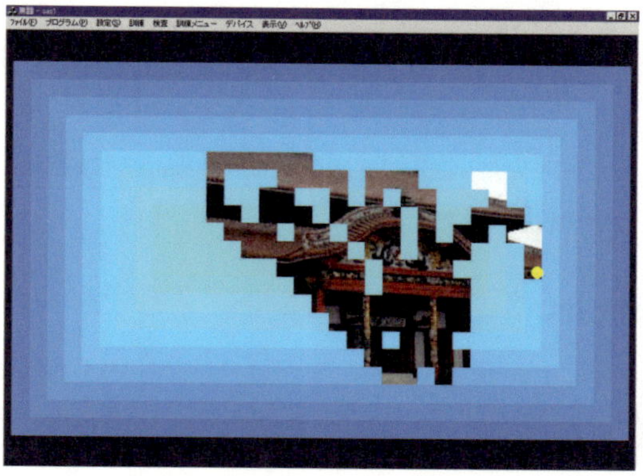

Fig. 6. Sweeping tiles

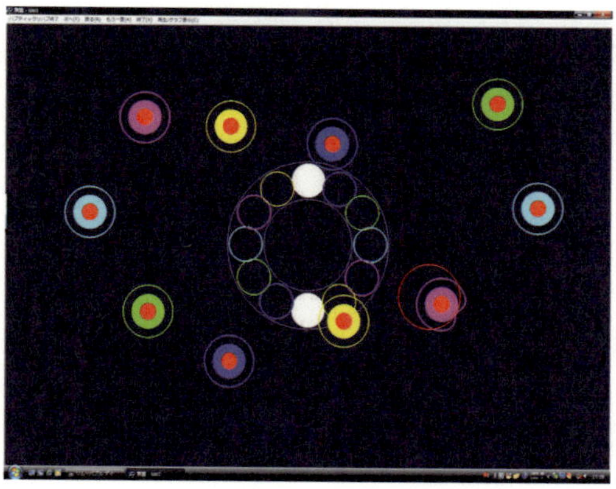

Fig. 7. Balloon operation

4.2 Evaluation program

The four evaluation programs can record time, grip position, velocity, error of the grip position, and so on. The contents of the programs are almost the same as those of the training programs.

One of the evaluation programs, "Wave", is described in this section. Two circles and a sine-wave-shaped line are shown in the display (Fig. 8). The circles are connected with a wavy line. The user tries to move the cursor from one circle to the other while staying on the line. The amplitude and the cycle of the wave can be changed.

In addition, game-like evaluation programs for the children to use are also prepared. The details are introduced in the next section.

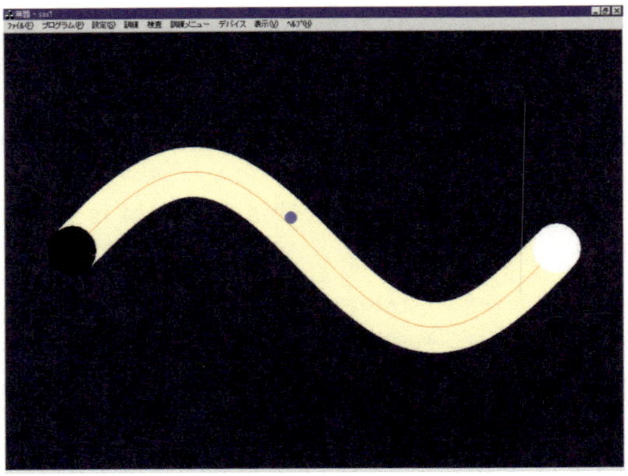

Fig. 8. "Wave" program for evaluation

5. Materials and methods

The haptic device system, consisting of the haptic device and rehabilitation software, was designed for functional and cognitive rehabilitation. The system was tested in experiments to apply and evaluate the haptic system as therapy.

5.1 Subjects

Twenty-seven subjects from the same kindergarten initially participated in this experiment. The age of the subjects ranged from 4 years 7 months to 6 years 3 months, and the average was 5 years 5 months. All subjects were right handed and one subject wore glasses. Of these 27 subjects, the experimental data of only 20 subjects (8 males and 12 females) were used, as explained below.

Informed consent was obtained from all parents of the test subjects and from the kindergarten staff. The experiment was approved by the Research Ethics Committee of Tokyo Metropolitan University.

5.2 Tasks and protocols

The experiment was carried out in the playroom of the kindergarten that the children attended. Test subjects were positioned in a chair (seat height: 290 mm, back height: 510 mm) in front of a desk (height: 470 mm, width: 1200 mm, length: 750 mm) that they regularly used. The haptic device and the display were placed on the desk, as shown in Fig. 9.

The test subjects were asked to play the evaluation program. The goal of this program, called "Starfish", was to move the starfish from the right end to the left end of the display along the thick blue curve with a red centerline as quickly and precisely as they could. This program is a variation of the "Wave" program mentioned in the previous section. The display image is shown in Fig. 10. The experimenter asked the subject to bring the starfish back home quickly because a big fish is after it. Also, the user pays attention to sea urchins along the edge of the thick curve. The sea urchins can prick the starfish with their needles. In the experiment, the subjects tried three different haptic force settings. One is viscosity force, which is related to the velocity of the grip motion. The other one is assistance force, which guides the cursor to the target position. The last one is no force is applied. The experiments included another two different trial programs before the "Starfish" program. A total of 10 minutes was spent for each subject. After playing the experimental game, an interview was carried out.

Fig. 9. Subject in the experiment

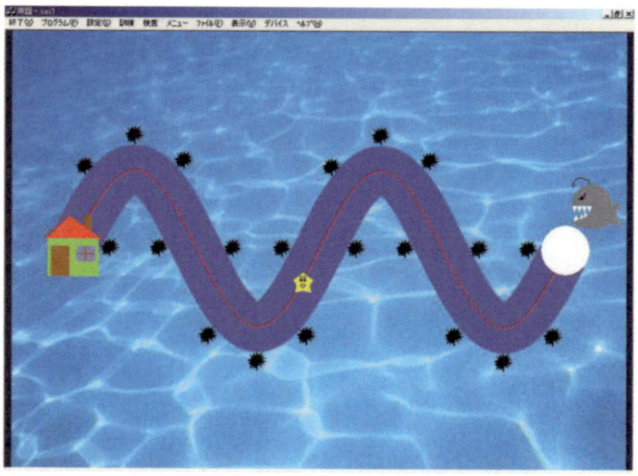

Fig. 10. "Starfish" program used in the experiment

6. Results

6.1 Comparison of time and error

The experimental data of four subjects could not be used due to the subjects' misunderstanding of tasks and some mistakes in the system setting. The data of another three subjects were statistically eliminated. Of these three, two subjects moved the grip too quickly and had large errors, and another subject moved the grip too slowly and took a long time to play the game. Thus, the data of a total of 20 subjects were compared for duration time, grip (cursor) position error from the center of the wave line, and subject age.

Fig. 11 shows the relationship between the duration time and age with the three variations of applied haptic force. The horizontal axis is expressed as the log of the age. No significant correlations are confirmed. For example, the highest correlation, $R^2 = 0.0029$, is in the case of "no force applied".

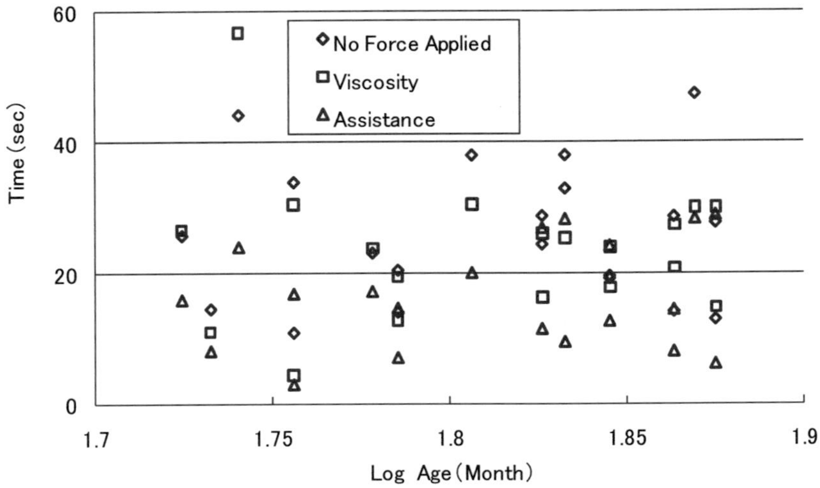

Fig. 11. Relationship of age of subjects and duration time

Fig. 12 shows the relationship between the root mean square (RMS) error of the grip position and the age with the same three variations of applied haptic force. The horizontal axis is again expressed as the log of the age. The correlations are negative in all cases. The RMS errors of the older subjects are lower than those of the younger subjects. The highest correlation, $R^2 = 0.330$, is confirmed in the case of "no force applied". In the case of "viscosity", the correlation is $R^2 = 0.256$. The case of "assistance force" has the lowest correlation, $R^2 = 0.102$.

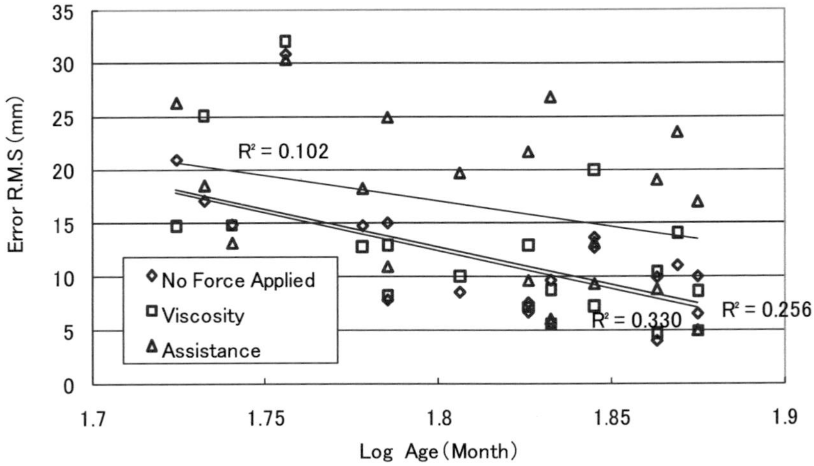

Fig. 12. Relationship of age of subjects and RMS error of the grip position

Fig. 13 shows the relaxation between the duration time and RMS error of the grip position with the three variations of applied haptic force. The horizontal axis is represented as the log of the duration time. All correlations are negative. This tendency is the same as that confirmed in a previous experiment by adult subjects. The correlation for "viscosity" is $R^2 = 0.464$, that for "assistance force" is $R^2 = 0.400$, and that for "no force applied" is $R^2 = 0.239$. The slope of the regression line of "viscosity" is steeper than those of the other two cases. This result means that the viscosity force assists the precise grip position control. In contrast, the assistance force assists the grip movement toward the designated position, which allowed the user to move the grip quickly. However, a short duration time generally incurs a large position error.

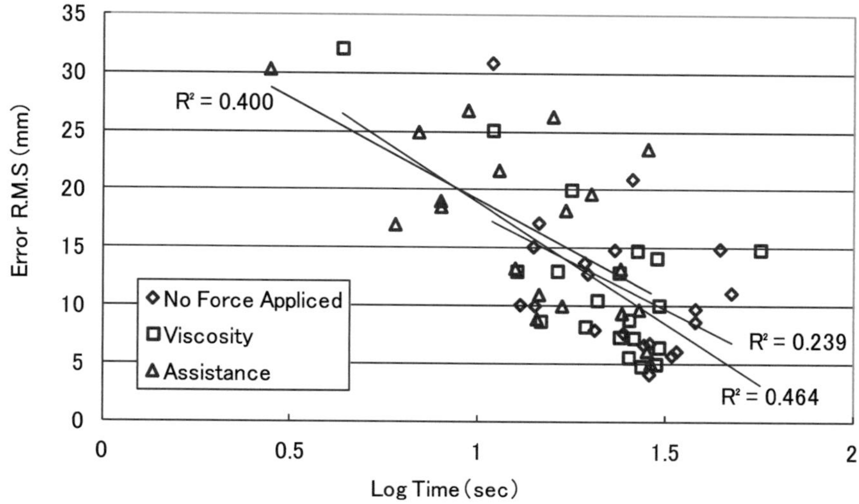

Fig. 13. Relationship of duration time and RMS error of the grip position

		Time	
		increased	decreased
RMS error	increased	1	11
	decreased	6	2

(a) Viscosity

		Time	
		increased	decreased
RMS error	increased	0	15
	decreased	2	3

(b) Assistance

Table 1. Number of subjects showing a difference in duration time and RMS error of the grip motion for "no force applied" and one other force. (a): "No Force Applied" and "Viscosity", and (b): "No Force Applied" and "Assistance".

Table 1 shows the number of subjects showing a difference in duration time and RMS error for "no force applied" and another force. The experiments were always done in the same order. Thus, if the training affected the results, the subjects would move the grip more quickly (duration time decreases) and more precisely (RMS error decreases) for "no force applied". Table 1 (a) indicates the case of "viscosity". The RMS error increased and the duration time decreased for 11 subjects (55%). In the case of "assistance", shown in Table 1 (b), the RMS error increased and the duration time decreased for 15 subjects (75%). Conversely, in (a) the duration time increased for 7 subjects (35%) in the case of "viscosity" and in (b) for 2 subjects (10%) in "assistance". The RMS error decreased for none of the subjects. In other words, the relationship between the duration time and RMS error has the same tendency of the previous results, and so the training effect can be excluded from consideration.

The difference of duration time and the difference of RMS error of the grip position are plotted in Fig. 14. This figure confirms the high correlation of "assistance". The average duration time of "viscosity" is -2.31 sec and that of "assistance" is -9.76 sec. The average RMS error of "viscosity" is 0.38 mm and that of "assistance" is 4.89 mm. In both cases, the significant difference was confirmed by a T-test ($p<0.05$).

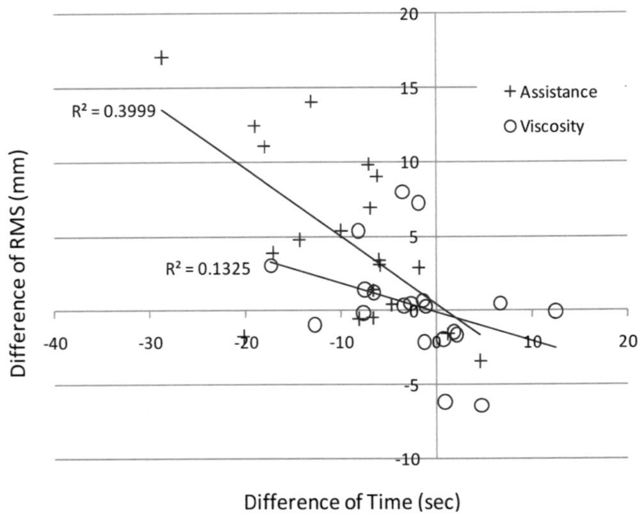

Fig. 14. Relationship between the difference of duration time and difference of RMS error of "viscosity" and "assistance"

6.2 Interview

A post-experiment interview was carried out for all subjects. 19 subjects answered the question "How was this game?" The subjects could answer freely about her or his impression of the experimental program. The vocabulary of their explanations was limited because they were young. The most common answers were "fun" (12 subjects), "interesting" (9 subjects), and "easy" (3 subjects). All subjects who gave an answer had a positive impression.

Two subjects gave both positive and negative impressions. Subject A (age 4 years 9 months, male) said, "Fun, but one of the pre-experiment programs was not interesting. It was too easy." Another subject B (age 5 years 8 months, male) said, "Fun, but I was tired." Subject A moved the grip quickly and finished tasks more quickly than average. In contrast, subject B moved slower than average and had less error than average. However, in the case of "assistance", subject B moved quickly and the error increased. This could be a sign of fatigue (Table 2).

Simple questionnaires were also used. We asked two questions: "Are you good at sports?" and "Are you good at TV games?" The subjects were categorized into a "good at" group and a "not good at" group. Table 3 shows the comparison of the group results and the average results. There are no significant differences. However, the "Good at Sports" and the "Good at TV Games" groups tend to have a shorter duration time than that of the "Not Good at Sports" or "Not Good at TV Games" groups. Due to the shorter duration time, the RMS error of the "Good at" group is larger than that of the "Not Good at" group. The "Good at Sports" group and the "Not Good at Sports" group can generally be expressed as "active" or "non-active" personality groups. The tendency of their motions may be quick, however the results are a shorter duration time and a larger RMS error. The "Good at TV

Games" group may be more familiar with computers and playing TV games. Therefore, they do not operate the grip and program carefully.

	No Force Applied		Viscosity		Assistance	
	duration time	RMS error	duration time	RMS error	duration time	RMS error
Subject A	10.93	30.83	4.35	32.04	2.79	30.27
Subject B	38.11	9.7	25.39	8.76	9.4	26.77
Average	26.01	11.71	23.7	12.08	16.25	16.6

Table 2. Comparison of results between subjects with negative impressions and the average

	No Force Applied		Viscosity		Assistance	
	duration time	RMS error	duration time	RMS error	duration time	RMS error
Good at Sports	23.47	14.11	23.37	13.63	11.8	18.51
Not Good at Sports	30.28	9.82	14.34	12.45	19.28	16.86
Good at TV Game	24.08	12.15	22.18	12.36	15	16.43
Not Good at TV Game	29	11.03	25.97	11.66	18.11	16.84
Average	26.01	11.71	23.7	12.08	16.25	16.6

Table 3. Comparison of results between "Good at Sports", "Not Good at Sports", "Good at TV Games", and "Not Good at TV Games" groups and the average

7. Discussion

No correlation was found between the age and the duration time. The assumed reason is the range and the variation of the subjects' ages. Some younger subjects could not clearly understand the instruction, "Keep cursor (starfish) inside the thick wavy line" and operated it impulsively. Some older subjects understood the purpose of the program, "Try to keep moving the cursor on the center of the thick wavy line" and tried to do it carefully. Therefore, when the subjects are younger or they are not developing as expected, the experimenter should explain the task using easy words and be careful to make sure the subjects understand.

In the comparison between "no force applied" and "viscosity" or "assistance" applied, the duration time with the "assistance" force was shorter than that of the other cases. In the "assistance" case, it was observed that the upper limb of the subjects seemed to be pulled by the haptic device. Thus, the "assistance" force may prevent voluntary motion. However, for children who have problems with voluntary upper-limb movement or hand-eye coordination, the guiding force can help move her or his upper limb (grip) to the designated point. This assistance can stimulate motion and cognitive function. The suitable level of assistance and how it is involved in therapeutic training should be discussed in the future.

The error of motion decreased according to age. It was confirmed that error and age have a negative correlation. From observations, it was also confirmed that most of the older subjects tried to move the cursor along the center of the thick wavy line in the "Starfish" program. Thus, the results were reasonable. However, children at 5 years of age start to write Japanese characters and Arabic numbers as preparation for elementary school. Therefore, a simple line-drawing task should be easy for them to understand.

The negative correlation for the duration time and the grip position error was confirmed in the two different cases of applied force and no force applied. The tendency was the same as that in previous research for young adult to elderly subjects. To move the cursor in a smooth and fast manner, the subject must see the cursor, recognize its position, and move the direction of the cursor by moving his or her upper limb to the appropriate position. Usually, this ability is obtained by visuomotor experience beginning at birth. Moreover, improved and refined actions increase with the increase of experiences. In many cases, developmental disorder children lack many skills. They have a problem with hand-eye coordination due to their learning difficulties and lack of sensory-motor experiences. From the viewpoint of occupational therapists, upper-limb motion depends on stability and control of the trunk and shoulder. Therefore, they focus on improving posture, stability, and shoulder control before using therapeutic tools. During operation of the haptic device system, the users held their trunk in median antigravity. The upper limb was held in the air, and the fingers were used to hold the grip. Shoulder and elbow joint motion were involved with the motion of the grip. Especially, moving one's hand on a smooth curving trajectory, as in the experimental programs, requires coordination of multiple functions, direction control by the shoulder joint, and position adjustment of the elbow joint. Thus, the haptic device system, which uses upper-limb motion with visuomotor involvement, can be effective for hand-eye coordination training.

8. Conclusions

We developed a rehabilitation system using a haptic device that integrates both motion and sensory therapy. The system is designed to maintain the user's interest during a rehabilitation activity and also to provide a quantitative evaluation for occupational therapists. From the results of experiments with kindergarten children, a negative correlation of duration time and motion error was confirmed in the two different cases of applied force and no force applied. In addition, the motion error decreased according to age. It was found that this developed system effectively motivated and evaluated hand-eye coordination.

9. Acknowledgment

I would like to acknowledge the generous support received from Dr. Takagi and the students of the Tokyo Metropolitan University and Shibaura Institute of Technology who assisted in the experiments conducted during this research.

10. References

Krebs I. H, Hogan N, Aisen L. M, Volpe T. B. (1998). Robot-Aided Neurorehabilitation. *IEEE Transactions on Rehabilitation Engineering*, vol.6, No.1, pp. 75–627.

Shor C. P, Lum S. P, Burgerk G. C, Van der Loos M. F. H, Majmundar M, Yap R. (2001). The Effect of Robotic-Aided Therapy on Upper Extremity Joint Passive Range of Motion and Pain, *Assistive Technology Research Series*, vol.9, pp.79–83.

Kahn E. L, Averbuch M, Rymer Z. W, Reinkensmeyer J. D, Comparison of Robot-Assisted Reaching to Free Reaching in Promoting Recovery From Chronic Stroke. (2001), *Assistive Technology Research Series*, vol.9, pp.39–44.

Furusho J, Koyanagi K, Ryu U, Inoue A, Oda K. (2003). Development of Rehabilitation Robot System with Functional Fluid Devices for Upper Limbs. *International Journal of HWRS*, vol.4, No.2, pp.23–27.

Takahashi Y, Terada T, Inoue K, Ito Y, Lee H, and Takashi K. (2003). Upper-Limb Rehabilitation Exercises Using Haptic Device System. *International Journal of HWRS*, vol.4, No.2, pp.18–22.

9

Development of a Detailed Human Spine Model with Haptic Interface

Kim Tho Huynh[1], Ian Gibson[1,3] and Zhan Gao[2]
[1]*National University of Singapore,*
[2]*Nantong University,*
[3]*Centre for Rapid and Sustainable Product Development, Leiria,*
[1]*Singapore*
[2]*China*
[3]*Portugal*

1. Introduction

The human spine is an important structure, providing strength and support as well as permitting the body to bend, stretch, rotate and lean. It is also a vulnerable part of our skeleton open to disease and injuries like whiplash, low back pain, scoliosis etc. Whiplash is a frequent consequence of rear-end automobile accidents and has been a significant public health problem for many years with injury to one or more ligaments, intervertebral discs, facet joints or muscles of the neck. Low back pain is a very common disease and strongly associated with degeneration of intervertebral discs (Luoma et al., 2000) seen in people with sedentary jobs spending hours sitting in relatively fixed positions, with the lower back forced away from its natural lordotic curvature. This causes health risks of the lumbar spine, especially for the three lower vertebrae L3-L5. 80% of people in the United States will have lower back pain at some point in their life (Vallfors, 1985). Scoliosis is a less common but more complicated spinal disorder, being a congenital 3D deformity of the spine and trunk affecting 1.5-3% of the population. In severe cases, surgical correction is required to stabilize the scoliosis curvature. Studies into the treatment of these spinal diseases have played an important role in modern medicine. Many biomechanical models have been proposed to study dynamic behavior and biomechanics of the human spine, to develop new implants and new surgical strategies for treating these spinal diseases.

2. Related works

Biomechanic models can be divided into four categories: physical, *in-vitro, in-vivo* and computer models. Computer models have been extensively used because they can provide information that cannot be easily obtained by other models, such as internal stresses or strains. They can also be used for multiple experiments with uniform consistency, lowering experimental cost, and simulating different situations easily and quickly. Multi-body and finite element models, or a combination of the two are the most popular simulation tools that can contribute significantly to our insight of the biomechanics of the spine.

Finite element models (FEMs) are helpful to understand underlying mechanisms of injury and dysfunction, leading to improved prevention, diagnosis and treatment of clinical spinal problems. FEMs often provide estimates of parameters that *in-vivo* or *in-vitro* experimental studies either cannot or are difficult to obtain accurately. FEMs are divided into two categories: dynamic study and static study models. Models for static study generally are more detailed in representing spinal geometries (Greaves et al., 2008; Kumaresan et al., 1999; Natarajan et al., 2007; Teo & Ng, 2001; Yoganandan et al., 1996). They can predict internal stresses, strains and other biomechanical properties under complex loading conditions, but they generally only consist of one or two motion segments and do not provide effective insight for the whole column. Dynamic study models generally include a series of vertebrae connected by ligaments and disks modeled as springs (Maurel et al., 1997; Ng & Teo, 2005; Pankoke et al., 1998; Schmidt et al., 2008; Seidel et al., 2001; Zander et al., 2002). They predict locally the kinematic and dynamic responses of a certain part of the spine under load. FEMs have also been widely used to study scoliosis biomechanics (Aubin, 2002; Gignac et al., 2000; Lafage et al., 2004; Schlenk et al., 2003). Understanding of the biomechanics of spine deformation helps surgeons formulate treatment strategies for surgery and design and develop new medical devices. Being complex, FEMs of scoliotic spines are usually restricted to 2D models or simplified 3D elastic beam element models. Although preliminary results achieved are promising, extensive validation is necessary before using the models clinically.

Multi-body models have advantages like less complexity, less demand on computational power, and relatively simpler validation requirements. They possess potential to simulate both kinematics and kinetics of the spine effectively. Rigid bodies are interconnected by various joints. Multi-body models can also include many anatomical details while being computationally efficient. The head and vertebrae are modeled as rigid bodies and soft tissues are usually modeled as massless spring-damper elements. Such models are capable of producing biofidelic responses and can be broken down into two categories: car collisions and whole-body vibration investigations. In the former, displacements of the head with respect to the torso, accelerations, intervertebral motions, and neck forces/moments can provide good predictions for whiplash injury (Esat & Acar, 2007; Garcia & Ravani, 2003; Jager et al., 1996; Jun, 2006; Linder, 2000; Stemper et al., 2004; Van Der Horst, 2002). In the latter, multi-body models are helpful for determining the forces acting on the intervertebral discs and endplates of lumbar vertebrae (Fritz, 1998; Luo & Goldsmith, 1991; Seidel & Griffin, 2001; Verver et al., 2003; Yoshimura et al., 2005). In both cases, multi-body models focus either on the cervical or the lumbar spine. Since spine segments are partially modeled in detail, it is impossible to investigate the kinematics of the thoracic spine region. In other words, global biodynamic response of the whole spine has not been studied thoroughly.

Although finite element and multi-body models are powerful tools used to study intrinsic properties of injury mechanisms, other techniques have been developed to obtain deeper understanding of biomechanical properties of medical diseases. One such technique is *computer haptics*. The word *haptics* was introduced in the early 20th century to describe the research field that addresses human touch-based perception and manipulation. In the early 1990s, the synergy of psychology, biology, robotics and computer graphics made computer haptics possible. Much like computer graphics is concerned with rendering visual images, computer haptics is the art and science of synthesizing computer generated forces to the user for perception of virtual objects through the sense of touch. Simulation with the addition of haptics may offer better realism compared to only a visual interface. In recent years, haptics has been widely applied in numerous VR environments to increase the levels of realism. Especially, haptics has been investigated at length for medical education and surgical simulations, like surgical planning and laparoscopic surgical training (Basdogan et al., 1998; Forest et al., 2004; Gorman et al., 2000; Seitz et al., 2004; Williams et al., 2004).

Haptics has been widely utilized in medical fields, but little has been applied to spinal diseases. Integrating haptics into spine models means surgeons can investigate biodynamic responses of whole human spine which either have not been investigated enough in the literature or are limited to partial spine segments. Understanding biodynamic behaviour of the whole human spine is beneficial to wheelchair design applications for the disabled. When applying forces to a certain vertebra of the spine under fixed constraints on sacrum and selected vertebrae, users such as surgeons or clinicians can feel force feedback from the spine as well as examine its locomotion. These results are useful for designing suitable and comfortable wheelchairs for the disabled with specific abnormal spinal configurations. In addition, by simulating in a haptically integrated graphic environment, orthopaedic surgeons can gain insight into the planning of surgery to correct severe scoliosis. Different rod and brace designs can be experimented with using this virtual environment. Furthermore, the surgeons may be able to understand the change in force distribution following spine fusion procedures, which can also assist in post-operative physiotherapy. The objective of this chapter is to present the development of a detailed human spine model with a haptic interface, which can be useful for investigating various medical applications.

3. Overview of human spine structure

The spinal column (Figure 1) extends from the skull to pelvis and is made up of 33 individual vertebrae that are stacked on top of each other. The spinal column can be divided into 5 regions: 7 cervical (C1-C7), twelve thoracic (T1–T12), and five lumbar vertebrae (L1–L5) in the lower back, five bones (joined together in adults) to form the bony sacrum, and 3-5 bones fused together to form the coccyx or tailbone.

Intervertebral discs (Figure 2) are soft tissue structures situated between each of the 24 cervical, thoracic, and lumbar vertebrae of the spine. Their functions are to separate consecutive vertebral bodies. Once the vertebrae are separated, angular motions in the sagittal (forward, backward bending) and coronal planes (sideway bending) can occur.

Facet joints are paired joints which are found in the posterior of the spinal column (Figure 3). The surfaces of each joint are covered by cartilage which helps to smooth the movement between two vertebrae. Certain motions are facilitated by these joints, such as: bending forward, bending backward and twisting. In addition, people can feel pain if the joints are damaged because of the connected nerves. Some experts believe that these joints are the most common reasons for spinal discomfort and pain.

The neural elements (Figure 4) consist of the spinal cord and nerve roots. The spinal cord runs from the base of the brain down through the cervical and thoracic spine. The spinal cord is surrounded by spinal fluid and by several layers of protective structures, including the dura mater, the strongest, outermost layer. At each vertebral level of the spine, there is a pair of nerve roots. These nerves go to supply particular parts of the body.

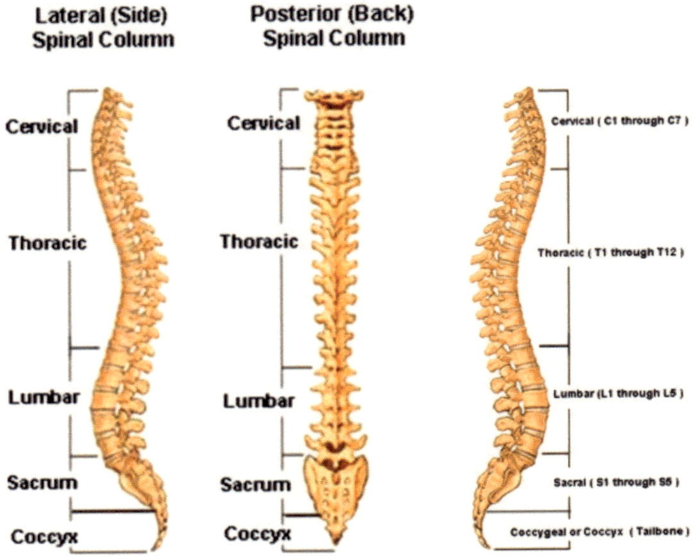

Fig. 1. Spinal column

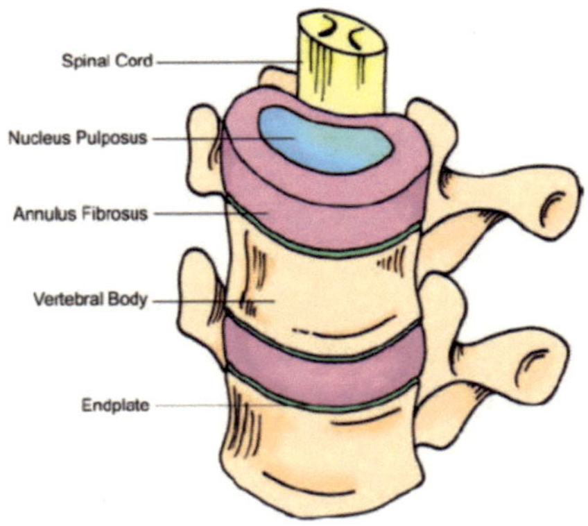

Fig. 2. Intervertebral discs

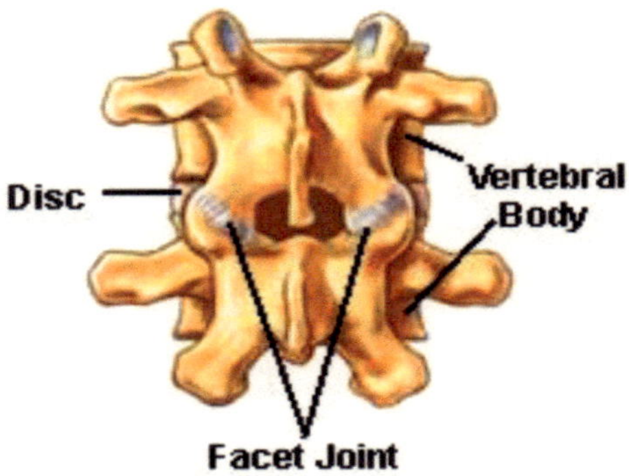

Fig. 3. Facet joints of the spine

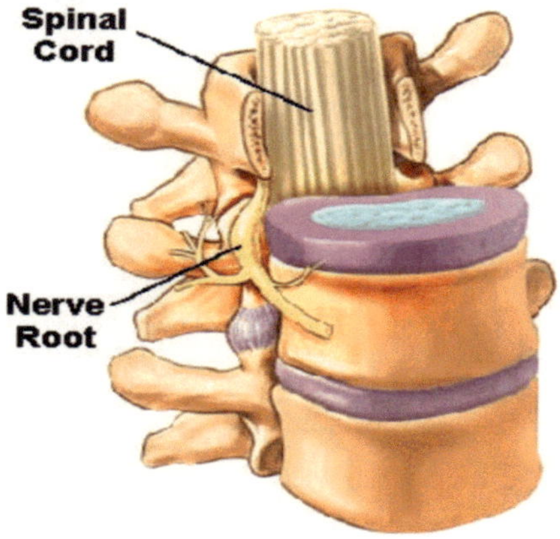

Fig. 4. Nerve roots and spinal cords

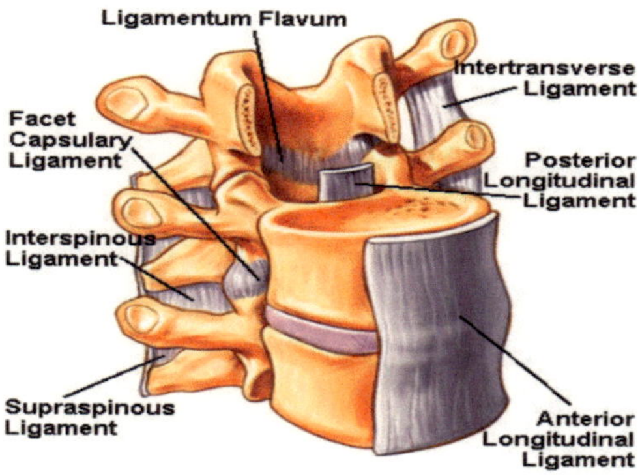

Fig. 5. Various ligaments of the spine

Ligaments enable the spine to function in an upright position, and the trunk to assume a variety of positions. There are various ligaments attached to the spine, with the most important being the anterior longitudinal and the posterior longitudinal ligaments (Figure 4), which run from the skull to the base of the spine (the sacrum). In addition there are also many muscles attached to the spine, which further help to keep it stable. The majority of the muscles are attached to the posterior elements of the spine.

4. Finite element modeling of the spine

In context of most researchers mainly focusing on modelling partially the spinal regions, the construction of a finite element model of the human spine can be useful for clinicians to investigate clinical problems by predicting its biomechanical behaviour. A beam finite element (FE) spine model for haptic interaction is built based on a solid FE spine model, which is created in offline finite element analysis (FEA) software. The mechanical properties of the beam FE spine model are tuned so that its deformation behavior is very similar to that of the offline solid spine model. Furthermore, the online beam FE spine model is greatly simplified as compared to the offline solid FEA model and hence more appropriate for real-time simulations. Haptic feedback is provided in the real-time simulation of the beam FE spine model, in order to enhance the human-computer interaction. Based on the results of spine deformation obtained from the haptic online FE simulator, the offline FEA spine model again is used to reproduce the same deformation and hence to provide more detailed deformation and vertebrae's stress/strain information, which the haptic beam FE model is not capable to provide. Figure 6 shows the architecture of the system.

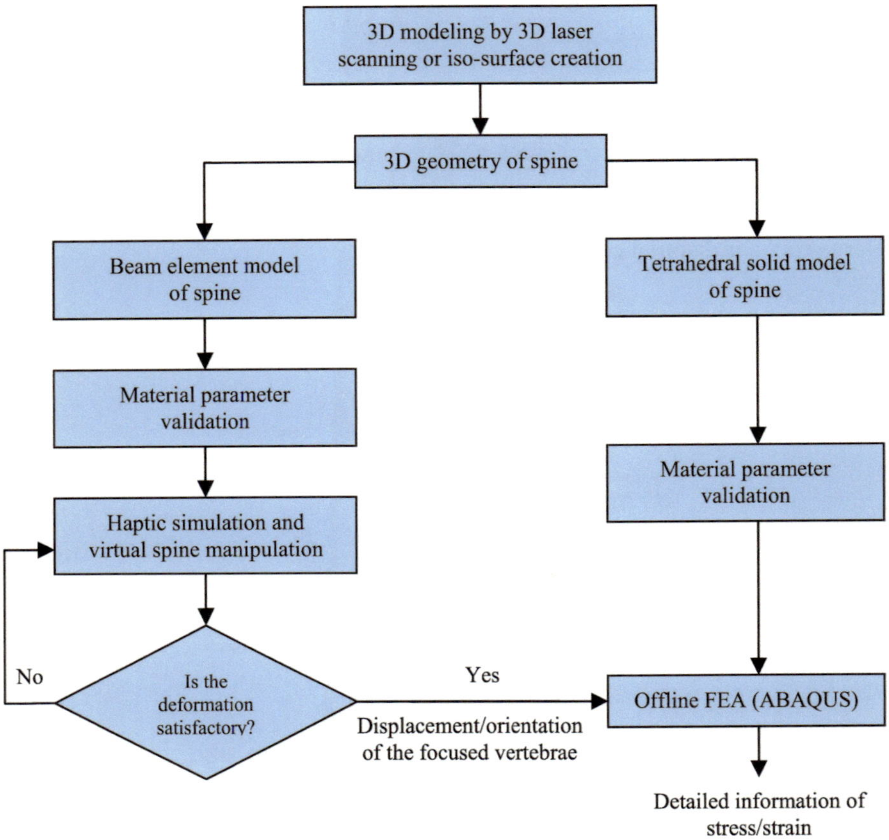

Fig. 6. Architecture of the modelling system

Effective haptic interaction requires a high updating rate of around 1kHz and only a simple FE spine model can be used without significant latency. FE solvers for haptic interfaces are often restricted to linear or simple non-linear solutions. Most research on FE simulation of the spine uses tetrahedral or brick element types in order to obtain thorough representations of spinal deformation. However, a haptic interface's requirement for high updating rate makes it difficult to use solid elements in the haptic virtual environment, because these often result in huge numbers of elements and nodes. Therefore, a beam element was chosen for this real-time haptic simulator. The beam element type provides very limited information concerning stress and strain of vertebrae or inter-vertebral discs, which is potentially important for representing realistic behaviour. In order to provide stress/strain information of spinal deformation, commercial FEA software (in this case ABAQUS) is employed using a tetrahedral element and computed offline. The complete simulation is achieved in two steps. Firstly, simulation in the online haptic simulator obtains quick, intuitive but relatively rough results. The displacement and deformation of the spine from the haptic simulator is then input to the offline FEA application for further detailed analysis. This offline computation is carried out when there is no direct haptic interaction and sufficient computational time.

Initially, two types of FE models, beam element and tetrahedral element models, were created based on 3D models of scanned vertebrae. Material properties of FE models should be validated before simulation. In the haptic simulator, a user can push or pull any vertebra in any arbitrary direction to observe the resulting deformation of the whole spine. After the user is satisfied with the deformation of spine model in haptic simulator, the displacements of some focused vertebrae are input to the offline commercial FEA application for more detailed simulation and the results of stress and strain information can be obtained.

4.1 Geometric modeling of vertebrae

In order to create a geometric model, a healthy spine is preferable to a specific diseased one. For our system, a resin spine prototype (Budget Vertebral Column CH-59X Life Size 29" Tall), which is cast from a Chinese-Singaporean cadaver, was digitized to create the geometric model of the spine (Figure 7(a)). A common method used to build computer models of the spine is by stacking computed tomography (CT) images sequentially to develop and discretize the 3D solid model. However, with this method, the computer model does not properly represent the surface geometry of the highly irregular vertebra, especially its posterior part. For this reason we used laser scanning of the individual surfaces of the model vertebrae to generate the initial point-cloud data set as can be seen in Figure 7(b). Spline (NURBS) surface models were then constructed based on the polygonal meshes generated from the scan data (Figure 7(c) and (d)). These NURBS models can then be used as templates for CAD model generation. Customized models can be obtained by modifying these templates according to dimensional specifications taken from individual patients (Mastmeyer et al., 2006). Once the geometric models of vertebrae have been prepared, FE models can be constructed according to these geometric models.

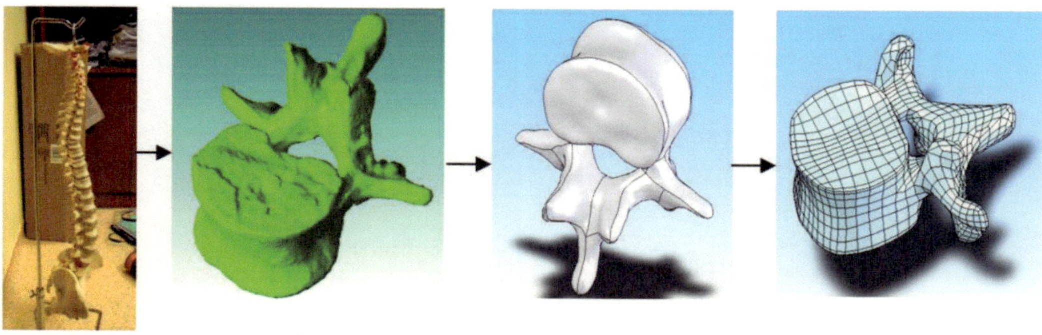

(a) (b) (c) (d)

Fig. 7. Process of geometric modeling

4.2 Finite element modeling for haptic rendering

A major concern is the high updating rate that is required for haptic rendering. Low rates can result in instability or vibration when using the haptic device. The FE model for haptic interaction is simplified and optimized so that the number of elements and nodes is kept as small as possible. In the haptic interface, spines are represented by beam elements. A similar strategy of simulating spines with beam elements can be found in (Lafage et al., 2004). Figure 8 shows the construction of a rigid beam element FE model of a vertebra. Points A and B are the center points of the upper and lower endplates of the vertebral body. Points C and D are the left and rightmost points of the transverse processes. Point E is the rearmost point of the spinal process. Vertebrae are represented using these rigid beams. Point A and B are then connected to intervertebral discs. Point C, D and E are to be connected to specific ligaments. Figure 9(a) and (b) show side and front views of a section of the assemblage of the spine finite element model and explanation is expressed in Figure 9(c).

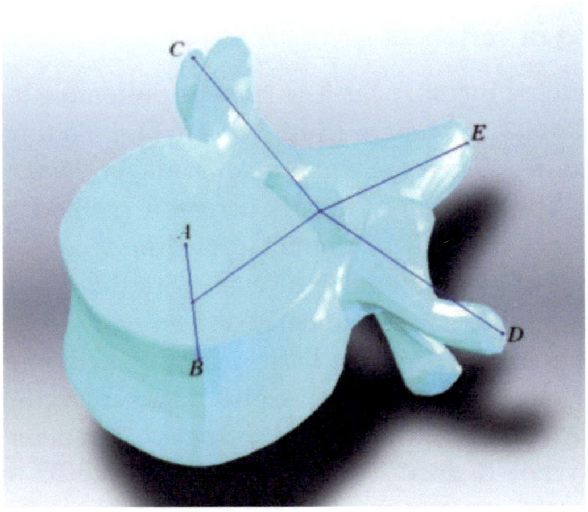

Fig. 8. Structure of beam element model of a vertebra

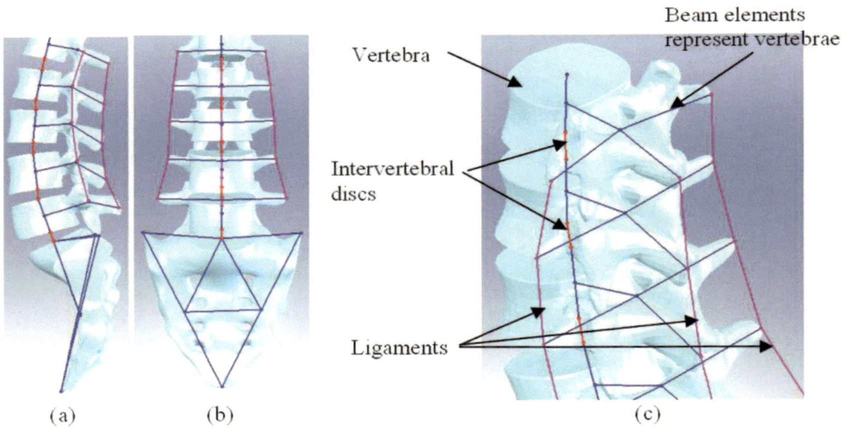

Fig. 9. Composition of finite elements of the spine

Our vertebrae are considered rigid and only the intervertebral discs (IVDs) and ligaments are deformable. The beam element of IVDs is of cylinder type. The flexural moments of inertia (I_y, I_z) of beam elements for IVDs are calculated from the intervertebral discs' geometries. An analogy with the beam theory allows Young's modulus to be expressed as a function of the disc stiffness in bending (K_f), obtained from in-vitro experiments (Lafage et al., 2004). Similarly, the torsion moment of inertia was expressed as a function of the disc stiffness in torsion (K_t), obtained from in-vitro experiments (Lafage et al., 2004). Ligaments were modeled using tension-only truss elements. Two ligaments for connecting transverse processes and one ligament for connecting the spinous process were created. The sacrum is also included as a quasi-rigid body composed of a set of stiff beams. The material properties of ligaments and disks can be found by reference to (Lafage et al., 2004).

4.3 Finite element models for offline FEA

The purpose of the offline FEA is to gain information on the stress/strain relationships of vertebrae and IVDs. The FE model should be sufficiently delicate and precise in order to achieve this. Normal vertebral body models have a cancellous core covered by a cortical shell of approximately 1.5mm thickness. The thickness of most IVDs is around 10mm. The nucleus pulposus of the IVD is modeled as an incompressible material comprising 40% of the total disc volume. The models of the nucleus, the annulus and the vertebral bodies are assembled with tie constraints between the interacting surfaces. Besides vertebral bodies and IVDs, ligaments play an important role in spinal biomechanics and stability. The seven intervertebral ligaments were incorporated and modeled with truss elements. The ribcage is currently not included in this FE model.

Since two FE models are employed in this system, their deformation under the same boundary conditions should be coherent. Therefore, the mechanical properties of spine FE models must be carefully tuned in order to ensure deformations from both models match. A similar approach of material property adjustment can be found in (Lafage et al., 2004). Since the offline FEA is considered as more accurate than the online FE simulator, its results can serve as a standard, meaning the mechanical properties of the beam element model should be adjusted according to the behaviour of a solid FE spine model. The iterative process of mechanical personalization is engaged in the commercial FEA package. Firstly, the offline element spine model is applied with a force of 40N on the T1 vertebra. The force direction is from the rear to the front. The displacement of each vertebra is recorded and serves as the template. Then, the same load and boundary conditions are applied to the online beam element spine model. Differences between the beam element model and the template solid element model are quantified. Mechanical characteristics of soft tissues of the beam element spine are then tuned manually and locally until the difference between the two simulations tend to less than 5 degrees for the vertebral orientation and 10mm for the vertebral bodyline. The mechanical properties to be tuned here include: the stiffness of ligaments; the Poisson's ratio, the shear stiffness and the torsional stiffness of intervertebral discs.

4.4 The reproduction of haptic simulation result in the offline FEA simulator

Although the haptic real-time simulation of the beam FE spine model helps us to understand better the kinematics of the whole thoracolumbar spine, it provides very limited information concerning stress and strain of vertebrae. If a full picture of the deformation behavior of the spine is required, it is important to study and obtain the information of stress/strain of vertebrae. Therefore, offline simulations following the haptic simulation are necessary to carry out and provide this useful information. Our system allows the user to pick interesting moments of particular spine shape during haptic simulation and reproduce the similar deformation of spine in the offline FEA simulator for greater detail. By this means, the user can obtain desired spine deformations conveniently in the haptic simulator and then observe every detail of stress/strain of vertebrae in the offline FEA simulator.

A straightforward way to reproduce the same deformation in the offline FEA simulator is to record the position and orientation of each vertebra along the spine and then apply the positional constraints to every vertebra of the offline spine model. However, this greatly increases the risk of finite element computation error because of too many constraints involved. In practice, we found this method almost always makes the FEA solver fail to converge. Another plausible way is to record the force vector and the vertebrae under the load in the haptic simulator and reproduce the same load condition in the offline FEA simulator. However, the deformation of spine is not solely determined by the load due to the high non-linearity of the spine. Plus, during surgery, the forces are often not directly applied to a vertebra; instead, surgeons often manipulate instruments, which are linked to one or multiple vertebrae. Therefore, this method is not feasible.

Our solution is firstly to record the position and orientation of vertebrae which are directly under the external forces or are constrained during the haptic simulation, then apply the position and orientation constraints only to these vertebrae in the offline FEA simulator. The position and orientation of a vertebra can be represented with the positions of point A ~ E of the vertebrae's beam elements model (shown in Figure 8). The procedure of reproducing the deformed spine in the offline FEA simulator is as follows:

a. Locate the vertebrae under external forces in the haptic real-time simulation.
b. Build the transformation matrix by comparing the original position and the current position of point A ~ E of the vertebrae.
c. Transform the vertebrae and set the constraints in the offline FEA simulator.
d. Simulate the deformation.

5. Human spine modeling in LifeMOD

5.1 Introduction to LifeMOD simulation software

Recently, many software applications have been developed for impact simulation, ergonomics, comfort study, biomechanical analysis and surgical planning. Such software enables users to perform human body modeling and interaction with the environment where the human motion and muscle forces can be simulated. These tools are very useful for simulating the human-machine behavior simultaneously. LifeMOD from Biomechanics Research Group is a leading simulation tool that has been designed for this purpose.

The LifeMOD Biomechanics Modeler is a plug-in module to the ADAMS (Automatic Dynamic Analysis of Mechanical Systems) physics engine, produced by MSC Software Corporation to perform multi-body analysis. It provides a default multi-body model of the skeletal system that can be modified by changing anthropometric sizes such as gender, age, height, weight etc. The created human body may be combined with any type of physical environment or system for full dynamic interaction. The results of the simulation are the human motion, internal forces exerted by soft tissues (muscles, ligaments, joints) and contact forces at the desired location of the human body. Full information on the LifeMOD Biomechanics Modeler can be found online (LifeMOD).

In following subsections, the developing process of a detailed musculo-skeletal spine model is presented thoroughly. This process includes five main stages such as generating a default human body model, discretizing the default spine segments, implementing ligamentous soft tissues, implementing lumbar back muscles and adding intra-abdominal pressure.

5.2 Generating a default human body model

The usual procedure of generating a human model is to create a set of body segments followed by redefining the fidelity of the individual segments. The body segments of a complete standard skeletal model are first generated by LifeMOD depending on the user's anthropometric input. The model used in this study was a median model with a height of 1.78 m and a weight of 70 kg created from the internal GeBod anthropometric database. By default, LifeMOD generates 19 body segments represented by ellipsoids. Then, some kinematic joints and muscles are generated for the human model. Figure 10 shows the base model in this study.

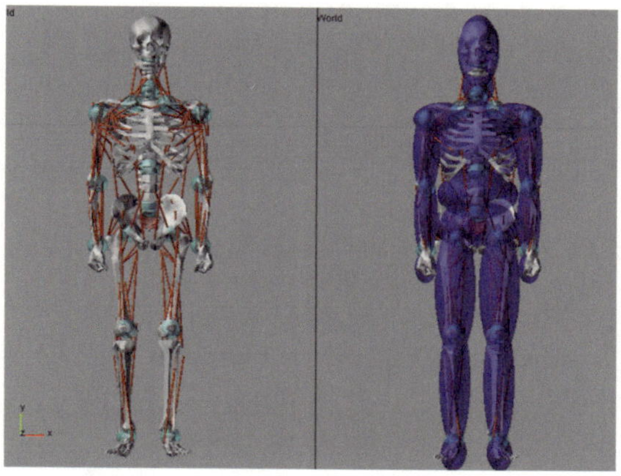

Fig. 10. Default human body model

5.3 Discretizing the default spine segments

To achieve a more detailed spine model, the improvement of the default spine model mentioned above is required and can be done in the three following steps: refining the spine segments, reassigning muscle attachments and creating the spinal joints.

From the base human model, the segments may be broken down into individual bones for greater model fidelity. Every bone in the human body is included in the generated skeletal model as a shell model. To discretize the spine region, the standard ellipsoidal segments representing the cervical (C1-C7), thoracic (T1-T12) and lumbar (L1-L5) vertebral groups are firstly removed. Based on input such as center of mass location and orientation of each vertebra, the individual vertebra segment is then created. Figure 11 shows all ellipsoidal segments of 24 vertebrae in the cervical, thoracic and lumbar regions after discretizing.

The muscles are attached to the respective bones based on geometric landmarks on the bone graphics. With the new vertebra segments created, the muscle attachments to the original segment must be reassigned to be more specific to the newly created vertebra segments. The physical attachment locations will remain the same. Figure 12(a) and (b) shows the anterior and posterior view of several muscles in neck/trunk regions. Table 1 lists attachment locations of these muscles.

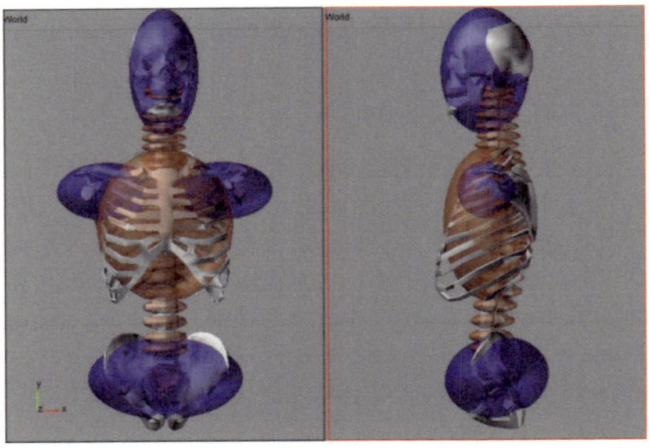

Fig. 11. Front and side view of the complete discretized spine

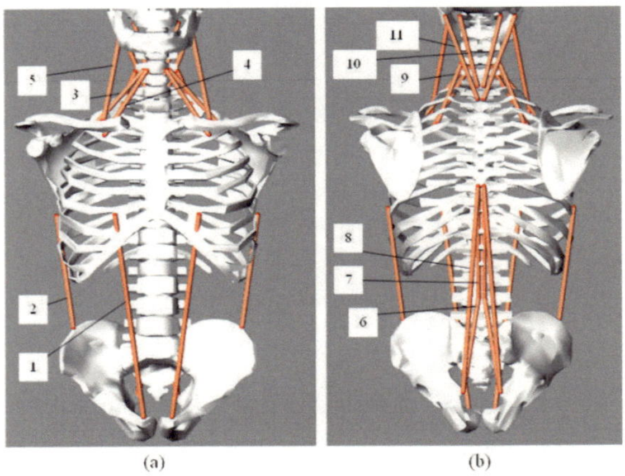

Fig. 12. Neck and trunk muscle set: (a) Anterior view; (b) Posterior view

Index	Muscle	Attach proximal	Attach distal
1	Rectus abdominis	Sternum	Pelvis
2	Obliquus externus	Ribs	Pelvis
3	Scalenus medius	C5	Ribs
4	Scalenus anterior	C5	Ribs
5	Sternocleidomastiodeus	Head	Scapula
6	Erector spinae 2	L2	Pelvis
7	Erector spinae 3	T7	L2
8	Erector spinae 1	T7	Pelvis
9	Scalenus posterior	C5	Ribs
10	Splenius cervicis	Head	C7
11	Splenius capitis	Head	T1

Table 1. Attachment locations of neck and trunk muscle set

It is necessary to create individual non-standard joints representing intervertebral discs between newly created vertebrae. The spinal joints are modeled as torsional spring forces and the passive 3 DOFs jointed action can be defined with user-specified stiffness, damping, angular limits and limiting stiffness values. These joints are used in an inverse dynamics analysis to record the joint angulations while the model is being simulated. The properties of the joints can be found in the literature (Moroney et al., 1988; Panjabi et al., 1976; Schultz et al., 1979; Schultz & Ashton-Miller, 1991).

5.4 Creating the ligamentous soft tissues

To stabilize the spine model, interspinous, flaval, anterior longitudinal, posterior longitudinal and capsule ligaments are created. Figure 13 displays various types of ligaments attached to vertebrae in the cervical spine region

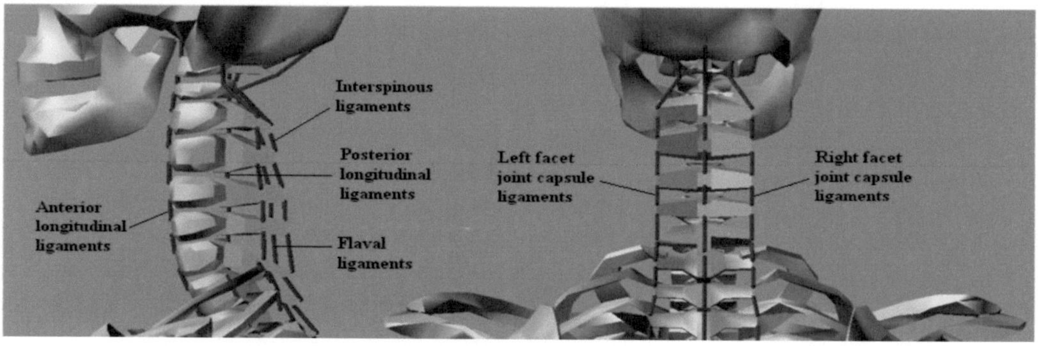

Fig. 13. Various types of ligaments in the cervical spine

5.5 Implementing lumbar muscles

Multifidus muscle: The multifidus muscle is divided into 19 fascicles on each side according to descriptions by the group of Bogduk (Bogduk et al., 1992a; Macintosh & Bogduk, 1986). The multifidus can be modeled as three layers with the deepest layer having the shortest fibres and spanning one vertebra. The second layer spans over two vertebrae, while the third layer goes all the way from L1 and L2 to posterior superior iliac spine (Zee et al., 2007). The rather short span of the multifidus fascicles makes it possible to model them as line elements without via-points (Figure 14(a)).

Erector spinae muscle: According to (Macintosh & Bogduk, 1987; 1991), there are four divisions of the erector spinae: longissimus thoracis pars lumborum, iliocostalis lumborum pars lumborum, longissimus thoracis pars thoracis and iliocostalis lumborum pars thoracis. The fascicles of the longissimus thoracis and iliocostalis lumborum pars lumborum originate from the transverse processes of the lumbar vertebrae and insert on the iliac crest close to the posterior superior iliac spine (Zee et al., 2007). The fascicles of the longissimus thoracis pars thoracis originate from the costae 1-12 close to the vertebrae and insert on the spinous process of L1 down to S4 and on the sacrum. The fascicles of the iliocostalis lumborum pars thoracis originate from the costae 5–12 and insert on the iliac crest. Since muscles of the two pars thoracis are automatically generated by LifeMOD, only muscles of the two pars lumborum need to be added to the model as shown in Figure 14(b).

Psoas major muscle: The psoas major muscle is divided into 11 fascicles according to different literature sources (Andersson et al., 1995; Bogduk et al., 1992b; Penning, 2000). The fascicles originate in a systematic way from the lumbar vertebral bodies and T12 and insert into the lesser trochanter minor of the femur with a via-point on the pelvis (iliopubic eminence) (Figure 14(c)). Bogduk found that the psoas major had no substantial role as a flexor or extensor of the lumbar spine, but rather that the psoas major exerted large compression and shear loading on the lumbar joints (Bogduk et al., 1992b). This implies that the moment arm for the flexion/extension direction is small and hence the via-points for the path were chosen in such a way that the muscle path ran close to the centre of rotation in the sagittal plane.

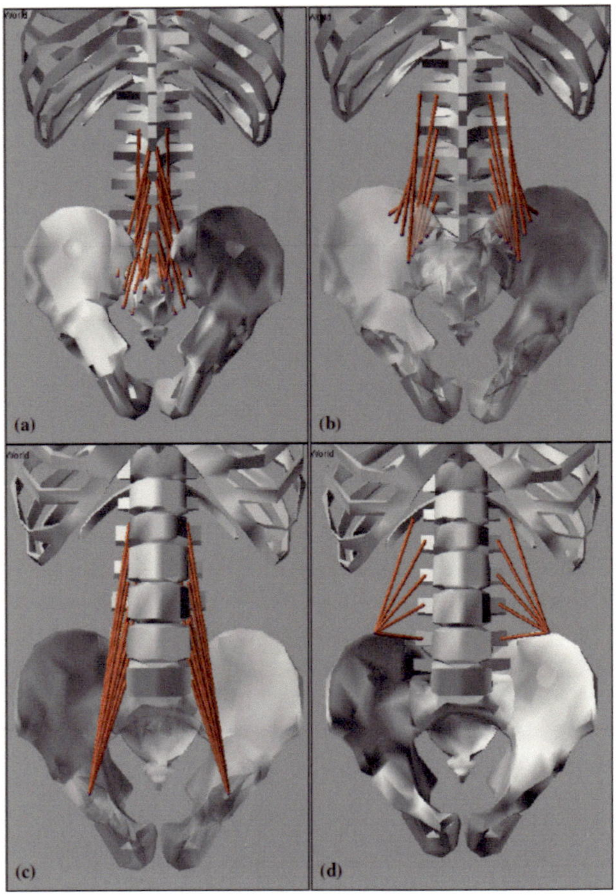

Fig. 14. (a) multifidus muscle (b) erector spinae pars lumborum muscle (c) psoas major muscle (d) quadratus lumborum muscle

Quadratus lumborum muscle: For modelling the quadratus lumborum, the description given by Stokes and Gardner-Morse was followed (Stokes & Gardner-Morse, 1999). They proposed to represent this muscle by five fascicles. The muscle originates from costa 12 and the anterior side of the spinous processes of the lumbar vertebrae and has in the model a common insertion on the iliac crest (Figure 14(d)).

Abdominal muscles: Two abdominal muscles are included in the model: obliquus externus and obliquus internus. Modelling of these muscles requires the definition of an artificial segment with a zero mass and inertia (Zee et al., 2007). This artificial segment mimics the function of the rectus sheath on which the abdominal muscles can attach (Figure 15(a)). The obliquus externus and internus are divided into 6 fascicles each (Stokes & Gardner-Morse, 1999). Two of the modeled fascicles of the obliquus externus run from the costae to the iliac crest on the pelvis, while the other four originate on the costae and insert into the artificial rectus sheath as can be seen in Figure 15(a). Three of the modelled fascicles of the obliquus internus run from the costae to the iliac crest, while the other three originate from the iliac crest and insert into the artificial rectus sheath (Figure 15(b)).

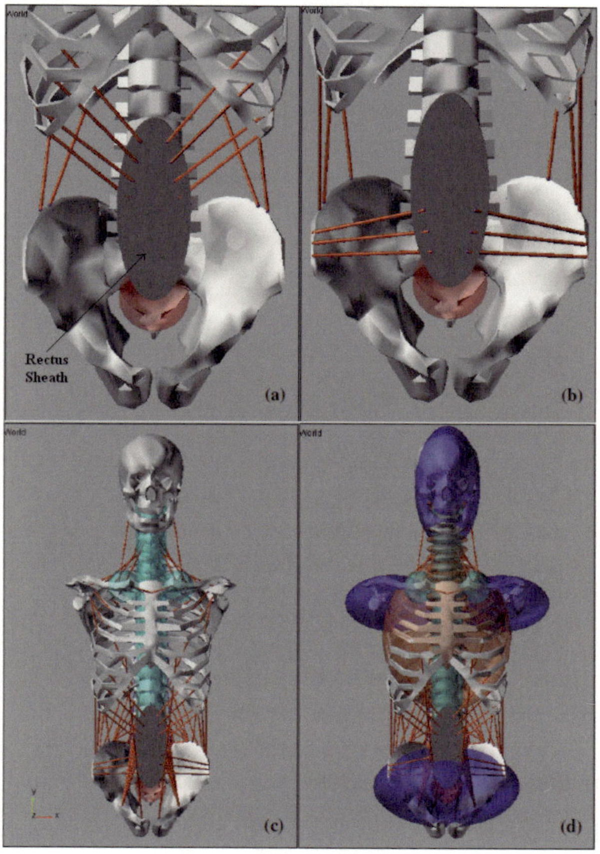

Fig. 15. (a) external oblique muscle (b) internal oblique muscle (c) detailed spine model in skeleton mode (d) detailed spine model in ellipsoid mode

5.6 Adding intra-abdominal pressure

Since LifeMOD and ADAMS provide tools that only generate concentrated or distributed forces, it is not possible to implement directly intra-abdominal pressure into the spine model. To overcome this difficulty, a new approach to intra-abdominal pressure modeling is proposed. Initially, an equivalent spring structure able to mimic all mechanical properties of intra-abdominal pressure such as tension/compression, anterior/posterior shear, lateral shear, flexion/extension, lateral bending and torsion is created (Figure 16). After that, the translational and torsional stiffnesses of the spring structure are determined. Finally, since adding this spring structure into the spine model is quite troublesome, a bushing element that can specify all stiffness properties of the structure is used instead (Figure 17).

Fig. 16. The spring structure used in the spine model

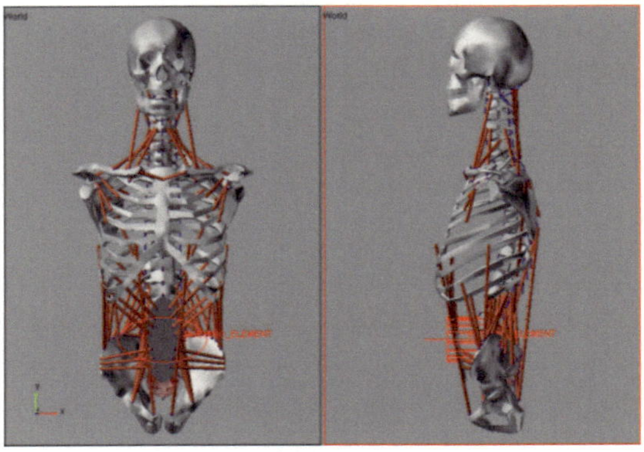

Fig. 17. An equivalent bushing element replacing the spring structure

5.7 Validation of the detailed spine model

To validate the detailed spine model presented above, two approaches are used and presented as follows:

- With the same extension moment generated in upright position, axial and shear forces in the L5-S1 disc calculated in the model are compared to those obtained from Zee's model (2007) and experimental data (McGill & Norman, 1987).
- While a subject holds a crate of beer weighing 19.8 kg, the axial force of the L4-L5 disc is computed and compared with in-vivo intradiscal pressure measurements (Wilke et al., 2001).

In the first approach, a gradually increasing horizontal force was applied onto the vertebra T7 of the spine model from posterior to anterior in the sagittal plane. From this force, axial and shear forces as well as the moment about the L5-S1 disc were calculated. Zee's model estimated an axial force of 4520 N and shear force of 639 N in the L5-S1 disc at a maximum extension moment of 238 Nm. Meanwhile, to obtain the same extension moment, the external force that needs to be applied in the present model is 1260 N. Corresponding with this force, axial and shear forces obtained in the model were 4582 N and 625 N, respectively. This is in accordance with the results presented by McGill et al. (1987) who found axial forces in the range of 3929–4688 N and shear forces up to 650 N.

In the second approach, a comparison was made with in-vivo intradiscal pressure measurements of the L4–L5 disc as reported by Wilke et al. (2001). They measured a pressure of 1.8 MPa in the L4–L5 disc while the subject (body mass: 70 kg; body height: 1.74 m) was holding a full crate of beer (19.8 kg) 60 cm away from the chest. The disc area was 18 cm^2 and based on this the axial force was calculated to be 3240 N. The same situation was simulated using the spine model in this research. The estimated axial force was 3161.6 N. This is a good match considering the fact that no attempt was made to scale the model to the subject in this study. Body mass and body height of the subject in this study are quite similar to the body mass and height used in the model.

6. Haptic interface for spine modelling

6.1 Haptic rendering

Haptic rendering is the process of applying forces to give the operators a sense of touch and interaction with physical objects. Typically, a haptic rendering algorithm consists of two parts: collision detection and collision response. Figure 18 illustrates in detail the procedure of haptic rendering. Note the update rate of haptic rendering has to be maintained at around 1000 Hz for stable and smooth haptic interaction. Otherwise, virtual surfces feel softer. Even worse, the haptic device vibrates.

To observe the locomotion and study dynamic properties of the spine model quickly, conveniently and more realisticly, haptic technique can be integrated into a spine simulation system. In this study, for two types of spine models developed using finite element method as well as multi-body method in LifeMOD software, the haptic rendering process has two main stages: the rigid stage and the compliant stage. Without pressing the stylus button of the PHANToM device, the users can touch and explore the whole spine model since it is considered to be rigid throughout. After the users locate a specific vertebra where he/she wishes to apply force, they can then press the PHANToM stylus button and push or drag the vertebra in any direction to make the whole spine model deform. Once the stylus button is pressed, the system switches from rigid stage to compliant stage. The haptic rendering algorithms in these two stages will be clearly presented in the following sections. Figure 19 shows the complete haptic simulation process in the system.

6.2 Haptic rendering method for the rigid stage of the spine models

In real-time haptic simulation, users can only interact with the spine model by manipulating a rigid virtual object considered as a probe on the computer screen. At present, a simple probe such as a sphere is used in this study. In the rigid stage, a common haptic rendering method is used for the aforementioned types of spine models. Since this interaction carries out at a high update rate of 1 kHz, the chosen haptic rendering method needs to be reasonable and effectively computational. As presented above, the haptic rendering method includes two phases: collision detection and collision response. For the collision detection, the simple algorithm proposed by James Arvo (1990) is utilized to check intersection between the probe and the spine model through axis-aligned bounding boxes (AABBs). Figure 20 illustrates all AABBs of a vertebra intersecting with the spherical probe.

For collision response, the algorithm developed by Gao and Gibson (2006) is used to determine force feedback. An important prerequisite in this step is that intersecting points with the spherical probe have to be specified. Figure 21 shows intersecting points during colliding process between the probe and a vertebra.

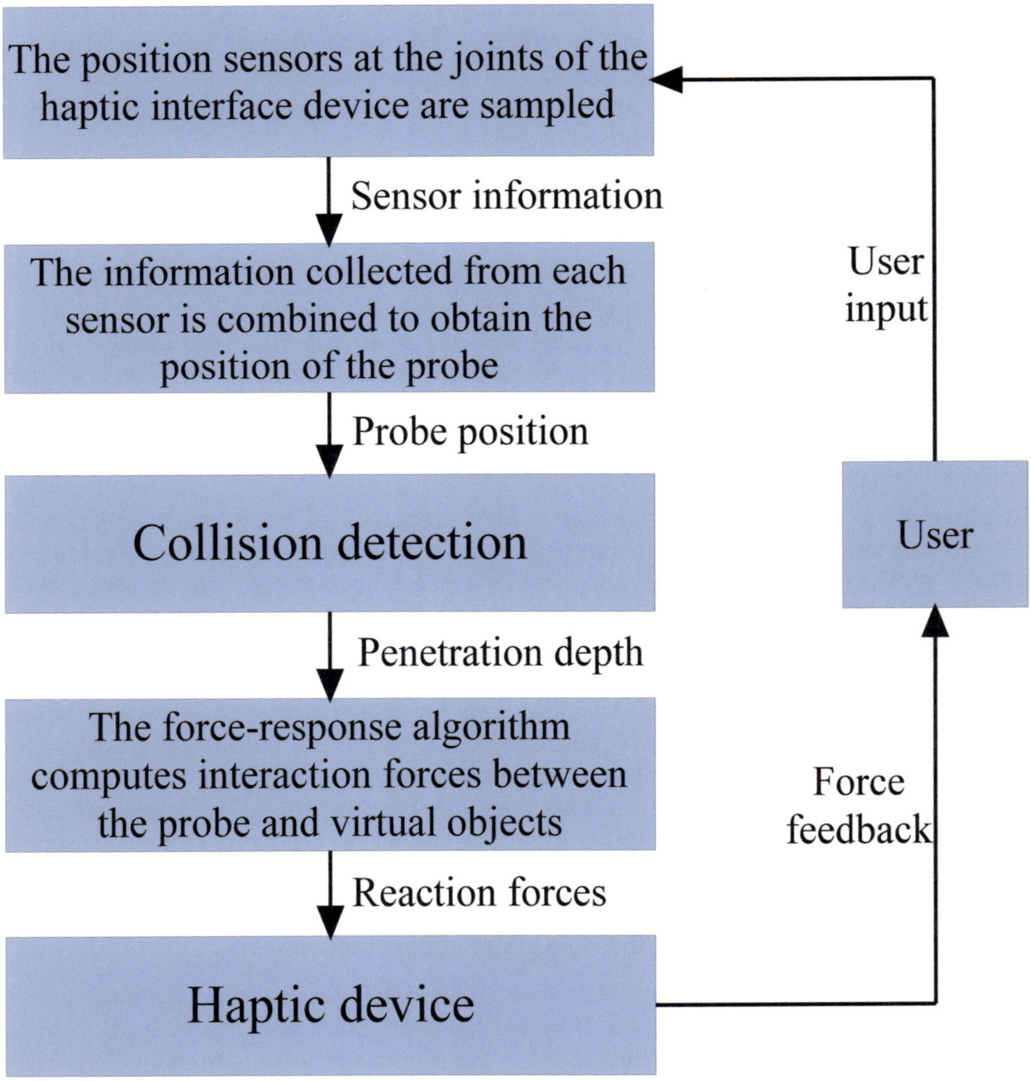

Fig. 18. Procedure of haptic rendering

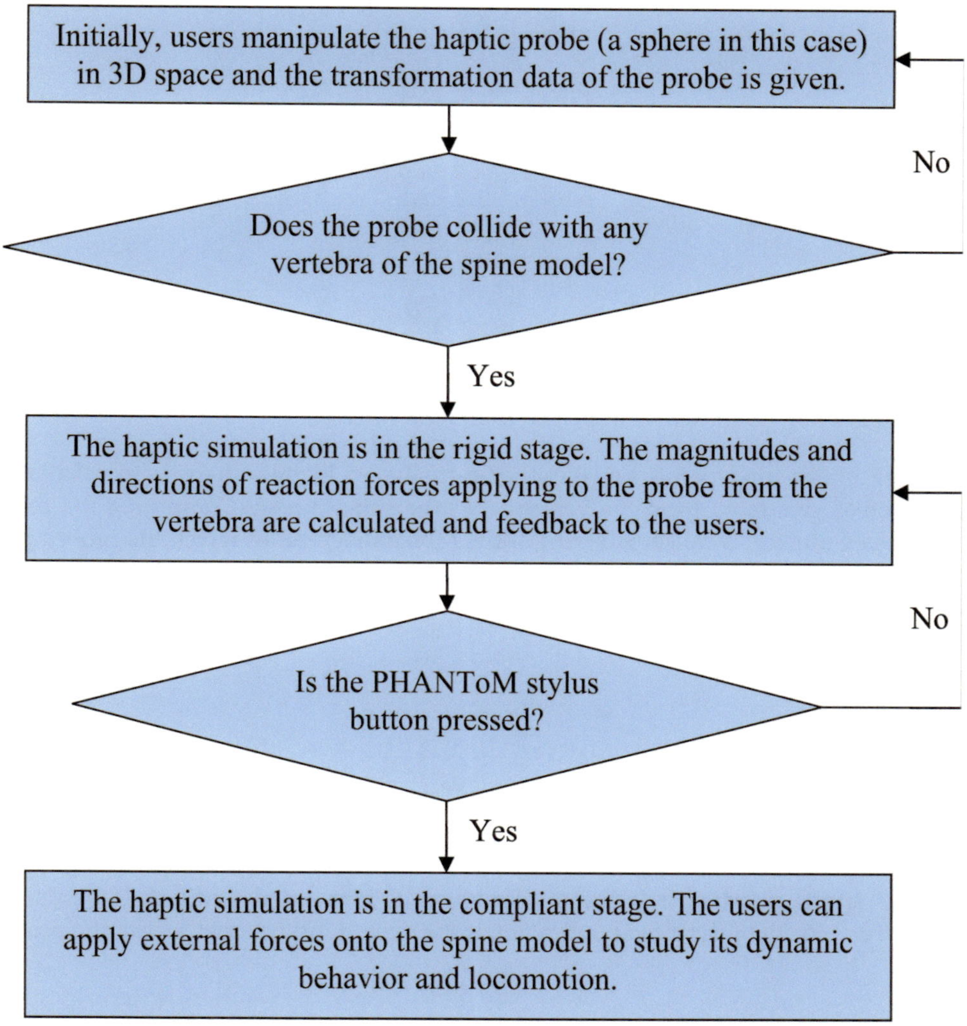

Fig. 19. Complete haptic simulation process in the system

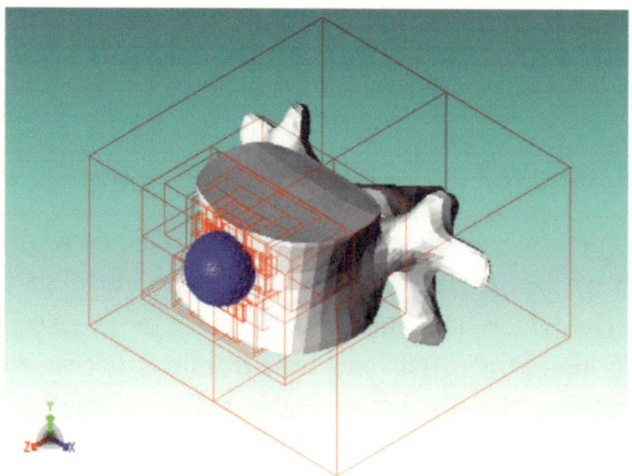

Fig. 20. Collision between the probe and a vertebra of the spine model

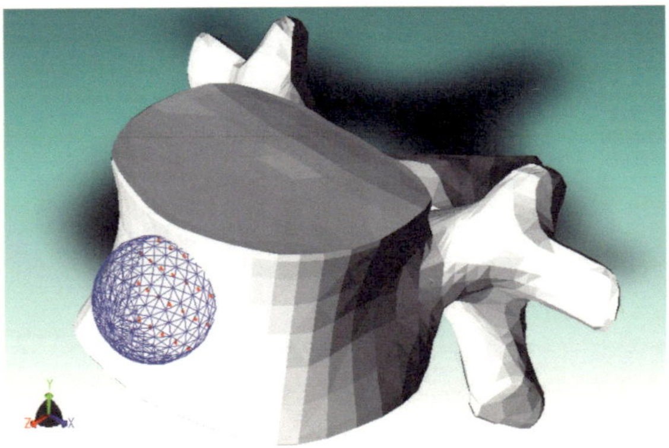

Fig. 21. Intersecting points betweenthe probe and the vertebra

After these intersecting points are found, the final step in this phase is to calculate the reaction forces generated from the vertebrae of the spine model. Computing the reaction forces of the vertebrae is concerned with finding force magnitudes which the probe applied to the intersecting points on the contact surface areas of the vertebrae and force directions at those points. The magnitudes and directions of reaction forces can be computed by the equations as follows:

$$|F| = \frac{\sum_{i=0}^{n}\left(k * s_i - d * \dot{s}_i\right)}{S_{MaxSec}} \tag{1}$$

$$S_{MaxSec}$$

where k is spring constant, s is the displacement of intersected point, d is the damping factor, is the velocity of the intersected point, is the maximum sectional area of the probe.

$$\vec{F} = \frac{\sum_{i=0}^{n} \vec{N}_i * s_i}{n} \tag{2}$$

where n is the number of surface sampling points inside probe, N_i as the normal vector of surface sampling point and s_i as the depth.

6.3 Haptic rendering method for the compliant stage of the spine models

After the users locate a specific vertebra where he/she wishes to apply force, they can then press the PHANToM stylus button and push or drag the vertebra in any direction to make the whole spine model deform. Once the stylus button is pressed, the system switches to another haptic rendering algorithm that uses the stretched-spring model. A virtual spring is set up connecting the vertebra and the haptic cursor. The spring has two hook points: one is on the vertebra and the other is the haptic cursor. Both of the hook points displace during spine deformation. The force magnitude is determined by the length of the virtual spring and stiffness while the force direction depends on the vector of the virtual spring.

6.3.1 Finite element spine model

In this stage, the haptic interface has two components: haptic rendering and an FE solver. The function of the haptic rendering component is to provide haptic feedback to the user when the user virtually deforms the spine model. The FE solver evaluates the deformation of the FE spine model according to the user's force input.

To solve the FE deformation problem, an explicit Newmark integration method is employed. The theory of elasticity consists of a set of differential equations that describe the state of stress, strain and displacement of each point within an elastic deformable body. A relationship between the deformation of the object and the exerted forces can be established by synthesizing those equations. The equation governing the resulting deformation from external forces is:

$$M\ddot{u} + D\dot{u} + R(u) = F \tag{3}$$

$$3n \times 3n$$

where u is the 3n-dimensional nodal displacement vector; and are the velocity and acceleration vectors respectively; F is the external force vector; M is the mass matrix; D is the damping matrix; R(u) represents the internal force vectors due to deformation; n is the number of nodes in the FE model.

If deformation is assumed to be small, a linear elastic model can be used to approximate linear strain:

$$\varepsilon_x = \frac{\partial u}{\partial x} \tag{4}$$

$$\gamma_{xy} = \frac{\partial u}{\partial y} + \frac{\partial v}{\partial x} \tag{5}$$

where x, y and z are the independent variables of the Cartesian frame, and u, v and w are the corresponding displacement variables at the given point.

Because the internal force vector is linear with respect to the nodal displacement vector, this leads to a constant stiffness matrix, which can be pre-computed. However, this solution does not consider geometric non-linearity and is only fit therefore for linear and small deformation situations. The linear strain model introduces distortions for large global deformations. In the model the deformation of the spine is rather large and therefore the linear strain approximation is not suitable. We model the deformation using the Green strain as follows:

$$\varepsilon_x = \frac{\partial u}{\partial x} + \frac{1}{2}\left[\left(\frac{\partial u}{\partial x}\right)^2 + \left(\frac{\partial v}{\partial x}\right)^2 + \left(\frac{\partial w}{\partial x}\right)^2\right] \tag{6}$$

$$\gamma_{xy} = \frac{\partial u}{\partial y} + \frac{\partial v}{\partial x} + \left[\frac{\partial u \partial u}{\partial x \partial y} + \frac{\partial v \partial v}{\partial x \partial y} + \frac{\partial w \partial w}{\partial x \partial y}\right] \tag{7}$$

The other 4 terms of the strain are defined similarly. The algorithm equations are:

$$\dot{u}_{n+1} = \dot{u}_n + \frac{\Delta t}{2}\left(\ddot{u}_n + \ddot{u}_{n+1}\right) \tag{8}$$

$$u_{n+1} = u_n + \dot{u}_n \Delta t + \frac{\ddot{u}_n}{2}\Delta t^2 \tag{9}$$

$$M\ddot{u}_{n+1} = F_{n+1} - R(u_{n+1}) - D\dot{u}_{n+1} \tag{10}$$

Zhuang's mass concentration method is employed to approximate the distributed mass in real-time (Zhuang & Canny, 2000). To avoid inverting a large sparse matrix at each time step, Zhuang's method approximates the force matrix M with a diagonal matrix. Diagonalization results in approximating the mass continuum as concentrated masses at each nodal point of the finite element model. This simplifies the nonlinear system of equations used to form a set of independent algebraic equations that can be solved with relatively high updating rate.

A prototype system has been implemented. Although the FE model of the spine is a simplified beam model, the updating rate of FEM evaluation is still far below the 1000 Hz required for effective vibration-free haptic rendering. The FE model has 472 elements and 473 nodes and the time step of the explicit integration is 0.02 second. The updating rate is approximately 200 Hz using a PC graphic workstation. To avoid vibration due to the updating rate discrepancy, a force interpolation method (Zhuang & Canny, 2000) was adopted to smoothen the force feedback. Haptic feedback between two simulated states is linearly interpolated at a suitably high frequency. However, at time t_n, we do not have the information of t_{n+1}. Zhuang's solution uses an intentional delay of an FEM deformation time step, up to 1/100s. User experimentation found that such a small lag in time is within the tolerance of human perception for virtual interaction with soft objects.

6.3.2 Multi-body spine model

Different from the finite element spine model whose locomotion is directly calculated in the haptic simulation, the multi-body spine model in the compliant stage utilize the pre-interpolated displacement-force functions of all vertebrae to conveniently compute the movement of the spine. Based on the magnitude of the haptic external forces applied by the users, dynamic properties of all vertebrae can be easily calculated via these functions and the locomotion of the whole spine model can be rapidly observed.

The purpose of interpolating displacement-force functions of all vertebrae is to facilitate computational process of dynamic properties of the spine model during haptic simulation. To do that, some constraints are imposed on the spine model. The pelvis is fixed in 3D space. Then, constant forces are applied on each specific vertebra in the thoracic region in each axis-aligned direction during simulation. The force magnitude is gradually increased with an equal increment in subsequent simulations. Corresponding to each value of force, dynamic characteristics of all vertebrae (e.g. translation, rotation) can be automatically obtained using the plots in LifeMOD as a reference. The dynamic properties are recorded after the spine model is stabilized. Based on these recorded dynamic properties, displacement-force relationships can be interpolated using the least-squares method and expressed in terms of polynomial functions. Figure 22 illustrates the graph of a dynamic property of vertebra T1 under forward forces in sagittal plane of the spine model. In these figures, each series of markers presents each dynamic property of one vertebra obtained in the simulations and the continuous line closely fit to that series is the corresponding interpolated line.

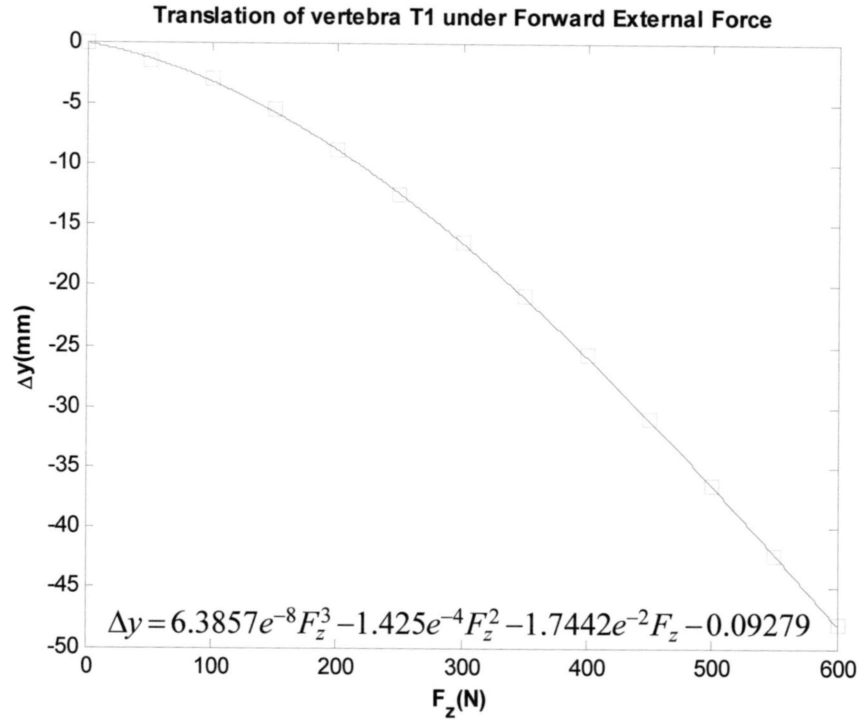

Fig. 22. Relative translation Δy of T1 versus forward force

7. Applications

7.1 Haptic simulation of the finite element spine model

Initially, without pressing the stylus button, the user can touch and explore the spine model since it is considered to be rigid throughout. Then, the user can control the probe to apply external forces in any arbitrary direction onto any vertebra by pressing the stylus button to observe the locomotion and study dynamic properties of the spine model. Figure 23 shows the haptic real-time simulation of the finite element spine model under lateral bending. During this real-time simulation, the displacement, rotation and deformation of the spine can be recorded and then input to the offline FEA application for further detailed stress/strain and deformation behaviour analysis of IVDs as well as vertebrae.

7.2 Studying stress/strain of the finite element spine model in a prone position

As presented above, all dynamic properties of the spine model recorded during the haptic simulation can be provided as input of offline FEA simulator for further detailed analysis. In this section, an example of spine manipulation is demonstrated. A human body is prone on a horizontal table and a downward force is pushed on T12 vertebra. Therefore, the spine is also in prone position. All 6 DOFs of the pelvis are constrained and 2 DOFs of the T1 on the horizontal plane are constrained in order to simulate the situation where the prone posture torso is constrained by a horizontal plane underneath the torso. In the haptic simulator, downward pressing forces are applied to the T12 vertebra by the user through the PHANToM device. Figure 24(a) shows the beam element spine model at initial status without any deformation.

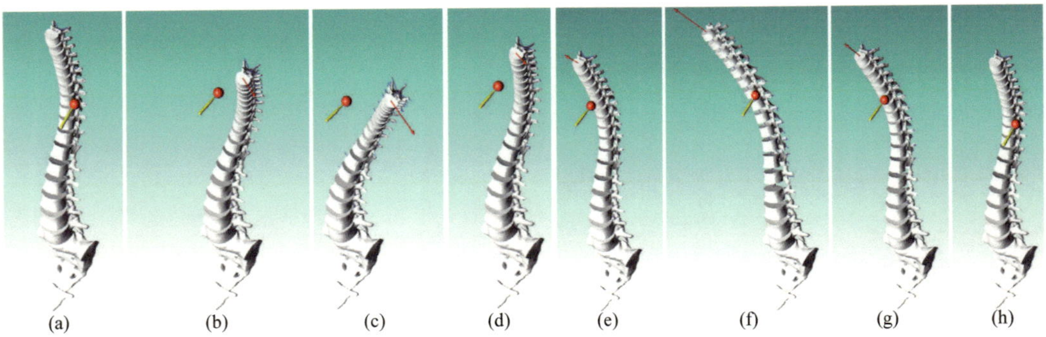

Fig. 23. The haptic real-time simulation of finite element spine model

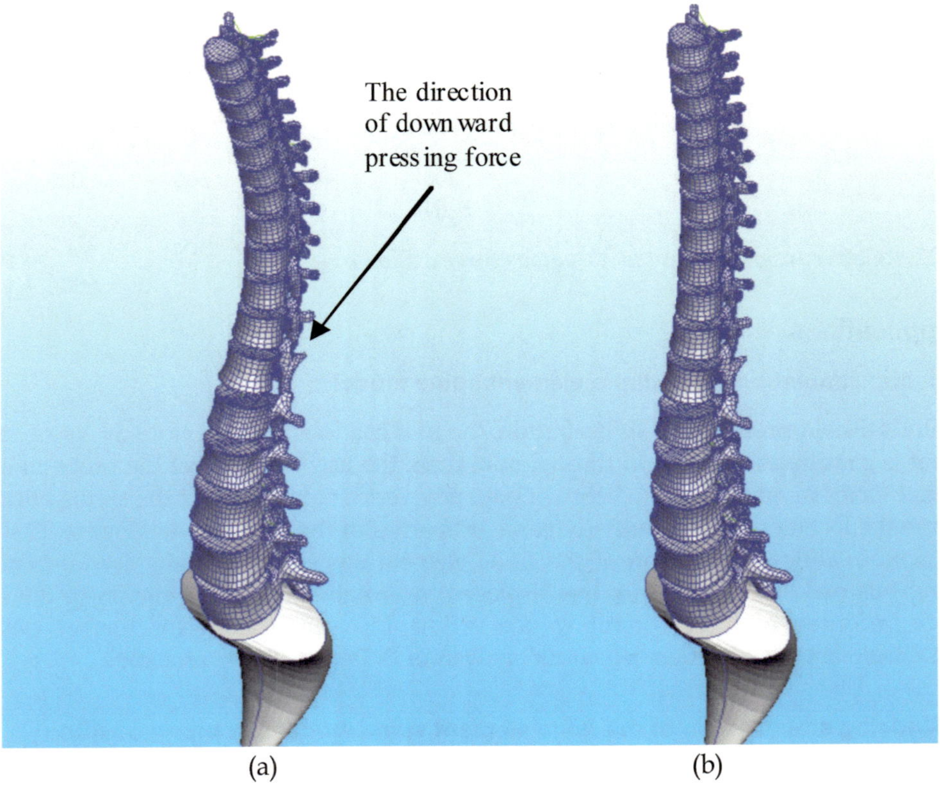

Fig. 24. Spine manipulation in the haptic real-time simulator

Figure 24(b) shows the spine model under deformation. The deformation is then recorded and the displacement of the focused vertebra, T12 in this case, is obtained and input into the offline FEA solver. Figure 25 shows the result from the ABAQUS offline FEA solution. Only T9 to the pelvis is shown because this region is the most interesting region if a pressing load is applied on T12. The offline FEM model consisted of cortical bones, cancellous bones, bony end plates and the intervertebral discs. The disc's annulus was represented as a composite of collagenous fiber embedded in a matrix of base substance. The nucleus was modelled as an incompressible inviscid fluid. Because intervertebral discs often experience large deformation and strains under compressive loading, the materials of the FEM spine model were non-linear. Figure 25(a) shows the tetrahedral FE model without deformation. Figure 25 (b) and (c) show the von Mises stress distribution after deformation.

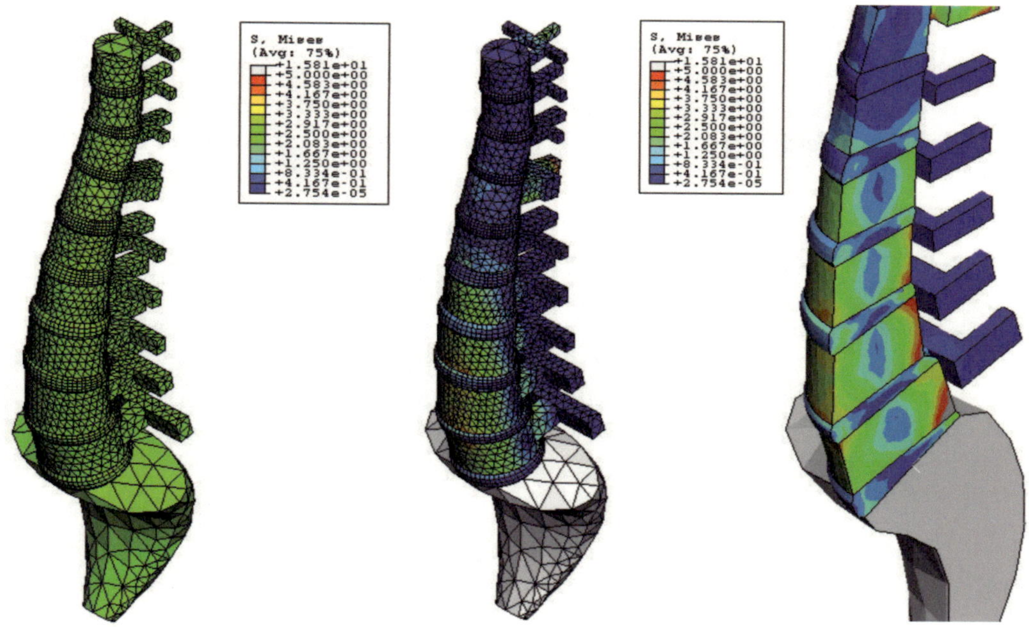

(a) (b) (c)

Fig. 25. Offline FEA simulation

7.3 Investigating dynamic properties of the spine model under external haptic forces

Since the finite element spine model for the haptic simulation is represented with beam element which is in fact highly simplified, it is difficult to describe precisely the dynamic properties of the real spine. Compared to this finite element spine model, the detailed musculo-skeletal multi-body spine model developed in LifeMOD can provide better information of biodynamic behaviour of the spine. Since LifeMOD software takes account of other components (such as head, ribcage, muscles, ligaments so on), the locomotion of the spine model will become much more realistic. Furthermore, by simulating the spine model in a haptically integrated graphic environment, the users (such as surgeons, trainers) can quickly and conveniently observe the locomotion as well as gain insight into the dynamic behaviour of the spine.

The long-term goal of this study is to develop a haptically integrated simulation platform for investigating post-operative personal spine models constructed from LifeMOD. The first step in this study is to develop a haptic interface for a detailed normal spine model whose dynamic properties are obtained from LifeMOD. Figure 26 illustrates the analysis of some dynamic properties of the spine when applying force on vertebra T1 in x-axis direction.

The next step in the study is to develop a post-operative detailed spine model. The operation conducted on the spine model can be spinal fusion or spinal arthroplasty. By using this haptically integrated graphic interface, assessing biomechanical behavior between natural spines and spinal arthroplasty or spinal fusion becomes more convenient. This will help orthepaedic surgeons understand the change in force distribution following spine fusion procedures, which can also assist in post-operative physiotherapy. In addition, the surgeons can gain useful insight from this system in the planning of surgery to correct severe scoliosis. Different designs of rods and braces can for example be experimented with using this virtual environment. It is also considered that this system may assist physiotherapists and other practitioners when designing cushioning and supports for wheelchair-bound and other clients suffering from asymmetric spinal disorders.

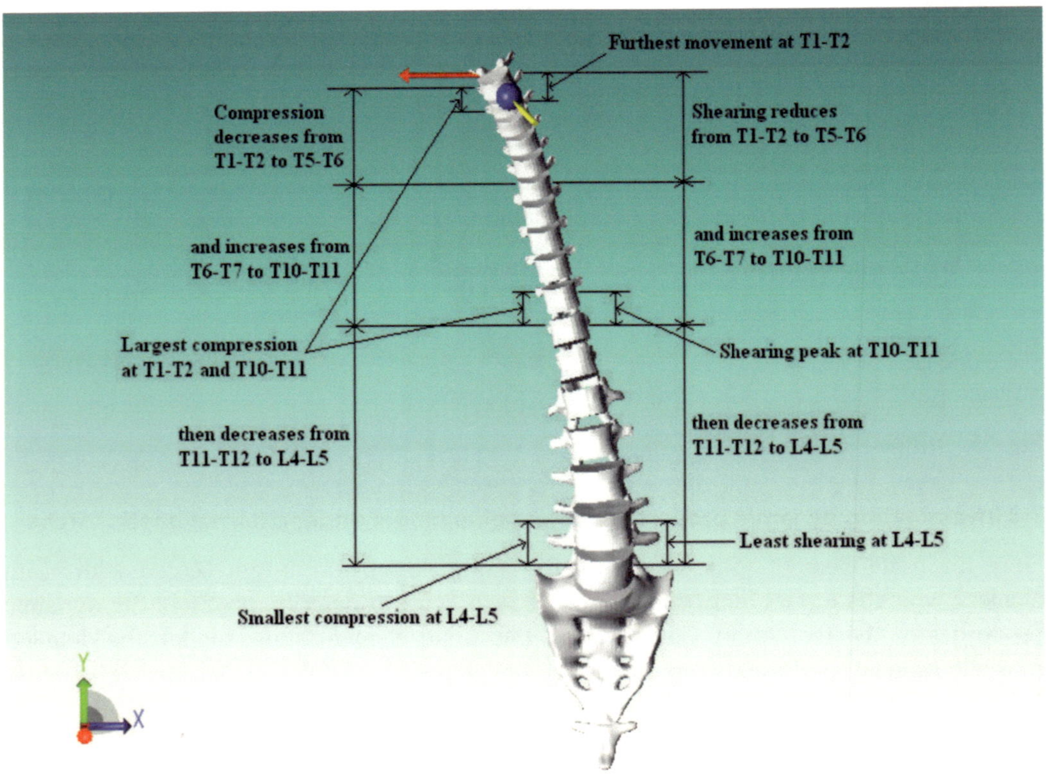

Fig. 26. Analyzing translational properties of the spine model under lateral force on T1

8. Conclusion

In general, we have presented the process of modelling human spine. Initially, a beam FE spine model for haptic interaction is built based on a solid FE spine model, which is created in offline finite element analysis software. Although there are some limitations on not fully taking into account soft tissues, this beam FE model is able to simulate global dynamic behaviour of the whole spine, Subsequently, an entirely detailed musculo-skeletal muti-body spine model using LifeMOD Biomechanics Modeler is completely developed to solve the limitations aforementioned and reliably validated by comparing simulation results with experimental data and in-vivo measurements. Moreover, to enhance more realistic interaction between users (such as trainers, clinicians, surgeons) and the spine model during real-time simulation, haptic technique is integrated into a graphic interface. Based on this, exploration of the spine model becomes much more realistic since the users can manipulate the haptic cursor to directly touch, grasp and even apply external forces in any arbitrary direction onto any vertebra to observe the deformation of the spine. In such a simulation interface, users can quickly and more conveniently study the locomotion and dynamic behaviour of the spine model.

9. References

Andersson E., Oddsson L., Grundstrom H. et al. (1995). The Role of the Psoas and Iliacus Muscles for Stability and Movement of the Lumbar Spine, Pelvis and Hip. *Scandinavian Journal of Medicine and Science in Sports*, Vol. 5, No. 1, pp. 10-16.

Arvo J. (1990). A Simple Method for Box-Sphere Intersection Testing. *Graphics Gems*, pp. 335-339.

Aubin C.E. (2002). Scoliosis Study Using Finite Element Models. *Studies in Health Technology and Informatics*, Vol. 91, pp. 309-313.

Basdogan C., Ho C.H., Srinivasan M.A. et al. (1998). Force Interaction in Laparoscopic Simulations: Haptic Rendering of Soft Tissues. *Stud. Health Technol. Inform.*, Vol. 50, pp. 385-391.

Bogduk N., Macintosh J.E. & Pearcy M.J. (1992a). A Universal Model of the Lumbar Back Muscles in the Upright Position. *Spine*, Vol. 17, No. 8, pp. 897-913.

Bogduk N., Pearcy M.J. & Hadfield G. (1992b). Anatomy and Biomechanics of Psoas Major. *Clinical Biomechanics*, Vol. 7, No. 2, pp. 109-119.

Esat V. & Acar M. (2007). A Multi-Body Model of the Whole Human Spine for Whiplash Investigations.

Forest C., Delingette H. & Ayache N. (2004). Surface Contact and Reaction Force Models for Laparoscopic Simulation. *In International Symposium on Medical Simulation*, Vol. 3078, pp. 168-176.

Fritz M. (1998). Three-Dimensional Biomechanical Model for Simulating the Response of the Human Body to Vibration Stress. *Journal of Medical & Biological Engineering & Computing*, Vol. 36, No. 6, pp. 686-692.

Gao Z. & Gibson I. (2006). Haptic Sculpting of Multi-Resolution B-Spline Surfaces with Shaped Tools. *Computer Aided Design*, Vol. 38, No. 6, pp. 661-676.

Garcia T. & Ravani B. (2003). A Biomechanical Evaluation of Whiplash Using a Multi-Body Dynamic Model. *Journal of Biomechanical Engineering*, Vol. 125, No. 2, pp. 254-265.

Gignac D., Aubin C.E., Dansereau J. et al. (2000). Optimization Method for 3d Bracing Correction of Scoliosis Using a Finite Element Model. *European Spine Journal*, Vol. 9, No. 3, pp. 185-190.

Gorman P., Krummel T., Webster R. et al. (2000). A Prototype Haptic Lumbar Puncture Simulator. *Studies in Health Technology and Informatics*, Vol. 70.

Greaves C.Y., Gadala M.S. & Oxland T.R. (2008). A Three-Dimensional Finite Element Model of the Cervical Spine with Spinal Cord: An Investigation of Three Injury Mechanisms. *Annals of Biomedical Engineering*, Vol. 36, No. 3, pp. 396-405.

Jager M., Sauren A., Thunnissen J.G.M. et al. (1996). A Global and Detailed Mathematical Model for Head-Neck Dynamics. *SAE Tech. Pap. Ser.*

Jun Y. (2006). A Computational Model of the Human Head and Cervical Spine for Dynamic Impact Simulation.

Kumaresan S., Yoganandan N. & Pintar F.A. (1999). Finite Element Analysis of the Cervical Spine: A Material Property Sensitivity Study. *Clinical Biomechanics*, Vol. 14, No. 1, pp. 41-53.

Lafage V., Dubousset J., Lavaste F. et al. (2004). 3d Finite Element Simulation of Cotrel-Dubousset Correction. *Computer Aided Surgery*, Vol. 9, No. 1-2, pp. 17-25.

Lifemod Biomechanics Modeler [cited; Available from: http://www.lifemodeler.com/].

Linder A. (2000). A New Mathematical Neck Model for a Low-Velocity Rear-End Impact Dummy: Evaluation of Components Influencing Head Kinematics. *Accident Analysis and Prevention*, Vol. 32, No. 2, pp. 261-269.

Luo Z.P. & Goldsmith W. (1991). Reaction of a Human Head-Neck-Torso System to Shock. *Journal of Biomechanics*, Vol. 24, No. 7, pp. 499-510.

Luoma K., Riihimaki H., Luukkonen R. et al. (2000). Low Back Pain in Relation to Lumbar Disc Degeneration. *Spine*, Vol. 25, No. 4, pp. 487-492.

Macintosh J.E. & Bogduk N. (1986). The Morphology of the Human Lumbar Multifidus. *Clinical Biomechanics*, Vol. 1, No. 4, pp. 196-204.

Macintosh J.E. & Bogduk N. (1987). 1987 Volvo Award in Basic Science: The Morphology of the Lumbar Erector Spinae. *Spine*, Vol. 12, No. 7, pp. 658-668.

Macintosh J.E. & Bogduk N. (1991). The Attachments of the Lumbar Erector Spinae. *Spine*, Vol. 16, No. 7, pp. 783-792.

Mastmeyer A., Engelke K., Fuchs C. et al. (2006). A Hierarchical 3d Segmentation Method and the Definition of Vertebral Body Coordinate Systems for Qct of the Lumbar Spine. *Medical Image Analysis*, Vol. 10, No. 4, pp. 560-577.

Maurel N., Lavaste F. & Skalli W. (1997). A Three-Dimensional Parameterized Finite Element Model of the Lower Cervical Spine: Study of the Influence of the Posterior Articular Facets. *Journal of Biomechanics*, Vol. 30, No. 9, pp. 921-931.

McGill S.M. & Norman R.W. (1987). Effects of an Anatomically Detailed Erector Spinae Model on L4/L5 Disc Compression and Shear. *Journal of Biomechanics*, Vol. 20, No. 6, pp. 591-600.

Moroney S.P., Schultz A.B., Miller J.A.A. et al. (1988). Load-Displacement Properties of Lower Cervical Spine Motion Segment. *Journal of Biomechanics*, Vol. 21, pp. 767-779.

Natarajan R.N., Williams J.R., Lavender S.A. et al. (2007). Poro-Elastic Finite Element Model to Predict the Failure Progression in a Lumbar Disc Due to Cyclic Loading. *Computers & Structures*, Vol. 85, No. 11-14, pp. 1142-1151.

Ng H.W. & Teo E.C. (2005). Development and Validation of a C0-C7 Fe Complex for Biomechanical Study. *Journal of Biomechanics*, Vol. 127, No. 5, pp. 729-735.

Panjabi M.M., Brand R.A. & White A.A. (1976). Mechanical Properties of the Human Thoracic Spine as Shown by Three-Dimensional Load-Displacement Curves. *Journal of Bone and Joint Surgery*, Vol. 58, No. 5, pp. 642-652.

Pankoke S., Buck B. & Woelfel H.P. (1998). Dynamic Fe Model of Sitting Man Adjustable to Body Height, Body Mass and Posture Used for Calculating Internal Forces in the Lumbar Vertebral Disks. *Journal of Sound and Vibration*, Vol. 215, No. 4, pp. 827-839.

Penning L. (2000). Psoas Muscle and Lumbar Spine Stability: A Concept Uniting Existing Controversies. Critical Review and Hypothesis. *European Spine Journal*, Vol. 9, No. 6, pp. 577-585.

Schlenk R.P., Kowalski R.J. & Benzel E.C. (2003). Biomechanics of Spinal Deformity. *Neurosurg Focus*, Vol. 14, No. 1, pp. 1-10.

Schmidt H., Heuer F., Claes L. et al. (2008). The Relation between the Instantaneous Center of Rotation and Facet Joint Forces - a Finite Element Analysis. *Clinical Biomechanics*, Vol. 23, No. 3, pp. 270-278.

Schultz A.B., Warwick D.N., Berkson M.H. et al. (1979). Mechanical Properties of Human Lumbar Spine Motion Segments-Part 1: Responses in Flexion, Extension, Lateral Bending and Torsion. *Journal of Biomechanical Engineering*, Vol. 101, pp. 46-52.

Schultz A.B. & Ashton-Miller J.A., *Biomechanics of the Human Spine*, in *Basic Orthopaedic Biomechanics*, V.C. Mow and W.C. Hayes, Editors. 1991, Raven Press: New York. p. 337-374.

Seidel H. & Griffin M.J. (2001). Modelling the Response of the Spine System to Whole-Body Vibration and Repeated Shock. *Clinical Biomechanics*, Vol. 16, No. 1, pp. 3-7.

Seidel H., Hinz B. & Bluthner R. (2001). Application of Finite Element Models to Predict Forces Acting on the Lumbar Spine During Whole-Body Vibration. *Clinical Biomechanics*, Vol. 16, No. 1, pp. S57-S63.

Seitz H., Tille C., Irsen S. et al. (2004). Rapid Prototyping Models for Surgical Planning with Hard and Soft Tissue Representation. *International Congress Series*, Vol. 1268, pp. 567-572.

Stemper B.D., Yoganandan N. & Pintar F.A. (2004). Validation of a Head-Neck Computer Model for Whiplash Simulation. *Medical and Biological Engineering and Computing*, Vol. 42, No. 3, pp. 333-338.

Stokes I.A. & Gardner-Morse M. (1999). Quantitative Anatomy of the Lumbar Musculature. *Journal of Biomechanics*, Vol. 32, No. 3, pp. 311-316.

Teo E.C. & Ng H.W. (2001). First Cervical Vertebra (Atlas) Fracture Mechanism Studies Using Finite Element Method. *Journal of Biomechanics*, Vol. 34, No. 1, pp. 13-21.

Vallfors B. (1985). Acute, Subacute and Chronic Low Back Pain: Clinical Symptoms, Absenteeism and Working Environment. *Scandinavian Journal of Rehabilitation Medicine. Supplement*, Vol. 11, pp. 1-98.

Van Der Horst M.J. (2002). Human Head Neck Response in Frontal, Lateral and Rear End Impact Loading: Modeling and Validation.

Verver M.M., Hoof J.V., Oomens C.W.J. et al. (2003). Estimation of Spinal Loading in Vertical Vibrations by Numerical Simulation. *Clinical Biomechanics*, Vol. 18, No. 9, pp. 800-811.

Wilke H.J., Neef P., Hinz B. et al. (2001). Intradiscal Pressure Together with Anthropometric Data – a Data Set for the Validation of Models. *Clinical Biomechanics*, Vol. 16, No. 1, pp. S111-S126.

Williams R.L., Srivastava M., Howell J.N. et al. (2004). The Virtual Haptic Back for Palpatory Training. *Proceedings of the 6th international conference on multimodal interfaces.*

Yoganandan N., Kumaresan S., Voo L. et al. (1996). Finite Element Modeling of the C4-C6 Cervical Spine Unit. *Medical Engineering Physics*, Vol. 18, No. 7, pp. 569-574.

Yoshimura T., Nakai K. & Tamaoki G. (2005). Multi-Body Dynamics Modelling of Seated Human Body under Exposure to Whole-Body Vibration, Vol. 43, No. 3, pp. 441-447.

Zander T., Rohlmann A., Klockner C. et al. (2002). Comparison of the Mechanical Behavior of the Lumbar Spine Following Mono-and Bisegmental Stabilization. *Clinical Biomechanics*, Vol. 17, No. 6, pp. 439-445.

Zee M.D., Hansen L., Wong C. et al. (2007). A Generic Detailed Rigid-Body Lumbar Spine Model. *Journal of Biomechanics*, Vol. 40, No. 6, pp. 1219-1227.

Zhuang Y. & Canny J. (2000). Haptic Interaction with Global Deformations. *ICRA '00. IEEE International Conference on Robotics and Automation.*

10

Training Motor Skills Using Haptic Interfaces

Otniel Portillo-Rodriguez[1,2], Carlo Avizzano[1],
Oscar Sandoval Gonzalez[1,3], Adriana Vilchis-Gonzalez[2],
Mariel Davila-Vilchis[2] and Massimo Bergamasco[1]
[1]*Perceptual Robotics Laboratory, Scuola Superiore Sant'Anna, Pisa,*
[2]*Facultad de Ingeniería, Universidad Autónoma del Estado de México, Toluca,*
[3]*Instituto Tecnológico de Orizaba, Orizaba,*
[1]*Italy*
[2,3]*México*

1. Introduction

Skill has many meanings, as there are many talents: its origin comes from the late Old English scele, meaning knowledge, and from Old Norse skil (discernment, knowledge), even if a general definition of skill can be given as "the learned ability to do a process well" (McCullough, 1999) or as the acquired ability to successfully perform a specific task.

Task is the elementary unit of goal directed behaviour (Gopher, 2004) and is also a fundamental concept -strictly connected to "skill"- in the study of human behaviour, so that psychology may be defined as the science of people performing tasks. Moreover skill is not associated only to knowledge, but also to technology, since technology is -literally in the Greek- the study of skill.

Skill-based behaviour represents sensory-motor performance during activities following a statement of an intention and taking place without conscious control as smooth, automated and highly integrated patterns of behaviour. As it is shown in Figure 1, a schematic representation of the cognitive-sensory-motor integration required by a skill performance, complex skills can involve both gesture and sensory-motor abilities, but also high level cognitive functions, such as procedural (e.g. how to do something) and decision and judgement (e.g. when to do what) abilities. In most skilled sensory-motor tasks, the body acts as a multivariable continuous control system synchronizing movements with the behavioural of the environment (Annelise Mark Pejtersen, 1997). This way of acting is also named also as, action-centred, enactive, reflection-in-action or simply know-how.

Skills differ from talent since talent seems native, and concepts come from schooling, while skill is learned by doing (McCullough, 1999). It is acquired by demonstration and sharpened by practice. Skill is moreover participatory, and this basis makes it durable: any teacher knows that active participation is the way to retainable knowledge.

The knowledge achieved by an artisan throughout his/her lifelong activity of work is a good example of a skill that is difficult to transfer to another person. At present the knowledge of a specific craftsmanship is lost when the skilled worker ends his/her working activity or when other physical impairments force him/her to give up. The above considerations are valid not only in the framework of craftsmanship but also for more general application domains, such as the industrial field, e.g. for maintenance of complex mechanical parts, surgery training and so on.

The research done stems out from the recognition that technology is a dominant ecology in our world and that nowadays a great deal of human behaviour is augmented by technology. Multimodal Human-Computer Interfaces aim at coordinating several intuitive input modalities (e.g. the user's speech and gestures) and several intuitive output modalities.

The existing level of technology in the HCI field is very high and mature, so that technological constrains can be removed from the design process to shift the focus on the real user's needs, as it is demonstrated by the fact that nowadays the user-centered design has became fundamental for devising successful everyday new products and interfaces (Norman, 1986; Norman, 1988), fitting people and that really conforming their needs.

However, until now most interaction technologies have emphasized more input channel (afferent channel in Figure 1 The role of HCI in the performance of a skill), rather than output (efferent channel); foreground tasks rather than background contexts.

Advances in HCI technology allows now to have better gestures, more sensing combinations and improve 3D frameworks, and so it is possible now to put also more emphasis on the output channel, e.g. recent developments of haptic interfaces and tactile effector technologies. This is sufficient to bring in the actual context new and better instruments and interfaces for doing better what you can do, and to teach you how to do something well: so interfaces supporting and augmenting your skills. In fact user interfaces to advanced augmenting technologies are the successors to simpler interfaces that have existed between people and their artefacts for thousands of years (M. Chignell & Takeshit, 1999).

The objective is to develop new HCI technologies and devise new usages of existing ones to support people during the execution of complex tasks, help them to do things well or better, and make them more skilful in the execution of activities, overall augmenting the capability of human action and performance.

We aimed to investigate the transfer of skills defined as the use of knowledge or skill acquired in one situation in the performance of a new, novel task, and its reproducibility by means of VEs and HCI technologies, using actual and new technology with a complete innovative approach, in order to develop and evaluating interfaces for doing better in the context of a specific task.

Figure 2 draws on the scheme of Figure 1, and shows the important role that new interfaces will play and their features. They should possess the following functionalities:

- Capability of interfacing with the world, in order to get a comprehension of the status of the world;
- Capability of getting input from the humans through his efferent channel, in a way not disturbing the human from the execution of the main task (transparency);
- Local intelligence, that is the capability of having an internal and efficient representation of the task flow, correlating the task flow with the status of the environment during the human-world interaction process, understanding and

predicting the current human status and behaviour, formulating precise indications on next steps of the task flow or corrective actions to be implemented;

- Capability of sending both information and action consequences in output towards the human, through his/her afferent channel, in a way that is not disturbing the human from the execution of the main task.

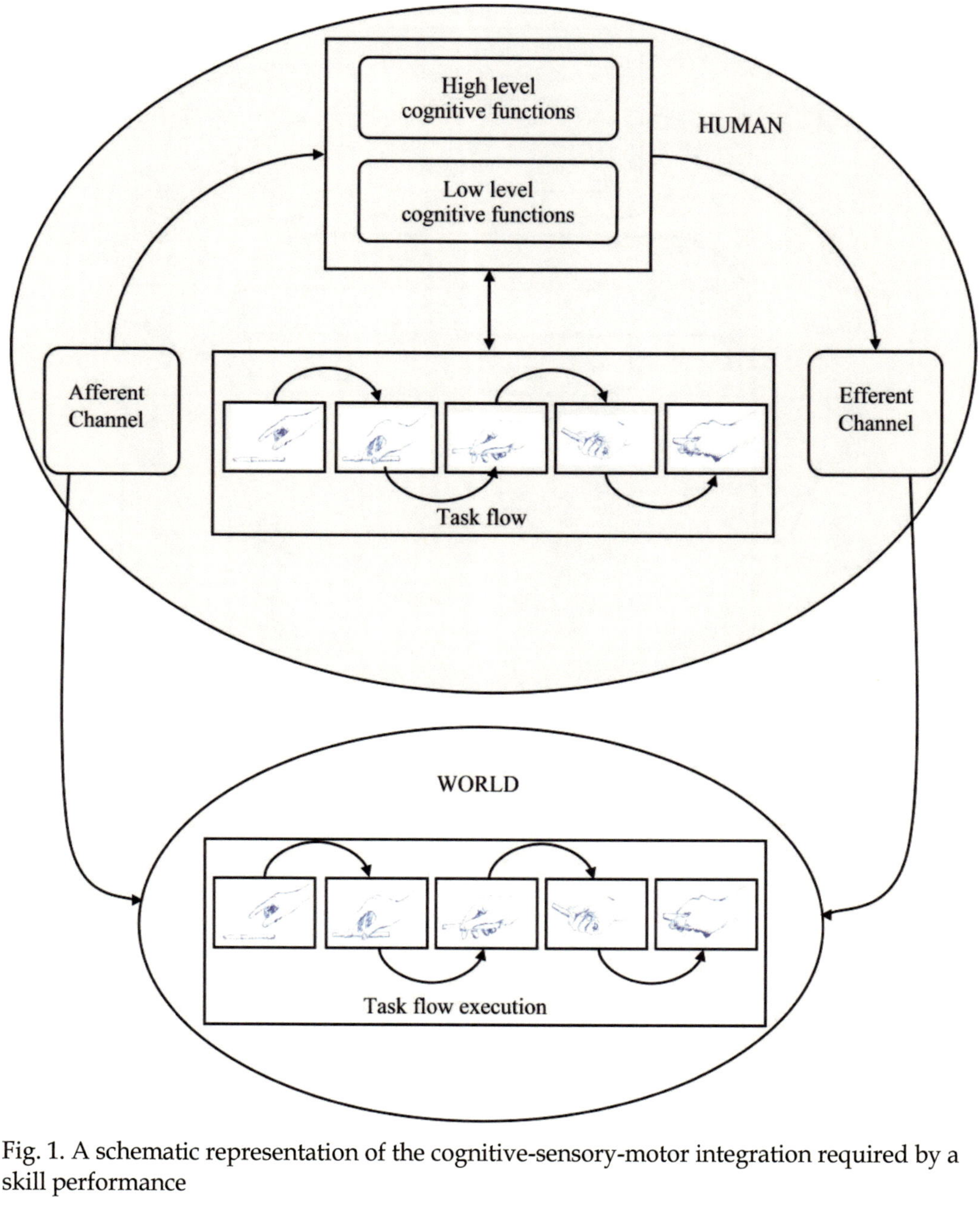

Fig. 1. A schematic representation of the cognitive-sensory-motor integration required by a skill performance

We desire improving both input and output modalities of interfaces, and on the interplay between the two, with interfaces in the loop of decision and action (Flach, 1994) in strictly connection with human, as it is shown clearly in Figure 2. The interfaces will boost the capabilities of the afferent-efferent channel of humans, the exchange of information with the world, and the performance of undertaken actions, acting in synergy with the sensory-motor loop.

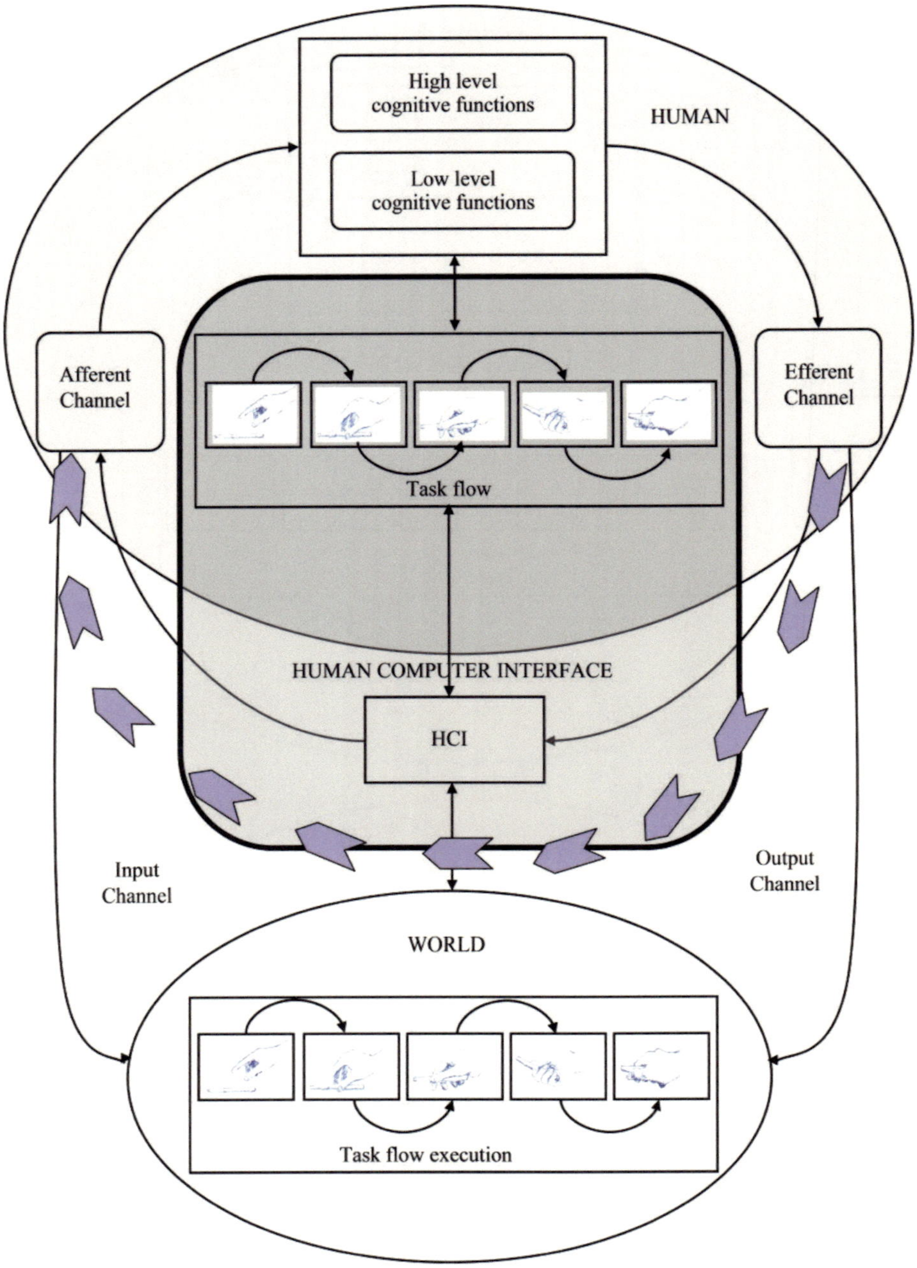

Fig. 2. The role of HCI in the performance of a skill

Interfaces will be technologically invisible at their best -not to decrease the human performance-, and capable of understanding the user intentions, current behaviour and purpose, contextualized in the task.

In this chapter a proposal of one multimodal interface for the transferring of skills, it will be described. The interface is called Haptic Desktop System (HDS), it was specifically projected for the training of motor skills specifically virtual fixtures. The HDS is an integrated system that merges haptic functionalities and Video Display Terminal (VDT) systems into one. It has been designed to provide visual and haptic perceptual information in order to avoid high mental loads and enable natural interaction with the user. Two applications to assist to human users to develop their motor skills to draw simple sketches were developed. The basic idea is generate a virtual template trajectory that the user must follow assisted with the force feedback capabilities of the HDS. In the first application, the virtual templates are generated from a given image file using image processing techniques, the templates are obtained and sent to the HDS controller which in combination with a graphical user interface (GUI) permits to the user to "fill" (follow) the virtual template. In the second application the templates are generated in a more dynamic way; the basic idea is to build a sketch using a set of virtual geometrical templates (VGT). The application currently allows drawing three types of VGTs: circles, lines and arcs. The user decides when and where request the assistance of the HDS to drawn a geometric shape. Based on the results we have demonstrated that the use of haptic interfaces improves and accelerates the acquiring of sketching skills.

2. Haptic desktop

The Haptic Desktop System (HDS) developed at PERCRO is our multimodal interface solution for design simple sketches. In Figure 3 a conceptual representation of this interface is shown, the user can freely design sketches inside the workspace of the interface which correspond with the superficies of a screen, enabling to the interface render the haptic and visual feedback in the same point in the 2D space.

2.1 Design guidelines

Two types of design guidelines have been employed during the preliminary definition of the system: qualitative and performance guidelines. According to qualitative guidelines the device had to show ergonomic features, which make the use of the system very comfortable. These guidelines have regarded: the workplace, the quality of the visual feedback, the aesthetics of the system, and the modality of interaction. Another very important guideline is the reduction of mental load during the use of the device.

The system design and control should allow the user to feel and control haptic interaction just below his fingertips, while directly viewing the effects of his actions on the computer screen (co-location). Specific state of the art analyses [Jansson & Öström, 2004] have verified that co-location greatly enhances the user performances in HCI while reducing the mental load of the interaction. The haptic device has therefore to be calibrated in order to collimate the position of the usage tool (end-effector), with the pointer within the computer screen. The accuracy provided in design, should ensure that the sensitivity of the system is far beyond the pixel resolution of the screen.

These guidelines have steered the main design choices of the system: the presence of the haptic interface should minimally interfere with the visual feedback and therefore it was decided to make use of transparent materials for building; all cables and connection should be hidden to the user; the device should offer the possibility of using a common pen as an interaction tool or the possibility of changing the end part with different tools; the device should be able in any case to replace and substitute the mouse in all its basic functions (point, select, click,...); the kinematic of the device should be designed in order to not interfere with the user limbs, it should preferably move in the opposite space with respect the user; the device, whenever unused, has to be closable in order to left the desktop free.

According to performance guidelines the device should have the following characteristics: a comfortable workspace wide enough to allow user to interact in writing operation: the workspace estimated had to cover at least the same dimensions of a notebook (270 x 360 mm); for design and writing related applications a typical position resolution well below 1 mm was identified. Backlashes were not allowed in kinematic design. A set of preliminary experiments, carried out with pens in writing-and-contour-following-tests suggested a target continuos force of about 1-1.5N. Similar tests outlined a maximum residual mass of 0.2 Kg.

A high isotropy of the mechanical parameters (manipulability ellipsoid ~1) was required all over the workspace in order to reduce the distortion effects and to maximize the exploitation of the motors. In order to achieve high control bandwidth and facilitate the system maintenance and development a high degree of integration with the hosting OS was required.

Finally, in order to reduce the cost related to the system manufacturing two features were required to the system design: simplicity and possibility of manufacturing with low precision (low cost) technologies such as the laser cutting..

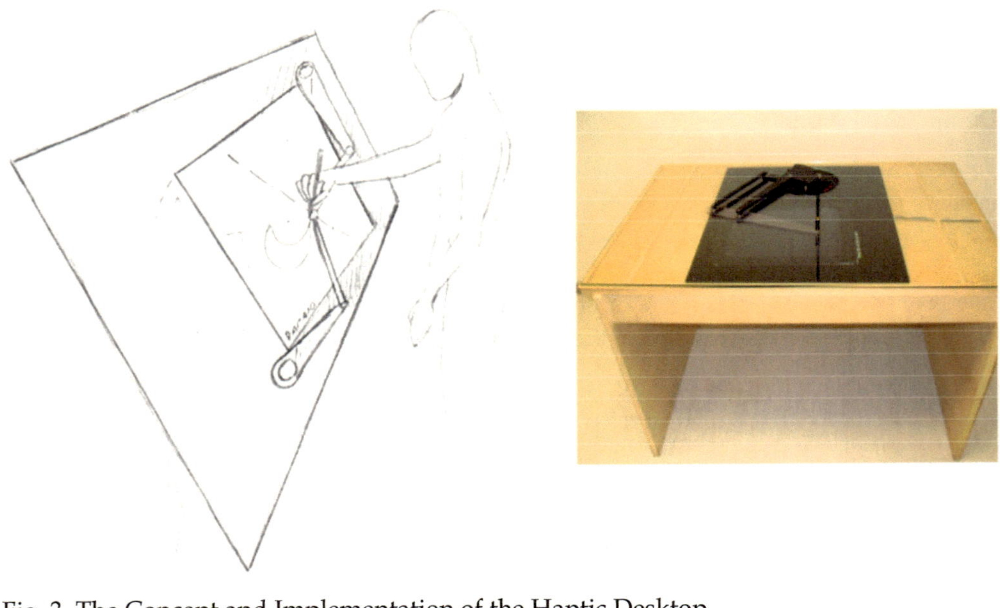

Fig. 3. The Concept and Implementation of the Haptic Desktop.

2.2 Design of the haptic device

An LCD monitor of the proper size and resolution 34x27 cm (1024x768 pixels) was chosen and integrated within a desktop plane. The haptic device is a 2DOF system which employs and hybrid serial parallel kinematic structure. This solution behaves an end-effector, which slides over the monitor and desk plane in correspondence with the computer pointer. The specific kind of materials adopted has chosen in order to reduce the friction factor among surfaces.

In order to improve the performances of the haptic device (transparency, manipulability, workspaces, reflected mass), the following solutions to the design guidelines mentioned previously have been adopted:

- Both actuators have been grounded and attached to the base link. As in parallel manipulators, the grounding of the motors allows to reduce the amount of movable masses and to increase the overall stiffness. The specific serial parallel design was used for transmitting the actuation to the end effector and to solve the typical workspace limitations of parallel devices (Frisoli, Prisco, Salsedo, & Bergamasco, 1999);
- Brushed DC motors have been selected: the amount of target force in this kind of applications is limited to few newtons; therefore the iron-less construction of the rotor allows the best compromise of performances.
- Capstans and metallic in tension tendons have been used as means of transmission of forces from the actuators to the joints. This solution allows completely avoiding geared transmission for the reduction of the transmission ratio, and therefore to avoid the backlash and friction issues related to this kind of solutions.

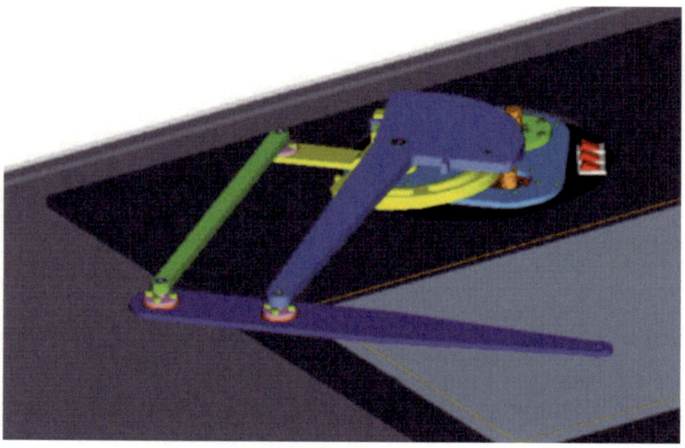

Fig. 4. Assonometric view of the haptic interface.

The structural parts have been realized with light materials (aluminium, plastic) and the specific design used allows the system to correctly operate even in presence of medium tolerance manufacturing.

The whole system has been designed to be integrated with the work-plane of a desk: the computing unit, the power supply, the motors and the electronics for the control of the haptic interface have been placed under the desktop so that the desk plane is completely free and the operator has direct access only to the visual and haptic systems.

Figure 4 shows an assonometric view of the design prototype: in this system, on the desk plane only the required mobile parts of the interface are present; a new design of the prototype allows moving event the capstans and motor pulleys below desk plane. Three buttons have been left near the haptic base in order to control the computing-unit power, to enable force feedback, and to switch on/off the desk light.

2.3 Optimization of the design

In order to evaluate the proper length of link 1 and link 2, a preliminary analysis was set. As basic assumption we required that the device should cover the whole workspace of the LCD while maintaining a good factor in the manipulability ellipsoid. The variation of the condition number of the manipulability ellipsoid (while the system moves over the workspace) was considered in this design phase. A script procedure was initially set up to estimate the conditioning number all over the workspace when links' sizes and interface position were changed.

In Figure 5, the best-case solution is graphically represented. The workspace areas have been coloured by the value of the condition number (c). The colour type changes at each tenth of unit. Central area has values between 0.9 and 1, second area values range between 0.8 and 0.9 and the third area values range between 0.7 and 0.8. More than 90% of the overall workspace has c>0.9.

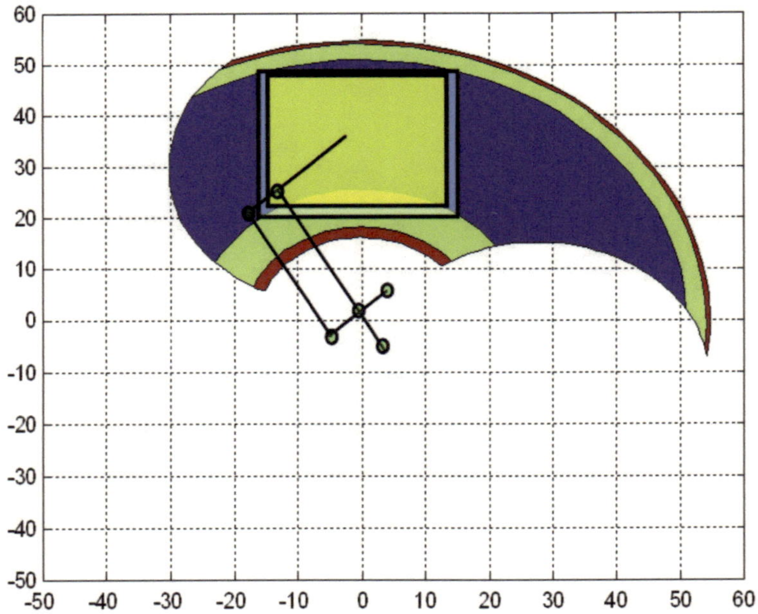

Fig. 5. Workspace evaluation

In Figure 6, the haptic desktop workspace in case of link 1 length equal to 300mm and link 2 length equal to 270mm is shown. Two capstans are used for reducing the inertia of moving masses and for introducing a reduction ratio. These reduction ratios have been dimensioned to obtain a condition number in the middle of the workspace equal to 1.

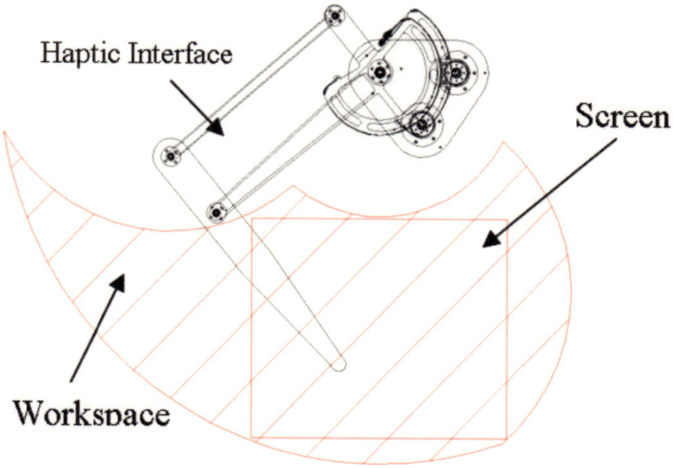

Fig. 6. Workspace of the haptic interface.

2.4 Components choice

The kinematics of the haptic interface has been determined according to the chosen link lengths and describe end-effector's coordinates referred to the central pivoting joint (Figure 7).

$$X_{ee} = -L_2 \cdot \cos(q_2) + L_1 \cdot \cos(q_1) \tag{1}$$

$$Y_{ee} = -L_2 \cdot \sin(q_2) + L_1 \cdot \sin(q_1) \tag{2}$$

From (1) and (2) L_1 and L_2 are the lengths of link 1 and link 2 while q_1 and q_2 are the angles referred to the joints. On the other hand, the end-effector's coordinates referred to the motors, q_1 and q_2 can be computed as follows:

$$q_1 = \frac{r_1}{R_1} \cdot \theta_1 \tag{3}$$

$$q_2 = -\frac{r_2}{R_2} \cdot \theta_2 \tag{4}$$

From (3) and (4) are the rotations of the two actuators, r_1 and r_2 are the radii of motor pulleys and R_1 and R_2 are the radii of the capstans. Using the above relationships it was possible to identify the commercial components to be used within the haptic device (motor type and size, sensors, etc). The homogeneity of the conditioning number has allowed us to size out the design by using the workspace centre as reference point. Maxon motor 3557024CR was used for actuation. With this solution the Haptic Interface can generate on user's hand up to 3 N of continuous forces and 5 N of peak forces. To detect device motion 1024 counter per cycle optical encoders where adopted with a 4X decoding. Such a choice leads to a spatial sensitivity of about 30μm at workspace centre (pixel size is about 300μm).

The design of the hardware system is characterized by its compactness and low cost. The HD is composed by a Single Board Computer (SBC) with Windows XP, a LCD screen and a Haptic Interface actuated by two DC motors (Figure 8).

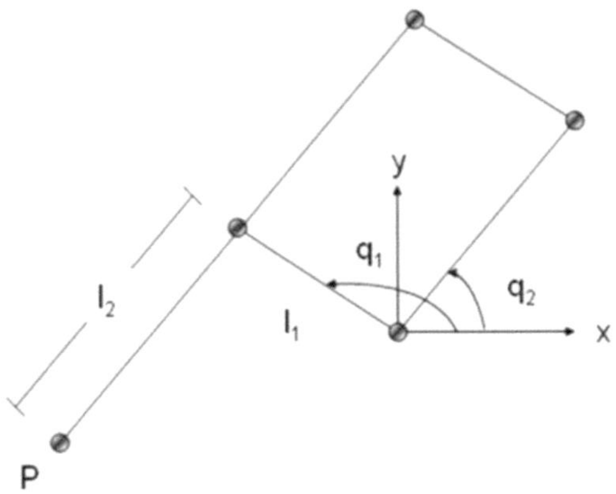

Fig. 7. Kinematics of the system

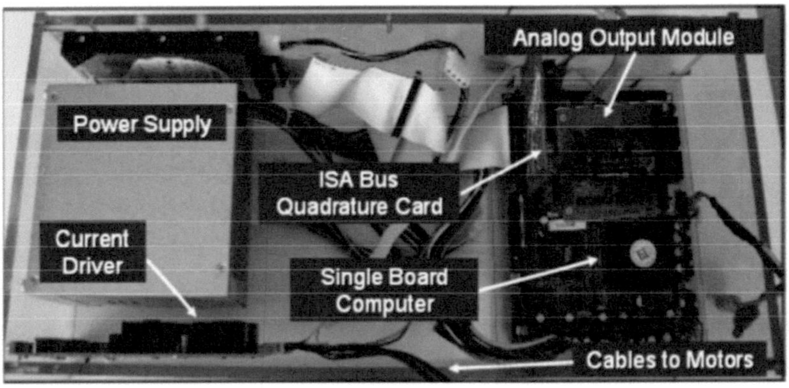

Fig. 8. Hardware unit has been designed to fit into a small acrylic box.

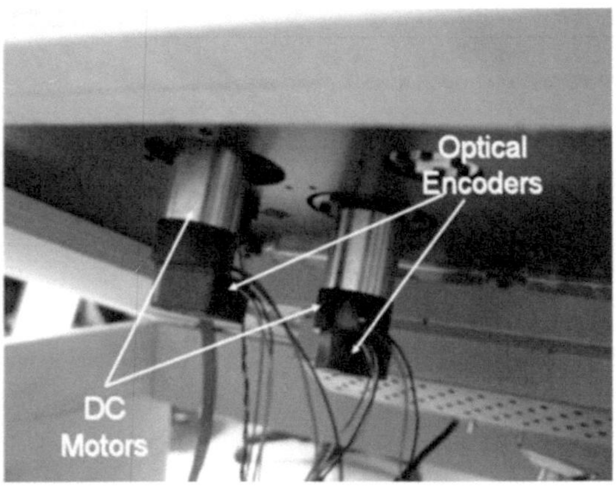

Fig. 9. The DC Motors and Optical Encoders are mounted on the rear of the desk.

The encoder signal is read using an ISA Bus Quadrature Encoder Card attached to the SBC. The current to motors is generated by using a PC/104 module with two channel analog outputs (AX10415) and a custom-made current driver which is fed by the power supply of the computer (Figure 9). The Figure 10 shows the system's architecture.

2.5 Control system

The base control system of the HD has been designed and implemented with Matlab™ Version 6.5 and Simulink Version 5.0. Due to the restrictions of Windows operating system to execute "hard" real-time applications; the Matlab´s Real-time Workshop provides two solutions to implement the real-time controller without adding additional hardware to the system: Real-Time Windows Target (RTWIN) and Generic Real-Time Target (GRT).

The Real-Time Windows Target uses a small real-time kernel to ensure the real-time application runs in real time. The real-time kernel runs at CPU ring zero (privileged or kernel mode) and uses the built-in PC clock as its primary source of time. In order to share the data from the Real-Time Windows Target kernel to the outside world (i.e. graphical system), an S-function was written as a SimViewing device which lets the creation of a shared memory by means of a static library. Such S-function does not compile into real-time code but acts as a Simulink External mode interface instead. This is due under the real-time kernel, the Win32 API cannot be executed as a component of the real-time application. One drawback of this implementation is that the updating time of the data send to the external application is too low, although the real-time control loop can achieve frequencies up to 2k Hz.

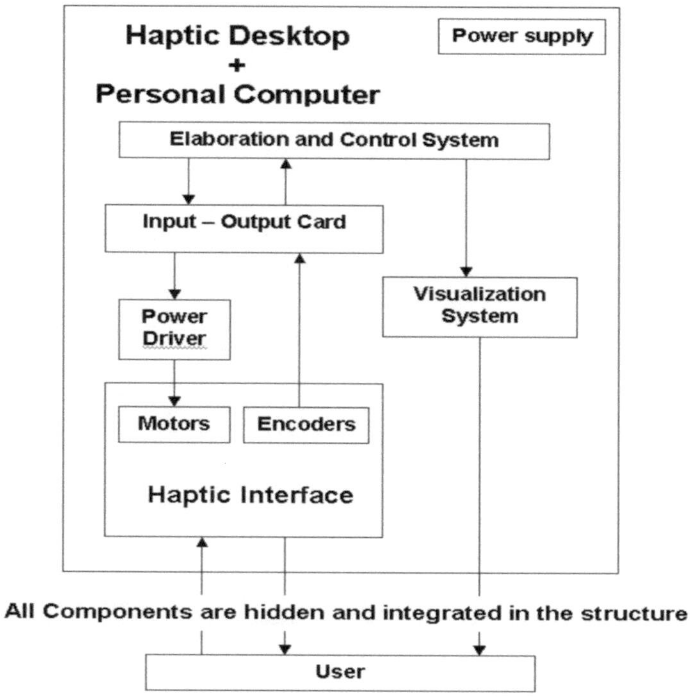

Fig. 10. Architecture of the system.

On the other hand, the Real-Time Workshop provides a generic real-time development target. The generic real-time (GRT) target provides an environment for simulating fixed-step models in single or multitasking mode. A program generated with the GRT target runs the control model as a stand-alone program under the computer. The real-time execution is achieved by controlling the real-time clock using the multimedia timers (such capability can be done by modifying the grt_main.c file). Such timers have the highest resolution under the Windows OS, with a minimum resolution of 1 millisecond. The data is shared with the graphical application also by a static library (Figure 11).

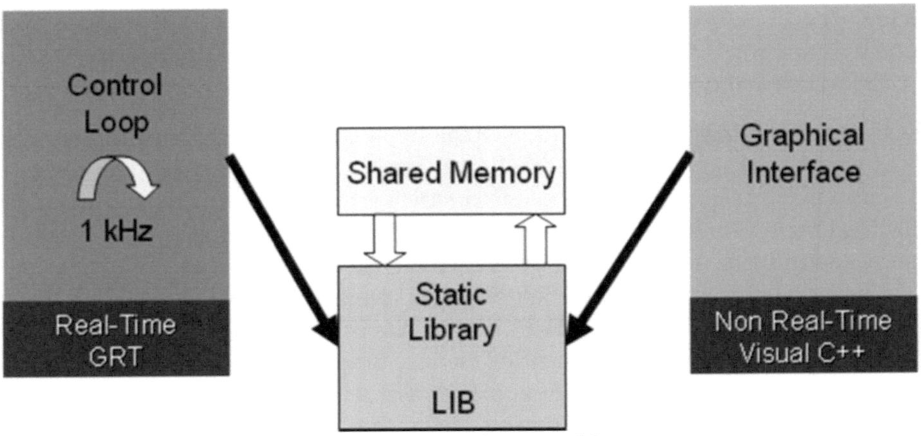

Fig. 11. Shared memory is managed by means of a static library

A calibration phase of the HI has been implemented to measure correctly the joint positions so that we can assure the coincidence between the haptic and graphical information. This phase consists on moving both links, using a velocity control, into a well know configuration (Figure 12), where the difference between the real joint position (q_1= 130º and q_2= 170º) and the measured joint position is computed and used to correct the signal coming from the encoders.

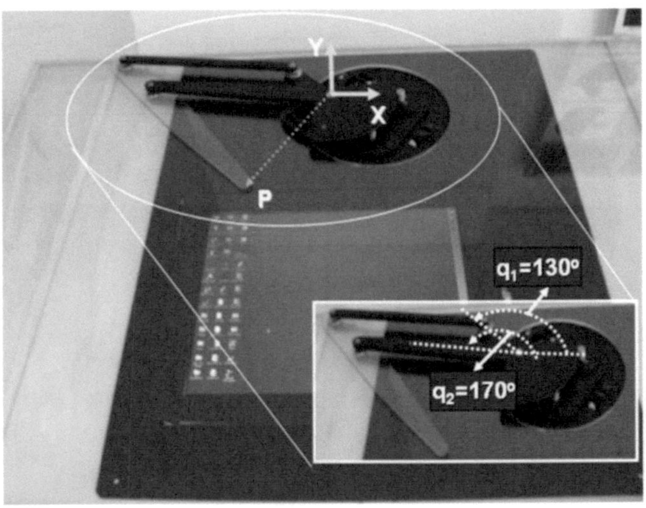

Fig. 12. The reset position for calibrating the HI is shown.

In the case of the GRT, the I/O ports cannot be accessed directly, due to the restrictions of the OS. This problem can be solved by using the PortTalk utility which allows the permissions to the real-time code to access the I/O ports. Therefore, at this moment, we have implemented the base control by compiling the system model under the generic real-time target, with a sampling frequency of 1k Hz.

This control system was implemented on the same architecture of the target application system. This device was made by an embedded PC (PIV 1.4GHz 1 GB RAM). Specific I/O board for detecting the encoder position and for generating the DAC command to be forwarded to drivers where implemented on the ISA and PC104 busses offered by the embedded board. The desktop backside was designed in order to host motors, power supply, hard disk, power drivers, mother boards and IO boards, all within a minimal regular square box as shown in Figure 9. The high integration achieved has allowed us to implement all control procedures and drivers within the hosting OS kernel (Windows XP).

Several functional control solutions are available to use the system: a basic mouse replacement toolkit allow to make use of the system interface to control the pointer position within the screen and interact to the GUI; it is also possible to directly control the hardware device by software and or control CAD; a set of functionalities libraries also implement main feature to facilitating integration within application.

2.6 Graphical system

In order to access the resources of the operating system, the mouse functionalities have been replaced by computing the end-effector position and by reading the signals coming from the buttons attached to the HD. Just after the real-time control is started, the system cursor is controlled, by using the mouse Win32 APIs, so that the contact point position is used to refresh cursor's position.

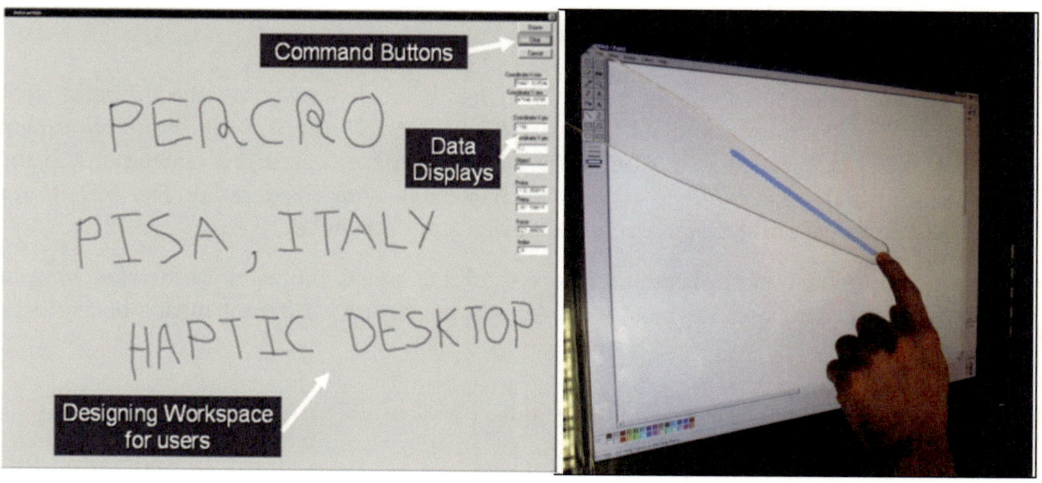

Fig. 13. The drawing interface window is shown.

As it was explained before, the contact position is computed by the real-time application and then, it is transferred to the shared memory. Then, the non-real time application developed with Visual C++, obtains the position and transform it to screen coordinates.

Furthermore, the non-real time application displays an interactive drawing window where the user can draw any kind of shapes or write words by changing grasping the HI and by controlling the command buttons (Figure 13).

3. A transfer skill system for teaching how to draw to unskilled persons

As mentioned previously, the core idea is to use the HDS as a tool capable of interacting dynamically with the human on the basis of the action he decides to perform. The use of an automated system in the skill transfer process has several advantages: the process could be repeated indefinitely with a high level of precision, time and location flexibility, the user can improve its performance without the assistance of a teacher and his progress can be evaluated numerically through automated procedures.

The HDS aims to be an interactive bi-directional skill transfer system that can emulate the presence of a human assistant, guiding the user movements on the trajectories chosen by the user himself (Figure 14).

Fig. 14. Haptic Interfaces as assistant of abilities

In our previous research (Solis et al., 2002) it has been demonstrated the influence that proportional feedback programmed into haptic interface (HI) can have in the development of motor skills, in spite of this experiment was neither co-located nor coherent with the visual stimuli and only could assist to drawn a circle with fixed radio. The HD is our multimodal interface solution for teaches to design simple sketches.

We have developed two applications where the HDS assists the users in the sketching of simple drawings. The user interacts with the system through different means of feedback (visual, force, audio).

3.1 Assisting to sketch using fixed templates

In order to present fixed templates to the users, we have developed an application that transforms the principal edges of a given input image file (jpg, bmp, tiff, etc.) into trajectories for later HDS interpretation, this way the "trajectories" are generated without any kind pre programming. The first process applied to the image is a median filter to remove the possible noise present, then a equalization and binarization is done (Pratt, 1991), after that, to detect its edges a Canny edge detector (Canny, 1986) is used, then the resulting edges are s segmented using label connected components in a binary image (Haralick & Shapiro, 1992), subsequently its components that are not more longer than a minimum predefined size are erased. The remaining components are converted to one pixel wide curves applying on them the morphological thin operator (Haralick & Shapiro, 1992).

a) Original image file

b) Processed Image "Trajectories"

c) Haptic and Visual Feedback

d) Visual Feedback

Fig. 15. The HDS live a virtual tutor.

Finally, the coordinates of the remaining objects (virtual templates) are converted to the HDS reference system controller and stored in a segment memory, which is shared with the HDS controller. The Figure 15a shows an example of original jpg image and Figure 15b shows the results of the image processing.

The GUI displays the processed images and assists to the user to interact with the templates. The application is controlled through four buttons, the first two (top to bottom, Figure 15c) acts like the left and right mouse buttons, the third cleans the screen and the fourth toggles the force feedback. The user can move the HDS's end effector (HEE) freely in all its workspace until he presses the first button. On button press, a blue dot is drawn in the end effector position (visual feedback) and a collision detection algorithm looks for collisions between the HEE position and any template (trajectory) inside a radius of 40 mm from the HEE center.

If a collision is detected, the HDS responds using force feedback to maintain the HEE constrained to the nearest point of the contacted template. Force feedback is generated with the following control law:

$$F = -K_P \Delta - K_v \dot{\Delta} \tag{5}$$

Where Δ is the distance between the HEE Position and its nearest point on the template, and K_P and K_v should be small enough to allow a free movement along the trajectory while creating a force feedback outside the trajectory, its values where find experimentally. When the HDS exerts a force of two Newtons or more, the user receives an auditory feedback.

Figure 15c shows a user interaction with the application: it is possible to see the coherence and colocation between haptic and graphical information. The visual feedback presented to the user is shown close up in Figure 15d.

3.2 Assisting to sketch using interactive templates

A second application was developed in order to assist to drawn sketches interactively, the HDS's audio feedback, coherence and co-location between haptic and graphical information are exploited. The GUI developed is minimalist and simple to use (Figure 16). At the moment it can assist to design three different types of virtual geometrical templates (VGTs): straight line, circle and arc. The use of the buttons in order to control the application, the collision detection algorithm and the auditory cues have the same behaviour, that its fixed template counterpart.

The user can move the HEE freely in all the workspace and drawing a free sketch when the first button is pressed. When the user decided to drawn a VGT with the assistance of the HDS, he first, must indicate the VGT's first point, pressing the second button and choosing of a menu the VGT that he want drawn (Figure 16a); this first point could be; a) the beginning of a straight line, b) beginning of an arc or c) the center of a circle. Once that the first point has been selected, he must move the HEE to another position inside the GUI and with the first button must to mark the second and third points depending on which VGT has been selected. The second point is the end of the straight line if a line VGT has been chosen, on other hand if circle VGT was selected, the second point is used to calculate the radius respect to the first point and then generate a circumference around it. If arc VGT is chosen, the three points marked are united interpolating a second order spline curve.

Once that all the control points have been defined, the application draws a virtual "template trajectory" (Figure 16b), after that, the user can move the HDS's end effector (HEE) freely in all its workspace until he presses the first button. On button press, a blue dot is drawn in the end effector position (visual feedback) and a collision detection algorithm looks for collisions between the HEE position and the virtual template. Similarly to the fixed template application, the HDS maintains its HEE constrained to the nearest point of the contacted template and draws a blue line.

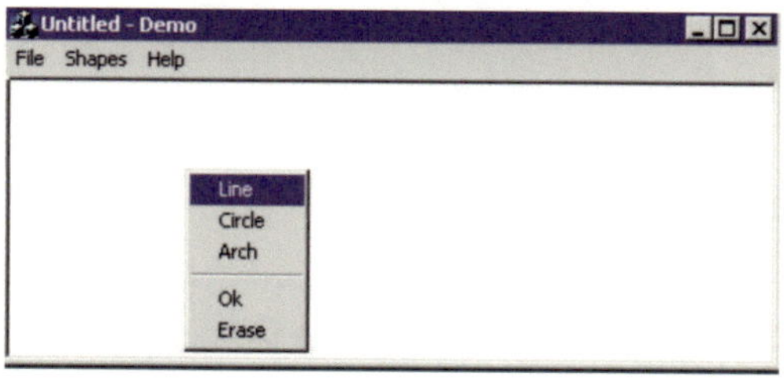

(a) Choosing between three different geometric primitives (straight line, circle and arc).

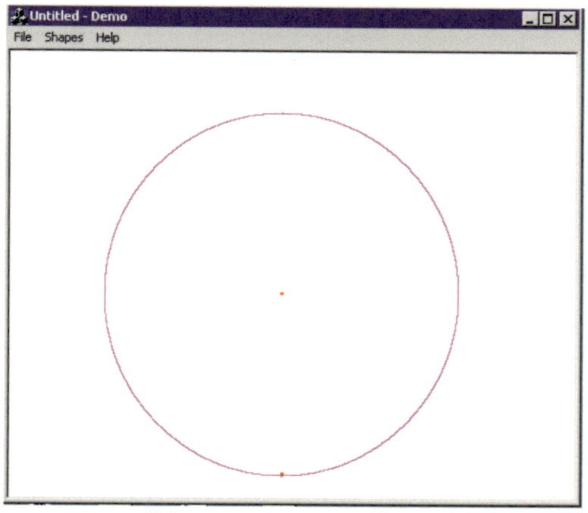

(b) A circle "template"

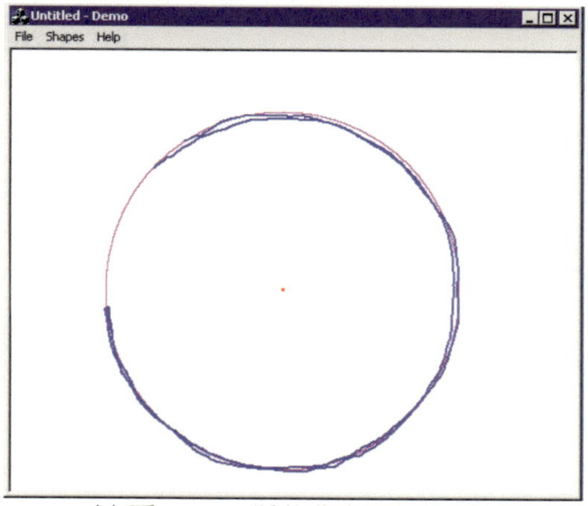

(c) The user "fills" the template

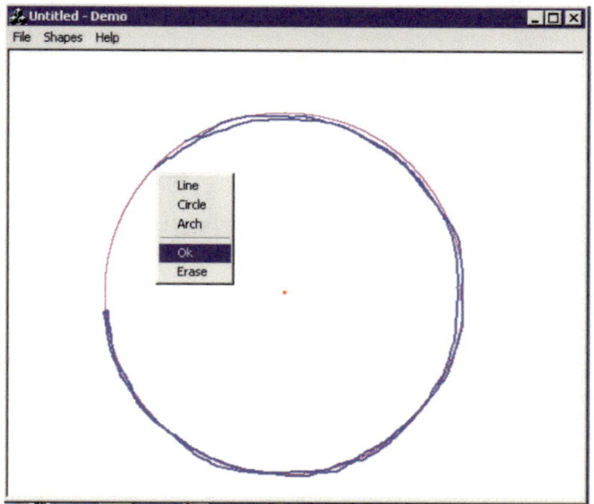

(d) The user decides to finalize with assistance of the HDS

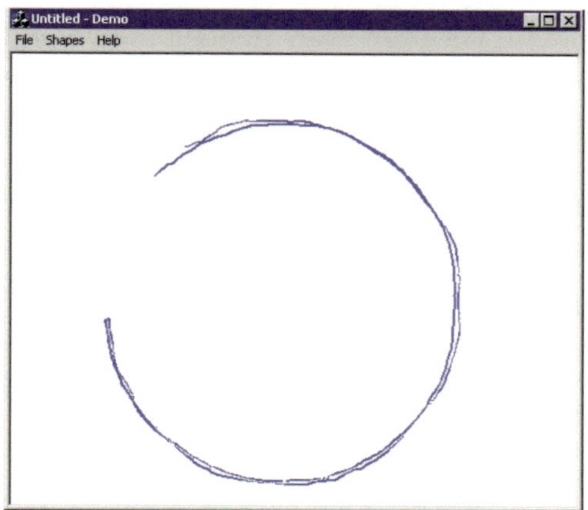

(e) Final sketch without "template"

Fig. 16. Interaction with the HDS assistant.

When the user desires finalize with the HDS's assistance, he must press the second button and indicates using a menu, if erase the line recently drawn or maintains it; if he decides maintain it, the virtual template will be erased and only the line drawn made remains (Figure 16.e). In order to design more complex sketches is necessary repeat all the precedent steps and depending of the ability of the user can draw more complex design.

4. Experiment to validate sketching skills for fixed templates

To check that the users learn sketching faster when they are provided with force feedback, we carried out the following test: The image used in the experiment is shown in the Figure 17b, which is based on the original image shown in the Figure 17a. The test image was chosen due it has the basic components of more complex designs (lines, curves, circles, squares, etc).

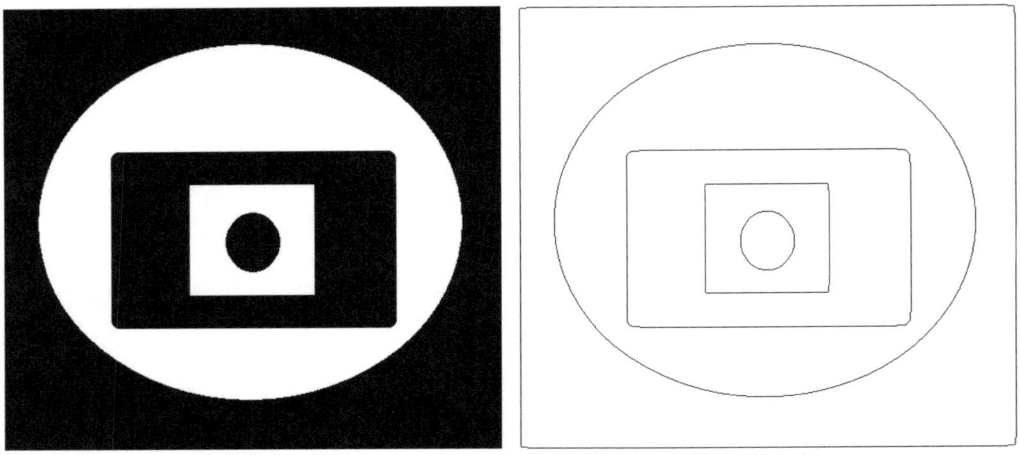

(a) Original (b) Processed Image

Fig. 17. Test Image.

We requested to 10 users to trace the test image seven times as precisely as possible in terms of position. Since this task should model free drawing, no restriction on completion time or effector velocity was imposed. The users were divided in two groups of 5 members. At the beginning of each experiment, the users had five minutes for drawing on the test image in order to become familiar with the HDS. The users of the first group were stimulated only with visual feedback throughout the experiment. The users of the second group were stimulated with visual feedback on every trial, and they received the force feedback only in the second, fourth and sixth trials.

We used the performance parameter described by (6) to measure if user learning of drawing skills was indeed accelerated. The PSD parameter involves the time, velocity, distance and error (between the HEE Position and the point on the trajectory nearest to the HEE) when the user is drawing.

$$P_{SD} = \frac{\int_o^t |\Delta| dt}{L = \int_0^t v dt} \quad (6)$$

4.1 Results

In the Figure 18, we present the normalized sum of PSD over the subjects of the two groups: the PSD sum for trial 1 has been made equal to 1.

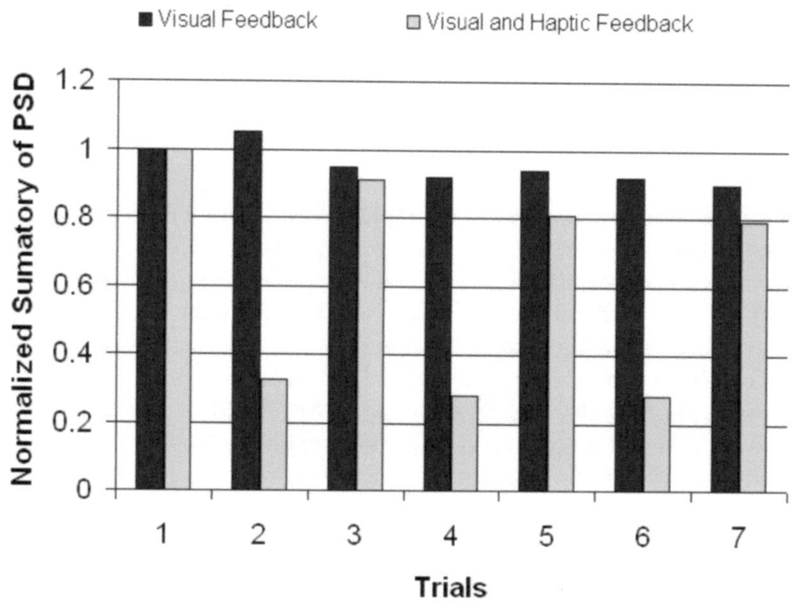

Fig. 18. Evolution of normalized sumatory of the PSD

We can obviously observe a strong difference between performances on trial 2, 4 and 6. What is more interesting, we can observe that for the Visual Feedback Only group, learning stops at Trial 4, while the Visual Feedback and Haptics group continues learning to Trail 7. Furthermore, at trial 7 the normalized sum of PSD is lower for the Visual Feedback and Haptics group, which leads us to conclude (within the limits of a small scale experiment with a small number of subjects) that Haptic feedback enables learning for a longer time and leads to better results for the task at hand.

We didn't validate the improvement of the user to drawn simple skills due there aren't restrictions about position, size of the sketch's traces. It is our first attempt to develop a more advanced assistant, which will have more virtual geometric templates and the auditory cues will be exploited more properly, i.e. vocal instructions.

5. Conclusions

The efficacy of the Haptic Desktop to transfer basic skills to drawn simples sketches was demonstrated through the use of two applications, in both the HD acts like a virtual teacher that uses its force feedback and collocated capabilities to retain the cursor's position (controlled by the end effector position) in contact the borders of predefined sketch. The sketch could be either fixed or interactive, the fixed ones are generated from images, and the interactive ones are generated by the user whom can decide where, how big and which primitive geometric element draw (circle, line or arch).

The experiment described in this chapter, showed that the use of force and visual stimuli helps to the user to drawn the simple sketches more quickly and with less errors, but more work must be done in order to enable to the interface to understand when and how the feedback stimuli have to be generated, to do it, it would be necessary obtain velocities and forces (magnitude and orientation) of the hand users and develop advanced algorithms that recognize the difference between drawn a primitive element as expert or novice. These algorithms are difficult to develop and possibly the variables to quantify the quality of the hand movement could be not enough.

6. References

Annelise Mark Pejtersen, J. R. (1997). Ecological Information Systems and Support of Learning: Coupling Work Domain Information to user Characteristics. *Handbook of Human-Computer Interaction*. North/Holland.

Flach, J. M. (1994). Beyond the servomechanism: Implications of closed-loop, adaptive couplings for modeling human-machine systems. *Symposium on Human Interaction with Complex Systems. North Carolina A&T State University.*

Frisoli, A., Prisco, M., Salsedo, F., & Bergamasco, M. (1999). A two degrees-of-freedom planar haptic interface with high kinematic isotropy" Robot and Human Interaction. *8th IEEE International Workshop on Robot and Human Interactive Communication*, (p. 297 - 302).

Gopher, D. (2004). Control processes in the formation of task units. *28th International Congress of Psychology*. Beijing, China.

Haralick, R., & Shapiro, L. (1992). *Computer and Robot Vision* (Vol. I). Addison-Wesley.

Jansson, G. J., & Öström, M. (2004). The Effects of Co-location of Visual and Haptic Space on Judgments of Form. *EuroHaptics*.

McCullough, M. (1999). *Abstracting Craft*. MIT Press.

M. Chignell, P., & Takeshit, H. (1999). Human-Computer Interaction: The psychology of augmented human behavior. In P. Hancock (A cura di), *Human performance and Ergonomics*. Academic Press.

Norman, D. (1986). *User-centered systems design*. Hillsdale.

Norman, D. (1988). *The design of everyday things*. New York: Basic Books.

Pratt, W. (1991). *Digital Image Processing*. John Wiley & Sons, Inc.

Solis, J., Avizzano, C., & Bergamasco, M. (2002). Teaching to Write Japanese Characters using an Haptic Interface. In Proceedings of the *10th International Symposium on Haptic Interfaces for Virtual Environment and Teleoperator Systems*. Orlando, FL.

Part 4

Haptics and Games

11

The Role of Haptics in Games

Mauricio Orozco, Juan Silva, Abdulmotaleb El Saddik and Emil Petriu
University of Ottawa,
Canada

1. Introduction

Today, playing a video game is a different story than what it was twenty years ago in many senses. Game consoles have steadily gained popularity not only among kids but also among other age groups. For example, today, the Xbox 360 from Microsoft comes with Kinect technology which is based on webcam built in system for users to control and interact with the console without the need for conventional game controller to bring entertainment and playing games to people of all ages. On the other hand electronic gadgets including smart phones have changed the way game controllers, pads, buttons, joy sticks can be used with the incorporation of haptic and sensing technologies. Additionally, impressive graphics and 3D rendering displays are creating virtual environments more realistic which have the potential to capture the gamer's attention all throughout the gaming process. As stated by Jurgelionis and others: "The increasing number of broadband users, and a demand for quality and diversity in entertainment services drives the development of new pervasive entertainment systems" (Jurgelionis et al., 2007). Indeed, they also stated that such entertainment systems should be accessible without any limits on time and location.

In the real world, people receive and disseminate information in three-dimensional space. Computers, through graphical user interfaces, allow users to perceive an imitated three-dimensional world that exists in the real world. Such a virtual world can be enhanced in a more complete imitation of the real space by the introduction of an artificial support technology called haptics. A haptic interface is a device that allows a user to interact with a computer by receiving tactile and force feedback. The interaction can embrace the entire body or only the tip of a finger, giving the user information about the nature of objects inside the world. The introduction of haptics permits one to enhance a vast spectrum of human tasks in a virtual environment.

Currently, haptic research and technology has been focused on designing and evaluating prototypes of different features and capabilities for the use in virtual environments. The evidence is that, some of these prototypes have become commercially available to the market. In that sense, applications of this technology have been invaded rapidly from devices that can interact with sophisticated graphical user interfaces (GUI's), games, multimedia publishing, scientific discovery and visualization, arts and creation, editing sound and images, the vehicle industry, engineering, manufacturing, Tele-robotics and Tele-operations, education and training, as well as medical simulation and rehabilitation.

For the time being we could argue that haptic research related to home entertainment and computer games has blossomed and impacted the development of technology during the past few years.

It is well-know that the game experience comprises four aspects: physical, mental, social, and emotional (El Saddik, 2007). It is on the physical aspects that, force feedback technology (haptics) enhances the game experience by creating a more realistic physical feeling of playing a game. This physical experience can be translated for example in improving the physical skills of the players, and imitating the use of physical artefacts. By using existing, well-developed game engine components—specifically, a scene graph library and physics engine - and augmenting them with the design and implementation of haptic rendering algorithms, it is possible to create a highly useful haptic game development environment.

This can be reflected in a rich environment which provides to players or users a higher sense of immersion as well as new and interesting ways to interact with the game environment. In addition this simulated world can be used to do research on applications such as physical rehabilitation, driving training simulation and more.

Currently, a diverse spectrum of games available in the market take advantage of the force feedback stimuli effects offered by mainstream haptic interfaces. Here we intend to give a broad view of past and present developments aimed at enabling game environment with haptic augmented interfaces, while discussing the strengths and weaknesses of such developments.

2. Machine haptics

In order to fully understand the potential and capabilities of haptics in the gaming environment, let us first look how the sense of touch has brought a more complex and appealing dimension the human computer interaction. Haptics was introduced, at the beginning of the 20th century by research work in the field of experimental psychology aimed at understanding human touch perception and manipulation. Psychophysical experiments provided the contextual clues involved in the haptic perception between the human and the machine. The areas of psychology and physiology provided a refreshed impulse into the study of haptics and it remained popular until the late eighties. Researchers have found that the mechanism by which we feel and perceive the tactual qualities of our environments are considerably more complex in structure than, for example, our visual modality. However, they opened up a wealth of opportunities in academic research and development to answer the many questions that the haptic cognition discipline has. Therefore the discipline that put in practice many of the theories developed in haptic perception domain were addressed by *machine haptics*.

Machine Haptics involve designing, constructing, and developing mechanical devices that replace or augment human touch. These devices, also called haptic interfaces, are put into physical contact with the human body for the purpose of exchanging (measuring and displaying) information with the human nervous system. In general, haptic interfaces have two basic functions; firstly, they measure the poses (positions and/or orientations) and/or contact forces of any part of the human body, and secondly, they display the computed reaction touch to a haptic scene that populates touchable virtual objects with haptic properties such as stiffness, roughness, friction, etc. Haptic interfaces can be broadly divided into two categories: force feedback devices and tactile devices. Force feedback devices display force and/or torque and enable users to feel resistive force, friction, roughness, etc. Tactile devices present vibration, temperature, pressure, etc. on the human skin and display textures of a virtual object or provide information such as showing direction, reading text, displaying distance, etc.

Turning to the robotics arena in the seventies and eighties, most researchers were considering the systems aspect of controlling remote robotic vehicles to manipulate and perceive their environments by touch. The main objective was to create devices with dexterity inspired by human abilities. Robotic mechanical systems with a human being in their control loop are referred to as Tele-manipulators, where an intelligent machine is expected to perceive the environment, reason about the perceived information, make decisions based on this perception, and act according to a plan specified at a very high level. In time, the robotics community found interest in topics including but not limited to: sensory design and processing, grasp control and manipulation, object modeling and haptic information encoding.

Meanwhile, terms such as tele-operation, tele-presence, tele-robotics and supervisory were used interchangeably by the robotics community until the mid-nineties. From those terms two were especially important to develop haptics systems; Tele-operation and Tele-presence. Tele-operation refers to the extension of a person's sensing and manipulation capabilities to a remote location. Tele-presence can be described as a realistic way that an operator feels while physically being at a remote site. Motivated by these concepts, the Tele-presence and Tele-operation research communities developed several projects in the several related fields such as the nuclear industry, sub-sea, space and the military markets.

In the early nineties, the use of the word haptics, in the context of computer haptics was introduced. Much like computer graphics, computer haptics is concerned with the techniques and processes of generating and displaying haptic stimuli to the user. In fact, computer haptics uses digital display technology as a medium for physically tangible interaction where objects can be simulated in an interactive manner. This new modality presents information to the user's hand and/or other parts of the body by exerting controlled forces through the haptic interface. These forces are delivered to the user depending on the physical properties of the objects that can be perceived. The hardware components of this interface play an important role in displaying these forces through the response sensors to the user. Unlike computer graphics, the behaviour of haptic interaction is bidirectional, due to energy and information flow in both directions from the user to the haptic interface and vice versa.

Only recently, have haptic technologies become integrated with high-end workstations for computer-aided design (CAD) and, at the lower end, on home PCs and consoles, to augment the human-computer interaction (HCI). Effectively this implies the opening of a new mechanical channel between human and computer so that data can be accessed and literally manipulated through haptic interfaces.

Nowadays, computer haptic systems can display objects of sophisticated complexity and behaviour; thanks to the availability of high-performance force-controllable haptic interfaces, affordable computational geometric modeling, collision detection and response techniques, a good understanding of the human perceptual needs, and a dramatic increase in processing speed and memory size. With the commercial availability of haptic interfaces, software toolkits, and haptics-enabled applications, the field of human-haptics interaction is experiencing an exciting exponential growth.

3. A roadmap to haptic interfaces in games

Haptic research in the realm of home entertainment and computer games has blossomed during the past few years. The game experience comprises four aspects: physical, mental, social, and emotional. In particular, force feedback technology enhances the physical aspects of the game experience by creating a deeper physical feeling of playing a game, improving the physical skills of the players, and imitating the use of physical artefacts. Plenty of games available in the market take advantage of the haptic effects offered by mainstream haptic interfaces. Car racing games can be enhanced when players drive over a rough section of road by receiving vibrations in their joysticks or steering wheels. However, how did we come to realize such novel interfaces that enhance our gaming experience? In this section we present a roadmap to past and present work, which can give a picture of how haptic interfaces came to be what they are today.

3.1 Evolution of the videogame industry

It is know that Egyptians were playing games since around 3000 BC when an expedition in 1920s by Sir Leonard Wooley found two board games in tombs. Thus the Royal Game of Ur gets its name from the two game boards which are associated with first dynasty of Ur (before 2600 BC). Each of the game boards contains a set of twelve squares and a set of six cases which were linked by a bridge of two cases (for review consult "Histoire des jeux de sociéte by Jean Marie Lhéte, 1994). The rules of the game are very similar to backgammon, the goal is to introduce seven pawns and move them along to designated path and be the first to have them also out of the game. At this point it is possible to state that games have existed along the existence of humanity. Thus many games have remained as they were designed but the way to play them has changed radically. The sole relationship between human societies with games can fill entire books.

The video game industry itself could be dated from the late 19th century, more precisely in 1889 when Fusajiro Yamauchi established a company called Marufuku to distribute and manufacture a Japanese playing card game-Hanafuda. In the 1950s Marufuku company became Nintendo which means 'leave luck to heaven". Meanwhile in the USA, Martin Bromley buys slot machines and creates a game rooms concept named Service Games(SEGA) (Kent, 2001).

Later on, David Rosen opens a business in Japan and he starts shipping photo booths. Then Rosen imports coin-operated electron mechanical games machines to launch this industry in Japan. At the beginning of 60s, a student from Massachusetts Institute of Technology(MIT), Steve Russell developed an interactive game computer called Spacewar.

At the time Rosen Enterprises merges with Services Games to become Sega Enterprises. Then, in mid sixty's Ralph Baer starts interactive television games at Sander Associates meanwhile Sega in Japan was charging $0.25 cents per play arcade games to overcome with the high shipping costs, which then eventually become the standard price for playing arcade games. In 1970 Magnavox licenses Rapl Baer's television game from Sander Associates and a year later released as Odyssey based on Ping-Pong Baer's game. In the mid 1970's Atari designed a prototypical Home Pong unit and Namco starts creating video games.

In the late 70's Atari released the video game computer system known as 2600 and Mattel introduced a line of LED-based handled video games, also Nintendo released its first home video game in Japan. In 1979 Atari releases Asteroids, which became an all time bestselling game and Mattel Electronics introduces the Intellivision game console. In addition Milton Bradley released Microvision, the first handled programmable game system. In the 80's the practice of selling home versions of arcade machines hits the business. The same year Pac-Mac was released which is the most popular game by Namco (Kent, 2001).

In 1983 Cinematronics released Dragon's Lair, the first arcade game to feature laser-disc technology. One year later Nintendo released the Family Computer (Famicom) in Japan and then become in the USA the Nintendo Entertainment System(NES). In the mid 80s Tetris was created by Alex Pajinov and also Atari released the 7800 game console. Later on NEC released the 16 -bit/8 -bit hybrid PC-Engine game console in Japan and Sega unveils 16-bit Meha Drive game console. Early 90s Sega ships SEGA CD peripheral for Genesis game console. In 1993 Atari launches the 64-bit Jaguar and Id software publish Doom for PCs. One year later Sega releases 32X, a peripheral device that increases the power of the Genesis. In mid 90s Sony releases PlayStation in the United States and Nintendo Virtual Boy and also unveils the 64-bit Nintendo game console in Japan. At the late 90s Sega releases Dreamcast game console in the USA. In 2000 Sony released PlaStation 2 and Micorosft unveils plans for XBOX. in 2001 Nintendo release GameCube and Microsoft Xbox worldwide (Kent, 2001).

Development of video games industry has also been based on a close relationship with the well established amusement industry (Kent, 2001). To extend such criteria, Kent has stated that pinball games had made a huge impact in the development of videogame and computer industry in general. In his book he assumes the position that the creator of *Baffle Ball* game David Gottlieb was a great influence in the development that we know today as video game. In the first stage of development the *Baffle Ball* game was used with no electricity and it was built in a countertop (worktop) cabinet and had only one moving part the plunger. Players could enjoy the game by spending a penny[1] and get seven balls to try into scoring holes. *Baffle ball* was successful at the time that Gottlien created a company to deal with a shipping load of 400 cabinets per day.

Later on, competition was in place, thus this industry in the 70s had five game manufactured companies to place and distribute equipment in restaurants, bar, bowling and stores. On the other hand the development of computers was growing fast from the 60s when the computers occupied the whole room to the introduction of transistor which replaced the vacuum valves and later on the silicon chips which replace the transistors making computers more robust and fast. Thus more academic society and students were involved in the development of computer languages and interaction. The first game was created by engineers at Sander Associate a contractor company. The game was created from idea of which a hard-wired logic circuit projected a spot flying across the screen. The original idea was for players to catch the spot with manually controlled dots. Over time, the

[1] A penny is a coin or a type of currency used in several English-speaking countries. It is often the smallest denomination within a currency system source: Wikipedia 2011

player's dots evolved into paddles and the game became "ping-pong". One the main developers of this concept was Baer who sold the idea to Magnavox but they first of outrageously priced and poorly advertised at the time that this game had gone almost unnoticed until Magnavox released later on as Odyssey which change dramatically the way to play games (Kent, 2001).

3.2 Enhancing the experience with the sense of touch

In a first generation we started out with the modest beginnings of Pong, a two dimensional simulated table tennis where players were only allowed to move the game-paddle vertically to control a moving dot, or Pac-man which through a maze eats Pac-dots, Tetris and video pinball, video games. Then we moved to a second generation with the Super Mario Brothers where the player controlled Mario in a one-player control based strategy and a second player acted as Mario's brother Luigui in a second controller approach. The game was intended to race through the Mushroom Kingdom, survive the main antagonist Browser's forces and save the princess Toadstool, Wolfenstein 3D, Command and Conquer, Microsoft Flight, then to Quake the first shooter video game which was released on June 1996. The game engine of Quake popularized many advances in the 3D game domain such as polygonal modeling instead of pre-rendered sprites, in addition pre-rendered lightmaps and also allowing end user to partially program the game (QuakeC). Then half-life, World of Warcraft.

In this new era of gaming, we have moved far from the Pong game trend, to more realistic virtual scenarios. Particularly, such perception of reality can be enhanced by the development of computerized games influenced by technology such as haptics to make the entertainment more sophisticated.

The first work on development of haptic devices such as joysticks was carried out at Massachussetts Institute of Technology (MIT) and University of North Carolina at Chapel Hill (UNC), which resulted in a 3-DOF device that simulates an object's inertia and surface texture (Minsky et al. 1990).

Currently, vibration feedback joysticks and steering wheels from companies like Logitech are widely used as input devices in video games. In this sense, haptic research has introduced new forms of complexity in the development of games by emulating the user experience based on this particular bidirectional feedback. Pioneering attempts at introducing modern haptics to gaming include Haptic Battle Pong (Morris et al. 2004), a pong clone with force-feedback that, thru haptics, displays contact between a ball and a paddle using the PHANTOM Omni device (Sensable 2010). The PHANTOM is used to position and orient the paddle and to render the contact between the ball and the paddle as physical forces.

Nilsson and Aamisepp (Nilsson and Aamisepp, 2003) worked on the integration of haptics into a 3D game engine. They have investigated the possibility of adding haptic hardware support to Crystal Space, an open source 3D game engine.

By using existing, well-developed game engine components such as Unity 3D, a scene graph library and physics engine, and augmenting them with the design and implementation of haptic rendering algorithms, it is possible to create a highly useful haptic game development environment. This can result in a rich environment, which provides players or users with a higher sense of immersion, as well as new and interesting ways to interact with the game environment (Andrews et al. 2006). In addition, this simulated world can be used to do research on applications such as physical rehabilitation, driver training simulations, and more.

There is also a haptic device called HandJive designed for interpersonal entertainment (Fogg et al.1998). The concept is described as a handheld object that fits in one hand and allows remote play through haptic input and output. It communicates wirelessly with similar devices, and provides haptic stimuli. In fact, haptic devices are becoming more accessible to the average computer and console user and will play an important role in providing innovative forms of entertainment. As further evidence, in 2008, Novint Technologies introduced the Novint Falcon device, which is affordable, even for mainstream consumers (Novint 2010). This device is now integrated with several popular video games.

4. Haptic controllers

4.1 Force feedback wheels

Although drivers obtain a substantial amount of information from driving from vision, information from other sensory modalities may also provide relevant information about the state of the car or even the surrounding environment (Liu & Chang, 1995). Force feedback steering racing wheels provides mainly realistic resistance to the wheel rotation and providing precise throttle response. This is achieved by emulating the real steering system through a mechanism that also provides vibration feedback. From a tele-operatiing system perspective, the energy which flows between the driver and the vehicle front wheel through the mechanical linkage can be considered to be mainly effort and flux exchange which corresponds to force and velocity (Mohellebi et al, 2001).

In addition driving-simulators fidelity is usually defined by the quality of its visual and motion cueing system (Katzourakis et al. 2011). Katzourakis experimented that the quality of driving-simulator's haptic cues are very important and rely on the hardware and control properties of the system design. Despite the hardware characteristics there is also important to consider the model of vehicle dynamics. An experimental work was carried out by Toffin et al in order to answer questions such as how do drivers use the force appearing on the steering wheel when driving in curves?. Well, they have found that a wide range of adaptation results that occurs mainly at the haptic level rather than in the internal model of the vehicle dynamics. Many features provided by commercial force feedback steering wheels is based on exclusive design and technology proprietary of IMMERSION Technologies.

In 1992 Thrustmaster Enzo Ferrari Force Feedback Racing wheels was released which did not provide a satisfactory sense of precise force feedback for some users. In 1998 Logitech the leading company of gaming controllers for PCs and consoles released the Logitech Formula™ Force GP racing wheel with more than one million sales worldwide and actually it was the first force feedback wheel found in any game console. The force feedback in racing wheels attracted a more sophisticated method for racing aficionados immersed in more realistic playing environments.

In 2002 Logitech introduces a Speed Force Feedback wheel for GameCube. In 2005 the R440 Force Feedback Wheel from Saitek has busted open the doors to affordable racing fun. In

2006 more realistic racing simulators and more affordable appeared in the scene. For instance the Logitech G25 wheel offers advanced features which, until now, could be found only in specialized or custom-made racing simulators that sometimes cost thousands of dollars to assemble, thus introduced the industry's first two-motor force-feedback mechanism with the G25 wheel console, providing stronger and more precise feedback as well as 2 1/5 rotation feature(900 degrees). With a second motor, the directional forces are more realistic and evenly distributed throughout the wheel - drivers will feel everything from the banks in the road to impact with walls, structures and other cars.

In 2007 things were tuned up with Forza Motorsport 2 on the Xbox 360 using the Microsoft Wireless Force Feedback Wheel. Force feedback is an extremely useful haptic interface. It provides real-time info on several key aspects of Forza Motorsport 2's physics model. Obviously, force feedback simulates the steering wheel torque created by having the front tires on different terrain types, such as asphalt, rumble strips, or grass. It also simulates load balance between tires as well as slippage. At the end of 2007, Saitek has launched its new R660GT Force Feedback Wheel, a USB racing wheel with force feedback and switchable gearstick. The R660GT wheel comes with a solid G-clamp to securely fix the wheel to a desk, and the soft handle finish ensures a strong grip. Its setup includes pedals that can be customized to suit the driver, so that they can operate independently of each other or can be combined to suit different games or a player's driving style. Unlike most other driving wheels, the R660GT pedals accurately reflect the positioning of pedals in a real car, pivoted from the top rather than the bottom, whilst the brake offers more resistance than the accelerator. 2009 is the era of wireless, therefore Logitech Speed Force Wireless Racing Wheel Works With EA's Highly Anticipated Racing Game Need for Speed™ Undercover.

4.2 Joysticks

The joystick has been the principal fight control in the cockpit of many aircraft, particularly military fast jets. It has also been used for controlling machines such as cranes, trucks, underwater unmanned vehicles, and wheelchairs but also very popular to control video games. It is an input device consisting of a stick that pivots on a base and reports its angle or direction to the device it is controlling. Its origins date since early 20th century and are related to the aviation pioneers where its mechanical origins are uncertain but the term "joystick" was coined to Robert Loraine.

An arcade ticks is a large-format controller for use with home game consoles or computers. Most joysticks are two-dimensional, having two axes of movement (similar to a mouse), but one and three-dimensional joysticks do exist. An analog joystick is a joystick which has continuous states, i.e. returns an angle measure of the movement in any direction in the plane or the space (usually using potentiometers) and a digital joystick gives only on/off signals for four different directions, and mechanically possible combinations (such as up-right, down-left, etc.). Digital joysticks were very common as game controllers for the video game consoles, arcade machines, and home computers of the 1980s.

The force feedback joystick is similar to ordinary ones however it has in addition a couple of electrical motors and gear train or belt system and microprocessor. The X-axis and Y-axis shafts are connected to the stick both engage a belt pulley. The other end of the belt for each axis engages a motor's axle. In this setup, rotating the motor axle will move the belt to pivot the shaft, and pivoting the shaft will move the belt to rotate the motor axle. The belt's function is to transmit and amplify the force from the motor to the shaft. One thing that differentiates force feedback joysticks from traditional joysticks is the lack of a centering spring. This spring keeps the joystick's neutral position in the middle (at 0,0 in terms of the x- and y-axis). Force feedback joysticks do not have the traditional centering spring; instead they rely on small servos or motors to push the joystick into the center of the range of movement

In 1977, the Atari 2600 game console was launched with a joystick that had one button to use. In 1978 a patent was released which disclosed a joystick controller that includes a plurality of pressure actuated switches disposed about the axis of the joystick handle. The ZX Interface 2 was a peripheral from Sinclair Research for its ZX Spectrum home computer released in September 1983. It had two joystick ports that were mapped to actual key presses and the hardware came with ROM cartridge which was very limited. Released in 1987, the Atari XE Game System (XEGS) came with a detachable keyboard, joystick, and light gun. Essentially, the XE was a repackaged Atari 65XE, hence the compatibility with almost all Atari 8bit software and hardware.

In 1989 a joystick handle which is telescopic like a car antenna was released. This joystick can save space when not in use and it can save space when packed for shipment. The joystick length is customizable to the individual user's input needs as described. Another type is a miniature joystick incorporated into the functional area of the keyboard. This miniature joystick has been successfully incorporated into a number of laptop computers. In 1995, Dear Ace Pilot The Phoenix Flight and Weapons Control System by Advanced Gravis is getting lots of raves among gamers. It's fast, ergonomic and completely programmable with 24 buttons that can map to keyboard or joystick functions.

Microsoft's latest Force Feedback 2 Joystick comes complete with feature rich enhancements and new force feedback effects. The most practical aspect of the force feedback in this game is that if the plane stalls in flight, the stick will shake just like in a real aircraft. You can also feel the thud when the landing gear retracts. The force feedback for these events is rather small - while you can feel the stick shake when the gear retracts, it isn't something that is going to disturb your control over the joystick. It's the small details like these, the added sensations, that will add to the gaming experience.

In 2004, Logitech is introducing its latest controller for the PlayStation 2 - the Logitech Flight Force joystick during the 2004 International Consumer Electronics Show in Las Vegas. For an immersive experience, the three-component Logitech Flight System G940 features a force feedback joystick, dual throttle and rudder pedals and has more than 250 programmable button options integrated into a fully featured HOTAS (or Hands On Throttle-and-Stick)

4.3 Game pads

It is the most common kind of game device that provides input in a computer game or entertainment system used to control a playable character or object. Its design was conceived to be hold in both hands with thumbs and finger used to press buttons to provide input. Thus the main goal of game controller is to govern the movement/action of payable body/objects in a video computer game. Gamepads usually feature a set of action buttons handled with the right thumb and a direction controller handled with the left. Later on some common additions to the standard pad include shoulder buttons placed along the edges of the pad.

Third generation of video game controllers included the Nintendo Entertainment System (NES) featured a brick-like design, Master System which has a similar design as NES and the Atari 7800. The fourth generation included Genesisi Mega Drive by Sega, TurboGrafx-16/PC-Engine and the Super Nintendo Entertainment System which had a more rounded dog-bone like design and added two more face buttons, "X" and "Y", arranging the four in a diamond formation.

In the Fifth Generation the Apple Bandai Pippin had a short live console designed by Apple Computer Inc. The Atari Jaguar was the first and last Atari console to employ the modern gamepad. Another example is the Neo Geo CD which was similar in shape and size to Sega Genesisi/Mega Drive game pads. Other examples include, The Sega Saturn, whose control pad introduced an analogue stick and analog triggers, Virtual Boy controller designed to use dual joypads, which was envisioned to control objects in a 3D environment. Sony developed a four direction D-pad, four actions were referred not by color or letter/number like most pads instead were colored shapes; triangle, circle, cross and square. The basic design and layout was based on that of Nintendo's SNES controller, as the PlayStation was originally developed as a CD add-on for the SNES, before becoming a console in its own right. It was the default pad for the first year of the PlayStation, until the release of the Dual Analog. It was often cloned for PC gamepads. The Nintendo 64 started to have both an analog stick and a D-pad. It has the traditional A,B,L and R buttons, along with a Z trigger button on its underside.

4.4 Haptic vests and jackets

Originally designed for medical investigation, Physician Mark Ombrellaro developed a haptic vest that enabled the wearer to feel the impact of bullets, explosions and/or even hand taps in the trunk of the player's body. The 3RD Space Vest is commercialized by TN Games and is advertised as the only gaming peripheral device that allows you to feel what your game character feels. It works with pressured air to provide the player pressure and impact forces that can emulate a wide scope of direction and magnitude (TN Games, 2011).

Others have worked on similar systems, and although they have not focused on the application in games specifically, it is clear how such technologies could also be applied in a game scenario. In the University of Ottawa in Canada, Jongeun Cha and others have worked in a device to enhance teleconferencing. They developed a jacket that enhances communication with the physical and emotional connection by allowing participants give encouraging pats to one another (Cha et al, 2009). Similarly, researchers at the National University of Singapore developed the Huggy Pajama wearable system, where the remote communication between parent and child is enabled through virtual hugs. This is possible by using a doll with embedded pressure sensors as input device and a haptic jacket as the actuator for the hug at the other end. The hug is reproduced by air pockets and the experience is further enhanced by adding a heating element to the device to mimic the warmth of a hug (Teh et al, 2008).

5. Haptics in mobile gaming

With the advent of smart phones, and other personal and portable devices such as MP3 players and tablets, which everyday include a richer set of sensory, processing, and memory capacities, videogames have finally make the jump from good old PCs and Consoles to the mobile world. Smartphones and related devices are capable of rendering videogame graphics and sound in high definition, which aims at immersing the player in the game experience even with the limited size of the screen.

Because mobile video games are inherently restricted to small screens, game developers must rely on advanced user interface design to fulfill the input/output streams of media information necessary to play the game. Furthermore, most of the portable devices that serve as a platform for modern mobile games feature a touch screen as the main way of interaction with the device and its software interface. Most of the time such devices, either completely lack or, have very few physical buttons that the player can use to play the game. Even when physical buttons are present on the device, they are often located in places where using them as part of the game input controller makes it awkward for the player. In terms of haptic feedback, this is a limitation of such devices, since touch screens lack that physicality that players have grown used to with pc and other gaming consoles and their controllers.

To help with the lack of physical buttons and the sense of touch that they provide, mobile phones and devices are often capable of reproducing a vibration feeling. By controlling the moment, and duration of the vibration, to be synchronized with the touch of the screen, such mobile devices compensate the lack of hard buttons by giving a haptic feedback to the user whenever he/she presses a soft button on the touch screen. Although this is often good enough for common in-device tasks such as entering text on a virtual keyboard, from a gaming perspective the approach is very limited, as is the hardware available in most devices. Games require a higher degree of variation on the vibration to produce more rich and realistic experiences. Different levels of intensity, duration or even a specific vibration pattern must be applied for different events in the game play. The challenge in providing such degree of high definition on the haptic feedback is twofold. On one hand, hardware on the devices must be sufficiently advanced to permit the variation of intensity at which the internal motors will cause the vibration. And on the other the software must be sufficiently sophisticated to control the motors in such a way that a wide array of vibration effects can be rendered.

Research has been mostly focused in developing vibrotactile rendering techniques that can allow for a sophisticated touch feedback experience. Different algorithms have been tried to control the vibration motors and render the desired effects. Sang-Youn and others proposed a Traveling Vibrotactile Wave rendering technique which makes the effect of a traveliing sensation across the device display. It is based on controlling the vibrations of two motors, which permits to specify the location where the overlapping of two waves occurs. This control further allows the generation of a sensation of continuous flowing vibration by constantly changing the overlapping point, adjusting the timing of motor actuation. They tested their rendering technique with a ball rolling game (Sang-Youn, 2009). In another related work, they tested a miniaturized vibrotactile rendering system based on an eccentric vibration motor and a solenoid actuator, which generates vibrotactile information having a large bandwidth and amplitude. Their intention was to generate event-specific vibrotactile effects for a car racing game in a mobile device. The system could render human discernible effects for the events of collision, driving on a bump, and driving on a hard shoulder (Sang-Youn, 2006).

A good example on the latest advances in this direction is the MOTIV platform from Immersion. Their solution provides a TouchSense embedded controller technology to enables a high degree of control over the vibration motors of the device. On the software side, they provide MOTIV Integrator for OEMs to include in their devices a vibration profile manager that leverages on TouchSense, and MOTIV Software Development Kit to enable developers to build third party applications and video games that also take advantage of the high definition vibration effects provided by their platform (Immersion, 2011).

Another approach has been taken by Senseg, a company based in Finland whose latest haptic rendering solution is a promise to revolutionize the way we perceive computer generated haptic feedback on touch screens and other real world surfaces. Their E-Sense Technology is based on biophysics; where instead of having the device's surface vibrate, they create a sensation of vibration directly in the finger's skin by using an ultra-low electrical current from an electrode to produce a small attractive force. The modulation of that force allows the production of any number of touch sensations that can range from vibrations, clicks, textured surfaces and more. A direct implementation of this technology is in the mobile device industry, and the provided software APIs would allow the development of video games with a sophisticated array of touch sensations (Senseg, 2011).

In terms of evaluation of the effectiveness of the haptic feedback on mobile gaming, Chui Yin Wong and peers tested the playability of a mobile game, using a vibrotactile feedback soft keypad, against playing the same game with a hard physical keypad. According to their findings, although players had higher scores using the soft keypad, they reported a preference on using the hard keypad in term of a better experience in the game play (Chui Yin Wong, 2010).

6. Haptics and games for the visually impaired

Although haptics has proven to be a valuable technology to help gamers to have more immersive and realistic experiences, there is yet another type of game for which haptics is of essential value. Haptics is a very well suited type of interaction to address the problem of accessibility to games for the visually impaired.

There a currently different technologies that have improved the accessibility of electronic media to the blind people, such as automated reading software, voice synthesis, tactile displays with Braille and speech recognition. Yet, those are mostly focused in input/output of text and there is still some types of media that are still difficult to represent in a non-visual modality, particularly graphics (2D or 3D), which form the basis for any computer game. Computer haptics seems to be a suitable solution for this problem of game accessibility, but still there are plenty of problems and research to be done on the field. It is hard enough to have an accurate haptic representation of an object in a virtual world that can be properly recognized by someone who is not able to look at it, and even harder to do it for the multiple objects and events that need to be perceived during game play. In fact, in most instances the haptic interface must be accompanied by some audio feedback as a complement, as to no overload the user with haptic signals (Yuan, 2008).

There have been two main approaches to enable visually impaired individuals into computer games. The first one is to design games that are inherently designed and implemented with the purpose of not relying on visual feedback. That is games whose playability is completely subject to interaction based on audio or haptic clues.

A survey of strategies for making games accessible to the blind shows that audio is the most common used channel to either complement or substitute the visual channel (Yuan et al. 2010). AudioGames.net is an online community portal that has a repository of games whose interface is solely based on audio and the natural haptic interface of keyboard and mouse buttons (Audiogames, 2011). In terms of pure haptic games there are examples such as Haptic Sudoku for the blind, developed by Gutschmidt and others. In this technological solution they emulate visual perception completely by haptic perception. Players can feel the Sudoku board and scan the numbers by sense of touch using a haptic display, while audio cues alert the user of the outcome of their actions (Gutschmidt et al. 2010). Another example is Finger Dance, a sound based game for blind people. In FingerDance, user try to match musical rhythm patters to keystrokes in the keyboard. The game has no visual feedback at all (Miller et al. 2007).

The second approach is sensory substitution. In this case the cues that would normally come from the visual channel are replaced by haptic stimuli. This allows for the modification of currently existing games that were originally designed for non disabled individuals and adapted to be played by the blind.

Blind Hero is a typical example of a game where sensory substitution has been applied to a very well known video game (Guitar Hero from Red Octane). Guitar Hero is a rhythm action game that is played by using a guitar shaped input device with colored buttons on it that must be pressed following the corresponding visual cues that appear on the screen at the peace of some rock tune. In the modified version, Yuan and Fomer replaced the visual cues with haptic stimuli coming from a haptic glove that has small pager motors that stimulate the tip of each finger (Yuan and Fomer, 2008).

VI-Tennis and VI-Bowling are another example of sensory substitution from their analogous version of the Wii Console (Wii Sports, 2011). In this case the haptic interface is based on a motion sensing controller enhanced with vibrotactile and audio cues that allows the players detect the key events in game play. In the case of VI-Tennis the controller would provide vibrotactile feedback to reflect the event of the ball bouncing and the timeframe at which the ball should be hit in return, while audio cues were left the same they ware on the original Wii Tennis game (Morelli et al., 2010a). For the VI-Bowling they implemented a technique called Tactile Dowsing where the Wii Remote is used to sense the direction to where the bowling ball should be thrown. With the Tactile Dowsing the player moves the remote left and right in a horizontal pattern. The receiver will detect the motion of the remote and the software prompts a vibrotactile feedback on the remote in a pulsing pattern. The delay between vibrotactile pulses is regulated so that the closer the player points to the optimal direction of the throw, the lower the delay and vice versa. This way the player can sense the direction the same way by trying to position the remote in a direction that has a near continuous vibrotactile feedback (Morelli et al., 2010b).

7. Haptics and serious games

In general, the term "Serious Games" refers to computer video games that are used with a purpose beyond or other than entertainment. However some discussion has been going on for some time about the formal definition and some other details about what may or may not constitute a serious game.

According to a definition stated by the people on the Serious Games initiative, started in 2002 by Ben Sawyer and others (Serious Game Initiative, 2011), a serious game can be defined as follows:

> *"applications of interactive technology that extend far beyond the traditional videogame market, including: training, policy exploration, analytics, visualization, simulation, education, health, and therapy."*

Serious games have been developed for many areas, including education, government, military, corporate, healthcare, politics, religion and arts. Haptics technology has been present to different extent in the majority of these areas. However, we argue that two of the most prominent serious games application areas where the advantages of haptic technology can really be appreciated are healthcare and education.

7.1 Healthcare

In this particular area there has been great interest in research how computer haptics technology can assist in rehabilitation process of people who has had some damage to their motor skills, while playing a game. The combination of the properties inherent to computer haptics (force and tactile feedback) with the appealing and motivating factor offered by Virtual Environments have provided a framework for the development of various rehabilitation systems that often involve the patient, and the therapists.

Haptic Hand writing sessions and Ten Pin Bowling are two examples of haptic assisted game applications developed by Xu and others at the University of Shanghai for Science and Technology in China. Their Ten Pin Bowling is intended for training of the motor function of post-stroke patients, based on Virtual Reality. They also demonstrate that haptic based hand writing is an efficient way to improve motor skills, postural stability, control and hand to eye coordination (Xu et al, 2010).

Jack and others worked on serious games rehabilitation using a haptic glove. In their work, the interaction with a virtual environment is enabled by using a CyberGlove and a Rutgers Master II-ND (RMII) force feedback glove. The Virtual Environment was designed to promote the training rehabilitation of a specific parameter of hand movement: range, speed, fractionation or strength. Their system would adapt to the level of rehabilitation achieved by the patient (Jack et al. 2001).

Similarly Huber and collaborators developed a home based tele-rehabilitation system for children with Hemiplegia. They made modifications to a play station game console to support the use of a haptic glove and their custom made virtual environment game. The game consisted in making specific hand movements to scare away butterflies that would appear on the virtual environment (Huber et al. 2008).

Broeren et al. Studied the effects of virtual reality and haptics in stroke rehabilitation by using a VR station loaded with a library of games and a hand held haptic stylus device. User interacted with the virtual objects of the games, while the workstation collected data about the 3D hand movements of the patients. They found that the enhanced rehabilitation experience was highly motivational to the patients (Broeren et al. 2008).

7.2 Education

In the education field, most of the work has been towards providing a more immersive and hands-on approach to learning class content. In particular chemistry is one of the subjects often targeted thru haptic assisted learning tools (Fjeld and Voegtli, 2002).

As a good example, Sato and others designed a haptic grip and an interactive system with haptic interaction as a teaching aid. They focused on the interaction between two water molecules by constructing an environment to feel Van der Waals force as well as electrostatic force with haptic interaction (Sato et al. 2008). In a similar way, Comai and collaborators propose a framework for the implementation of haptic bases systems for chemistry education (Comai et al 2010).

A second point of interest for haptics in education is that of learning hand writing skills. Eid and others seveloped a multimedia system for learning hand writing in different languages. The system is based on a haptic stylus controlled by software in such a way that it can guide the movement of the learner in an analogous way that a teacher would hold his/her hand. The system supports various languages including Arabic and Japanese. The amount of strict guidance of the system can be adjusted so that overtime the user makes the writing by him/her self (Eid et al. 2007).

In a similar work, kindergarten children were subject to hand writing training using a Visuo-Haptic device to increase the fluency of handwriting production of cursive letters. Forty two children participated in the experiment that showed that the fluency of handwriting production for all letters was higher after the training with the tool than those children which were not subject to it (Palluel-Germain et al., 2007).

8. Summary

Computer video games have come a long way and have evolved from a pure graphics and visual rendering into a fully fledged multimedia experience. Videogames try to appeal to all senses of the human player. Video graphics are very sophisticated and the definition, speed and overall quality of the visual stimuli is at its best. Audio has become an integral part of any computer video game as well, from small audio clues about events on the game to full soundtracks that give character to the titles. We argue that video and audio were the dominant media channels in the videogame industry in what could be called the first generation of games.

In this new era where computers are miniaturized and with even higher capacities of processing and memory, developers and researchers have focused on extending the sensory experience to include the sense of touch. Initial implementations include vibrotactile feedback with a rumble effect on game input controllers. However, in an attempt to achieve a more immersive experience other haptics modalities have been explored, particularly force feedback. There are already haptic devices available in a consumer level market that have complex hardware implementation that allow for more realistic reactions from the controller to game dynamics and user actions.

Another trend on games has been mobility. The wide availability of low cost, high performance mobile phones and tablet PCs has created a whole new market for game titles that can be played on the go. Along with this trend haptic technology has been introduced even on those constrained environment by means of sophisticated algorithms that can create a whole array of vibrotactile effects for each type of game condition.

Finally, games have ceased to be a purely entertainment element. The so called serious games are making people to engage in more practical and meaningful activities (in the fields of education, government, military, corporate, healthcare, politics, religion and arts), while still having the fun that game play always brings. Even in these particular type of games, haptic technology promises to enhance the activity and may be even provide a type of interaction or achieve a specific goal that would not be possible by using any other media channel.

In the future, it can be expected that machine haptics will evolve and improve into a more robust technology reaching a wide spectrum of human endeavour. And we are sure that gaming in all of its forms will always be one of the fields where the haptics potential can be exploited.

9. References

Andrews S., J. Mora, J. Lang, W.S. Lee, "HaptiCast: a Physically-based 3D Game with Haptic Feedback", Proc. of Future Play 2006, London, ON, Canada, October 2006

Broeren, J., Bjorkdahl, A., Claesson, L., et al. Virtual rehabilitation after stroke. Studies in Health Technology and Informatics 136, (2008), 77-82.

Cha, Jongeun; Mohamad Eid; Ahmad Barghout; ASM Mahfujur Rahman; Abdulmotaleb El Saddik. (2009). HugMe: synchronous haptic teleconferencing. In Proceedings of the 17th ACM international conference on Multimedia (MM '09). ACM, New York, NY, USA, 1135-1136. DOI=10.1145/1631272.1631535 http://doi.acm.org/10.1145/1631272.1631535

Chui Yin Wong; Chu, K.; Chee Weng Khong; Tek Yong Lim; , "Evaluating playability on haptic user interface for mobile gaming," Information Technology (ITSim), 2010 International Symposium in , vol.3, no., pp.1093-1098, 15-17 June 2010 DOI: 10.1109/ITSIM.2010.5561513

Comai Sara, Davide Mazza, and Lorenzo Mureddu. 2010. A haptic-based framework for chemistry education. In Proceedings of the 5th European conference on Technology enhanced learning conference on Sustaining TEL: from innovation to learning and practice (EC-TEL'10), Martin Wolpers, Paul A. Kirschner, Maren Scheffel, Stefanie Lindstaedt, and Vania Dimitrova (Eds.). Springer-Verlag, Berlin, Heidelberg, 614-619.

Eid Mohamad A., Mohamed Mansour, Abdulmotaleb H. El Saddik, and Rosa Iglesias. 2007. A haptic multimedia handwriting learning system. In Proceedings of the international workshop on Educational multimedia and multimedia education (Emme '07). ACM, New York, NY, USA, 103-108. DOI=10.1145/1290144.1290161 http://doi.acm.org/10.1145/1290144.1290161

El Saddik, Abdulmotaleb. The Potential of Haptics Technologies IEEE Instrumentation Measurement, February, 2007

Fogg BJ, Lawrence D. Cutler, Perry Arnold, and Chris Eisbach. 1998. HandJive: a device for interpersonal haptic entertainment. In Proceedings of the SIGCHI conference on Human factors in computing systems (CHI '98), Clare-Marie Karat, Arnold Lund, Jo\&\#235;lle Coutaz, and John Karat (Eds.). ACM Press/Addison-Wesley Publishing Co., New York, NY, USA, 57-64. DOI=10.1145/274644.274653 http://dx.doi.org/10.1145/274644.274653

Fjeld M. and Voegtli B. 2002. Augmented Chemistry: An Interactive Educational Workbench. In Proceedings of the 1st International Symposium on Mixed and Augmented Reality (ISMAR '02). IEEE Computer Society, Washington, DC, USA, 259-.

Gutschmidt René, Maria Schiewe, Francis Zinke, and Helmut Jurgensen. 2010. Haptic emulation of games: haptic Sudoku for the blind. In Proceedings of the 3rd International Conference on Pervasive Technologies Related to Assistive Environments (PETRA '10), Fillia Makedon, Ilias Maglogiannis, and Sarantos Kapidakis (Eds.). ACM, New York, NY, USA, , Article 2 , 8 pages. DOI=10.1145/1839294.1839297 http://doi.acm.org.proxy.bib.uottawa.ca/10.1145/1839294.1839297

Huber, M., Rabin, B., Docan, C., et al. PlayStation 3-based tele-rehabilitation for children with hemiplegia. Virtual Rehabilitation, 2008, (2008), 105-112.

Jack, D., Boian, R., Merians, A.S., et al. Virtual reality-enhanced stroke rehabilitation. IEEE Trans. Neural Sys. And Rehab. Engr., 9, 3 (2001), 308-318.

Jurgelionis, A., Bellotti, F., IJsselsteijn, W. and de Kort, Y. (2007) Evaluation and testing methodology for evolving entertainment systems. Proceedings of ACE 2007 International Conference on Advances in Computer Entertainment Technology, Workshop 'Methods for Evaluating Games - How to measure Usability and User Experience in Games'. ACM.

Katzourakis, D.; Gerard, M.; Holweg, E.; Happee, R.; , "Design issues for haptic steering force feedback on an automotive simulator," IEEE International Workshop on Haptic Audio visual Environments and Games, 2009. HAVE 2009., vol., no., pp.1-6, 7-8 Nov. 2009 doi: 10.1109/HAVE.2009.5356141

Kent, Stephen L. The Ultimate History of Video Games: From Pong to Pokemon--The Story Behind the Craze That Touched Our Lives and Changed the World. hree Rivers Press; 1 edition (October 2, 2001)

Miller Daniel, Aaron Parecki, and Sarah A. Douglas. 2007. Finger dance: a sound game for blind people. In Proceedings of the 9th international ACM SIGACCESS conference on Computers and accessibility (Assets '07). ACM, New York, NY, USA, 253-254. DOI=10.1145/1296843.1296898 http://doi.acm.org.proxy.bib.uottawa.ca/10.1145/1296843.1296898

Minsky, M., Ming, O., Steele, O., Brooks, F.P., and Behensky, M., Feeling and seeing: issues in force display, Proc. of the 1990 Symposium on Interactive 3D Graphics, pp. 235-241, 1990.

Mohellebi, H. Kheddar, A. Espie, S. (2009) Adaptive Haptic Feedback Steering Wheel for Driving Simulators. IEEE Transactions on Vehicular Technology, Volume: 58 Issue: 4. pp 1654 - 1666

Morelli Tony, John Foley, Luis Columna, Lauren Lieberman, and Eelke Folmer. (2010a). VI-Tennis: a vibrotactile/audio exergame for players who are visually impaired. In Proceedings of the Fifth International Conference on the Foundations of Digital Games (FDG '10). ACM, New York, NY, USA, 147-154. DOI=10.1145/1822348.1822368 http://doi.acm.org.proxy.bib.uottawa.ca/10.1145/1822348.1822368

Morelli Tony, John Foley, and Eelke Folmer. (2010b). Vi-bowling: a tactile spatial exergame for individuals with visual impairments. In Proceedings of the 12th international ACM SIGACCESS conference on Computers and accessibility (ASSETS '10). ACM, New York, NY, USA, 179-186. DOI=10.1145/1878803.1878836 http://doi.acm.org.proxy.bib.uottawa.ca/10.1145/1878803.1878836

Nilsson, D., and Aamisepp, H., Haptic hardware support in a 3D game engine. Master thesis,Department of Computer Science, Lund University, May 2003.

Palluel-Germain R., F. Bara, A. Hillairet de Boisferon, B. Hennion, P. Gouagout, and E. Gentaz. 2007. A Visuo-Haptic Device - Telemaque - Increases Kindergarten Children's Handwriting Acquisition. In Proceedings of the Second Joint EuroHaptics Conference and Symposium on Haptic Interfaces for Virtual Environment and Teleoperator Systems (WHC '07). IEEE Computer Society, Washington, DC, USA, 72-77. DOI=10.1109/WHC.2007.13 http://dx.doi.org/10.1109/WHC.2007.13

Sang-Youn Kim; Jae-Oh Kim; Kyu Kim; , "Traveling vibrotactile wave - a new vibrotactile rendering method for mobile devices," Consumer Electronics, IEEE Transactions on, vol.55, no.3, pp.1032-1038, August 2009 DOI: 10.1109/TCE.2009.5277952

Sang-Youn Kim; Kyu Yong Kim; Byung Seok Soh; Gyunghye Yang; Sang Ryong Kim; , "Vibrotactile rendering for simulating virtual environment in a mobile game," IEEE Transactions on Consumer Electronics , vol.52, no.4, pp.1340-1347, Nov. 2006 DOI: 10.1109/TCE.2006.273154

Sato Makoto, Xiangning Liu, Jun Murayama, Katsuhito Akahane, and Masaharu Isshiki. 2008. A haptic virtual environment for molecular chemistry education. In Transactions on edutainment I, Abdennour El Rhabili (Ed.). Lecture Notes In Computer Science, Vol. 5080. Springer-Verlag, Berlin, Heidelberg 28-39.

Teh, James Keng Soon; Adrian David Cheok, Roshan L. Peiris, Yongsoon Choi, Vuong Thuong, and Sha Lai. (2008). Huggy Pajama: a mobile parent and child hugging communication system. In Proceedings of the 7th international conference on Interaction design and children (IDC '08). ACM, New York, NY, USA, 250-257. DOI=10.1145/1463689.1463763 http://doi.acm.org/10.1145/1463689.1463763

Xu Zhaohong, Hongliu Yu, and Shiju Yan. 2010. Motor rehabilitation training after stroke using haptic handwriting and games. In Proceedings of the 4th International Convention on Rehabilitation Engineering \& Assistive Technology (iCREATe '10). Singapore Therapeutic, Assistive \& Rehabilitative Technologies (START) Centre, Kaki Bukit TechPark II,, Singapore, Article 31 , 4 pages.

Yuan Bei and Eelke Folmer. 2008. Blind hero: enabling guitar hero for the visually impaired. In Proceedings of the 10th international ACM SIGACCESS conference on Computers and accessibility (Assets '08). ACM, New York, NY, USA, 169-176. DOI=10.1145/1414471.1414503 http://doi.acm.org.proxy.bib.uottawa.ca/10.1145/1414471.1414503

Yuan Bei. 2009. Towards Generalized Accessibility of Video Games for the Visually Impaired. Ph.D. Dissertation. Univ. of Nevada, Reno, Reno, NV, USA. Advisor(s) Frederick C. Harris and Eelke Folmer. AAI3355610.

Yuan, Bei., Folmer, E., and Harris, F. C. Game accessibility; a survey. Universal Access in the Information Society 10, 1 (2010), 88-111.

Audio Games. Games based on sound. http://audiogames.net/. Retrieved June, 2011

Crystal Space 3D. http://www.crystalspace3d.org/. Retrieved June, 2011

Immersion. TouchSense Technology. http://www.immersion.com/products/motiv. Retrieved June, 2011.

Novint Technologies. http://www.novint.com/. Retrieved June, 2011

SensAble Technologies. http://www.sensable.com/. Retrieved June, 2011

Senseg. E-Sense Technology. http://senseg.com/technology/senseg-technology. Retrieved June, 2011.

TN Games. The 3rd Space Vest. http://tngames.com/products. Retrieved June, 2011